THE GEORGIA
ONE-DAY TRIP BOOK

*Like the rings of the Olympic symbol,
my life is linked forever with four people
who have enriched my world:
Harry Ockershausen, my father;
Jerry Bloch, my husband;
Alexis Ashley Smith, my daughter;
Anne Ockershausen, my sister.*

THE GEORGIA ONE-DAY TRIP BOOK

A New Way to Explore the
State's Romantic Past, Vibrant Present
and Olympian Future

JANE OCKERSHAUSEN

EPM Publications
McLean, Virginia 22101

Library of Congress Cataloging-in-Publication Data

Ockershausen, Jane.
    The Georgia one-day trip book : a new way to explore the
state's romantic past, vibrant present, and Olympian future /
Jane Ockershausen.
        p. cm.
    ISBN 0-939009-71-4
    1. Georgia—Tours.   2. Historic sites—Georgia—
Guidebooks.
I. Title.
F284.3.O25   1993
917.5804'43—dc20   93-5351
                                                               CIP

EPM Publications, Inc., 1003 Turkey Run Road
    McLean, VA 22101
Printed in the United States of America

Cover and book design by Tom Huestis
Cover photos courtesy of Georgia Department of Industry &
Tourism

Contents

THE GEORGIA ONE-DAY TRIP BOOK

======================ATLANTA METRO======================

PRESIDENTIAL PATHWAYS

HISTORIC HEARTLAND

CLASSIC SOUTH

PLANTATION TRACE

MAGNOLIA MIDLANDS

COLONIAL COAST

A New Way to Explore
the State's Romantic Past,
Vibrant Present and Olympian Future

Georgia On
My Mind

I started work on *The Georgia One-Day Trip Book* on September 18, 1990. The date is significant because it was the day the International Olympic Committee announced that Atlanta would host the 1996 Centennial Olympic Games. It seemed singularly appropriate for me to end my research in Savannah at the Olympic Flag Celebration. Along with thousands of cheering spectators, I watched for the first glimpse of the U.S. Coast Guard barque *Eagle* as it carried the multi-ringed Olympic flag up the Savannah River on September 10, 1992.

The most remarkable discovery I made during the two years I traveled through Georgia, the largest state east of the Mississippi River, was the incredible diversity of the day-tripping options in the state's nine travel regions. I was struck by the dramatic Tallulah Gorge region and the haunting beauty of Providence Canyon, Georgia's Little Grand Canyon. The serenity of the barrier islands—Cumberland, Sapelo, St. Simons, Jekyll—soothed my spirit. The tumbling waterfalls—Anna Ruby, Amicalaola, and Toccoa—and the quiet mountain trails afforded endless delights. The man-made beauty of communities like Athens, Madison, Macon and Milledgeville where antebellum homes sit along tree-lined streets offered me a glimpse of the Old South.

Georgia's history, dating from man's earliest days on this continent, is filled with drama. Prehistoric mounds at Etowah, Ocmulgee and Rood Creek are so old they have a mystical appeal: The story of the Cherokee Nation and its Trail of Tears still leaves the visitor shocked and dismayed. Because Georgia was one of the 13 original colonies, its historic sites trace much of the entire nation's development. The War Between the States left vivid reminders in Georgia, from the exciting railroad chase between the General and the Texas to the tragedy at Andersonville Prison Camp.

Even lifelong residents of Georgia will find new leisure options in these one-day trips. In planning your itinerary, it's helpful to read all the selections in the geographic region you plan to explore, since many of the attractions can be combined for one trip.

Be sure to check the Calendar of Events to see if there are special activities planned during the time of your visit. Sometimes visitors prefer to schedule trips at slower periods when there are fewer people; others go for the festivals and fairs that enliven parks and historic sites. If you plan to attend a specific event, call ahead to make sure it will be held. Hours of operation also change; so it's always a good idea to check before starting out.

The right time of year can make a difference in your impressions of many of these attractions. Spring is the time to catch the blanket of blossoming azaleas at Callaway Garden, Macon's cherry blossoms and the flowering bulbs in the fenced gardens of Historic Savannah. During the summer months the laser performance at Stone Mountain captivates visitors; the action at Six Flags Over Georgia excites them. The mountains around Blue Rocks, Dahlonega, Helen and the Tallulah Gorge blaze with color in the autumn. Shopping for holiday gifts becomes effortless at distinctive craft shops such as Mark of the Potter, Gourdcraft Originals, Happy Valley Pottery and many other craft shops. Even with Georgia's mild winters, the colder months are a good time to check out the amazingly diverse museums throughout the state. Don't miss the outstanding Michael C. Carlos Museum, the state-of-the-arts Fernbank Museum of Natural History, the exciting video presentation at the Chickamauga National Military Park and the recently completed museum at the Atlanta History Center, to name a few of Georgia's fine offerings.

Traveling through Georgia is a sensory treat. There is food for thought but also delicious food to sample. Many regions specialize in unique products: Few travelers can resist the sweet Vidalia onions from the Magnolia Midlands, Muscadine jelly and jam from Callaway in the Presidential Pathways region, Mayhaw Jelly from Plantation Trace area and an appetizing array of pecan and peach products. The regional cooking ranges from Low Country boil, Brunswick stew and seafood specialties in the coastal region to the delectable barbecues found throughout the state (try Sprayberry's in Newnan, Fresh Aire Bar-B-Que outside Indian Spring and Sconyers of Augusta). Southern cooking of the kind served at Mrs. Wilkes Boarding House in Savannah or the Dillard House Inn in Dillard is unrivaled. Excellent continental cuisine can be enjoyed at such diverse spots as the 1848 House in Marietta, Tiberios in Rome, Bon Cuisine in Pine Mountain and Trumps at the Georgian in Athens.

Some travelers are drawn to day tripping because it is an inexpensive way to travel. Many of the attractions provide lovely areas in which to picnic. Since most of the selections take only a few hours to see, they can be combined for a full day or weekend getaway and interspersed with al fresco meals and snacks.

When my first One-Day Trip Book was published in 1975, most

families did their traveling during an annual two-week vacation. By now one-day trips have become a popular option. Short excursions spaced weekly or monthly throughout the year offer an escape from the winter doldrums, a jump on spring, a wide array of outdoor summer recreation and a fall foliage fling.

One-day trips are enriching: They nourish the spirit and provide shared experiences that are long remembered. I hope your one-days are fun days!

J.O.

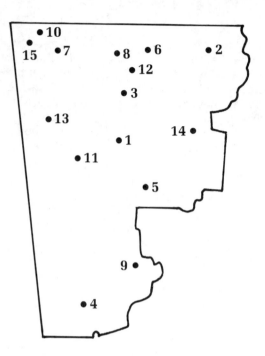

NORTHWEST MOUNTAINS

1. *Adairsville*
   Barnsley Gardens

2. *Blue Ridge*
   Toccoa Ranger District

3. *Calhoun*
   New Echota

4. *Carrollton*
   John Tanner State Park

5. *Cartersville*
   Allatoona Lake and Red Top
      Mountain State Park
   Etowah Indian Mounds
   William Weinman Mineral
      Museum and Air Acres
      Museum

6. *Chatsworth*
   Chief Vann House Historic Site
   Fort Mountain State Park

7. *Chickamauga*
   Chickamauga and Chattanooga
      National Military Park
   Gordon-Lee Mansion and Fort
      Oglethorpe

8. *Dalton*
   Crown Gardens and Archives

9. *Lithia Springs*
   Sweetwater Creek State
      Conservation Park

10. *Lookout Mountain*
    Rock City Gardens

11. *Rome*
    Chieftains Museum
    Martha Berry Museum and Oak
       Hill

12. *Rossville*
    Chief John Ross House and Park

13. *Summerville*
    James H. Floyd State Park

14. *Tate/Jasper*
    Tate House and Georgian
       Marble Festival

15. *Trenton*
    Cloudland Canyon State Park

—Northwest Mountains—

Georgia deserves credit for not ducking the harsh realities of the state's treatment of the Cherokees. Chieftains Trail winding through the state's northwest corner covers land once belonging to the Indian Nation. Many of the natural wonders of the region, such as Rock City and Fort Mountain, are woven into tribal tales.

It's surprising to hear at New Echota and Chieftains Museum, how closely the Cherokee system of government and education followed the U.S. government organization. The heartbreaking story of the Trail of Tears is regrettably unfamiliar to many students of American history.

The bitter and tragic war that divided North and South is also remembered in this region. Chickamauga and Chattanooga National Military Park, the nation's first military park, has an outstanding visual program about this two-day encounter and its aftermath. The story continues at the nearby Gordon Lee Mansion and along the Blue and Gray Trail.

Many visitors seek tranquility in Georgia's Northwest Mountains. Trails winding through the Toccoa Ranger District, Cloudland Canyon State Park and around Allatoona Lake offer diverse scenic appeal. Some of the most picturesque points in the region have been added by those who once lived here: the crumbling ruins and newly restored gardens at Barnsley, the pink-marbled Tate House, the waterwheel and campus buildings at Martha Berry and the walkways that make Rock City Gardens accessible.

Allatoona Lake and Red Top Mountain State Park

Thirteen Million People Can't Be Wrong!

Allatoona is one of the most picturesque and popular lakes in Georgia. Roughly 13 million visitors enjoy this 12,010-acre lake each year. Preliminary work began on the dam site in 1941, making it the oldest multi-purpose project in the U.S. Army Corps of Engineers' South Atlantic Division. World War II interrupted the work, and the dam did not become operational until January 1950.

The **Allatoona Dam** impounds run-off water from 1,100 square miles into a large, irregular lake with 270 miles of shoreline. Since the lake serves such a large drainage area, its level fluctuates dramatically. The record increase was 20 feet in one week, but three- and four-foot increases are common during heavy rains. The lake is on the Etowah River, a tributary of the Coosa River. If you are boating from November to February, watch out for submerged obstructions. During these months the lake is at its lowest, and the logs, stumps and rocks covered by the water can be hazardous. Boaters always need to exercise caution in the turbulent water immediately above and below the dam.

The **Allatoona Lake Visitor Center**, just outside Cartersville, has exhibits that trace the development of the dam and the history of the region. An eight-minute video tells the story of the dam construction, and an animated cutaway drawing of the dam shows how it operates (after you leave the Center you can walk across the top of the dam). The Visitors Center also provides details about the Civil War Battle of Allatoona Pass on October 5, 1864.

Before the Civil War this area was a center of milling and manufacturing. The town of Etowah was founded in the late 1830s by Jacob Stroup whose son built the Cooper Furnace. Georgia Congressman Mark Anthony Cooper purchased the iron works in 1847. Etowah also had a spike and nail mill, flour mill (it's said that the Queen of England use to order her flour from this gristmill), rolling mill, foundry, hotel and workers' homes. The town was connected to the Western Atlantic Railroad via a spur track, and the switch engine Yonah hauled freight back and forth. The Yonah was used by Fuller to try to catch the General in the Great Locomotive Chase during the Civil War (see Big Shanty Museum selection). General Sherman's troops destroyed the town of Etowah in 1864.

You can take the one-mile Laurel Ridge Trail from the Visitors Center down to the .7-mile Cooper Furnace Trail that leads to the remains of the old furnace. The Laurel Ridge Trail runs through the hillside and hollows along the north side of the Etowah River Valley. In the spring, wildflowers and mountain laurel bloom in profusion alongside the trail. After linking up with Cooper Furnace Trail, you will follow the railroad bed of the 19th-century mining train. You can also follow the service road from the Visitor Center parking lot down to the Cooper Furnace Trail, an easier route for some visitors than the two steep grades along the Laurel Ridge Trail.

The Cooper Furnace Day Use Area, has picnic tables, grills and a playground and is open year-round from 8:00 A.M. to sundown in the winter months and to 10:00 P.M. in the summer months. This is one of 19 day-use areas around the lake. Additionally there are 11 campgrounds with swimming beaches and eight city, county or state parks. Hunters also enjoy the abundant game in the forest along the lake shore. For hunting regulations check with the Resource Manager's Office at the Visitors Center.

Red Top Mountain State Park, located on a 1,950-acre peninsula along Lake Allatoona, is named for the rich red soil, a reminder of the land's early importance as an iron-ore mining region. The park contains remains of several old iron mines. Recreational opportunities at the park include swimming, boating, fishing and hiking. There are campgrounds and a 33-room lodge, a seven-mile trail, boat marina and picnic shelter. The lodge's Mountain Cove Restaurant overlooks the lake inlet. For information on accommodations at Red Top Mountain Lodge call (404)975-0055.

In addition to the marina at Red Top there are eight other marinas on the lake: Allatoona Landing (404)974-6089, Galts Ferry (404)974-6422, Glade (404)974-6710, Holiday (404)974-2575, Little River Landing (404)345-6200, Park (404)974-6063, Victoria Landing (404)926-7718 and Wilderness Camp (404)382-9066.

Directions: From I-75 take Exit 125, go east on Route 20 for a short distance and follow Route 294 N to the Allatoona Lake Visitors Center. For Red Top Mountain State Park take Exit 123 off I-75 and follow Red Top Mountain Road for two miles over Bethany Bridge and into the park.

Barnsley Gardens

Remarkable Ruins

Dramatically incongruous, the ruins of this immense mansion seem vaguely European though they stand not far from Adairsville. There are even tales of a ghost who haunts the grounds of Barnsley Gardens, an Italianate manor house built in the 1840s by Godfrey Barnsley. Stories claim that Godfrey arrived in Georgia from England with four shillings in his pocket and within ten years was one of the wealthiest men in the state. On Christmas Eve 1828, Godfrey married Julia Henrietta Scarborough, daughter of the Savannah shipping family that sent the first steamship across the Atlantic. When his much-beloved wife became ill with tuberculosis, Barnsley purchased 10,000 acres in the Northwest

Mountains, land he had discovered while on a tourist excursion to Lookout Mountain. The Barnsleys with their six children moved to a large, frame house beside a spring while their more elaborate manor house was built. But even the mountain air could not sustain Julia, who died in February 1845.

Godfrey Barnsley lost all interest in **Woodlands**, as he called his home to be, until he attended a seance and became convinced that Julia's spirit walked and talked to him in the gardens they once shared. He believed she advised him on the continuing construction of a 26-room Italian villa. Allegedly, her suggestion led to the use of red clay bricks for the exterior walls while numerous details concerning the design of the elegant interior woodwork were made at her request. The house was completed in 1857. Legends say Julia Barnsley's ghost still walks amid the boxwood each evening in the stillness of dusk.

Reports from acquaintances of Margaret Mitchell claim that she was thinking of Woodlands when she wrote of her fictional Tara, even though Woodlands was far from being a traditional antebellum plantation home. Woodlands had its personal brush with the Civil War in May of 1864 when it was occupied by Union troops under General J.B. McPherson. A close family friend, Confederate Colonel Richard Earle, was killed after he rode to warn the Barnsleys that the Yankees were on their way. Colonel Earle's grave is beneath the redwood tree behind the manor house. McPherson described Woodlands as "a little piece of heaven itself" and ordered his men not to damage the house, but stragglers and looters ransacked the estate after the main army had moved on. Barnsley as a British subject filed a list of damages in the amount of $155,000 with the British Consulate in Washington, but he never received reimbursement.

Barnsley's wealth was lost during the war. At the onset of the conflict he gave his fleet of ships to the Confederate navy and invested his money in Confederate bonds. His children and their spouses were never able to restore Woodlands to its former glory. By the time a tornado swept off the roof in 1906, the mansion had declined to the point where only costly repairs could salvage it. Finally all that remained were crumbling brick walls.

In 1988, Prince Hubertus Fuerst Fugger-Babenhausen of Bavaria purchased the property. Under his direction the Barnsley Gardens have been recreated, and although the manor house will never be rebuilt, the ruins have been stabilized and form a dramatic backdrop to the natural beauty of the estate.

The right, or kitchen, wing of the house survived over the years. Here the Barnsley descendants lived until 1942. Converted into a museum, the wing houses Barnsley family possessions. Artifacts from two archaeological digs on the grounds include reminders of the Civil War days and arrowheads and implements from the Indians that crossed this land more than a thousand years ago.

Efforts to restore the gardens to their appearance in the 1840s are aided by the extensive correspondence of Godfrey Barnsley, whose letters describe the plants and flowers he obtained for his estate. Great care has been lavished to return the 30-acre English-style pleasure garden to its pre-Civil War appearance. Woodland paths take you into a lost Arcadia where in the spring more than 200,000 daffodils bloom on a hillside that slopes to a lovely water garden. Another bank is planted with Confederate and Carolina jasmine, and a nearby meadow, seeded with wildflowers, resembles a Monet painting. There is also a bog, or sunken garden, and an heirloom rose garden. Barnsley reputedly grew every known variety of rose. Black swans again swim on the pond, and peacocks roam the grounds.

The old Barnsley boxwood maze has been replanted, and specimen trees, brought to Georgia by Barnsley's ships, can be appreciated once more now that the overgrown underbrush is gone. A new fountain stands in the middle of the boxwood parterre garden in the style of the Italian marble original.

Barnsley Gardens is open February through mid-December Tuesday through Saturday from 10:00 A.M. to 5:00 P.M. and Sunday the gardens open at NOON. Admission is charged. There is a cafe, gift and garden shop.

Directions: From I-75 take Exit 128 at Adairsville and travel west on Route 140 for 1.5 miles to Hall Station Road. Turn left on Hall Station Road for 5.5 miles to Barnsley Gardens Road and make a right. Take Barnsley Gardens Road for 2.5 miles, and the gardens will be on your left.

Blue Ridge and Toccoa Ranger District

Happy Trails to You

The mountainous area around the town of Blue Ridge is full of scenic beauty, best explored on a driving tour or a leisurely hike. If you're afraid of getting hopelessly lost by venturing off the main roads, stop at the Fannin County Chamber of Commerce at the corner of Route 515 and Route 5 or the Visitors Center in Downtown Blue Ridge and pick up directions for the three self-driving tours. These will get you *way* off the beaten track.

The first driving tour covers 37 miles and takes between 1½ to 2½ hours. Odometer readings between each set of directions or reference points help keep you from getting lost. The route gives you a glimpse of the powerhouse for the Blue Ridge Dam and takes you through a narrow mountain farm valley with old churches, dairies and farmhouses. You can stop and get a good look at an old Cherokee fish trap in the Toccoa River. Several recreational options can break up this drive. You can take a 4.2-mile side trip to the Benton Mackay Trail (white diamond-blazed general forest trail) or take a brief detour on a gravel road to the Lake Blue Ridge Recreation area where there are boat slips and campgrounds.

The second driving tour—for skilled drivers only—is a 69-mile, three- to four-hour trip into the wilderness. It leads through a scenic hardwood mountain forest to an isolated lake where you can swim. The route gives you access to a variety of hiking trails. The first spot you'll pass on your tour is **Mercier's Orchard Apple House**, which sells roughly 25 varieties of apples. Fannin County is noted for its Georgia apple orchards, and you'll want to pick up some fresh fruit, cider or other apple products. As you travel through the rolling farm valleys you'll pass several of the more than 100 small churches that serve these isolated congregations. After 11.2 miles you will leave the paved highway and continue the tour on gravel roads, some of which are narrow with a definite upgrade, so be alert for oncoming traffic. At this point the tour guide gives you the option of cutting short your drive and re-turning to Blue Ridge. If you continue to the top of Dyer Mountain, you'll have a spectacular view. Several trails intersect the road including the 5.6-mile Mountain Creek Trail and the easy 1.8-mile Chestnut Lead Trail, lined with wildflowers. Another easy trail is the 1.2-mile Lake Conasauga Trail. The Lake Conasauga Recreation Area is ideal for swimming in the hot summer. After traveling 32 miles, you will began your return to Blue Ridge.

The final driving tour winding through a deep forest has both a short and a long route. The former is an easy 30-mile drive that takes 1½ to 2½ hours, while the latter takes you to the edge of the Cohutta Wilderness and is for skilled drivers only. Part of the 32-mile round-trip drive is steep, narrow and rough and should not be attempted during the winter or early spring. Even in good weather this stretch will add an hour to your drive. In June this drive is most splendid because you will pass miles of rhododendrons, wildflowers and rushing waters. The Ocoee River is noted for its white-water rafting, and you can obtain details at the Fannin County Chamber offices. As you drive along the Cohutta Wilderness Area, you'll note several hiking trails leading off the gravel road.

If you want a complete listing of the recreational options available in the Chattahoochee National Forest stop at the **Toccoa Ranger District** in Blue Ridge on East Main Street in the Owenby Building. You can get material on the six developed camp-grounds: two are on Lake Blue Ridge, three on trout streams and one on the Toccoa River. Beside the Toccoa River campground there is a fishing access platform for handicapped visitors. There are other camping options available as well.

There are nine miles of single-track mountain bike trails as well as one-to four-day loop tours for bicyclists. For hikers the district has more than 100 miles of trails. An approach trail and the southern terminus of the Appalachian Trail is within the Toccoa Ranger District. Four trails lead to easily accessible waterfalls: Long Creek Falls, Fall Branch Falls, Sea Creek Falls and Little Rock Creek Falls. Rockhounds enjoy the region because Fannin and Gilmer counties are the only spots in the country where **staurolite** crystals, called "fairy crosses," can be found. (They are also found in Switzerland.) Staurolite is an iron-aluminum silicate that occurs as orthorhombic prisms and as twinned crystals. When the twinning is at 90 degrees it forms a perfect cross. Excellent specimens have been found near Mineral Bluff. Cherokee legend says these crosses were formed when the fairies wept at the death of Christ.

Other recreational options include hunting, horseback riding over 30 miles of trails and berry picking throughout the district in season. There is canoeing, tubing, rafting, swimming and fishing on the Toccoa River and swimming, waterskiing, sailing, snorkeling and fishing on Lake Blue Ridge. From this wealth of options it is hard to make a choice, but the opportunities can fill many one-day excursions.

The Toccoa Ranger District office is open Monday through Friday from 8:00 A.M. to 4:00 P.M., or you can call (706)632-3031. The office is in the Owenby Building in Blue Ridge.

While in Blue Ridge you may want to stop for lunch or dinner at The Merchants Hope Inn, an exact reproduction of the Wetherburn Tavern in Williamsburg, Virginia. Long-range plans are to create a colonial village, carefully reproducing other buildings and relocating 18th-century structures. Already in place is a private home copied from Colonial Williamsburg and the only maze to be found in Georgia, as well as the only hemlock maze known to exist. To arrange a tour call (706)632-9000.

Directions: Take I-575 north to the intersection with Route 515, then continue north to the town of Blue Ridge.

Chickamauga and Chattanooga National Military Park

Battlefield Video Scores Direct Hit

A key point to bear in mind considering military action in the Civil War is that in many battlefield situations no one knew what was going on. The generals frequently remained in their headquarters removed from the battlefields, connected to the action only by reports coming from the lines. Communication and intelligence gathering were severely limited. Armies often encountered one another unexpectedly as was the case at Gettysburg in July 1863.

After the summer action at Gettysburg and Vicksburg, the scene shifted to central Tennessee and northern Georgia. In the fall, Union General William S. Rosecrans's Army of the Cumberland faced Confederate General Braxton Bragg and his Army of Tennessee. They met just 12 miles south of Chattanooga, Tennessee, along the banks of the Chickamauga Creek in Georgia.

When contemplating the action at Chickamauga, remember that these commanders had been moving their armies and skirmishing non-stop for nine months. They were never granted a respite, and even competent commanders suffered battle fatigue and stress under these conditions.

The **Battle of Chickamauga** began on September 19, 1863. Bragg had 66,000 men, and Rosecrans's army was roughly 8,000 men shy of that. This battle was fought in dense woods and thick underbrush, which made it even harder than usual for the generals to keep track of their men. One of the brigade commanders, Confederate General Longstreet, traveled 900 miles to reinforce Bragg and arrived in the area at midnight. Next morning Longstreet led 50 percent of the Southern army over terrain he had never even seen.

There are different ways you can explore the battlefield. One way to trace the action of this two-day conflict is to take the seven-mile self-guided auto tour route. Secondly, you can rent an auto tape tour that covers 12 miles and takes a little over two hours to complete. During the summer months, a third choice is to join a ranger-led, car-caravan tour.

The fighting began just after dawn when the two armies met at Jay's Mill. The bitter, hand-to-hand struggle lasted all day and eventually spread south over a four-mile area. With darkness, the Union troops fell back to the area in front of the LaFayette Road, now U.S. 27.

Stop 1 on the auto tour route orients visitors to the battlefield. There are monuments and markers along the road denoting the location of units and batteries. The silver metal tablets trimmed in blue represent the Union positions, and red-trim stands for the Confederates. Most of the 1,400 monuments and historical markers were put in place by veterans of this battle. To gain a better understanding of the action, it helps to know that there were usually three brigades per division, and three or four regiments for each brigade with ten companies per regiment and roughly 100 men in each company when they were at full strength. By the time they reached Chichamauga companies were down to 35 or 40 men.

Stop 2 marks the spot where at about 9:30 A.M. on September 19th Lt. General Leonidas Polk's Confederate troops attacked General Thomas's corps. Thomas's men had worked all night building breastworks to protect against the next day's Confederate assault. The strength of Polk's attack forced Rosecrans to shift troops to support Thomas. This created a problem on the Federal line.

As you move down Battle Line Road you'll come to Stop 3 where a mix-up in communication caused Rosecrans to issue unwise orders to General Wood. Rosecrans was incorrectly informed that Brigadier General John M. Brannan's division was out of position, so Wood's division was ordered to fill Brannan's spot. On another day Wood might have questioned the command, because if he pulled his men it would leave a gaping hole in the Federal lines. But earlier that morning Rosecrans had blisteringly chastised Wood, accusing him of disobeying his orders. Still smarting from these remarks, Wood followed Rosecrans's orders and pulled his men out of line. General Longstreet's troops charged through the gap, past the Brotherton Cabin (which is still standing) and across the field to the Federal line. Stop 4 marks the position of Longstreet's breakthrough.

The monument at Stop 5 indicates troop position on the first day of battle. At the next stop an 85-foot monument honors Union Colonel John Wilder and his valient but vain efforts to stop Longstreet's veterans. The monument stands where Rosecrans had his headquarters. A platform at the top of the monument affords an overview of the battlefield. After the war, Wilder settled in Chattanooga, and in 1876 the townspeople elected him mayor. Stop 7 offers another view of Longstreet's breakthrough and indicates where the Union right retreated. The last stop is Snodgrass Hill where General George H. Thomas won the nickname "Rock of Chickamauga." He is credited with saving the Union army by his stand on Snodgrass Hill. It is ironic that Thomas was never fully trusted by Lincoln or Grant because he was born in Virginia. His family disowned him when he took up arms for the Union cause.

Legend has it "Chickamauga" is a Cherokee word meaning "River of Death": all too appropriate, as the water did run red after this battle. There were 34,000 casualties and 3,969 deaths; some companies lost most of their officers. The 22nd Alabama regiment lost 55 percent of its soldiers and almost half of its officers, and the 20th Georgia lost 17 of 23 officers.

To get a vivid picture of what it was like for the soldiers at Chickamauga, watch the new 26-minute state-of-the-arts multimedia dramatization of the battle (there is a charge but it is well worth it). This five-screen presentation gives you a strong sense of immediacy by its use of holographic figures and surround sound that picks up the woodland noises as well as the sounds of battle. The production even creates the illusion of gunfire with bright white lights and wisps of smoke.

It is fitting that this battlefield has one of the best dramatic visual programs in the national military park system because this was the nation's first national military park. The park was conceived by General H.V. Boynton and Ferdinand Van Derveer, veterans of the Army of the Cumberland, when they visited the battlefield in 1888. Enlisting support from both Union and Confederate veterans, they saw their idea realized on August 19, 1890, when it passed both Houses of Congress on the same day and was signed into law by President Benjamin Harrison.

The **Chickamauga and Chattanooga National Military Park's Visitor Center**, which houses the 355-piece Fuller Collection of American Military Arms, is open from 8:00 A.M. to 5:45 P.M. Memorial Day to Labor Day. It closes at 4:45 P.M. the rest of the year; closed on Christmas Day. Other sections of the park, such as Point Park and Lookout Mountain, are in Tennessee. They cover the action of November 23-25 when the Union forces struck back at Orchard Knob, Lookout Mountain and Missionary Ridge winning the battles for Chattanooga and preparing the way for an invasion of the South.

Directions: From I-75 take Exit 141, Route 2, to the intersection with Route 27 and make a left. Follow Route 27 into the Chickamauga and Chattanooga National Military Park. The Visitor Center is on your right.

Chief John Ross House and Park

Cherokee Chieftain

John Ross was born in Indian Territory on October 3, 1790. Reports on his exact birthplace vary. Some list it on the Coosa River at Tahnoovayah; others claim he was born in the area that became known as Rossville, originally Turkey Town. John Ross or Coowescoowe, the Egret, as he was called by his mother's people, was born to Mary (Molly) McDonald, Scotch-Cherokee, and Daniel Ross, a Scotsman. He was only one-eighth Cherokee, but while he was young he was brought up as an Indian among the Cherokees, who called him Tsan-usdi, which meant Little John.

In 1803, when his mother died, John Ross and his eight brothers and sisters moved into their maternal grandparents' house, now the **Chief John Ross House**. Their grandfather, John McDonald, built this two-story log house in 1797. The house stood beside the fresh waters of Poplar Springs on the old Cherokee trading path to Augusta.

With the young people in the house, it became the first school in north Georgia. Their father hired a tutor for his children and other Cherokee youngsters. Having obtained this educational grounding, John Ross attended an academy in Kingsport, Tennessee. All his life John Ross worked to improve the educational level of the Cherokee people.

After completing his education, Ross returned to his grandfather's house and made it the operating headquarters for his various business undertakings. He operated a supply depot and warehouse at Ross's Landing, the settlement founded by his father Daniel Ross, which grew into the town of Chattanooga, Tennessee. At the age of 23, Ross married the widowed Elizabeth Brown Henley. Quatie, as she was called, was nearly a full-blood Cherokee. They lived in what is now the John Ross House for 13 years before moving to a large plantation near Rome, Georgia.

Although the house you will tour is original, in 1962 it was moved log by log from its location on Route 27 (there is a historic marker at the site) to its present position beside Poplar Spring. The house, now a National Historic Landmark, still contains some of John Ross's furniture like the table and glassware in the kitchen and the bed, which was once in his Oklahoma home.

The house was also one of the first post offices in the area. John Ross was appointed postmaster in 1817, and settlers from Ross's Landing came to this house to collect their mail when it was delivered every two weeks by the Nashville-Augusta stagecoach. You'll see an old post office desk as you tour the upstairs.

Downstairs are reminders of Ross's years as Principal Chief of the Cherokees from 1828 to 1866. Before that, from 1819 to 1826, in a building adjacent to this log cabin, he presided over the Cherokee National Council. As a tribal leader, John Ross made numerous trips to Washington on behalf of the Cherokee Nation. His first meeting with a U.S. president was in 1816 when he met President Madison. He fought in vain against federal and state encroachment on Cherokee land. But once gold was discovered by a young Cherokee in Dahlonega in 1828, any hope of keeping their land was lost. In the early 1830s Georgia began stripping the Cherokees of their land and their rights. In 1838 the Cherokees remaining in Georgia were rounded up, placed in stockades and then force marched to Oklahoma. Many died during the summer confinement, and roughly a quarter, or 4,000, died on what was called the Trail of Tears.

Ross's wife Quatie died along the route after she gave her only blanket to a needy child and caught pneumonia. Ross, who tried to help his people as he led them west, survived the trek. He established a new home in Oklahoma and married a Philadelphia widow, Mary Stapler. Ross died on a trip to Washington, D.C., on August 1, 1886. His portrait was unveiled at the Georgia State Capitol in 1990.

The Chief John Ross House is open June through September on Monday through Sunday from 1:00 to 5:00 P.M.; closed on Wednesdays. There is no admission, but donations are welcome.

While you are in Rossville you can enjoy the more than thirty rides at Lake Winnepesaukah, an old-fashioned family-style amusement park. This 110-acre park is noted for the Cannon Ball Roller Coaster and for its summer Sunday concerts. The park also has miniature golf, arcade games, a fun house as well as gift shops and picnic groves. For ticket information call (706)866-5681. The park is on Lakeview Drive at the end of McBrien Road in Rossville.

Directions: From I-75 take I-24 west toward Chattanooga then exit on Rossville Boulevard south, U.S. 27. Continue south on Route 27, Rossville Boulevard, approximately 2½ miles to the city of Rossville. You will cross the Tennessee/Georgia state line at this point. Proceed to the fourth traffic light at Spring Street and turn right. Go one block to the stop sign and you will be facing the John Ross House. A historic marker is located at the intersection of Spring Street and U.S. 27.

Chieftains Museum and Rome

The Glory that is Rome

The Cherokee Nation was located in part within the state of Georgia. The Indians had their own alphabet, culture, government and leaders, one of whom was Major Ridge. While his first name is not known, he gained his military rank during the Battle of Horseshoe Bend in 1814.

Born in Tennessee around 1771, Ridge moved to the Rome area around 1794 and built a log cabin on a grassy riverbank of the Oostanaula (meaning shoaly) River, where he ran a ferry and trading post. In 1828 his successful business ventures enabled him to enlarge his home, transforming it into a typical Piedmont planter's house. (The house has been turned into the Chieftains Museum.)

In 1835 Major Ridge was sent to Washington to discuss the removal of the Cherokees from the Southeast to the West. He did not speak for the entire tribe since he was merely a regional chief. Part of the negotiations for the treaty to relocate the Cherokees, which Ridge eventually signed, took place at his home in

Rome, and thus it is considered the spot where the infamous Trail of Tears began.

The Cherokee nation categorically rejected the treaty that President Andrew Jackson discussed with Major Ridge. After John Ross (see John Ross selection) was temporarily jailed, Ridge went to Washington and signed a treaty with the federal government. Roughly 400 Cherokees agreed to sell their land, and they left for Oklahoma in the spring of 1837. All who did so were considered traitors by the Indians. It was Ridge's son John, a lawyer for the tribe, who established the law mandating the death penalty for those who sold their property. On June 22, 1830, on the Oklahoma reservation, Major Ridge was murdered for his crime against the Cherokee Nation.

Being a Cherokee, Major Ridge had never had legal title to his home in Rome, and once he and his family left for Oklahoma, the property was included in the land lottery and passed through several owners. Legend has it that Union troops tried to destroy the house during the war, but the logs were so well constructed they withstood their efforts.

Today the Chieftains Museum is on the National Register of Historic Places and is included on the list of National Historic Landmarks. One of the stops on northwest Georgia's Chieftains Trail, it is now a museum with an extensive collection of Cherokee Indian history. Artifacts go back to the 16th-century King Site. In prehistoric time the Mound Builders came through this area, as did DeSoto and his men.

Museum exhibits also focus on the Civil War. By the time the Union army reached Rome, most people had refugeed (the term used in Georgia for fleeing the path of the oncoming Yankees) to safety. The nearly deserted Rome was not burned by the Union army. Besides the historical exhibits, the modern wings of Chieftains Museum sponsor shows of regional artists. On the grounds you can see the *Myra H.* riverboat, capturing the days when the ferry ran up and down the Oostanaula. There is also an archaeological dig behind the house on the original location of the trading post owned by Ridge and his friend George Lavendar. Chieftains Museum is open Tuesday through Friday 11:00 A.M. to 4:00 P.M. and Sunday from 2:00 to 5:00 P.M.

The Chieftains Museum is just one of the sights of **Rome**. The town, like its Roman counterpart, is built around seven hills and is situated on two rivers, the Etowah and Oostanaula, which meet in downtown Rome to form the Coosa that flows into the Gulf of Mexico. This Georgia city also has its Capitoline Wolf Statue, which stands in front of City Hall. It was a gift to the city in 1929 from Benito Mussolini. Another Roman landmark common to both cities is the clock tower, which still keeps time. It too is on the National Register of Historic Places. At the city's Visitor Cen-

A replica of original Etruscan art, this Capitoline Wolf Statue was a gift from ancient Rome to Rome, Georgia.

ter, in a converted railroad depot and caboose, you can obtain a taped walking tour of Rome's historic "Between the Rivers" district.

The city is also noted for its parks. At the Lock and Dam Park on the Coosa River you can rent canoes, try your luck at the fishing pier or overnight at the campgrounds (706)234-5001. Georgia's first National Natural Landmark, Marshall Forest, is in Rome. Maclean Marshall, naturalist and philanthropist, gave the Nature Conservancy 220 acres of forest and fields. The old-growth forest has never been cut and is home to over 300 species of plants and numerous varieties of birds and mammals. Five nature trails lead into the forest, but only the Braille Trail is now open to the public. This self-guided trail takes about 30 minutes to explore. For information on guided walks call Dr. Mark Knauss at (706)291-4298.

While in the Rome area you should take the time to visit nearby **Cave Spring**. The town, noted for its quaint Victorian and Gothic Revival homes, has more than 90 buildings and sites on the National Register of Historic Places. Another reason to visit is the abundance of antique shops, more than 40 specializing in antiques and collectibles. During the summer months you might want to take a dip in the state's second largest pool, and one of only five built in the shape of the state. Another cool spot is the cave at Rolater Park, which is open daily from Memorial Day to Labor Day.

Directions: From I-75 north take Exit 125, Route 411 west, into Rome, where it merges with Route 20/27. Chieftains Museum is at 501 Riverside Parkway, 1.5 miles from downtown Rome. Once you reach the center of Rome, take a right at the Visitor Center and then turn left on Reservoir Street and right on Riverside Parkway. The museum will be on your left. For Cave Spring go south on Route 27 then southwest on Route 411/53 to the small community nestled in the Appalachian foothills. For information on all the attractions in Rome stop at the Visitors Center off Route 27 north and Route 20 west. For additional information call the center at (800)444-1834.

Crown Gardens and Archives

Peacock Alley

Dalton's distinction as the Carpet Capital of the World grew from an earlier fame: it was once the Bedspread Capital of the World. For years travelers called the section of Highway 41 between Dalton and Cartersville, Peacock Alley or Bedspread Alley—Row, Line or Boulevard. To learn about the link between these two businesses visit Crown Gardens and Archives Museum in the 1884 Crown Cotton Mill office building.

Crown Cotton Mill, Dalton's first large manufacturing plant, was made from clay bricks fired on the grounds. The land once was occupied by Chief Redbird whose grave is alleged to be under the railroad bed that runs beside the mill. When a train wrecked going around a curve near his grave, locals claimed that he was haunting the tracks.

The village that surrounds the once prosperous Crown Cotton Mill is now a National Historic District. In the Crown Gardens Museum, operated by the Whitfield-Murray Historical Society, a bedspread exhibit shows how the chenille spreads were made.

It all started when 12-year old Catherine Evans Whitener, visiting her cousin in McCuffy, Georgia, admired a homespun bedspread, probably created in the candlewicking method. This technique used white cords that resembled candle wicks. A pioneer variation on this method was to fluff out the ends of the threads to make a design. Three years later Catherine decided to make a spread like the one she remembered, and on seamed flour sacks she used a method that became known as tufting (locals pronounce it turfing). Catherine's spreads, which she made for $2.50 each, became popular. She soon taught others how to tuft, and a cottage industry developed with haulers delivering supplies and picking up spreads. During the Depression entire families worked to make these bedspreads. From about 1925 into the early 1970s, colorful spreads hanging outside on clotheslines beside farmhouses and cottages was a common sight. By far the most popular pattern featured two peacocks with bright tail feathers.

At Crown Gardens volunteers demonstrate how these spreads were made and show you the machines that converted this cottage industry into an even bigger business in the 1930s and 40s. You'll see examples of various patterns and even some of the secondary products made from chenille including robes and jackets. The museum displays one of the two bedspreads used in *Gone With the Wind*. After World War II the tufting machines used to mass-produce the bedspreads were adapted to make tufted carpeting and a multi-billion-dollar business evolved. Dalton became the carpet capital of the world. Today there are more than 100 carpet outlets in town.

The museum has another collection of furnishings and memorabilia that focuses on black heritage. A third exhibit has artifacts from the Civil War, and finally there is an extensive local genealogical collection. Another major focus of the museum is the collection honoring Dalton native and Georgia's Poet Laureate Robert Loveman. A room is furnished with items from his home at 205 N. Thornton Avenue. Loveman, a local character, liked to engulf youngsters in his huge black cape and quote them poetry. One of Loveman's most enduring works is the lyrics to "Georgia," the state song for years before the honor shifted to "Georgia On My Mind."

The Crown Gardens and Archives are open daily Tuesday through Friday from 10:00 A.M. to 5:00 P.M. and Saturday from 10:00 A.M. to 3:00 P.M. The Hamilton House, at 701 Chattanooga Avenue, is also part of the Crown Mill Historic District. John Hamilton built this clay-brick house in 1840 on land he purchased from Chief Redbird. In 1863 the house served briefly as the headquarters of Confederate General Joseph H. Lewis. When the Union army entered Dalton they used the Hamilton House as a hospital. The house is not open for tours. You can, however, tour the Blunt House at 506 S. Thornton Avenue, home of Dalton's first mayor. To tour this historic house contact the Historical Society at (706)278-0217.

If you are in Dalton around meal time, you can combine dining with another important aspect of the town's past by stopping at the **Dalton Depot**. Dalton was a significant stop on the Western and Atlanta Line, built in the 1840s to connect the Chattahoochee and Tennessee rivers. The Dalton Depot stands on the exact center of the city. The center marker can still be seen in the restaurant's entranceway.

Begun in 1852 the depot linked Dalton with Atlanta and with the newly opened Cherokee land in North Georgia. During the Civil War, the depot was one of the stops the General passed as it raced to escape Captain Fuller aboard the Texas (see Big Shanty selection). The Dalton Depot, a transportation hub for 138 years, is now listed on the National Register of Historic Places. The renovation into a restaurant has been imaginatively achieved, and diners can still see trains whizzing past the station—roughly 26 scheduled runs a day. The Dalton Depot is at 110 Depot Street in the heart of town (706)226-3160.

Directions: From I-75 take Exit 136. Head east into Dalton on Route 76/52, W. Walnut Avenue, then turn left on Thornton Avenue. Continue through the central business district. Turn right on Tyler Road and cross the railroad tracks. Turn left on Chattanooga Avenue and continue to Crown Gardens and Archives one block on your left.

Etowah Indian Mounds

Standing the Test of Time

Before Jean Auel began writing her multi-volume series *The Earth's Children*, archaeologists were the only ones with more than a sketchy idea about the life of prehistoric people. The idea of more than two thousand prehistoric people living in a thriving town in the northwest Georgia mountains is amazing. Visitors to the Etowah Indian Mounds gain an understanding of the people who lived in this region between 1000 and 1500 A.D. from the 30-minute video, Lost in Time, which you should see before exploring the mounds and the museum exhibits.

The video takes you back to the Ice Age and the time when hunters trekked from the Arctic Circle across a land bridge to the North American continent. It moves from the Archaic Period to the Woodland Period, when these prehistoric people began farming. This was when the Mississippi People emerged. The Indians who built the Etowah mounds were part of this group. The largest town of the Mississippi culture was in what is now Collinsville, Illinois, while the northernmost site was in Wisconsin. **The Mound People** ultimately evolved into the Creeks and other recognized Indian tribes.

After putting the Mound People into a historical time frame, go out and see the village site. Once you've seen the mounds, the museum artifacts uncovered when portions of the mound were excavated will have more significance. Only 8 percent of the 52-acre village site has been excavated.

The Etowah village site was the largest and most important of the tribal communities along the Etowah River and the center of political and religious life for the Etowah Valley. As you walk from the museum towards the village site you will see a model mound. The cutaways reveal how the mounds were built in layers. When a chief died they burned his temple, added another layer to the mound and erected a new temple.

It is easy to see the perimeters of the village because it is surrounded on three sides by a defensive moat and on the fourth by the Etowah River. The moat was nine to ten feet deep, and just inside (although no longer standing) was a protective palisade of upright logs. This fence stood approximately 12 feet tall. The combination of moat and fence made the village virtually secure against attack by spears, arrows and clubs. Village chiefs vied for power and for land, so protection was essential.

Before crossing the moat notice the borrow pit (a second pit is just a short distance from the first). The pits resulted from the removal of thousands of basketfuls of dirt used to build the mounds. Thousands of tribal villagers lived in the flat area you see within the compound.

As you approach the largest mound on your right **(Mound A)** you will notice a slight rise in the path that indicates the edge of the ceremonial plaza. This large square was constructed of packed red clay, which was also used to build the ceremonial center of the mound complex.

The plaza stands in front of the 63-foot-high ceremonial platform mound, which is roughly the height of a six-story building
and three acres in circumference at its base. The 105 steps are
positioned where once there were steps built into the mound,
which was originally approximately 75 feet high. Unlike the
reconstructed ceremonial earthlodge you see at Ocmulgee National Monument in Macon (see selection), there isn't a room
inside the mound. If you climb to the top of the mound you will
be standing where a ceremonial temple once stood, but there are
no ruins or reminders. This great temple mound has not been
excavated. If you look down at the south side (or walk around
the base to that side) you will see a small platform built into the
mound. This might have been used by the leaders of the Etowah
people to watch ceremonies or to address the villagers.

Although smaller, Mound B was also a temple platform. A
thorough excavation has not been done on this mound, but test
pits reveal it was used for burials. Remains of deer, turkey, turtles, plants and fish were discovered in trash pits on the west
side of the mound. The major excavation work done at Etowah
was conducted at **Mound C**. It was thoroughly studied, then
painstakingly restored. Archaeologists discovered 350 burials in
Mound C and found the Indian leaders interred in costumes and
with ceremonial objects. From this field work much information
was obtained about life in this village. Most of the museum's
artifacts were found in Mound C, including the world-famous
marble mortuary figures.

If you have time before returning to view the museum collection, take the path to the river bank to see the rock shoals and
fish traps visible when the water level is low. The "V" shaped
traps were formed from piled stones. The Indians caught gar,
drum and catfish in woven baskets at the point of the "V." From
the trail winding along the riverbank, you'll see vegetation much
like what the Etowah people relied on to supplement the food
they grew, like walnut, hickory and persimmon trees. The Indians used the river cane you'll see growing here to make arrow
shafts and for thatch in roofing and in making floor mats.

In the **museum** drawings suggest what the Etowah people
looked like: Surprisingly, they were almost six feet tall. The
tombs yielded agricultural tools, food gathering utensils, hunting
and fishing implements and ceremonial objects used in their
rituals. The most exciting discovery was that of two effigy figures
carved out of marble that once stood watch over the burial site.
These remarkable statues are a haunting reminder of the Etowah
people. The Etowah Indian Mounds are open year-round on
Tuesday through Saturday from 9:00 A.M. to 5:00 P.M. and on
Sunday from 2:00 to 5:30 P.M. There is a nominal admission fee.

Directions: From I-75 take Exit 124 and follow Route 61/13 south then turn left on Indian Mounds Road. The site is only six miles southwest of the interstate.

Fort Mountain State Park

Mysterious Ruins

On a wind-swept summit in the Cohutta Mountain range an 855-foot-long **ancient rock wall** remains a mystery to scholars, historians and archaeologists. More than a hundred years have passed since it was discovered, but its origin is still shrouded in secrecy.

This prehistoric wall's history is steeped in legends. One explanation is that the wall was built by Indians around 500 A.D. as a fortification or as a ceremonial site. Similar walls are scattered in the highlands of Tennessee and in other parts of the southeastern United States. Since prehistoric Indians worshiped the sun, the fact that the wall extends along a precipice on the east side of the mountain and due west to a similar point on the other side meant that the sun rises on one end of the wall and sets on the other side. Supporting the theory that it was used for ceremonial purposes is the lack of artifacts in or around the wall; all objects used in ancient ceremonies were taken away when the Indians moved to a new location.

Another theory is that the wall was built by Welsh explorers in the 14th century to protect them from the Indians. The legendary Welsh Prince Madoc reputedly sailed into Mobile, Alabama, roughly 500 years ago and then traveled north through the Fort Mountain region. Petrogylphs in the southeast have been linked to Madoc's passage.

Legend even claims that the wall was built by the explorer De Soto. Although this idea once enjoyed wide support, more recent research disputes it since De Soto did not remain in the area long enough to need or build a defense system.

Cherokee myth tells of "Moon-eyed" people, a race of light-skinned people who could see in the dark, who came to the region and built the wall. Since the Cherokees have either brown or black eyes, the myth could refer to a race of blue-eyed people, perhaps Welsh or Spanish.

Most archaeologists lean towards the prehistoric Native-American explanation. Today the wall is only two feet to six feet in height, but experts think it was once considerably higher. Every 30 feet, circular pits are built into the wall. A steadily inclined trail up the mountain starts at the **Fort Mountain State Park** parking area and takes hikers to the wall.

The 1,932-acre state park has five main trails; the major one goes to the stone wall and loops past a stone tower built by the Civilian Conservation Corps. Another popular trail skirts around a 17-acre lake; while a third follows Gold Mine Creek. An 8.2-mile Cahutti backpacking trail gives hikers an in-depth exposure to Fort Mountain.

There are camping sites for both recreational vehicles and tents, as well as 15 cottages. The park gates open at 7:00 A.M. and close at 10:00 P.M. For additional information call (706)695-2621.

Just three miles down the road from Fort Mountain State Park is the Cohutta Lodge, (706)695-9601, a mountain-top hotel and restaurant for those who enjoy hiking but not camping. To the north of Fort Mountain State Park is the 34,100-acre **Cohutta Wilderness Area**. The Fannin County Chamber of Commerce in Blue Ridge, (706)632-5680, can supply information about a variety of mountain cabins adjacent to the Cohutta Wilderness and the Chattahoochee National Forest, many of which overlook trout streams. At Sunnybrook Bend Cabins, just eight miles northwest of Blue Ridge, each cabin has a secluded hot tub overlooking the sparkling Little Fighting Town Creek. Within the Cohutta Wilderness, fisherman can try their skill hooking three species of trout and the Coosa bass, found only in the unpolluted upland headwaters of the Conasauga and the Jacks rivers. Hikers and backpackers also enjoy the unspoiled, rugged beauty of this mountain refuge where elevations range from 950 to 4,200 feet. You can also call the U.S. Forest Service in Chatsworth, (706)695-6736, for information on the Cohutta Wilderness Area.

Directions: From I-75 north take Exit 126, Route 441 north. At Chatsworth turn right on Route 52 for the entrance to Fort Mountain State Park.

Gordon-Lee Mansion and Fort Oglethorpe

Good Side Bets

Flanking Chickamauga National Military Park are two sites of interest to travelers. Just three miles south of the park is the Gordon-Lee Mansion, and immediately to the north is the now deactivated Fort Oglethorpe.

Three days prior to the Battle of Chickamauga the Union army used the Gordon-Lee Mansion as their headquarters, but once the fighting began and the casualties mounted they converted it into their main hospital. The completely restored and furnished house is now a National Historic Site. It is open for tours and overnight guests.

James Gordon began building his antebellum mansion in the early 1840s. He lived on the grounds in a log cabin until 1847 when the elegant brick mansion was completed. A log cabin still stands on the grounds, although it is not the original one. James Gordon moved out while the Union troops occupied his home and moved back in after the battle. The floors are original and when you tour the house you can still see blood stains in the library floor. The Union surgeons used this room as their operating theater. A sense of perfect harmony and tranquility now echoes through these rooms where long ago men screamed in outrage against the tides of war that swept them here. Locals claim 40 wagon loads of severed limbs were hauled away from the house. This estimate is not unreasonable when you consider that the bloody two-day battle on September 19 and 20, 1863, cost the Confederates 18,000 men and Federal casualities numbered 16,000.

Today delicate antebellum antiques once more fill the rooms. The oldest piece in the house is the 1741 mirror in the library. There are also several interesting examples of reverse painting on glass: The portraits in the parlor of George and Martha Washington are executed in this fashion. The parlor also has a portrait of James's grandson Gordon Lee, a noted Georgia legislator, who lived here until his death in 1927. Dying childless, Gordon Lee left his property to the local school. In 1974 the house was acquired by Dr. Frank Green of Chattanooga who restored it, opened it as a house museum in 1976 and expanded it in 1989 into a bed-and-breakfast inn.

Overnight guests enjoy breakfast in the dining room, which has an Oriental mural painted on the wall. The bedrooms are also filled with antiques, although the only original piece of furniture in the house is the High Victorian-style mirror in the downstairs bedroom. Although there is a metal tub in the room, guests enjoy the luxury of modern facilities in the six rooms.

Both guests and visitors should take the time to peruse the collections in the upstairs museum room. There are Indian artifacts, memorabilia from the Civil War era and old newspaper clippings about the house.

On the grounds there is an original slave cabin, one of six brick slave houses. The garden has also been restored. The grounds have a historical significance that predates the house. Before Andrew Jackson's proclamation that relocated the Cherokee Indians in Oklahoma, this was the site of a Cherokee courthouse. Once the Indians were driven west the courthouse was used by the white settlers as their seat of government. James Gordon obtained his 2,500 acres from the "lottery tracks" held to distribute Indian land.

Tours of the mansion are given from Memorial Day through

Labor Day, Tuesday through Saturday from NOON until 5:00 P.M. and on Sundays from 2:00 to 5:00 P.M. Admission is charged. For information on accommodations call (706)375-4728.

Just before you enter the Chickamauga National Military Park you will pass **Fort Oglethorpe** on your right. This fort built in 1902–1904 became a post for the Sixth U.S. Cavalry on July 4, 1919. After the cavalry left in 1942 it became a WAC training center until it closed in January 1946. The former parade field is now listed on the National Register of Historic Places. One of the former officers' quarters is now a bed-and-breakfast called the Captain's Quarters, (706)858-0624.

Also on the parade field is the small Sixth Cavalry Museum where you'll see old photographs of the fort as well as old army vehicles, uniforms, a field tent and equipment plus a Cobra helicopter on the roof. Interested visitors can view a 30-minute film on the history of the Sixth Cavalry and Fort Oglethorpe. Museum hours are weekdays, except Wednesday, 10:00 A.M. to 4:00 P.M. and Saturdays 1:00 to 4:00 P.M. Donations are appreciated.

Directions: From I-75 take Exit 141, Route 2, to the intersection with Route 27 and make a left. Follow Route 27 through the Chickamauga National Military Park and turn right on Lee & Gordon Mill Road. Continue on that to Cove Road. The Gordon-Lee Mansion is at 217 Cove Road. Fort Oglethorpe is on your right on Route 27 immediately before the entrance to the military park.

Lookout Mountain and Cloudland Canyon State Park

Up Among the Clouds

Tucked in the western corner of the state is Lookout Mountain, part of the Cumberland Plateau. This mountainous region runs parallel to the Appalachian Chain. Lookout Mountain extends for a hundred miles through three states: 76 miles in Alabama, 3 miles in Tennessee and 21 miles in Georgia.

Mountains in the Cumberland Plateau are flatter than the Blue Ridge Mountains in the northeastern part of the state. Lookout Mountain is a typical "flat mountain" produced by mountain folding during the Paleozoic era. This process produced one of the best caving regions in the country. Ellison's Cave on Pigeon Mountain, not far from Lookout Mountain, is the deepest cave you'll find east of the Mississippi River. In the Tennessee portion of Lookout Mountain you can visit Raccoon Mountain and Ruby

Falls, two caves that attract thousands of visitors each year. A multi-highway, multi-state parkway covers what the region boasts is "America's most scenic 100 miles."

One of the most scenic spots on Lookout Mountain is the 2,200-acre **Cloudland Canyon State Park**, straddling a deep gorge cut into the mountain by Sitton Gulch Creek. Elevations in the park range from 1,800 at the highest vantage point to 800 feet above sea level. The best way for most visitors to see the park is to take the 4.9-mile West Rim Loop Trail that follows the edge of the canyon rim. An overlook along this trail lets you see the park's three gorges. To reach this trail drive to the western side of the gorge where the cottages are located. If you walk about 200 yards past cottage #15 you will reach the overlook and from there you can pick up the trail. A short 0.3-mile Waterfall Trail leads to two waterfalls on Daniels Creek. Although it is a short trail there are 400 wooden steps down to the falls. There is also a 6-mile loop Cloudland Back Country Trail. Primitive campers can overnight along this trail, but be sure to obtain a permit at the park office before setting off.

One way to enjoy Cloudland Canyon if you don't have the time or the energy to take these hikes is from the picnic area where there are splendid vantage points from which to view the canyon. Near the picnic area, you'll find a children's playground. The park also has tennis courts and a swimming pool. There are 16 rental cabins, but they require long-range planning as they are often booked up to 11 months in advance. You might have better luck with the 75 tent and trailer sites and the 30 walk-in campsites.

Cloudland Canyon is open daily 7:00 A.M. to 10:00 P.M. The park office is open 8:00 A.M. to 5:00 P.M. For information call (706)657-4050. Cloudland Canyon State Park is only 17 miles from Rock City, and along the way you will pass the Lookout Mountain hang-gliding launch site. The hang-gliding headquarters offers lessons, sales and service. Call (706)398-3541. Most travelers are not interested in taking part in this spine-chilling sport, but they do find it fascinating to watch the colorful hang gliders take off into the void. The action is best in the spring and fall, but on any pleasant day you're apt to see one or two enthusiasts.

Directions: From I-75 heading north take Exit 133 and follow Route 136 west to LaFayette. The park is 18 miles west of La-Fayette on Route 136.

Martha Berry Museum and Oak Hill

Miracle in the Mountains

Everyone has read lists of the most admired and respected women in America, but one name deserves to be included and is not. Seldom beyond the boundaries of northwest Georgia is Martha Berry's name remembered. You'll discover the inspirational story of her interest in educating mountain children when you visit **Berry College** in Rome, which she founded to continue the educational program she had begun in the formative grades.

To appreciate all that you will see, make your first stop the Martha Berry Museum. Be sure to take the time to watch the touching 28-minute movie about Martha Berry. She was born at Oak Hill, and her family home is included in the museum tour. Just outside the museum is a small log cabin that Martha used as a study. While reading in the cabin one day in the late 1890s, she looked up to see several young children looking in the window, watching her while she read. Martha Berry invited them in and read Bible stories to them. Soon the mountain children were coming to her cabin to hear her read the Bible, and her Sunday school classes became the precursor to the Berry Schools. She expanded her schooling to the elementary levels, then into an accredited high school and ultimately founded Berry College, a boys' college begun in 1902.

In 1910, just before visiting Berry College, President Theodore Roosevelt wrote a letter praising her efforts but asked, "What are you doing for mountain girls?" By the end of that year Berry College was expanded to a coeducational facility.

The Martha Berry Museum has photographs and memorabilia from the earliest days of the college. Martha's father gave her 82 acres of land which she later used to begin her school. Henry Ford underwrote, and personally supervised the construction of, a magnificent complex of Gothic buildings on the campus. Andrew Carnegie also provided financial support and encouraged other industrialists to do the same. In the museum you will see the dress that Miss Berry wore when she was presented to the King and Queen of England. You'll notice it does not have a train, which she insisted on renting, refusing to pay an excessive amount for such vanity. College lore claims that from that date on she wore her presentation gown to the weddings of all her students.

The Martha Berry Museum also has one of the region's finest art collections. Martha's sister, Eugenia Berry Ruspoli, married an Italian prince and moved to Italy where she collected furniture, paintings and objets d'art. A substantial portion of her collection that she gave to the museum is displayed in the Ruspoli Room.

After touring the museum, your next stop should be **Oak Hill**, on a hilltop overlooking the museum. This antebellum plantation was built in 1847 and acquired by Martha's father, Captain Thomas Berry, in 1859 just before he married Frances Rhea. Martha, born in 1866, was the second of eleven children.

During the Civil War, Union soldiers camped on the grounds of Oak Hill. Though not confirmed, tradition has it that Oak Hill was not damaged but that some outbuildings were burned before the troops departed. A fire in the 1890s, however, did damage the second floor. All of the furnishings are original Berry family pieces. Her father's room has remained much as it was at his death in 1887. Her mother's bedroom also remains unchanged. Martha's own room reveals a great deal about her character. It is utterly Spartan; there are no rugs, no curtains and no decorations. It was obviously not a room in which she spent much time. Preserved just as it was in 1942 when Martha lived here, the house does not look like a museum.

Adjacent to the house is the carriage house with some vintage vehicles including a 1914 Ford touring car, a 1917 Model-T and a 1940 Mercury as well as the family surrey and buggy. Be sure to take the time to explore the gardens. Springtime is particularly delightful with the flowering cherry trees, a gift from the Japanese government. There are also azaleas, flowering bulbs and an extensive hemerocallis collection. Formal areas include the goldfish garden, sundial garden and a unique sunken garden. The greenhouse is also open for tours.

The museum and Oak Hill are open from 10:00 A.M. to 5:00 P.M. Tuesday through Saturday and from 1:00 to 5:00 P.M. on Sunday. A nominal admission is charged. You may prefer to stop at the museum and pick up an audio tour tape and map of the Berry campus. This is not just another campus: It is the nation's largest campus with 26,000 acres encompassing nature trails, lakes, forests and gardens.

One of the highlights of the campus is the **Ford Complex** built around a reflecting pool. The architect who designed the Gothic buildings in this quadrangle also did the College Chapel, modeling it after Christ Church in Alexandria, Virginia. Martha Berry, who died at age 76, is buried beneath a pecan tree just south of the chapel.

Another campus landmark is the Roosevelt Cabin where Martha Berry lived for almost five years, between 1902 and 1907, because she said life at Oak Hill made her too lazy. It received its name after President Theodore Roosevelt had lunch here with Miss Berry on October 8, 1910.

One section of the campus is called the **Log Cabin Campus**,

A pool on the grounds of Berry College reflects the Gothic splendor of the Ford Complex.

with student-constructed buildings still in use. The Barnwell Chapel, built in 1911 with hand-hewn logs, is an architectural gem. A scenic three-mile drive takes visitors from the main campus to the mountain campus where you may arrange to see the House O'Dreams atop Lavender Mountain. Students built this retreat in 1926 for the college's 25th anniversary with funds donated by Mrs. Emily Vanderbilt Hammond. The grounds are landscaped like the Ruspoli's Castle Nemi in Italy.

Just down Lavender Mountain is the Old Mill. The mill is 42 feet in diameter, making it among the world's largest overshot-waterwheel mills. This photographer's delight is appealing in every season.

When Martha Berry moved her group of children from her log cabin study she began giving classes in Possum Trot Church, also part of the mountain campus. The church was built around 1850, but it wasn't until around 1900 that Martha began using it for Sunday school and then as a grammar school. She painted the scriptures that visitors see on the wall. Possum Trot is considered the "cradle of Berry College."

Berry College, to the roughly 1,700 undergraduates who attend, is more than an historical, cultural and natural attraction. The students value it as one of the top liberal arts colleges in the country. Visitors should stop at the Handicraft Shop and Weaving

Studio from 8:30 A.M. to 5:00 P.M. Monday through Friday and watch the students. A selection of fine hand-crafted work is sold at the shop.

Directions: From I-75 north, take Exit 125 to Route 20/411 to Rome. In Rome, take Route 20/27 to the entrance of Berry College at the intersection of Route 27 and the Georgia Loop 1 intersection. From I-75 south, take Exit 129 to Route 53 then pick-up Georgia Loop 1 west. The entrance to Martha Berry College will be on the left immediately before the light on Route 27.

New Echota and Vann House State Historic Sites

Cherokee National Capital

In 1830 the Cherokee Nation stretched across a 10-million-acre tract of land in what is now northwest Georgia, northeast Alabama, southern Tennessee and North Carolina. Five years earlier the Cherokee legislature established a national capital they called New Echota. The name honored a much-loved town of the Cherokees in present-day eastern Tennessee called Old Chota.

New Echota was a thriving town with a 60-foot-wide main street and side streets almost that size. Along these generous thoroughfares Cherokee surveyors laid out 100 town lots and a two-acre public square. Government buildings included the Council House and the Supreme Courthouse. The Cherokees adopted a government system like the federal government, complete with a written constitution, elected leaders and a supreme court. By 1830 there were 20 buildings and 50 permanent residents at New Echota.

In 1828 the *Cherokee Phoenix*, the world's first Indian language newspaper began weekly publication out of New Echota's National Printing Office. The Cherokee language was transformed into written form in 1821 by Cherokee scholar and leader Sequoyah, who spent 12 years creating a syllabary from the symbols used in the Cherokee language. They were the first North American Indian tribe to have a written language. The bilingual *Cherokee Phoenix* was published from February 21, 1828, until May 31, 1834.

When you visit the **New Echota State Historic Site** you'll see a 15-minute video that gives the history of this capital and its painful legacy as the military headquarters for the U.S. Army during the removal of the Cherokees on their Trail of Tears. You can hear the Cherokee language spoken and see Sequoyah's symbols as part of the museum's exhibits.

The staff lead guided tours of the original and reconstructed buildings at New Echota Tuesday through Saturday. Times are 9:30 and 11:00 A.M. and 1:30 and 3:00 P.M. Sunday tours are at 2:30 and 4:00 P.M. These are the only times you can enter the buildings; at other times you can take a self-guided walking tour of the village.

The first of the nine stops on your tour is a small hewn-log cabin typical of the ones Cherokees in the village built in the mid-1830s. On the average, a Cherokee cultivated 11 acres, with corn as the principal crop. Stop two, is the crossroads of what was once New Echota. After the Cherokees were sent west, the town fell into ruin, and the buildings were burned or torn down. A few buildings survived sufficiently to be restored; others have had to be rebuilt on their old foundations. This is a continuing project, and additional restoration is planned if funding can be obtained.

Next on your tour are four stone markers indicating the location of Elias Boudinot's house. He was the editor of the Cherokee Phoenix from 1828 to 1832. Boudinot married Harriet Gold from New England. Just up from his house site is the reconstructed printing office. A printing press similar to the original still turns out copies of the historic Cherokee newspaper, and each family on the tour is given a page. You can purchase a four-page copy of the paper.

The **Vann Tavern**, stop five, was moved to this location from the Gainesville area. It is an original Cherokee structure, built in 1800 by James Vann, as a tavern, inn and store. The small opening under the staircase was an old-fashioned version of take-out service for those travelers the proprietor would not allow inside. All of the tavern furniture is over a hundred years old, and the price list on the wall harkens back to earlier days, listing room and board for 25 cents, clean sheets 10 cents and whiskey 12½ cents a shot.

Samuel Worcester's home has been restored as stop six on your walking tour. Worcester was a Presbyterian minister sent to New Echota by the American Board of Commissioners for Foreign Missions in Boston. This Board also paid the cost of setting up the printing office. Worcester arrived at the Cherokee capital in 1827 with his wife and four children. The family quarters were on the first floor of his house, the school and church on the second floor. Worcester was forced to leave his mission station in 1831, when he was sentenced to four years' hard labor for defying a state law calling for whites living on Cherokee lands to register with the government. Elihu Butler, who also worked with the Cherokees at New Echota, was sentenced along with Worcester. After Worcester served his sentence he followed the Indians west and spent the rest of his life working among the

Cherokees. As a footnote to this story, in·November 1992, Governor Zell Miller posthumously pardoned the two Christian missionaries, Samuel Worcester and Elihu Butler, thus correcting a miscarriage of justice.

One of the stockades built by federal troops to imprison the Cherokees until their forced march west was just south of Worcester's house. There were 13 stockades in Georgia. Many of the Cherokees who were rounded up were given no chance to gather their personal possessions. The mortality rate in these concentration camps was high. Four thousand more Cherokees died on the Trail of Tears.

If you have time you can interrupt your tour and take the nature trail leading off the tour route. It winds through the woods alongside a stream.

Stop seven is the Rogers House. A one-story log house has been built here, like the one owned by John Rogers, a white man who married a Cherokee woman. This cabin is not furnished, so you can enter even if you are not taking part in a guided walk.

One of the most important stops on your tour is the Supreme Court Building, stop eight. This reconstructed two-story frame building served not only for the Supreme Court but also as a church and school. Visitors are welcome to walk in and explore.

The last stop marks the spot where the Council House once stood. Now on the drawing boards for reconstruction, this capitol building housed the General Council, a legislature made up of two houses, and the National Council with 32 delegates plus a select 13-member National Committee. Bills had to pass both houses to become law. The General Council selected the executive branch under Cherokee law.

New Echota Historic Site is open at a nominal charge Tuesday through Saturday 9:00 A.M. to 5:00 P.M. and Sunday 2:00 to 5:30 P.M. Closed on Mondays, Thanksgiving, Christmas and New Year's Day.

One of the most significant events of the year at New Echota is the annual **Cherokee Indian Homecoming Festival** in mid-September. Cherokees return to New Echota to take part in traditional dancing, storytelling, music, song, language demonstrations, blowgun shooting and craft demonstrations including beadmaking, woodcarving, basket weaving and fingerweaving. For more information call (706)629-8151.

Explore yet another aspect of Cherokee life and culture just 20 miles from New Echota at the **Chief Vann House State Historic Site**. This classic, pillared, brick mansion is called the "Showplace of the Cherokee Nation." Built in 1804 by Chief James Vann, the owner of the tavern that was moved to New Echota, the house has lovely interior wood carvings and a noteworthy cantilevered stairway.

Chief Vann was vitally interested in education, and he brought Moravian missionaries to the Cherokee Nation to educate the young. He also encouraged the Cherokees to adopt the Christian religion, although he himself had three wives. In 1808 he shot his brother-in-law in a duel and was killed the following year as punishment for his crime.

His son, Joseph, inherited the house and his father's businesses, but when he hired a white man to work for him the state of Georgia confiscated the house. It was awarded to a white during the land lottery of 1834.

The house is now filled with period furnishings and can be toured Tuesday through Saturday from 9:00 A.M. to 5:00 P.M. and Sunday 2:00 to 5:30 P.M. A nominal admission is charged.

Directions: From I-75 take Exit 131 east on Route 225 for one mile. You can continue on Route 225 to Chief Vann House or get back on the interstate and go north to Exit 136. Take Route 52 east. The Chief Vann House is at the intersection with Route 225.

Prater's Mill

Down By The Mill Pond

I feel sorry for you if, as a small child
You neve experienced the thrill
Of loading the wheat when the threshers had gone
And heading for Old Prater's Mill.

The Model 'A' truck was a sight to behold
Loaded with big sacks of wheat
The sack that was highest on top of the load
Was the one I chose for a seat.

I viewed the landscape from the throne of a queen
Chug-a-lug thru valleys a'er hills
And I couldn't wait to once more see the ducks
On the Pond behind Old Prater's Mill.

This opening to Julia Willene Bowers's *Memories of Prater's Mill* evokes the same sense of nostalgia that visitors have when they come to this bright red, three-story mill. An enthusiastic group of volunteers has restored this 1855 mill built by Benjamin Franklin Prater. He started by processing grains for the region's farmers but soon added a cotton gin. Eventually Prater's business interests expanded to include a saw mill, syrup mill, general store, blacksmith shop and camping shed.

Now all that remains is the old mill (and the 1898 Prater's

Store), but it is again in working order. It is the only one remaining of the 32 gristmills that served Whitfield County in 1879. The Prater family operated this mill into the 1950s, when it was sold out of the family. It continued in operation until the 1960s when the building and machinery gave out. In 1971 the all-volunteer Prater's Mill Foundation undertook to restore the mill. Their efforts have led to the mill being listed on the National Register of Historic Places.

The group's major fund-raising activities are the semi-annual Prater's Mill Country Fairs on Mother's Day weekend in May and the second weekend in October, the only time you can tour the mill, watch it in operation and purchase corn meal and whole wheat flour. This mill is unusual in that the water wheel lies flat in the mill pond, unlike the traditional upright water wheel. The wheel is a water-powered turbine, which was more efficient than an over-shot water wheel. The mill was built of hand-hewn heart pine timbers with mortised and pegged joints. You can even see where B.F. Prater signed the main beam, but he isn't the only one to leave his autograph. Over the years other millers and their customers scrawled their names and dates on the walls and steps, in what volunteers now call "genealogical graffiti."

The **Prater's Mill Country Fair** is one of the most popular events in the Northwest Georgia Mountains. Over 150 artists and craftsmen demonstrate and sell their wares. Quilts, ironware, ceramics, hooked rugs, porcelain painting, brooms and a myriad of other folk crafts are available. Fair goers enjoy a feast of country cooking that includes warm, sweet cornbread made from water-ground meal, plus churned ice cream, pit-cooked barbecue, homemade vegetable soup, boiled peanuts and funnel cakes.

There's also plenty of entertainment throughout the weekend-long event including storytellers, jugglers, country bands, dulcimer players, cakewalk and square dancers. Youngsters can enjoy pony rides, canoeing and the live farm animals. There is also an antique engine display. Appropriately, the fair also includes a Civil War encampment because the mill grounds served as a campsite for soldiers from both the North and South. Six hundred Union men camped here on February 23, 1864, and 2,500 Confederates in the spring of that year on April 13th.

During the fair the now restocked Prater's original general store is also open. Also on the grounds are Shugart's Cotton Gin that has been relocated from Cohutta, Georgia, and the Westbrook family hay barn moved from another location in Dalton. Workers at the fair recreate the bedspread display, known as Peacock Alley, that once hung on clotheslines besides shops and homes along U.S. Highway 41 (see Crown Gardens and Archives selection). Peacock-decorated hand-tufted bedspreads once again flutter in the Georgia breeze.

Although the buildings are only open during the fair, the grounds are open the rest of the year at no charge. Visitors can picnic, canoe and fish. For additional information on the Prater's Mill Country Fair call (706)275-MILL.

Directions: From I-75 take the Tunnel Hill-Varnell Exit 138. Take Route 201 north towards Varnell, then make a right on Route 2 and continue 2.6 miles to Prater's Mill on your left.

Rock City Gardens

Rock of Ages

Nature created the impressive formations at Rock City, but Garnet and Frieda Carter popularized them. The acreage that became Rock City was acquired by the Carters in 1924 when they optioned 300 acres to begin a luxury real estate development called Fairyland atop Lookout Mountain. While her husband spent the latter part of the 1920s on his development project, Frieda began collecting wildflowers and shrubs to plant along a path she marked off through massive stone skyscraper formations to the peak of the promontory.

Before long Garnet Carter became interested in his wife's project, and he and his assistants extended and enlarged her pathways and opened Rock City Gardens to the public in 1932. Carter's marketing genius resulted in one of the most successful advertising campaigns in American business history. Clark Byers painted the first Rock City sign on a barn roof in 1936; by the time he painted his last in 1968 more than 800 barns had big bold letters urging travelers to "See Rock City." (There are still 85 barns left, four in Georgia.) The slogan, which eventually appeared on bumper stickers, door mats, ash trays, birdhouses, ice coolers and a myriad of other items, became part of rural Americana.

Today there are ten acres to explore at Rock City. Visitors set their own pace on the self-guided tour and cover the equivalent of six city blocks. More than 400 different wildflowers, plants and shrubs native to the area grow amid the rocky formations. Spanning a 90-foot crevice is a 180-foot swinging bridge. For timid visitors there is also a stone bridge that crosses over to the promontory known as **Lover's Leap**, where according to Cherokee legend the brave warrior Sautee, from a far tribe, was thrown to his death and his lover the Princess Nacoochee leapt after him. The view from the 1,700-foot bluff is spectacular. On a crystal clear day you can see seven states (Tennessee, Kentucky, Virginia, North Carolina, South Carolina, Georgia and Alabama).

The origins of the rock formations go back a billion years to

According to Cherokee legend, star-crossed lovers Sautee and Princess Nacoochee met their deaths from this promontory (now Lovers Leap, Rock City Gardens).

the creation of the igneous and metamorphic base rock. Approximately 600 million years ago at the start of the Paleozoic era streams carried layer after layer of sand, silt and clay into large water-filled basins called geosynclines creating large formations of limestone. Prehistoric earthquakes toppled large rock boulders, and passageways between the massive rocks were created by two sets of joints at right angles to each other.

By the late Paleozoic and early Mesozoic eras the area where Lookout Mountain stands was a deep valley between high mountains. During the next several million years the folding and faulting occurred that produced the Appalachian Mountain Chain. Then, a mere one million years ago, a great ice age advanced and retreated. Though Lookout Mountain was not covered by ice, the frost action contributed to the breaking apart of the blocks of sandstone at Rock City. The layers of sandstone hold the broken cliffs that prove so alluring at Rock City.

After visitors wiggle through narrow passageways just wide enough to permit access and enjoy unusual formations like the mushroom rock and the 1,000-ton balanced rock, there is still more to see. Rock City has two man-made creations that children particularly enjoy. One is **Fairyland Caverns** completed in 1947. Favorite stories are depicted in colorful scenes that are brilliantly illuminated with black light. A popular favorite in the caverns is the crystal falls made of sparkling crystal rocks. Next is **Mother Goose Village** with a ten-foot-tall castle surrounded by such childhood favorites as Jack and Jill, Little Bo Peep and the Three Little Kittens.

Christmas is celebrated with The Legends of Christmas starting December 1 and continuing until New Year's Day. A 16-foot star hangs from Lover's Leap, and throughout the garden various legends are depicted, like the legend of the Christmas wreath. A shepherd girl wanted to present a gift to the Holy Child and, having nothing else, fashioned a tiny crown of green leaves from a nearby bush. She cried at the meagerness of her gift as she gave it to the Infant Jesus, but when He touched the wreath her tears gleamed like scarlet berries.

Rock City is open daily, except Christmas Day. Summer hours are 8:00 A.M. to sundown; from September to June it opens at 8:30 A.M. Admission is charged. The Big Rock Cafe is open from 9:00 A.M. to 6:00 P.M., and there are several well-stocked gift shops.

Directions: From I-75 take the Chattanooga exit onto I-24. Traveling westbound on I-24 take Exit 178; then take the Lookout Mountain exit and follow Rock City signs to TN Route 58 that will take you up Lookout Mountain to Rock City.

Tate House and Georgia Marble Festival

Pink Palace

The pink marble mansion on the quiet country road outside Tate in Pickens County is as startling and anachronistic as the Emerald City of Oz. Built in 1926 of rare Etowah pink marble, the house positively glows on a brilliant sunny day.

The story behind this mansion goes back to 1834 when the Cherokees were evicted from this land and it was acquired by Samuel Tate. Lot 147, purchased by Tate, included the tavern built by Ambrose Harnage, who was half Cherokee. A spring house, from the Harnage years, stands along the Old Federal Road cut through the mountains in 1817 when Andrew Jackson went down to Florida to fight the Seminoles.

Samuel Tate moved his family to his 27-acre holding and began mining marble. His son Steve brought the railroad to the quarries and put Tate—the town that developed around the marble mines—on the map. The eldest of Steve Tate's 19 children, later called Colonel Sam Tate, consolidated the marble business under his control in 1917. On his travels around the world, Colonel Sam carried with him two pieces of marble, and he challenged fellow travelers to distinguish between the **Georgia marble** and marble he claimed was from the Taj Mahal. What few realized was that both pieces were actually Georgia marble!

In the early 1900s, building in the area was at its peak. Famous architects often visited Tate to select marble for their buildings and monuments, and all kidded Colonel Sam because he lived in a frame house. So after spending almost three years selecting matching pieces of delicate pink marble, Colonel Sam Tate built his two-story mansion. The house was constructed of 12" × 15" × 36" blocks, impossible to duplicate today. The marble columns were originally made for the U.S. Capitol but didn't quite fit, so they were sent back and Tate added them to his house.

Colonel Tate moved into his palace in 1926 with his brother and sister but spent only 12 years in residence before dying in 1938 at the age of 78. Colonel Sam, his brother Luke, and sister Flora, all died without marrying, and the house stood empty for more than 25 years. It fell into disrepair, vandals stole the furniture and a whiskey still operated in the attic. By the 1970s the house was covered with vines and the pink marble disfigured by moss and mildew. But when Ann Laird saw the old mansion in 1974, she fell in love with it and restored it to its former glory. After four years Mrs. Laird and her children were able to move into the mansion, only to discover that they had no privacy because everyone who passed the house wanted to see inside it.

When Mrs. Laird remarried and moved to Florida the house was again empty, but only briefly. With the support of her husband, Ann Laird began decorating the house and restoring the gardens. In 1985 the house opened as a bed-and-breakfast with five elegant suites plus nine private cabins, each with its own fireplace and hot tub.

Throughout the year weddings, parties and family reunions are scheduled in the gardens and restaurant of the Tate House, now on the National Register of Historic Places. Recreational opportunities for guests include tennis courts, a heated swimming pool and horseback riding and white-water rafting available nearby. For information outside Georgia call (706)735-3122; within the state call (800)342-7515. You don't have to overnight to tour the house, which is open 11:00 A.M. to 5:00 P.M. Wednesday through Saturday. A champagne brunch is served every Sunday from 11:00 A.M. to 3:00 P.M.

The first weekend in October is one of the most popular visiting times, as guests like to combine a stay at the Tate House with a visit to the **Georgia Marble Festival**. During the festival you can tour the world's largest pit marble quarries, watch sculptors from across the country compete in a marble sculpture contest, browse through arts and crafts and enjoy mountain music and country clogging. There are usually road races, an air exhibit, golf tournament, historical tour and a festival parade. For additional information call the Pickens Chamber of Commerce at (706)692-5600.

Directions: Take I-75 north from Atlanta towards Marietta. Then pick up I-575 and head north to Tate, exit on Route 108 east, then onto Route 53 for the Tate House. For the Georgia Marble Festival, from Tate take Route 5 / 53 north to Jasper where most of the festival activity takes place.

William Weinman Mineral Museum and Air Acres Museum

In and Around Cartersville

The William Weinman Mineral Museum is included on the Chieftains Trail because the mineral wealth of the region was used by the Native American population in their ceremonial observances. A simulated limestone cave with trickling waterfall is the museum's focal point. Visual appeal is just one thrust of this exhibit; its other purpose is to explain how caves are formed and show visitors the type of fossils that are found in this Northwest Georgia Mountain region.

There are cases filled with cut gemstones including a group of rare amethysts. Another display focuses on gems and minerals found in this region. Other collections include the petrified wood exhibit and the meteorite and tektite display. Indian artifacts discovered locally are also displayed, some of which date back to the Archaic period around 8,000 B.C.

In a shed behind the museum you can pan for gold. The museum also has a selection of videos. Hours are Tuesday through Saturday from 10:00 A.M. to 4:30 P.M. and Sunday 2:00 to 4:30 P.M. Admission is charged and there is an additional fee for panning. The museum's gift shop has an attractive array of items including interesting jewelry.

The Bartow History Center in downtown Cartersville concentrates on people. Starting with the Cherokees, moving through the pioneers in the 1800s and the Civil War period, the exhibits show the historic and the colorful personalities who have lived in Barstow County. Well-known residents included evangelist Reverend Sam Jones; General P.M.B. Young, Ambassador to the Court of Tsar Nicholas; Boston Red Sox homerun-record holder Rudy York; missionary Lottie Moon; author Corra Harris; first female Senator Rebecca Felton; satirist Bill Arp and felon Pretty Boy Floyd.

The museum's artifacts preserve the folklife and culture of the area. Housewares and domestic curios date back to the 1820s, and clothes and uniforms reveal the personal side of the great epoch periods of history. Letters, photographs, oral histories and documentaries give first-hand accounts of the events that occurred in this community. The Bartow History Center and Shop are open Tuesday through Saturday 10:00 A.M. to 4:00 P.M. There is no admission charge.

Several blocks down the street is **Roselawn**, which focuses on two local residents. This colorfully restored Victorian mansion was the home of evangelist Samuel Porter Jones, for whom the Memorial Methodist Church in town is named and for whom Ryman Auditorium in Nashville was built. The house is furnished with period pieces and exhibits Reverend Jones's memorabilia and writings and memorabilia of Rebecca Latimer Felton, who in 1922 was the first woman to serve in the U.S. Senate. Roselawn is open Monday through Friday from 10:00 A.M. to 5:00 P.M. A nominal donation is requested.

One block over from Cherokee Avenue is Cartersville's Main Street and the first outdoor painted wall sign for Coca-Cola. This landmark wall of the Young Brothers Pharmacy was painted in 1894 by an innovative Coca-Cola syrup salesmen named James Coudon. Over the years the sign was painted over. In fact, more than 25 layers of paint were removed before this roughly 100-

year-old advertisement was uncovered. The pharmacy, built in 1881, has an exhibit on the restoration of this advertising first.

From Main Street heading west on Route 61 you'll see the **Air Acres Museum** on your left at the Cartersville-Bartow County Airport. This collection of U.S. military aircraft is owned and operated by private volunteers who wanted visitors to remember the old war planes from WW II, Korea and Vietnam. They call their first acquisition, a B-52 Mitchell Bomber, the *Georgia Girl*. Less than 30 B-52s remain flying out of what was once a fleet of nearly 10,000 planes. The biggest plane in the collection is the Navy's P2V Neptune, a land-based, anti-submarine aircraft. The Stearman Pt-17 Trainer is the oldest aircraft at the museum.

Spanning generations in flight are two of the museum's aircraft: a Douglas A-26 Invader, a bomber used in WWII, Korea and Vietnam; and the Vintage Beech C-45 Expeditor, designed in the late 1930s. Many are still in use today as civilian cargo planes. Other aircraft at the museum include trainers, such as the North American T-6 Texan and T-28 Trojan, and the Cessna T-37 "Tweety Bird." What's different about the planes at Air Acres is that the pilots who organized the museum in 1981, known as The Georgia Boys, fly these vintage craft in air shows across the country.

Several aircraft in their collection are on static display only, including a glider, a gyrocopter and an Army OV-1D Mohawk that was used in Vietnam. Within a large hanger there are additional displays: old uniforms, parachutes, wooden props and other aviation memorabilia. The museum is open Tuesday through Friday from 9:00 A.M. to 5:00 P.M. A nominal admission is charged.

One final point of interest, about ten minutes from Cartersville, is the Euharlee Covered Bridge. This much-photographed bridge was built in 1886, making it the oldest covered bridge in the state.

Directions: For the Weinman Mineral Museum take Exit 126 off I-75. The museum is right at the interstate behind the Holiday Inn off Route 411. Continue on Route 411 into Cartersville and take Route 41 to East Cherokee Avenue and turn right. The Etowah Historical Museum is at 319 East Cherokee Avenue. Continue to 224 West Cherokee Avenue for Roselawn. Air Acres Museum is on Route 61. Cartersville also can be reached from Exit 124 off I-75, which leads directly into the town's Main Street. For the Euharlee Covered Bridge take Route 113/61 to Euharlee Road and turn right, then make a left on Covered Bridge Road.

Regional Trails and State Parks

Blue Gray Trail

Length: 130 miles
Gateways: You can access the trail via I-75 south at Chattanooga,
Tennessee, via I-20 East at Atlanta and via I-20 west at Tallapoosa.
Theme: Civil War Sites
Background: This trail winds through the northwest corner of
Georgia, from Tenneesee's Chattanooga to Atlanta. During the Civil
War dramatic events occurred throughout this region, and this trail
was created to encompass these historic sites.
Highlights: (see individual selections where starred *)
*Chickamauga Battlefield: The bloodiest two-day battle of the war
was fought over this northwest Georgia and eastern Tennessee
territory.
Ringgold Depot: Battle of Ringgold Gap in 1863 was fought to give
the Confederates time to establish a defense line around nearby
Dalton.
Confederate Cemetery in Resaca: Mary Green, her sister and two
former slaves buried two fallen soldiers amid the flowers in their
garden.
Adairsville Depot: Part of the Great Locomotive chase (see Big Shanty
selection), this depot is where Captain Fuller boarded The Texas.
*Cyclorama: Circular painting depicting Battle of Atlanta, and home
of The Texas.

Chieftains Trail

Length: 150 miles
Gateways: You can reach the trail via I-75 south at Dalton, via
Highway 5/515 south at Blue Ridge and via I-75 north at Marietta.
Theme: Native American Heritage sites
Background: In the Northwest Mountains this trail traces the story of
the Native American Indians who once lived here. This was
designated a State Historic Trail in 1988 as part of the 150th
anniversary of the Trail of Tears.
Highlights: (see individual selections where starred *)
*New Echota: Cherokee capital.
*Chieftains Museum: Home of Cherokee leader, Major John Ridge.
*Etowah Indian Mounds: 400-year-old ceremonial town of Mound
People.
*Weinman Mineral Museum: Collection of Indian artifacts from
Archaic period.
*Tate House: 27-acre estate that was part of homeland of Cherokees.

*Fort Mountain: The origin of this 855-foot-long ancient rock is
shrouded in mystery.
*Chief Vann House: 1804 Federal-style brick mansion called the
Showplace of the Cherokee Nation.

State Parks

Cloudland Canyon State Park, Trenton (see selection)
Fort Mountain State Park, Chatsworth (see selection)
James H. "Sloppy" Floyd State Park, Summerville; two fishing lakes,
rental, camping, picnic facilities and playground, (706)857-5211
John Tanner State Park, Carrollton; wooded park with lake offering
bicycle and walking trails, canoe and fishing boat rentals, cottages
and camping, fishing and swimming, (706)832-7545
Red Top Mountain State Park, Cartersville (see selection)
Sweetwater Creek State Conservation Park, Lithia Springs; 250-acre
fishing reservoir, boat ramp and dock, canoe and fishing boat
rentals, hiking trails, picnic facilities and playground, (404)944-
1700

NORTHEAST MOUNTAINS

1. **Baldwin**
   Habersham Vineyards
   Smithville
2. **Blairsville**
   Brasstown Bald
   Helton Creek Falls
   Track Rock Gap
   Vogel State Park
   Walasi-Yi Center
3. **Braselton**
   Chateau Elan Winery
4. **Clarksville**
   Mark of the Potter
   Moccasin State Park
5. **Cleveland**
   BabyLand General Hospital
   Gourdcraft Originals
6. **Dahlonega**
   Crisson Gold Mine and
      Cavender Castle Winery
   DeSoto Falls Scenic Area
   Gold Museum and Consolidated
      Gold Mine
   Mountain Magic Trail
7. **Dawsonville**
   Amicalola Falls State Park
   Burt's Pumpkin Farm
   Elliot Museum and Dawsonville
      Poolroom
8. **Elberton**
   Bobby Brown State Park
   Granite Museum and Georgia
      Guidestones
   Lake Richard B. Russell State Park
9. **Gainesville**
   Elachee Nature
      Science Center
      and Georgia
      Mountains
      Museum

10. **Hartwell**
    Hart State Park and Hartwell
       Lake
11. **Helen**
    Alpine Helen and Museum of
       the Hills
    Anna Ruby Falls
    Country Crafts
    Historic Gold Mines
    Unicoi State Park
12. **Hiawassee**
    Georgia Mountain Fair and
       Reach of Song
13. **Homer**
    Banks County Courthouse and
       Jail
14. **Jefferson**
    Crawford W. Long Medical
       Museum
15. **Lake Lanier Islands**
16. **Lavonia**
    Tugaloo State Park
17. **Mountain City**
    Foxfire Museum and Black Rock
       Mountain State Park
18. **Tallullah Falls**
    Tallulah Gorge
    Terrora Park
19. **Toccoa**
    Toccoa Falls
    Traveler's Rest State Park
20. **Winder**
    Fort Yargo State Park

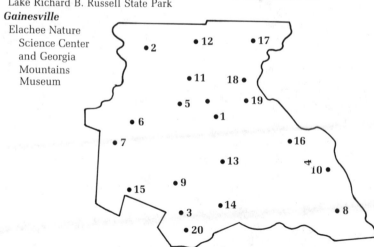

—Northeast Mountains—

The impressive number of natural attractions in the northeastern part of Georgia is hard to match. Few travelers hesitate to detour miles to see a tumbling waterfall: hence the appeal of this region where you'll find the spectacular double falls at Anna Ruby; the series of five falls along the DeSoto Falls Trail; Amicalola, the highest waterfall east of the Mississippi River; the splendid drop at Toccoa Falls and the three falls that cascade down the canyon walls of Tallulah Gorge.

For some adventurers who came to this region the beauty was in the gold that could be extracted from the land. Reminders of Georgia's gold rush can be seen at Dahlonega's Gold Museum and Consolidated Gold Mine or on tours of the mines around Helen. Visitors can try panning either at Helen or the Crisson Gold Mine.

For other settlers the soil yielded liquid gold in the form of fine wine, as you'll learn when you visit Chateau Elan, Habersham Vineyards and Castle Cavender. Many visitors to the area find treasure in the hand-crafted work done at such spots as Mark of the Potter, BabyLand General and shops in Helen and Smithville.

Mysteries intrigue visitors, from the petroglyphs carved by prehistoric people on five rocks at Track Rock Gap to the curious Georgia Guidestones, the instant Stonehenge monoliths commissioned by an unknown donor. But there is no mystery about why travelers head for these mountains; the explanation is found in these 24 appealing day trips.

Alpine Helen and Museum of the Hills

Georgia's Old Country

Helen is a theme park without the rides. Everything else is in place: quaint Bavarian crafts, Old World cuisine and music, Alpine architecture and plenty for the daytripper to do. This mountain village is an outstanding example of how a determined group of local citizens can transform a sleepy community into a tourist bonanza.

When Unicoi State Park (see selection) was established in the mid-1950s, tourists began arriving in this northeast mountain region. At that time, behind the houses in Helen, you were likely to see cow barns, pigpens and chicken coops. Over the years these disappeared and efforts were made to beautify the town but were never highly successful and the town's Main Street remained lined with a row of dull, block-like structures.

Helen, Georgia's version of an Alpine village, celebrates the nation's largest Oktoberfest.

In the mid-1960s a group of local businessmen were having a luncheon discussion about rejuvenating Helen when someone suggested turning the town into an Alpine village. This idea became reality in January of 1969 when many existing buildings were embellished with Alpine designs; eventually new Bavarian structures were added. While some visitors prefer the natural scenic beauty of the mountains, those who yearn for something different find Helen a picturesque alternative, and it is one of the most popular destinations in the region.

Confirmed shoppers spend all day browsing the craft and import shops of **Alpine Helen**. Gourmet food, clothes, jewelry and household items from Norway, Austria, even the British Isles and the Philippines fill the shop shelves. You can buy cuckoo clocks, beer steins, nutcrackers and smokers, Hummels and a score of other collectibles. There's also a factory outlet village with such popular brands as Gitano, Bass, London Fog, Corning Revere, Cape Isle Knitters and others.

Helen has nearly 30 restaurants. One of the most popular during the summer months is The Courtyard Restaurant on the Chattahoochee River. You're almost close enough to pluck tubing enthusiasts from the water as they float past. One of the finest spots in town is Paul's Restaurant, which also overlooks the river. Another waterside dining spot is the Hofbrauhaus. At the Alt Heidelberg you can enjoy regional cuisine while being entertained by an oom-pah band and high-spirited dancers, and every Saturday is an Oktoberfest celebration. The whole town celebrates this colorful pageant Thursday, Friday and Saturdays from early September until October. During the month of October the festivities take place every day but Sunday. It's the nation's largest Oktoberfest with parades, Alpine cloggers and oom-pah bands from Europe and from across the country.

A treat for young visitors is a stop at the **Museum of the Hills** on Helen's Main Street in the heart of the village. In addition to colorful dioramas telling the "Story of Helen" and how people in this region lived at the turn of the century, there is a fantasy kingdom with such nursery characters as Cinderella, Pinocchio, Snow White, Goldilocks, Old King Cole and many more. Small children can walk up the steps of the castle where Sleeping Beauty rests and look down at the Gingerbread House. The Museum of the Hills is open May through November from 10:00 A.M. to 9:00 P.M. From December through April the hours are 10:00 A.M. to 7:00 P.M.

Directions: From I-85 take I-985/Route 365. Continue on Route 365 for about 20 miles past Gainesville. At the intersection with Route 384 turn left and take Route 384 for 20 miles to Route 75. Turn right on Route 75 and follow into Helen. It becomes the Main Street, and you will pass the Museum of the Hills.

Amicalola Falls State Park and Burt's Pumpkin Farm

Tumbling Waters and No Picking Allowed

Talk about user-friendly, Georgia's highest waterfall, the 729-foot Amicalola Falls, is clearly visible from the park's parking lot. Older visitors and the handicapped can sit in their vehicles and relish one of the state's most scenic spots. At the base of the falls to the right of the parking lot is a serene reflecting pool, a popular spot for anglers to try their luck.

Amicalola is a Cherokee word meaning tumbling waters. To get a sense of how steep their tumbling path really is, the most precipitous waterfall east of the Rocky Mountains, drive up the sharply graded road to the top of the falls. A short walk along a planked path leads to the fall's overlook.

For those who want more exercise there are 3½ miles of hiking trails around the falls and through the mountain area. You can even take an eight-mile trail leading from Amicalola Falls to Springer Mountain, the southern end of the Appalachian Trail, a pathway from Georgia to Maine.

Amicalola has 4 playgrounds, 6 picnic shelters, 17 tent and trailer sites and 14 rental cottages (for camping and lodging information call (706)265-8888). The park's 57-room lodge overlooks the Blue Ridge Mountains.

Park naturalists schedule interpretative programs throughout the year, including a spring wildflower walk in April, the Appalachian Falls celebration in May, Summer's End Tradin' Days in August and Wilderness Survival Workshop in September. The year's special programs end with the busy month of October when the park hosts an overnight backpacking trip, a Native American Heritage Appreciation Day and a Fall Forest Festival.

Continuing west on Route 52 from Amicalola just ⅜ of a mile will bring you to **Burt's Pumpkin Farm**. If you are visiting the falls between September and the Thanksgiving season be sure to stop and see the farm's fall decorations. You can join one of their two-mile hayrides, through the farm's pumpkin fields, across a covered bridge and ending with a striking view of Amicalola Falls. The farm's roadside store shows a short video on how the pumpkin farm was started and how to harvest and cook pumpkins. This is not a pick-your-own farm, but there is a wide range of sizes available for purchase as well as freshly harvested squash and gourds. Burt's is also gaining a reputation for great popcorn. In December the farm is decorated for Christmas, and holiday handicrafts are on sale. The haywagon is ablaze with lights and follows a glitteringly lit path through the woods. Children delight in this unusual holiday wagon ride.

Directions: From I-75 north take Route 575 north to first traffic light, Route 108. Turn right on Route 108 and go to four-way stop; go straight through and pick-up Route 53. Stay on Route 53 for appromixately 20 miles and then turn left on Route 183 for about 17 miles. There will be signs to direct you to the park entrance.

Anna Ruby Falls, Unicoi State Park and Vogel State Park

Three Sites to Fall For

The Chattahoochee National Forest offers a myriad of recreational and scenic opportunities, including three popular parks: Anna Ruby Falls, Unicoi and Vogel State Parks.

The twin falls at Anna Ruby, arguably the most splendid in the state are formed by the juncture of Curtis and York creeks as they flow down Tray Mountain. The first of the falls is created as Curtis Creek drops 153 feet and the second, when the York Creek joins and drops another 50 feet. At the base of falls the two creeks become Smith Creek and flow downhill to become Unicoi Lake. A 1,600-acre protected scenic area surrounds the falls. Within this area visitors enjoy hiking trails and eight picnic groves. Much of this land once belonged to Colonel John H. (Capt'n) Nichols who purchased it after the Civil War. The falls are named for his only daughter.

The area is particularly appealing in the spring when the mountain laurel and rhododendron bloom. A wide variety of wildflowers and flowering shrubs also grow here and can be enjoyed as you hike the trails. There is a paved, steeply-graded .4-mile trail from the parking lot to the foot of the falls. Benches along the path and an observation deck at the base of the falls provide a place to rest and to enjoy the view. More enthusiastic hikers take the 4.6-mile Smith Creek Trail that begins at the base of the falls and travels down the mountainside to Unicoi State Park. Both native and stocked trout can be caught in Smith Creek. Anna Ruby Falls Scenic Area is open daily year-round from 7:00 A.M. to 8:00 P.M. The gift shop is open from 10:00 A.M. to 5:00 P.M.

At nearby **Unicoi State Park** there is a 53-acre lake and a beach. Swimming, boating and fishing are all popular options. The park has a lodge, 30 cottages and 96 tent and trailer sites. The restaurant serves meals buffet style and there are picnicking facilities

DeSoto Falls Scenic Area near Vogel.

with tables and grills. There are four lighted tennis courts and twelve miles of trails in the park.

Another state park, **Vogel**, lies to the west of Unicoi on yet another mountain lake. Although the area abounds with legends of buried gold, hikers along the 17 miles of trails are discouraged from digging for treasure. The reward is in the splendid scenery of this Blue Ridge Mountain refuge. The 280-acre park has 36 rental cabins, 110 tent and trailer sites, pioneer camping, picnic shelters, miniature golf, pedal and paddle boats for rent and mountain music programs on selected weekends. Locals like to claim that there is more variety of flora in this park than in Yellowstone. For additional park information or reservations call (706)745-2628.

Just south of Vogel State Park on Route 129-19 is a narrow gravel road (marked by a small sign reading Forest Service Road 118A) on the left. Take this road for 2.2 miles to a small pullout parking area and follow the trailhead on the right for the Helton Creek Falls Trail. This short, steep .3-mile trail follows Helton Creek to two waterfalls. You'll see the lower falls from both the top and bottom. The trail ends at the bottom end of the upper falls. Be careful around the falls; the rocks are extremely slippery.

Directions: From Atlanta take Route 19 north past Dahlonega. Vogel State Park is on Route 19/129 on the left. For Unicoi and Anna Ruby Falls travel 12 miles northwest of Dahlonega on Route 19 and turn right on Route 129 south. Travel about ten miles south and turn left on Route 75 Alternate to Helen. Route 75 Alternate ends at the Chattachoochee River Bridge in Helen. Turn right on Route 17/75 for ½ mile, then left on Route 356. There are signs for both Unicoi State Park and Anna Ruby Falls. Once you are on Anna Ruby Falls Road it is 4½ miles to the parking lot.

BabyLand General Hospital

Oh, You Beautiful Doll

In 1978 an old doctor's clinic in North Georgia became a place where dreams are realized. Babies are born before an enthusiastic crowd in this modest white and pink-trimmed, one-story frame hospital. LPNs, that's Licensed Patch Nurses, issue Imagicillin to aid in a Cabbage Patch delivery. The appropriately garbed doctors and nurses take their work seriously as do the younger onlookers who watch in wide-eyed wonder.

Hundreds of thousands of visitors a year watch the birth of these puffy-headed, pinched-face babies at BabyLand General Hospital where **Cabbage Patch Kids** originated in 1978. The idea for the dolls began a year earlier when Xavier Roberts, then a 21-year-old art student, combined the art of sculpture with Appalachian quilting skills to form life-size cloth babies that were described as ". . .so homely they're adorable." Visitors to craft shows throughout the Southeast were encouraged to adopt Roberts's "Little People." Growing demand prompted Roberts and five friends to pool their resources and open the old clinic as BabyLand General.

World-wide enthusiasm for these original soft-sculpture Cabbage Patch Kids has resulted in more than 500,000 adoptions. The earliest creations sold for as little as $30 and are now worth between $3,000 and $7,600. All Cabbage Patch Kids have birth certificates and adoption papers that are recorded at BabyLand General. About 25 offspring enter the world each day. If you plan to adopt a baby while visiting the hospital, you can even participate in "planned parenthood" by selecting the hair and eye color of the baby. Thrilled young visitors watch the birth of their very own babies (the babies are actually sewn and finished before the public ever sees them) at the Cabbage Patch and then recite the oath of adoption read to them by a BabyLand nurse. Many of the adopters are adults. A staffer says, "Children come in and grow up and adults come in and grow little."

The Cabbage Patch babies up for adoption range in price from $175 to $650, so if that is more than what you are prepared to pay you might want to discuss expense with your child before you arrive and perhaps decide instead on the Hasbro-licensed vinyl-faced dolls at the gift shop that are far less costly. These too are available for "adoption," over 71 million of these have been adopted world-wide. The shop also sells Xavier Roberts Furskins bears and Bunny Bees.

BabyLand General also performs cosmetic and corrective surgery for those who want to bring in, or send in, their dolls. Soiled, original Cabbage Patch babies are eligible for Bath Camps, two-week sessions that clean and tone the skin, the equivalent of a skin peel for dolls (this service is not available for the "Kids" from Hasbro).

BabyLand General Hospital is open Monday through Saturday from 9:00 A.M. to 5:00 P.M. and Sunday 1:00 to 5:00 P.M. at no charge. To discover the current "adoption fee" of original Cabbage Patch babies call (706)865-2171.

Xavier Roberts's creative company is called Original Appalachian Artworks Inc., and for those who want to stay in artistic surroundings while visiting in the Cleveland area, Roberts has built a Mediterranean-style luxury property, Villagio di Montagna, just outside the city. The marble, tile and glass blocks create a dramatic Art Deco design at this resort overlooking the Little Tesnatee River. The resort has an Olympic-size pool, rock grotto Jacuzzi and spa. For information call (706)865-7000.

Also in Cleveland, on Route 129 south, is the **North Georgia**

A LPN (Licensed Patch Nurse) aids in the "delivery" of a Cabbage Patch Kid at BabyLand General Hospital. Over 500,000 of the pinch-faced, cloth dolls have been adopted world-wide.

Candle Factory where you can watch skilled workers create sculptured candles. Each candle is hand carved then dipped into a special hardening glaze that protects the decorative outside layer. A small votive candle inside allows repeated use of these elaborate candles. The candles you see being made at this factory are shipped world-wide. Free demonstrations Monday through Friday from 8:00 A.M. to 4:30 P.M. and on Saturday from 10:00 A.M. to 2:00 P.M.

Directions: From Atlanta, take I-85 north to Route 985. Take Gainesville Exit 6, Route 129, turn left and follow through Gainesville to Cleveland, about 22 miles. BabyLand General is directly off Route 129 at 19 Underwood Street.

Banks County Courthouse and Jail

Keep Out of Trouble

Banks County, established in 1858, encompasses 216 square miles in northeastern Georgia. This region, in the foothills of the

Blue Ridge Mountains, was named for Dr. Richard Banks, a noted surgeon. In 1859 the county seat moved from Lebanon to Homer, and plans were made to build a courthouse. Construction began in March 1860, but the Civil War interrupted the work and the two-story brick building was not finished until the 1870s. The Banks County Courthouse is one of the oldest courthouses in the state. Slaves made bricks used in its construction from clay taken from a pit on the Hudson River a mile from the courthouse site. If you look closely, you may spot fingerprints left in the soft clay as the bricks were turned during the drying process. The white-columned building has a steep staircase leading to the entrance on the second floor.

Cases were heard in the courthouse for 115 years. In 1980 the building was placed on the National Register of Historic Places. The courthouse renovation is still in progress. Plans call for an archive room for genealogical research, a room with regional history and memorabilia, and the return of old court furnishings.

Across the street is the century-old **Banks County Jail** now repaired, repainted and restored. Although the downstairs serves as a meeting space, the second floor still looks as it did when prisoners occupied the barred-windowed cells. Young boys pay particular attention to the "hanging trap" with its rope and trap door where convicted murderers swung in the old days. Rumors say that two prisoners, one an ax murderer, were hung in this jail. Youngsters like to peer through the secret "viewing eye" where victims of violent crimes would identify their assailants in a line-up. When you see the jail's heavy metal doors you'll understand why jails were called slammers. This one was in use until 1972 and at its peak, 23 prisoners were crammed into the small holding areas.

Homer is also noted for three covered bridges. The 92-foot Kesler's Covered Bridge was built in 1925. Head north of Homer on Route 184 for ten miles then turn right and take Route 2196 east. Make a left turn and head south on Country Line Road for about one mile and you will see the bridge. The 46-foot New Salem Covered Bridge was build ten years earlier. To see that take Route 441 exit off I-85 and travel south for 1.5 miles. Turn left and go east on Route 59 for 2.5 miles and then turn right on Route 992 for a half mile. The last bridge, Lula Covered Bridge, is also called Blind Susie Bridge. Also built in 1915, it is the shortest of the three, only 35-feet long. Take Route 51 south of Homer. Just north of Lula turn onto gravel road Route 109, at Antioch Church, and travel one mile to the bridge.

Directions: From I-85 take Route 441 north approximately five miles to Homer. The courthouse is on the left facing Route 441.

Brasstown Bald, Walasi-Yi Center
and Track Rock Gap

Natural High

Brasstown Bald, the highest peak in Georgia, is near the southern end of the Appalachian Chain that begins in Maine. Geologists consider these the oldest mountains in the world, with the possible exception of a small range in northern Finland.

Brasstown Bald, also called Mount Enotah, rises 4,784 feet above sea level. The observation deck on the summit gives visitors a 360-degree view; on clear days you can see Atlanta's tall buildings, Clingman's Dome in Tennessee, plus part of both North and South Carolina. In the Mountain Top Theater, on 20-minute intervals, a 15-minute video shows the mountain in all four seasons. There is also an exhibit, "Man and the Mountain," that traces the history of the area. Brasstown Bald is open daily from Memorial Day through October and, weather permitting, on weekends in the early spring.

There is a shuttle bus from the parking lot to the Visitor Information Center. A nominal fee is charged for the ride. A steeply graded half-mile Summit Access Foot Trail also leads to the center. Three other trails begin at the parking lot. The shortest is the 4.5-mile Jacks Knob Trail that intersects the Appalachian Trail both at Chattahoochee Gap and at Red Clay Gap. The Arkaquah Trail descends along the mountain ridge for 5.5 miles to Track Rock Gap. Be warned the last mile is quite steep. The six-mile Wagon Train Trail leads to Young Harris. If you want to obtain interpretive materials on the diverse flora and fauna in the area, stop at the log cabin bookstore at the parking lot before beginning your hike.

Another great spot for books, hiking equipment, mountain crafts and refreshments is the **Walasi-Yi** (pronounced Wal-la-see-E) **Center**, not far from Brasstown Bald on Route 129. The Civilian Conservation Corp built this native stone, chestnut and knotty-pine inn in 1937. The natural construction materials blend the center into the scenic Georgia highlands. Walasi-Yi is at Neel Gap, and the Appalachian Trail passes under the center's roof, the only point on this 2,100-mile trail that is covered.

For more than 50 years hikers have been stopping at Walasi-Yi to send and receive mail. It generally takes between 4½ and five months to hike the entire Appalachian Trail, and only ten percent of those who start complete it.

If you want a less ambitious hike, Blood Mountain, Georgia's highest peak on the Appalachian Trail, is only a two-mile walk from Walasi-Yi. The mountain got its name from a battle that took place during the early months of the American Revolution. In July 1776, the Cherokees, angry because white settlers had moved into their lands, attacked the frontier settlers from Georgia to Virginia. Thousands of militiamen were sent after the Cherokees in retaliation, and by the end of September the Indians sued for peace. The Battle of Blood Mountain is thought to have occurred on September 19, 1776, between Major Andrew Williamson's forces and the Cherokees, with the Indians making their last stand at Blood Mountain.

Not too far from Brasstown Bald is **Track Rock Gap**, another site associated with Georgia's early Indian population. At the Track Rock Archaeological area you'll see a group of five rocks carved with petroglyphs. Prehistoric Indians may have carved the animals, crosses, circles and human footprints depicted here. A sixth rock is located on private land.

The Cherokees referred to the rock formations as Degayelun'ha, or "painted place" and also as Datsu'nalas gyn'yi, translated as "where there are tracks." According to Cherokee legend the Great Buzzard, who created the mountains when his wings raked across the mud and pushed and pulled on the earth's muddy surface, is responsible for the drawings. When the other animals from the sky vault came to see the damage the Great Buzzard had done, they landed and walked around before the mud dried, and their footprints became the petroglyphs at Track Rock.

You can see the rocks, protected by iron gratings, on the west side of Route S-2323 between U.S. Route 19 and Georgia Route 11, south of Blairsville, and U.S. Route 76 and Georgia Route 2, east of Blairsville. Signs indicate the location of Track Rock Gap. A historical marker explains the site.

On what was once a summer campground for the Cherokee Indians you'll find the 300-acre Track Rock Campgrounds. There are tent sites, RV hookups and rustic cabins. Recreational options include hayrides, fishing, hiking, swimming and riding. Horseback riding lessons are given and guided rides take you along mountain trails.

Directions: Take I-85 from Atlanta to Route 985. Take Route 985 north to Route 129 and head north to Cleveland. At Cleveland take Route 75 north through Helen and turn left on Route 180. After six miles turn right onto Route 180 spur for three miles to the Brasstown Bald parking lot. For Track Rock Gap continue past Route 180 spur for about five miles. Turn right onto Town Creek Road. Head north to the intersection with Track Rock Church Road and make a right. You will pass Track Rock Campgrounds on your right. When you reach Track Rock Gap Road make another right, and the archaeological area will be up the road on your left. To reach Walasi-Yi Center at Cleveland continue north on Route 129.

Chateau Elan

French-Style Country Outing

Chateau Elan looks like a 16th-century aristocratic French country retreat, but it's only thirty minutes from Georgia's bustling capital. Visitors can tour the winery, browse through the art gallery, dine in casual or elegant surroundings, enjoy a concert, explore the shops, test the golf courses, relax in the spa, stroll the nature trail, or horseback ride on the equestrian trail.

The chateau is not a copy of any one specific French country house but a blend of famous estates built between 1500 and 1576. Using design features popular during this early Renaissance period and 20th-century materials, Chateau Elan offers a combination of Old World elegance and New World know-how. When you enter the chateau, you are not in an elegantly furnished country house but rather on a stage set that recreates a French street. The chateau's ground floor is tiled with quarry stones, and there are wrought-iron fences and street lamps like those you'd see in Paris. A floating grand staircase leads to the skylight atrium and the second floor art gallery.

Chateau Elan's guided tour begins at the 46-foot-long **History of Wine Mural** that traces the art of wine making from ancient Egypt to Chateau Elan. At the start of your tour of the winery you'll see large containers of grapes, harvested from Chateau Elan's 2,600 acres. They grow six varieties of vitis vinifera: chardonnary, riesling, sauvignon blanc, cabernet sauvignon, merlot, cabernet Franc and two French-American hybrids chambourcin and seyval blanc. Self-explanatory signs explain the step-by-step process of wine making. Chateau Elan has been in production since 1984. The first vineyards were planted in 1983, and the first release of wines was in 1985. After only four years the output in 1990 was 30,000 cases.

After seeing how the wine is made, the next step is to taste their award-winning wines. In five years they've won 151 national and international awards. You'll use tastevins, small tasting cups introduced centuries ago by monks who made some of the earliest wines. These cups are stainless steel (so that no extraneous taste is added to the wine) and shallow so that you can swirl the wine. You can purchase your favorite in the adjacent Wine Market where you'll find a variety of wine-related items and books.

As you head upstairs to the **Art Gallery**, notice the four murals representing the different sides of the Place des Vosges, a much loved Parisian landmark in the Marais Quarter one of the city's most luxurious residential areas. On the lower level another mural depicts Le Gare Du Nord, and an exterior wall of the chateau's pavillon, a sheltered area for summer concerts, is painted with a nighttime view of Paris. The art gallery showcases regional and national artists.

The chateau's two restaurants offer both casual and elegant fare. At the open-air bistro-style Cafe Elan you can enjoy light fare as well as Sunday brunch from 11:30 A.M. to 3:00 P.M. On Thursday, Friday and Saturday by reservation only you can treat yourself to a five-course formal meal at Le Clos. There is also a restaurant at the Golf Club House open Tuesday through Sunday from 7:30 A.M. to 4:00 P.M. The spa's restaurant serves lunch daily. The chateau itself opens at no charge at 10:00 A.M. daily.

There are additional options once you familiarize yourself with the chateau. The ¾-mile St. Emilion Creek nature trail begins at the southwest corner of the chateau. In the spring the trail is enriched by blooming wildflowers: rose trillium, jack-in-the-pulpit, wild geraniums, bloodroot and pipsissewa. These flowers grow at the base of tulip poplar, oak, hickory, beech and other forest trees. The area is also noted for its fern varieties including the uncommon maidenhair fern.

After wine fanciers, the second most enthusiastic group of visitors at Chateau Elan are golfers. There are two public courses plus The Legends, a members-only course. The first par 71 championship 18-hole course opened in the summer of 1989. Associated with it is a driving range, six target greens and a three-hole practice loop. There is also a Regional Golf Digest Instructional School Facility and a second 18-hole championship course.

You can plan an hour or a week at Chateau Elan's European-style Spa. The health facility offers massages, mineral baths, herbal wraps, saunas and steam baths. For information you can call (404)867-8746.

From Memorial Day weekend through Labor Day there is a Saturday evening concert in Le Pavillon featuring fifties' and sixties' music under the stars. You can do more than just listen as there is a dance floor to encourage participation. Reservations are required, and there is a candlelit gourmet snack before the concert. Throughout the year Chateau Elan hosts special celebrations ranging from a St. Valentine's Dance to a July Spirit of France affair and culminating with the Christmas Lighting of the chateau in late November and December. Small chateau condominiums, a hotel and rooms at the spa are available if you want to overnight; call (404)867-0417 or in Atlanta call 339-9838.

Directions: From I-85 take Exit 48, Route 211. Turn left. The winery is just off the interstate at 7000 Old Winder Highway.

Clarkesville, Habersham Vineyards and Winery, Smithville and Mark of the Potter

High on Style

Clarkesville, established in 1823, was the first major resort town in northeast Georgia. In the town's historic district you'll see reminders of the 1830s, when wealthy residents of Savannah and Charleston began making their annual summer pilgrimages to the mountains' salubrious air.

There are 16 points of interest on **Clarksville**'s two-mile **walking tour**. Allow about an hour-and-a-half to complete. Many of the properties along the tour are private homes, but a few are open to the public. The first four tour listings are private homes built in a variety of architectural styles from Greek Revival to Queen Anne and Plantation Plain style. The next point of interest is Grace Calvary Episcopal Church, the sixth in the state to be admitted to the diocese. Nestled among the trees on the top of a small rise, the church is an excellent example of the Greek Revival period. The builder was Jarvis Van Buren, a cousin of the president. If you arrive between services take a look inside. The black walnut Erben organ is the oldest working pipe organ in the state. Next on the tour you'll see Gloaming Cottage, the home Jarvis built for himself in 1840. Its Gothic Revival style is unusual in this area.

Several more houses and two more churches are on the walking tour, as are two homes now open as bed-and-breakfasts. These are the most interesting because you can step inside. The Victorian-inspired, two-story, wood-framed 1901 Burns-Sutton House has a large wraparound porch and stained-glass windows. This historic inn, at 124 S. Washington Street, has a restaurant that serves lunch daily, dinner on Thursday, Friday and Saturday, breakfast on the weekends and Sunday brunch. The rooms are filled with period furnishings, and each of the seven guest rooms has its own unique appeal; call (706)754-5565 for current rates. Visitors also can stay at the Charm House Inn, a 1907 Greek Revival house. Both houses are on the National Register of Historic Homes. The inn overlooks Washington Street on Route 441. Call (706)754-9347 for additional information.

Another spot on the Clarksville tour that is open to the public is the Trolley Restaurant on the Square, built in 1907 as a drug store. The soda fountain, cabinets and paddle fans all date back to its earliest days. The turn-of-the-century decor makes this an interesting spot to dine. For quite a different dining experience try LaPrade's on Lake Burton in Clarkesville. This fishing retreat (they have rustic cabins to rent) serves family-style meals that are hard to beat. All three meals are bountiful buffet fare served on large platters to long tables of hungry customers. Breakfast is served from 8:00 to 9:00 A.M., lunch from 12:30 to 2:00 P.M. and dinner 7:00 to 8:00 P.M. It's a good idea to reserve a spot at the table; call (706)947-3313. In north Georgia call toll free (800)262-3313. It's open April through October from Thursday through Monday.

After eating at LaPrade's, stop at nearby **Moccasin Creek State Park** on the shore of Lake Burton. This 32-acre park is adjacent to Lake Burton Fish Hatchery where rainbow trout are bred to stock the streams of northeast Georgia. The park has a fishing pier, campgrounds, playground, picnic areas and a two-mile hiking trail.

Just south of Clarkesville in Baldwin is **Habersham Vineyards and Winery**. On the way you'll pass through Cornelia; the town center has the world's largest apple monument. A gigantic red apple sits atop a stone pedestal, a tribute to the immigrant farmers who established Georgia's apple-growing industry.

Habersham Winery, in the foothills of the Blue Ridge, began in 1980. Tours given of the wine-making operation include a stop in a tasting room. The Georgia muscadine is just one of Habersham's award winning wines. The winery is usually open Monday through Saturday from 10:00 A.M. to 5:00 P.M. and Sunday 1:00 to 6:00 P.M. They have a well-stocked wine shop with all kinds of interesting gourmet items and wine-related supplies.

Smithville, a collection of old-fashioned shops in Baldwin, is well worth including on your outing. The 1887 General Store is filled with curiosities like a medicinal chart that lists what you should take for worms, scrofula, catarrh and nervous disability. Notice the old barber chair. This model was only made for a short while because barbers kept tripping over the legs. There are old hats, books, kerosene lamps, garters, clocks and an assortment of local gourmet produce. Smithville's Gallery has upscale decorative items and antiques. The tiny chapel and 1909 gazebo add to the appeal of the village. If you make advance plans, you can have a wedding or renew your vows in this Lilliputian white-framed chapel; call (706)778-5709. The restored town pavilion is an ideal background for family photos. Also of interest is the 1840 log smokehouse now used as a visitors center and stocked with material about nearby Georgia attractions. Before you leave be sure to try the hand-dipped ice cream at the log cabin cafe. Smithville is just down Route 365 from Habersham Winery. It's open Monday through Saturday from 9:00 A.M. to 6:00 P.M. and Sunday 1:00 to 6:00 P.M.

Another type of handmade product is created at **Mark of the Potter**, just nine miles north of Clarkesville on Route 197, which winds along the Soque River. When you reach Mark of the Potter, spend a few minutes watching the river because you'll see trout the size fishermen always claim they almost caught. But be warned there is no fishing in this mill pond. A posted sign reads: "Notice to Poachers, Display name and phone number, Sheriff will notify next of kin." This well-known shop situated in a converted gristmill sells some of the state's finest hand-crafted pottery. All the stoneware is wheel thrown, and if you time your visit right, you can watch it being made. Mark of the Potter, the second oldest craft shop in Georgia, also sells hand-blown glass, weaving, ceramic jewelry and interesting wood and metal work. It is open 10:00 A.M. to 6:00 P.M. daily (except Christmas Day); in winter it closes an hour earlier.

Directions: From I-985 to Route 365 west and then take Route 441 north to Clarkesville. For Habersham Winery take Route 441 south of Clarkesville then bear right on Route 365. Moccasin Creek State Park is west of Clayton on Route 197.

Crawford W. Long Medical Museum

Parlor Game Clue to Painless Surgery

One of the ten milestones of modern medicine evolved, at least in part, from a party fad of the early 1840s. Crawford W. Long, who earned his college degree at what is now the University of Georgia at age 19 (he was only 14 when he entered), received his medical degree in 1839 from the University of Pennsylvania. After working in New York City hospitals, Dr. Long returned to practice in Jefferson where he had begun his medical studies. Some young men in Jefferson asked him to provide "laughing gas" for a party. Long remembered the effects of nitrous oxide and ether from hijinks at medical school, and he gave them sulphuric ether for their gathering.

As Long watched the participants bump into furniture, he noticed they seemed to feel no pain, even when they fell down. This observation led him to wonder if **ether** would make surgery less painful. Long had an opportunity to test his ground-breaking theory on March 30, 1842. James Venable, who had been in and out of Long's office with neck tumors but feared the pain of surgery, finally requested the removal of a cyst. Long asked Venable to inhale ether from a towel. When the surgery was complete, Venable insisted he had felt no pain. Subsequently Dr. Long successfully removed fingers and toes with minimal patient discomfort after administering ether as an anesthetic.

A Boston dentist used ether anesthesia in 1846 and tried to patent it, thus confusing the issue of who first introduced the technique. Long neglected to write about his discovery in the medical journals until 1849, but in 1877 (one year before he died) he was finally recognized nationally as the pioneer in his field. This belated acclaim helped offset the initial reaction to his first use of ether: ostracism. Ether was considered "black magic," and local lore claims that the black population of Jackson County ran and hid when they saw the doctor riding through the countryside on the way to visit a patient.

At the Jefferson museum you'll see a detailed diorama depicting Venable's surgery. There is a comprehensive exhibit on Crawford W. Long's life and a collection of memorabilia including his chess pieces and medical bags. Displays and models of early equipment explain the development of modern anesthesia. Flanking this main exhibit area are two additional buildings. In the Pendergrass Store displays expand on medicine in the 1840s and give visitors a look at a typical doctor's office and apothecary shop from that era. There is also a well-stocked 19th-century general store exhibit and historical displays.

Visitors enter through the Stovall building, once the office space for Dr. J. T. Stovall and now containing an exhibit on county history. This building also serves as the headquarters for the Jackson County Historical Society, whose genealogical research material is housed in the museum's library and archives, along with a sizable collection on medical history. If you have time there is a 30-minute "Fireside Theater" program on Dr. Long's discovery of anesthesia.

The Crawford W. Long Medical Museum is open Tuesday through Saturday from 10:00 A.M. to 1:00 P.M. and from 2:00 to 5:00 P.M. Sunday hours are 2:00 to 5:00 P.M. Admission is free, but donations are appreciated. For more information call (706)367-5307.

Just up Route 15/98 in Commerce is the **Tanger Factory Outlet Center** offering designer fashions including Liz Claiborne, Aileen, Harve Benard, Adolfo II, Gitano, Geoffrey Beene and others. Other outlet shops include Bass, Reebok, Just Kids, London Fog, Black & Decker, Fieldcrest Cannon, Corning Revere and Oneida.

Directions: From I-85 take Exit 50, Route 129, south for five miles to Jefferson. Turn left at the light in the center of town and left again immediately after the monuments. The museum is on the right at 28 College Street. To reach the Tanger Factory Outlet Center from I-85 take Exit 53, and it's just off the exit on Route 441. Open daily year-round.

Crisson Gold Mine and
Cavender Castle Winery

Solid and Liquid Gold

Reed Gold Mine in North Carolina claims the honor of the first gold strike in America back in 1799. Dahlonega and the Lumpkin County area boast that theirs was the region where the country's first major gold rush occurred in 1828.

Even the name Dahlonega is taken from the Cherokee word "dalanigeii" meaning yellow, after the gold the Indians discovered in and around Helen (see Historic Gold Mines of Helen selection). Once settlers found gold in the area, the population of Dahlonega and other nearby towns grew, and large-scale mines began operating. Gold was so plentiful around Dahlonega that many miners earned over $100 a day simply panning and using sluice boxes.

By the time gold was discovered in 1849 at Sutters Mill in California, the initial fervor of discovery had abated in the hills around Dahlonega. Although the town mayor insisted that "there's gold in them thar hills," the miners still headed for golder pastures. Mining continued in Lumpkin County, however, until the 1940s. There are those that claim there is still enough gold in the hills around Dahlonega to pave the square around the court house one foot deep in gold.

You can try your luck at prospecting at several places around town including the **Crisson Gold Mine** that dates back to 1847. Just 2.5 miles outside of town, this mine is owned by fourth-generation miners, who opened it for public gold panning in 1970. The family keeps an eye on visitors and is always ready to provide advice on the best techniques for gold panning.

Crisson Gold Mine is open daily. Summer hours are 10:00 A.M. to 6:00 P.M. Other months they close at 5:00 P.M. on weekdays. A nominal admission covers the first 14-inch pan of ore and instructions on how to proceed. They also sell a three-gallon bucket and a five-gallon bucket. The sizeable amount of gold dust you're apt to collect can be transformed into a unique reminder of your experience if you purchase a locket container. The gift shop staff will put your gold ore into the container for you. Another option is to prospect for gems. Crisson's has gem buckets in two sizes.

Several of the campgrounds around Dahlonega offer prospecting on their grounds. Hidden Valley Campgrounds, four miles northeast of Dahlonega, is spread out across 25 acres along Cavenders Creek. Over the years thousands of dollars worth of gold have been found in this creek bed. You also can pan for gold at Blackburn Park, seven miles south of town. If you want to experiment on your own, stop at The Prospector's Shack, on East Main Street at the northeast corner of the town square. This prospecting supply store has everything you'll need from how-to manuals to local maps, gold pans, sluices and shovels.

Across the street from Crisson Gold Mine is **Cavender Castle Winery** which sits atop Gold Mountain. This is Georgia's first bed-and-breakfast winery. Cavender Castle wines reflect the region; they offer Harvest of Gold, Nectar of Gold, Valley of Gold and Essence of Gold. You can take a winery tour, visit their tasting room and enjoy lunch on their porch-deck overlooking Mount Yonah, Three Sisters mountains and Black Mountain.

Directions: From Atlanta's I-285 take Route 400/19 north to Dahlonega. Turn left on Route 60 and proceed five miles into the center of Dahlonega's Downtown Historic District. Continue through the light and take Route 52E to the Route 19/60 connector road and go left 2.5 miles to Crisson Gold Mine on your right, or turn left for the entrance to Cavender Castle Winery.

Dahlonega Gold Museum and Consolidated Gold Mine

Tourists are Good as Gold

In 1838, ten years after gold was discovered in Lumpkin County, the federal government opened a branch mint in Dahlonega. The mint was closed by the Confederate States' government when the Civil War started. During its 23-year existence, 1.3 million gold coins were minted in one- to five-dollar denominations.

Coins from the Dahlonega mint are prized by collectors. Treasure hunters comb the hills in northern Georgia, hunting not only for gold nuggets in the streams but also buried and lost gold coins. This is a prime target for hobbyists armed with metal detectors, who are often rewarded by finding gold coins.

You can see what these coins look like in the **Dahlonega Gold Museum State Historic Site**, situated in the town's first courthouse. Besides the locally found coins and nuggets, including one that weighs over five ounces, the museum has exhibits on local mining techniques. A 30-minute film *Gold Fever* talks about the heyday of mining. Conversations with long-time Dahlonega mining families give the movie a personal flavor.

The locals explain that many of them "panned for money and farmed for food." Many never let go of the elusive dream of making the big strike. In 1848 most of the miners in this part of Georgia headed for California, but some like the Crisson family stayed. The Crissons own one of the few active gold mines in North Georgia (see Crisson Gold Mine selection).

Mining progressed from the simple to the complex. The first miners were equipped with only a shovel and a pan, but soon they had to tunnel to reach the veins of gold. Next, hydraulic mining was introduced and rivers of water washed the dirt away to expose the precious ore. Shaft mining was also used to expose veins deep in the earth.

The largest gold mine east of the Mississippi River at the turn of the century was **Consolidated Gold Mines**. It was one of approximately 100 mines within a two-mile radius of Dahlonega. Consolidated was organized in 1897, combining ten well-known mining properties as well as a tannery, saw mill and some in-town land. Construction of Consolidated's new stamp mill and chlorination plant started in 1899, and within two years *Engineering and Mining Journal* said that it was one of the best-equipped gold mines in the country.

Six years after it opened, Consolidated was a financial ruin, and the property was sold at a trustee sale recovering only $20,000 of a $175,000 debt. Theories abound to explain the failure: some say the owners knew nothing about mining, others that the college-trained engineers didn't know anything about Georgia ores, while still a third theory holds that it was a gigantic fraud to sell gold stock at inflated prices.

Consolidated is once again open, this time not for mining but for tourists. You can get a sense of what mining was like for the old-timers in Dahlonega by walking through the massive tunnel network. This mine is on the National Register of Historic Places, and there are exhibits on the early mining techniques and a collection of old tools. Tour guides for the 45-minute tour are actual miners; many helped with the excavation work removing the approximately 4,000 tons of dirt, debris and ore that filled the tunnels. Visitors can try their luck panning for gold at Consolidated. Knowledgable guides provide helpful hints.

Consolidated Mines is one mile east of Dahlonega on Route 19/60 N. Connector. Tours are given daily 10:00 A.M. to 6:00 P.M. Admission is charged. Take a light jacket as the temperature in the mine is around 60 degrees year-round.

One of the biggest annual events in Dahlonega is Gold Rush Days on the third full weekend in October. Beside such customary festivities as a parade and road race, this fun-filled weekend also includes a greased-pig contest, liar's contest, hog calling, a beard contest, black powder shoot, tobacco spitting and buffalo-chip throwing. There's entertainment, crafts, refreshments and gold panning.

This weekend brings out local crafters in profusion, but their works can always be found in the stores around the town square.

Nineteenth-century buildings around the town square recall
Dahlonega's golden days.

Native American work is featured at Chestatee Crossing. Anyone with a sweet tooth should check out the Fudge Factory. Book, map and nature lovers should drop by the History Store on the Public Square and North Parks Street. Mountain Christmas and Mountain Memories are filled with collectibles like German nutcrackers, Duncan Royal Santas, Budweiser Steins, Valencia porcelain, David Winter Cottages, Kystonia and much more.

If you get hungry try Caruso's for an Italian pizza, the Front Porch for watching the action while you enjoy a light lunch, or the Smith House for a family-style Southern meal with heaping platters of fried chicken, beef stew, about 10–12 vegetables, and desserts that have been popular for more than 70 years. Smith House also has a country store and a hotel for overnight guests (706)864-3566 or (800)852-9577. If you want to linger longer, check out the exquisitely decorated Mountain Top Lodge just outside town. Each room is uniquely furnished, and most guests who discover this hideaway are repeat customers. They even have a collection of personalized coffee mugs hanging from the kitchen ceiling for their frequent guests. Some of the rooms have fireplaces, and others have in-bath Jacuzzi tubs. A full country breakfast is served each morning. You can call David Middleton, (706)864-5257, for more information.

Directions: From Atlanta's I-285 take Route 400/19 north to Dahlonega. Follow Route 60 into town to the Public Square and the Gold Museum.

Elachee Nature Science Center and Georgia Mountains Museum

It's Your Gain

Elachee is the Cherokee word for new green woods, and the nature and science center is appropriately situated in the 1,500-acre Chicopee Woods Nature Preserve. The unpainted wood and glass of the center seem to blend and merge with its wooded setting. Opened in 1990, this center strives to enlarge visitors' understanding and appreciation of the natural world.

The science center conducts an active educational program within the school system. Walk-in visitors can peruse the center's exhibits, including a live animal collection, an exhibit on metamorphosis and another on regional birds. There is a nature trail and two teaching trails within a mile radius of the center. The trails are open 9:00 A.M. to 7:00 P.M. daily; they close earlier in winter. The nature center building is open Monday through Saturday 9:00 A.M. to 5:00 P.M. Admission is charged. For additional information you can call (404)535-1976. Nearby is the 18-hole public Chicopee Woods Golf Course.

The **Georgia Mountains Museum** at Green Street Station in nearby Gainesville tells the story of the people and the history of this region. Room after room of this old two-story fire station is filled with diverse collections. One of the first items you'll see is the podium built by Gainesville residents for President Roosevelt. He came to town in 1938 to dedicate the square that bears his name. The dedication culminated a rebuilding program after the devastating 1936 tornado wiped out much of the downtown area and killed 300 local residents.

Originally Gainesville was an Indian trading post called Mule Camp Springs. The museum's Native American room has artifacts that date back to the Woodland Period.

The museum staff tell a warming story in connection with the old medical instruments and equipment. Dr. Rogers, who seems to share some of the warmth we associate with television's Mr. Rogers, was associated with the local hospital. In the 1940s a rare quintuplet birth was successfully carried out at Dr. Roger's hospital, but due to the large number of children already at the family's home, Rogers decided to keep the quints at his hospital for six months. (This was not unusual in those days, and because Rogers worked on a "pay when you can" basis, the family agreed.) Dr. Rogers believed newborns needed three things: good food, health care and physical "loving."

To accomplish the last need, Rogers placed the babies at the entrance to the staff dining room and asked each nurse, as she took her meal break, to "love a baby." Most went one step beyond and held the infant during the entire meal. When the babies went home in six months they were well fed, healthy and admittedly "spoiled rotten."

The museum has an outstanding collection of North Georgia art, and a beautiful grouping of porcelain birds includes several Boehm creations. One of the most popular exhibits is the Ed Dodd Room. This Gainesville native created the Mark Trail comic strip, and it's easy to see that in many ways his fictional hero recreated Dodd's own travels and adventures. About the collection of hats he wore on his travels around the world, Dodd said, "A man's hat is indicative of his profession." Dodd was one of the earliest conservationists, and his love of nature is reflected in his remark, "An omnipotent being we call God, who runs this environment, does so by a process we call natural law. . .we had better conform to it or perish."

The museum also tackles such subjects as communications, weaving and spinning, pioneer life, black history, textiles, the poultry industry and local history. Two blocks away on Jesse Jewell Parkway between the Poultry Park and the Gainesville

Midland Depot is the Railroad Museum, which is also part of the Georgia Mountains Museum. To arrange a tour, call (404)536-0889.

Directions: From I-985 take Exit 4, Route 13, the Old Atlanta Highway, north to Elachee Drive, on the right after the golf course entrance. Elachee Drive leads into the nature preserve and to the parking lot for the Elachee Nature Science Center. For Green Street Station take Exit 6 off I-985 and head into Gainesville on Route 129. Turn left on Jewell Parkway for one block and then right on Green Street. The museum is on your right at 311 Green Street.

Elberton Granite Museum and Georgia Guidestones

Taking Attractions for Granite

Elberton has made its mark by being taken for granite: the town calls itself "The Granite Capital of the World." Today Elberton has 44 granite quarries and 150 monument manufacturing plants. Roughly a third of the granite used for monuments across the country comes from this area. The Elberton granite deposit is 35 miles long, six miles wide and about two or three miles deep containing an estimated six million tons of granite.

You'll see the wide variety of granite—a durable rock composite of feldspar, quartz and biotite—in the Elberton Granite Museum. You'll also learn the difference between granite and marble: The former was once molten rock while the latter is limestone that has been compressed and/or heated deep inside the earth. Marble is made of one mineral, calcite, and is softer than granite. Granite is one of the heaviest stones, weighing between 160 and 220 pounds per cubic foot—that's more than concrete but less than steel.

The museum's exterior is unprepossessing, but once inside you'll find an informative array of exhibits and some curiosities, like **Dutchy**, the first statue made of Elberton granite. This Confederate soldier memorial was unveiled in 1898 to a less than impressed citizenry. A lynch mob pulled the statue off its pedestal less than two years after the dedication. The immigrant sculptor who created Dutchy did not understand the distinctions in uniforms of the armies of the North and South. He carved a billed cap like Union soldiers wore and a long coat that certainly was not part of Confederate issue. The nickname came because indignant Elbertonians said the statue looked like "a cross between a Pennsylvania Dutchman and a hippopotamus." Dutchy was buried face down, a common practice indicating military dishonor, and was not exhumed until 1982 when the museum undertook the project.

Most of the exhibits tell the story of granite quarrying, and you'll see the clumsy looking tools of the trade. There is also an 11-minute tape program about touring a granite quarry. One of the interesting exhibits shows a variety of granite finishes: wire saw, diamond saw, shell rock, rock-pitched, stippled and polished. Also interesting is the Argo spire, an exterior exhibit. Measuring 51 feet, it's the longest single piece of granite ever quarried. It had to be cut, shaped and tapered without breaking.

Be sure to watch the short film about the **Georgia Guidestones**, before visiting this nearby mystery. There are few answers to visitors' questions about the Stonehenge monoliths that appeared suddenly in a field outside town in 1980. It is not clear who commissioned the stones or why.

What you will learn is that in 1979 a man, who called himself Mr. Christian, visited the president of the Elberton Granite Finishing Company and arranged for the Georgia Guidestones to be erected. Precise instructions were provided on their size, position and the context of the message each stone was to contain.

The stones are 19 feet, 3 inches high and weigh a total of 119 tons. There are four large tablets arranged in a spoke-like pattern with a smaller stone in the center and another lying across the top. All who view the stones note the resemblance to England's Stonehenge. Holes and slots in the stones accommodate astrological readings. A diagonal eye-level hole is drilled from the south to north side of the center column so that the North Star is always visible. Another slot, or window, aligns the positions of the rising sun at the summer and winter solstices and at the equinox so that at 12:00 the sun shines through a 7/8-inch hole onto a curved line to indicate noon. The capstone serves as a rough calendar. As the sun changes its position, the spot beamed through the hole tells the day of the year by its position on the south face of the center stone.

Four dead, or archaic, languages are used on the capstone: Sanskrit, Babylonian cuneiform, Egyptian hieroglyphics and classical Greek. The message reads: "Let These Be Guidestones to an Age of Reason." The ten "commandments" etched in the four tablets are written in eight languages: English, Russian, Hebrew, Arabic, Hindi, Chinese, Spanish and Swahili. Written on the giant monoliths are these maxims:

Maintain humanity under 500,000 in perpetual balance with nature.

Guide reproduction wisely—improving fitness and diversity.

Weighing 119 tons and resembling the monoliths at Stonehenge, the mysterious Georgia Guidestones are inscribed with messages in twelve languages.

Unite humanity with a living new language.
Rule Passion—Faith—Tradition—and all things with
   tempered wisdom.
Protect people and nations with fair laws and just courts.
Let all nations rule internally resolving external disputes
   in a world court.
Avoid petty laws and useless officials.
Balance personal right with social duties.
Prize truth—beauty—love—seeking harmony with the
   infinite.
Be not a cancer on the earth—Leave room for nature.

The Elberton Granite Museum is open at no charge daily 2:00 to 5:00 P.M., closed weekends from mid-November through mid-January when it is also closed on major holidays and the day before and after the holiday. The Georgia Guidestones can be visited at any time at no charge.
Directions: From I-85 take Lavonia Exit 58, and take Route 17 to Elberton. If you are traveling on I-20 take the Thompson Exit 59 and follow Route 78 to Washington, then Route 17 to Elberton. The museum is just a half-mile west of the downtown area on Route 17/77. For the Georgia Guidestones take Route 77 north for 7.2 miles and you'll see the stones on your right.

Elliot Museum and Dawsonville Poolroom

The Fast Track

NASCAR racing is big in Georgia, and so is Bill Elliot. One of the state's most popular racers, he's a five-time winner of NASCAR Winston Cup's "Most Popular Driver" award. Bill is the only driver to capture the "Winston Million" by winning three of the circuit's four major races in the 1985 season.

The Bill Elliot Museum in Dawsonville captures these and other great moments in this superb athlete's career. He's known as "Awesome Bill from Dawsonville." Racing fans and novices will enjoy the museum more if they take the time to watch the 45-minute video *Racing Into History*. In the film Bill Elliot takes you through the off-limits shop area where his cars are maintained and talks about his car and the races he's run. The museum has scores of blow-ups of photographs taken during and after some of Elliot's most important races.

Racing is a family preoccupation for the Elliots. Bill, his older brothers Ernie and Dan, and his father George are all involved in NASCAR competition. The Elliots started their NASCAR career in 1976, but it wasn't until 1981 when Henry Melling bought the team from George Elliot that they hit the big time. Two years later when Coors became a team sponsor, Bill Elliot became a full-time stock car racer.

During his career Bill Elliot has won 33 Winston Cup victories and 39 Winston Cup pole positions, meaning he had the best qualifying round. In 1987 Elliot set a world record on a closed course at the Alabama International Motor Speedway when he covered the course at a staggering 212.809 miles per hour. In 1988 he won the Winston Cup Points Championship, an award coveted by all NASCAR drivers. By the early 1990s Bill Elliot was third on the list of racing's all-time money earners with a career total of more than $10 million.

A collection of winning race cars fills the Bill Elliot Museum. Younger visitors particularly enjoy climbing into one of the cars for a photograph. You'll notice that the cars are different. That's because they are modified for different kinds of tracks: short tracks like Bristol and Martinsville, fast tracks like Charlotte and Daytona and road-type racing like Sears Point and Watson Glen.

Bill's mother Mildred started the museum, and like any proud parent she has filled display cases with her son's awards and with memorabilia sent to Bill by his fans. The museum is open at no charge from 10:00 A.M. to 4:00 P.M. daily except Wednesday and Sunday.

One place you may even find Bill Elliot himself when he is in town is the **Dawsonville Poolroom**, a spot filled with local color. This hangout, on East 1st Street, caters to families, tourists and locals. The walls are covered with pictures of Bill Elliot as well as parts from some of his cars like the tire from the Thunderbird Bill raced at the Southern 500 in Darlington, South Carolina, on September 1, 1985.

Directions: From I-75 north take Route 53 east to Dawsonville and turn left on Route 183 and the Elliot Museum will be on your left. If you continue a little farther on Route 53 past Route 183 turn-off, just past the courthouse on East 1st Street, you will see the Dawsonville Poolroom on your left. From I-75 south take Georgia Route 400, Highway 19, to Route 53 and turn left. Go past the courthouse on Route 53 to Route 183. Turn right on Route 183 and continue for 2.6 miles to the museum on the left.

Foxfire Museum and Village and Black Rock State Park

Creative Brush Fire

More than 25 years ago, Eliot Wigginton started teaching high school in the Appalachian Mountains of northeast Georgia. Under Wigginton's direction his English students wrote a quarterly magazine called *Foxfire*, named for a fungus that glows in the dark. The students' stories emphasized learning by doing and ranged from carpentry to folk medicine and music. Year after year the little quarterly operated on a shoestring, until in 1972 a selection of articles was published by Doubleday as the *Foxfire Book*. That was the beginning of an incredible success story. More than three million copies of the book have been sold and it was followed by 12 additional volumes.

Tape recorders and cameras help the high school students document the mountain skills that are their heritage. This approach stresses communication skills as well as practical skills like knowing how to build cabins and furniture, play folk instruments and grow and use the indigenous plants.

In Mountain City you can visit the Foxfire Museum where you'll see a collection of Appalachian artifacts that span the 19th and early 20th centuries. Most of the objects were obtained by the Foxfire students as they interviewed community members for their articles. The log cabin that houses the museum was reconstructed by students.

The first exhibits cover toys and amusements, many of them featured in various *Foxfire* volumes. In the sixth book you learn how Kenny Runion makes the woodpecker door knockers you'll see displayed. The same volume also features Dave Pickett's limberjack, a toy that develops a youngster's sense of rhythm and singing. There are also cornstalk toys, wood carvings, an ox yoke puzzle and a rag doll.

Judd Nelson was born in Georgia in 1911, and he is one of the last blacksmiths to know how to make a wagon. He made one for Foxfire, so the students could document the entire construction process. One of his wagons is displayed, as is a wagon jack used to lift the wagon to re-grease or change wheels. The expression, "the squeaky wheel gets the grease," was no more than an accurate reporting of when to grease the wheel.

Another exhibit area focuses on cabin building tools: broad axe, froe, mallet, buck saw, foot adze, auger, draw knife, glut and maul. There are also instruments used by blacksmiths like the traveler, cleaver, tongs, anvil and single tree. Another collection is of woodworking tools like the tongue-and-groove plane, plumb bob, jack plane, croze cutter, scorper and hewing hatchet.

The Foxfire Museum also rescued a mid-1800s gristmill from the Dahlonega area. The nearly derelict mill was moved and restored to its present site at the museum. It's interesting to learn that the expression "keep your nose to the grindstone" evolved because over-heated meal smelled bad and resulted in a glaze on the grindstone that interfered with grinding.

The museum's household items reveal much about life in the Appalachian area from the washboard and lye soap to the kitchen tools like the egg basket, bark berry bucket, sausage grinder, dish-rag gourd and the apple butter stir stick. Tools of various trades are displayed including logging, shoemaking, animal trapping and farming.

The Foxfire Museum is open Monday through Friday from 10:00 A.M. to 5:00 P.M. and Saturday from 10:00 A.M. until 4:00 P.M. On Wednesdays, from Memorial Day to Labor Day, the rangers at nearby **Black Rock Mountain State Park** lead a hike from the campground to the Foxfire Village, where rough-hewn cabins are used for the Foxfire instructional program.

Black Rock Mountain State Park is named for the sheer cliffs of dark granite in Georgia's highest state park. The 1,502-acre park sits astride the Eastern Continental Divide at an altitude of 3,640 feet. Overlooks provide visitors with a splendid 80-mile panoramic view of the Georgia Blue Ridge and southern Appalachian mountains. The rounded knobs, sheer ridge tops and rhododendron-sprinkled forest can be explored on the Tennessee Rock Trail, Ada-hi Falls Trail and James E. Edmonds Trail. Each season offers its unique appeal: In the spring wildflowers dot the trails; in the summer hillsides of mountain laurel and rhododendron are in bloom; the autumn foliage has its fans, and in winter the icy waterfalls have a delicate beauty. The park also has a 17-acre fishing lake, rental cottages, an RV campgrounds and picnic areas. The park is open 7:00 A.M. to 10:00 P.M. and the Visitor Center is open 8:00 A.M. to 5:00 P.M.

Not far from the Foxfire Museum in Mountain City is another gristmill worth visiting. The Sylvan Falls Mill on Taylor Chapel Road is a picturesque sight. This 27-foot waterwheel sits beside Sylvan Falls. The historic gristmill is still operational. The first mill was built in 1840 and operated until 1930; this mill was moved here from Tennessee in 1946 but was built in 1930. You can purchase wheat flour and cornmeal daily 9:00 A.M. to 5:00 P.M. Monday through Saturday from April through October.

If you want a taste of the natural world, stop at Penny's Garden on Blacks Creek Road in Mountain City. Penny and Don Melton make their own herb vinegars, jellies and mustards. They also sell herb plants, dried herbs and a variety of sachets and pot-pourri. You can pick up recipes that include their delicious raspberry vinegar or cinnamon basil vinegar. Their shop sells herb and flower books and an assortment of garden accessories. You can even buy their products by mail; call (706)746-6918 or 746-2298. They're open Monday through Saturday from 9:00 A.M. to 5:00 P.M.

If you continue north on Route 441 you'll reach one of the northeast mountain's most popular dining spots, the **Dillard House**. This four-star resort offers swimming, tennis, horseback riding, a farm animal zoo, entertainment and nearby square dancing. But it is the mountain cooking that inspires raves from repeat visitors. The tables are laden with farm-grown vegetables: hams, sausages and bacon cured in the Dillard smokehouse, homemade jams, jellies and relishes, fresh baked bread and homemade desserts. Breakfast is served 6:30 to 10:00 A.M., lunch from 11:30 A.M. to 5:00 P.M. and dinner from 5:00 until 8:30 P.M. On weekends meals are served continuously from 11:30 A.M. until 8:30 P.M. They have a store, so you can take some of the home-cooked treats with you when you leave. The Dillard family has been serving guests for over a century and they have become a regional tradition. Call (800)541-0671 or (706)746-5348 for more information.

Directions: From I-85 take Route 17 west until it intersects with Route 441 north. Follow Route 23/441 north to Clayton. Foxfire Museum is 2½ miles north of Clayton off Route 23/441 in Mountain City. Black Rock Mountain State Park entrance is also in Mountain City, signs will indicate turn off Route 441. In Rabun Gap just 2¼ miles west of Route 441 off Wollfork Valley Road is Sylvan Falls Mill. For Penny's Garden turn right off Route 441 onto Darling Springs Road, then bear left 6/10 of a mile and Penny's Garden will be on your left.

Georgia Mountain Fair and *Reach of Song*

State's Oldest, Longest and Most Down Home Fair

The Georgia Mountain Fair is a triumph of local pride, a showcase of the traditions and heritage of the North Georgia mountains. It started in Hiawassee as a three-day agricultural exposition in August 1950. In the intervening years it has expanded to a 12-day celebration of crafts, music and food. It's a chance for local residents to show off their produce and homemade products. The fair's midway vies for attention with the entertaining pig races, country music concerts, craft booths, clogging and square dancing exhibitions and much more.

For more than forty years the Towns County Lions Club has sponsored this popular August event. One constantly expanding area is the **Pioneer Village**. In this mountain village of yesteryear, you can visit a mercantile store where the shelves are stocked with products and goods your grandmother would recognize. There's also a furnished log cabin that brings back the days when settlers first came to these mountains. You can look in a one-room school house, smoke house, barn, corn crib, soap-making lean-to and an area where hominy, meat skin and apple cider are made. Quilters, blacksmiths and wood carvers are often hard at work.

As you continue along the path that winds through the fairgrounds, you'll pass the flower show pavilion, the three-building antique farm museum collection and the main exhibit area with 4-H, Homemakers' Clubs and extension center displays. Farther along the path is a moonshine still where demonstrations are held showing how illegal liquor was once made.

Another major exhibit area has more than 60 craftspeople demonstrating and selling their works. These skilled craftsmen offer an array of leatherwork, woodcarvings, jewelry, iron work, pottery and other artistic fare.

The fair's nominal admission includes the nightly musical performances by the best of the hill country's pickers and singers, Nashville performers, bluegrass groups, cloggers and gospel singers. You have to pay for the rides in the midway carnival area.

The fairgrounds are spread out along the shores of the 7,500-acre Lake Chatuge. A nature path follows the lake shore, and there are 188 campsites on the grounds and a host of recreational options including tennis, volleyball, basketball, playgrounds, fishing and boating.

The Georgia Mountain Fair is held annually in early August. Hours are Monday through Thursday 10:00 A.M. to 9:00 P.M. Friday and Saturday the fair stays open until 10:00 P.M. and Sunday it closes at 6:00 P.M. For more information call (706)896-4191.

The fairgrounds are also popular in late April when the Rhododendron Festival is held at the Fred Hamilton Rhododendron Garden, the state's largest rhododendron garden. On a hill overlooking Chatuge Lake the 400 varieties of rhododendron make a splendid spring showing. Flanking the garden's paths are more than 2,000 bushes. The garden, which also has azaleas and native wildflowers, is at its best from mid-April through late-May.

The next seasonal treat begins in mid-June and runs until early August. This is when Georgia's official historic drama, *The Reach of Song*, is presented at Anderson Music Hall, part of the Georgia Mountain Fairgrounds. This award-winning musical drama by Tom DeTitta (it was among the Top 100 North American events for 1992) tells the story of the people of Appalachia.

The state's official historic drama, The Reach of Song, *brings to life the joys of mountain living.*

It's told through the life and works of native writer and farmer Byron Herbert Reece. This North Georgia author and poet, a Pulitzer Prize nominee, lived from 1917 to 1958.

The words you hear are taken from scores of interviews and public meetings held over a two-year period in the mountains of North Georgia. Each line and each character is a legacy to someone's memory, insight or experience. The music and dance incorporated into the show are taken from traditional mountain refrains. This journey into the past takes you to quilting bees and mountain church services and introduces you to people who made all that they used, and used all they made. The show's message is expressed in Act II by one of the characters: "The most important thing to remember is where you came from. . .if you don't know where you came from, it's gonna be twice as hard gettin' where you're going."

The Reach of Song is a two-hour performance at 8:00 P.M. Tuesday through Saturday. There is limited reserved seating, general admission price, and tickets for children under 12. For more information call (706)896-3388 or (800)262-SONG.

Byron Herbert Reese whose words come to life in *The Reach of Song* taught English at Young Harris College. The college regularly presents Star Shows in the Rollins Planetarium.

Since there are so many evening options, it might be advisable to plan an overnight visit. One of the mountain's premier properties, Fieldstone Inn, is located right on Lake Chatuge three miles west of Hiawassee. This stone inn, a member of Great Inns of America, has 66 large rooms furnished with Early American antiques and replicas. The rooms have balconies providing scenic views of the lake or nearby mountains. The inn has a marina with rental boats and aqua cycles. There is also a swimming pool, lighted tennis courts and game areas where you can play shuffleboard, volleyball and horseshoes. The Fieldstone Restaurant overlooks the lake. You can call (800)545-3408 or (706) 896-2262 for additional information.

Directions: From I-75 take I-575 north to Canton, through Ellijay, Blue Ridge, Blairsville and on to Hiawassee. The Georgia Mountain Fairgrounds are off Route 76 in Hiawassee. Fieldstone Inn is also on Route 76.

Hart State Park and Hartwell Lake

A Heroine For All Times

Hart State Park and Hartwell Lake are just two of the spots in Georgia that commemorate Nancy Hart, a legendary Revolutionary War heroine. Fact and fiction are combined in the stories told about this six-foot-tall, muscular mountain woman.

A British soldier stationed in the Carolinas wrote, "Even in their dresses, the females seem to bid us defiance." This was certainly true of Nancy Hart who at the time of the war was living in upcountry Georgia with her husband and eight children. A fervid patriot, she was hostile to Tories, but when five or six stopped by her cabin one afternoon, legend has it that she cordially fixed them a meal and liberally served alcohol. When the liquor took effect she began slipping their muskets through a chinking space in the wall. The British noticed her efforts as she pushed the third gun through. When an angry Tory rushed her, Nancy shot him. Before the remaining Tories could react, Nancy's husband and his friends arrived at the cabin. She argued that shooting was too good for the surviving Tories, so they were hung from a nearby oak tree.

At the Hart State Park visitor center you will see exhibits relating to Nancy Hart's adventurous life. This 147-acre wooded park located on Hartwell Lake offers a variety of recreational options including swimming, boating, water skiing and fishing. Fishermen can try for largemouth bass, black crappie, bream, rainbow trout and walleyed pike in this 56,000-acre reservoir. There are three picnic shelters, two boat ramps, 65 campsites and a row of attractive newly-constructed lakefront cabins that are a real bargain to rent. The park also has a one-and-a-half mile nature trail and playgrounds. On Saturday nights during the summer there are truck-pulled hayrides with group sing-alongs.

Hart State Park is open 7:00 A.M. to 10:00 P.M. daily. Office hours are 8:00 A.M. to 5:00 P.M. The beach is open during daylight hours only. For camping and cabin information call (706)376-8756.

Just eight miles by water from the park is Hartwell Dam on the Savannah River. **Hartwell Lake**, created by the U.S. Army Corps of Engineers between 1955 and 1963, is one of the nation's three most visited Corps lakes. Hartwell Dam and powerhouse bordering Georgia and South Carolina is seven miles below the point where the Tugaloo and the Seneca rivers join to form the Savannah.

The concrete and earth Hartwell Dam extends more than three miles across the Savannah River. The concrete escarpment rises 204 feet above the river bed at its highest point and is 1,900 feet long. Earth embankments and dikes extend the dam on both sides of the river. There are 12 large spillway gates, each 40 feet wide and 35 feet high. One unique feature of this dam is that the generators are outdoors, an experiment to reduce operating costs.

Guided tours of the dam are given at no charge at 2:30 P.M. during the recreation season on Sundays and Wednesdays, as well as on Memorial Day, July 4th and Labor Day. Tours begin at the Resource Center, one mile south of the dam on Route 29. You'll be able to visit several major areas of the dam like the penstock floor, switchgear gallery and control room plus enjoy a panoramic view of Hartwell Lake from atop the dam. Taking a tour is the only way you can gain access to the top of the concrete portion of the dam.

There are additional recreational options available on the lake, including two marinas in the Georgia portion of the 962-mile shoreline. Corps-managed campgrounds, recreation area and boat ramps are available. For information call (706)376-4788. Two campgrounds are open for group camping only. There is a fishing pier at the base of the dam.

Directions: From I-85 take Exit 59, Route 77 south to Hartwell. Then take Route 29 north. Turn left on Ridge Road and proceed two miles to Hart State Park. Continue on Route 29 for approximately eight miles to get to the Hartwell Lake Natural Resource Management Center (U.S. Corps of Engineers office) and Hartwell Dam.

Helen's Country Crafts

Down Home Delights

In and around Alpine Helen (see selection), you'll find small shops specializing in homemade crafts in surroundings that offer eye-appealing diversions. Be sure to sample "Georgia ice cream" at **Nora Mill**. For out-of-state visitors this may be their first introduction to white-speckled grits. Herbert Hoover is said to have been partial to the white biscuits he tasted on his visit. You should also stock up on Nora Mill's specialty syrups, varieties unavailable elsewhere, like amaretto peach syrup, that are simply delicious. Nora Mill, an authentic working mill on the Chattahoochee River, still grinds meal with the original 1876 French burr stones.

In downtown Helen you'll discover **Betty's Country Store**, the oldest shop in town. Just inside the door is a wash tub full of marbles. The marbles sell for around $3.50 a pound, and Betty invites anyone who has lost their marbles to come in and replace them. Children delight in the multi-colored array, but their attention quickly turns to the candy-filled jars on the next counter. Though no longer costing a penny, these treats remind older visitors of youthful forays to old-fashioned drug stores. There is a tempting array of regional gourmet foods plus odds and ends that encourage browsing, including a collection of nearly a hundred cookbooks. Nearby at the Square in Helen, you'll find an eclectic array of Alpine shops selling imported items from Bavaria, Austria and other European countries.

If you head into Helen on Route 17 you'll pass several interesting spots in Sautee, just four miles east of Helen. The **Old**

Sautee Store has been operating for more than a hundred years. It now serves as a shop and museum with old fixtures, posters and items of merchandise that reflect its century-long business. It's one of the state's largest collections of old store memorabilia and is on the National Register of Historic Places. In the rear post office section of this store there is a Scandinavian gift shop featuring hand-carved trolls, crystal, dinnerware, sweaters, jewelry, embroidery and imported gourmet food items. There is also a Yule Log shop in an adjacent sod-house that features international Christmas items. The Old Sautee Store is open year-round weekdays and Saturdays 9:30 A.M. to 5:30 P.M. and Sunday 1:00 to 6:00 P.M.

Sautee was a Chickasaw brave. Traveling with a band from his tribe he strayed into this area, Cherokee territory, and met Nacoochee, daughter of a Cherokee chief. They fell in love and ran away to nearby Yonah Mountain to be together. When they returned to seek her father's help in establishing peace between the two tribes, the patriarch's answer was to throw Sautee to his death from the same mountain where the young pair had discovered their love. Forced to watch Sautee's fall, Nacoochee escaped her father's grasp and hurled herself over the cliff. (This same legend is told at Rock City Gardens, see selection.) Regretting his action, the chief buried the lovers together in a mound beside the Chattahoochee River. Two miles south of Helen on Route 75 is Nacoochee Mound, where legend claims the couple is buried. Seventy-eight skeletons have been unearthed in this burial mound that archaeologists believe predates the Cherokee occupation of the area. Later the Cherokees built a ceremonial dwelling on the site.

The area boasts two historic restaurants. For the most part, there has been an inn where the Sautee Inn now stands since the 1870s (between Helen and the Old Sautee Store). The present two-story inn was built in 1900 and opened to the public as the Sautee Inn in 1972. This acclaimed country gourmet restaurant serves bountiful buffets that many claim remind them of feasts at their grandmothers' house. The inn is open from early May until early November daily except Tuesday from 11:30 A.M. to 8:00 P.M. Light luncheons are served weekdays until 3:00 P.M. In March and April and from mid-December until just before Christmas it is open weekends only. Reservations suggested, call (706)878-2940.

Taking Route 255 north from Sautee, you will see the 1837 **Stovall House** on your right. On the National Register of Historic Places, this award-winning restaurant is included on a listing of the top 50 restaurants in the state and was recognized as the Restoration Project of the Year in 1985 by Georgia's Regional Planning Commission. The restaurant serves dinner Tuesday through Sunday as well as a Sunday brunch. There are five antique-filled guest rooms. Reservations recommended; call (706)878-3355.

Just up the road is the picture-perfect Stovall Mill Bridge spanning Chickamauga Creek. A small park invites you to enjoy the sparkling water and photograph this 1895 queen-rod truss bridge named for miller Fred Stovall, who operated a sawmill, gristmill and shingle mill along this creek.

There's one more spot that bears mentioning as it is not far from Helen and definitely worth seeing: **Gourdcraft Originals**. A museum displays unusual artistic gourd creations from American and international artists. The retail shop offers an array of distinctive items from small ornaments to decorative containers and planters. Few visitors can resist poking their heads into giant gourds to pose for the camera. If you want to take up gourdcraft you can purchase gourds and printed instructions. Stop in Monday through Saturday 10:00 A.M. to 5:00 P.M. and Sunday 1:00 to 5:00 P.M. from May through December. January through April it's open on weekends only, or by appointment; call (706)865-4048.

Directions: From Atlanta take I-85 north to Gainesville Exit 45, which is I-985/Route 365. Route I-985 ends, but Route 365 continues. Stay on it approximately 20 miles beyond Gainesville. At the traffic light at the intersection with Route 384 turn left and go roughly 20 miles to Route 75 and turn right. Continue on Route 75 for three miles to Helen. Nora Mill is on Route 17/75 in Helen. Betty's Country Store is on Main Street (Route 17/75).

The Sautee Inn and Old Sautee Store are located on Route 17. If you want to see the Nacoochee Mound stay on Route 75 when it splits off Route 17 just south of Helen, and you'll see the burial mound on your left. If you head north of Sautee on Route 255 you'll see both Stovall House and the Stovall Mill Bridge on your right. For Gourdcraft Originals head south of Helen on Route 75 and take Route 384, Duncan Bridge Road, east for two miles. It will be on your left.

Historic Gold Mines of Helen

Treasure in the Hills

Helen has more gold mines than any other city in the country. White settlers claimed they discovered gold in North Carolina and Georgia then later in California, but on the East Coast the Indians found it first. The Cherokees claim they found the precious metal in what became Helen as far back as 1,500 A.D. The first white man to explore the region, Hernando De Soto, arrived on May 23, 1540, in search of gold. Following the nation's oldest trail, the Unicoi Turnpike, De Soto with 500 Spanish conquistadors and 200 Cherokee bearers found their way to the Helen gold fields 26 years before the Spanish settled St. Augustine. Twenty years later a Spanish gold expedition led by De Luna mined gold in Helen.

The Cherokees never exploited the gold they knew was in the area around Helen, and the existence of this precious metal was forgotten until 1828 when a negro slave re-discovered gold in Duke's Creek starting Georgia's own gold rush. (Gold had been discovered in North Carolina in 1799 and was being mined at Reed Gold Mine outside Charlotte in 1803.) At the Nacoochee General Store the proprietor took in over three million dollars worth of gold in the years just after the Duke's Creek find. For a time the store was the largest private gold exchange in the United States. To cope with the gold mined in this region, in 1838 a federal mint was established in nearby Dahlonega. The gold fever in this region lasted about 20 years until it was supplanted by the news of gold in California.

The Cherokees had been well advised to keep quiet about the gold because its discovery by the settlers was the death knell of the Cherokee nation in Georgia. The desire for their land prompted President Andrew Jackson to order the U.S. Army to remove the Cherokees. Thus began the Trail of Tears that took those that survived to the Oklahoma territory (see New Echota selection).

A guided tour of Helen's historic mines includes a hand-dug Cherokee mine that reputedly dates back to 1510. Local legends claim that before the Cherokees left their homeland they gathered all their gold and hid it in one mine shaft and then sealed it so they could return and claim it. The Lost Treasure of the Cherokee may still be hidden somewhere in the hills around Helen.

Other mine sites on the tour include the 1828 gold camp of Thomas Clemson, who gained sufficient wealth to establish Clemson University. Captain John England's gold mine also yielded rich veins. At **Historic Gold Mine Tours of Helen** you can ride electric ore cars into the England gold mine. Guides will take you on a trail and point out the location of the Cherokee mines and those dating back to the first gold rush. After your tour you can try your own luck and pan for gold at the site of the early gold rush.

The creeks and rivers that yield such a rich lode also provide recreational opportunities in Helen. One of the most popular options is tubing on the Chattahoochee River. You can float past the Alpine delights of Helen on a two-hour trip or take an even longer trip at Alpine Tubing. Float trips run from Robertstown daily 10:00 A.M. to 6:00 P.M. You might want to throw a bathing suit and casual shoes in the car when you head for Helen because once you watch the folks floating under the main bridge in town you'll be tempted to join the fun. For details call (800)782-8823 or (706)878-TUBE.

Garden Tubing LTD., across from the Fest Halle in Helen, offers a 3½-mile ride, which can turn out to be an all-day ride. They also have a shorter hour-and-a-half float. They too operate from 10:00 A.M. to 6:00 P.M. weather permitting, call (706) 878-3472 for additional information. At the Wildewood Outpost at Sandy Bottoms off Route 384, just outside Helen, you can whitewater raft or canoe on the Chattahoochee River. There are rafts and canoes for two passengers, rafts for three and four and canoes for one; rates vary. Reservations are usually necessary; call (800)553-2715 or (706)865-4451. Their motto is: "Take only memories, leave only ripples, kill only time."

Directions: From the Atlanta area take I-85 north to Gainesville Exit 45, which is I-985/Route 365. Interstate 985 ends but Route 365 continues through Gainesville. Continue on Route 365 about 20 miles past Gainesville. A traffic light marks the intersection with Route 384; turn left on Route 384 and take it for 20 miles to the intersection with Route 75. Turn right on Route 75 and take it into Helen. In about three miles it becomes Helen's Main Street.

Lake Sidney Lanier

Inland Water Getaway

The 38,000-acre Lake Sidney Lanier is the most visited Corps of Engineers' lake in the country. This is a recreational Mecca with outstanding golf courses, a wide array of boat rentals, a water park, camping, picnicking, hiking, biking and horseback trails plus an assortment of overnight accommodations for those who want to spend a weekend or week enjoying the fun.

Georgia poet Sidney Lanier celebrated the beauty of the area in his poem "Song of the Chattahoochee." Walking along the shores of the lake named in his honor, visitors are tempted to break into song, or at least hum or whistle. The lake's 540-mile shoreline is a bountiful resource for nearby Atlanta city dwellers.

Swimmers enjoy the cool, clear water of Lake Lanier. The Corps parks do not have lifeguards, so be sure to swim with a friend or relative. While rafts are fun, make sure young children don't float too far from shore. It's easy to get out on the lake since ten marinas along the shore rent boats and water-ski equipment. The lake's Holiday Marina is the world's largest floating inland marina. The Corps also maintains 54 boat launching ramps for boat owners. Boating gives you an opportunity to explore the more than 100 small islands that are sprinkled freckle-like across the water. You may even pack a picnic and lunch al fresco on your own deserted island.

Picnickers are also welcome to use the Corps maintained grills that are conveniently located beneath the trees along the shore. Fishermen may even grill their catch. The area below Buford Dam, on the south side of the lake, is one of the best trout fishing areas in the state. Other game fish are striped bass, both large- and smallmouth bass and crappie.

One of the lake's most popular attractions is the **Lake Lanier Islands Beach** and **Water Park**. A single-admission day pass, or season pass, gives you access to all the action at the beach and water park. Here you'll find a white, sandy life-guarded beach, boats, mini golf and water slides. The 850,000-gallon WildWaves pool is the largest wave pool in the state. It boasts nine different kinds of waves. Young children have their own kiddie wave pool that's just part of their water playground. You have to arrive early to latch onto one of the free lounge chairs, or you can bring your own from home. The only extra expenses to figure on are refreshments, locker and inner-tube rentals.

In 1989 *Golf Digest* selected the Lake Lanier Islands Golf Club as one of the top five new resort golf courses in the U.S. You don't have to stay at the resort to play this 18-hole course, with all but five holes on the water. A round at Lake Lanier Islands includes a cart, complimentary tees, ball markers and a hand towel, and with all that the greens fee is highly competitive; call (404)945-8787 for tee time. Also on the lake is Stouffer PineIsle Resort Golf Course where the LPGA's Nestle World Championship was played from 1985 to 1989. If you want to know the tee times, call (404)945-8921.

Horseback riding enthusiasts can arrange hourly trail rides or lessons by calling (404)932-7233. Pony rides for young visitors are also available. Bikes can be rented to explore the 1,200 acres surrounding the lake by calling (404)932-7233. Boat rentals include houseboats, group party boats, ski boats, pontoons and sport boats. The Lanier Sailing Academy offers sailing lessons, sailboat and sunfish rentals and charters. To make your arrangements call (404)945-8810.

The action kicks-off on Memorial Day Weekend with a beach music concert; then throughout the summer there are concerts. One of the year's most popular and colorful events is the traditional Fourth of July concert and fireworks show. You can call (404)932-7275 for the current schedule.

There are also campgrounds at Lake Lanier Islands. These operate on a first-come, first-served basis and charge a nominal fee. For information call (404)932-7270.

Directions: From I-85 northeast of Atlanta, take I-985 to Exit 1 or 2 and follow the signs to Lake Lanier Islands.

Mountain Magic Trail

Paradise Found

Dahlonega's self-guiding auto-loop tour makes going around in circles fun. This scenic 12-stop tour has something for everyone—history, hiking, scenery, fishing, camping, horticulture and even prospecting.

The tour starts eight miles out of Dahlonega on Route 60 and Route 19 north. You'll see a pile of stones that legend claims is the grave of Princess Trahlyta. She reputedly lived with her tribe just north of here on Cedar Mountain. The mountain's sorceress had shared with the tribe the secret of the magic springs of eternal youth. But when a rejected suitor, Wahsega, carried Trahlyta far away from the springs, she lost her beauty. On her deathbed he promised to return her to her homeland and bury her near the magic springs. It is considered good luck to add a stone to her grave.

Between this stop and the next, you'll pass Woody Gap Trail. If you're traveling during wildflower season be sure to stop. About a mile in on this trail is a patch of wildflowers that is a springtime delight. Dockery Lake is the next stop, a hiking trail leads to a secluded three-acre lake. You can continue along the half-mile footpath around the lake. If you do, you're likely to spot deer and grouse. Trout fishing is a popular sport in this lake and along Pigeon Roost Creek and nearby Waters Creek. You also can connect with the Appalachian Trail from here. Picnic tables are available.

Picnicking is available at stop three, just up the road. You can sit at the picnic tables and enjoy the expansive view of the mountains from the Chestatee Overlook. You'll be looking out over the Chattahoochee National Forest. Yet another place to enjoy an al fresco meal is the Woody Gap Picnic area with tables beneath the tall, whispering pines. This is on the Appalachian Trail, so you can hike a short way and experience the attraction that lures outdoorsmen to travel the trail's 2,100 miles.

Continuing on your auto tour you'll next stop at Suches and Woody's Lake, another inviting mountain lake where the trout are the lure. Even without a fishing license you can fish by simply paying a daily fee. Yet another lake, Lake Winfield Scott, is stop six. Besides fishing, there is swimming and boating (if it's a small boat) on this tranquil lake. Hiking trails lead into the mountains and secluded campsites are available.

Sosebee Cove Scenic Area is noted for its verdant growth. Nature lovers appreciate the assortment of trees. You'll see yellow poplar, sourwood, white oak, hickory and others. The wildflowers are also in profusion including jack-in-the-pulpits, Dutchman's breeches, lady slippers and foam flowers.

Stop eight, Vogel State Park and the next stop, the Walasi-Yi Center at Neel's Gap are included in detail elsewhere in the book (see selections). Continuing on your scenic loop you'll come to stop ten, DeSoto Falls Recreation Area, where there are five waterfalls to enjoy. Summer is a particular treat as the banks beside the flowing water are abloom with fragrant rhododendron. Hiking trails, trout fishing and camping are available here.

Camp, picnic, trout fish and swim at Waters Creek Picnic Ground another stop within the Chattahoochee National Forest. The state has designated Waters Creek as a trophy trout stream, and anglers enjoy trying their luck here.

The last stop as you head back into Dahlonega on Route 19 is Crisson's Gold Mine (see selection) where you can see an old gold mine and try your luck, not at fishing, but at panning.

Your route takes you past Camp Glisson, a Methodist campground. Visitors are welcome to pull in and stop at the lovely Cave Creek Falls. You can drive right up to this splendid falls. On hot summer days you're apt to see people ignoring the no swimming signs and wading at the base of the falls despite the frigid temperature of the water.

For an auto-loop tour map and trail brochure, stop in Dahlonega at the Welcome Center on the town's Public Square. For a full package of things to do and places to stay in Dahlonega call the Welcome Center at (706)864-3711.

Directions: From Atlanta's I-285 take Route 400/19 north to Dahlonega. Pick up Route 60 to begin the auto tour loop. It will loop around to Route 180, then head south on Route 11/129 and back into Route 19.

Tallulah Gorge Park and Terrora Park

Oldest Natural Gorge in North America

Tallulah Gorge's natural beauty lures tourists; they come to peer into its depths and explore its mysteries. The Tallulah River in a series of splendid waterfalls drops 650 feet in just half a mile. In the first mile of the gorge the river drops 350 feet. At Tallulah Gorge Park you can see three of the four main falls: L'Eau d'Or, Tempesta and Hurricane. Only during heavy winter rainy seasons is Oceana, the fourth waterfall, visible. The torrent of water that once flowed over these falls is reduced by a hydroelectric dam.

The **Tallulah Gorge** is noteworthy as it is the only quartzite-walled gorge in the southern Appalachians. In 1819 David Hillhouse, one of the first to describe the falls, wrote that they were "one of the greatest curiosities in the United States." The gorge, often dubbed the Niagara of the South, is between 200 and 1,200 feet deep. The width varies from several hundred feet to a half mile across and it is two miles long.

When the Cherokees lived in this part of Georgia, they told stories about the gorge. The Indians believed that a cave on the precipitous side of the gorge was the door to the Happy Hunting Grounds because those who entered never returned. The Indians feared the little people they called Yunwi, who they thought lived in the gorge.

One of the most exciting stories told about the gorge is not myth but advertising hype. One of the area's first hotel developers, happened to be in the crowd watching Professor Leon walk across a tightrope wire in Atlanta. The developer hired Leon to walk a wire across the gorge. On July 24, 1886, before an estimated 5,000 onlookers Professor Leon began his walk from Inspiration Point, the highest point in the gorge. Halfway across the crevasse one of his guy lines broke; Leon fell but caught himself. He rested on the line, then got up and completed his walk. The walk was duplicated on July 18, 1970, by Karl Wallenda who covered a greater distance in less than 40 minutes.

The safest way to explore the gorge is along the **Tallulah Gorge Nature Trail**. The trail has seven major observation points. A brochure tells what you will see from each spot. As you walk the self-guided nature trail, you're apt to spot several of the gorge's rare and endangered plants. If you are going to hike into the gorge, it is recommended that you stop at Georgia Power's Terrora Park Visitors Center and view an educational videotape about the gorge. Georgia Power states that the hazardous terrain, flash floods and other dangerous elements make the gorge unsafe for hikers.

If you do hike into the gorge it is suggested that you wear long pants and heavy shoes. Rattlesnakes and other poisonous species live in the gorge's rocky crevices. You also should pack a first-aid kit, flashlight and whistle. Be sure to allow enough time to hike out of the gorge by nightfall and be alert for flash floods.

Terrora Park is across the highway from Tallulah Gorge Park. Georgia Power operates the center, and there is a multi-media display on electricity's role in the region's development. There also are exhibits on mountain crafts: quilting, potting and woodworking. Within the park's 300-acres is trout-stocked Tallulah

Lake. Visitors can enjoy the 63-acre lake's sandy beach, try their luck from the fishing pier, play tennis, camp, hike or watch younger children play on the swings and sliding boards. The Visitors Center is open Monday through Saturday 9:00 A.M. to 5:00 P.M. and Sunday 1:00 to 5:00 P.M. For camping information call (404)754-3276 or call the Visitors Center at (706)754-3276.

Directions: From I-85 north from Atlanta to Exit 45. Follow I-985 north from Gainesville, where I-985 turns into Route 365 north. Stay on this road until it turns right toward Toccoa at the Tom Arrendale Interchange. At this interchange, continue straight on U.S. 441 north for 11 miles to Tallulah Falls and the park.

Toccoa Falls

You Don't Have to Learn to Enjoy the Falls

Toccoa is the Cherokee word for beautiful, and the spectacular falls on the campus of this Christian college in the foothills of the Great Smoky Mountains merit the name. The 186-foot-high falls are 29 feet higher than Niagara, though much narrower. Originally there was a lake above the falls, but after 39 people were killed in 1977, when the earthen dam collapsed, both the lake and the dam were eliminated. The falls are fed by Toccoa Creek, considered a federal waterway because it is a tributary of a river that forms the boundary between two states.

Visitors approach the falls by passing through a gift shop, where a nominal admission fee is collected. On a Sunday, after viewing the waters, you can stop for lunch at the Gate Cottage Restaurant at the foot of the falls. Another option is to head back into Toccoa and lunch at the Simmons-Bond Inn, (706)886-8411, 130 W. Tugalo on Courthouse Square, noted for its quiche and key lime pie. This 1903 house on the National Register of Historic Places is also a bed-and-breakfast inn, as is the attractive Greek Revival Habersham Manor House at 326 W. Doyle Street (706)886-6496.

Toccoa is one of Georgia's attractive Main Street cities. A short self-guided walking tour route takes you past nine points of interest including the Habersham Manor House, Simmons-Bond Inn and the Stephens County Historical Headquarters and Museum at 313 S. Pond Street. You can pick up a map at any of these sites.

Not far from the college on Pond Street is Henderson Falls City Park, a 25-acre park with lighted tennis courts, picnic areas, playground and its own scenic falls. The park has nature and bike trails.

Directions: Take I-85 north, and then take Route 17 north to Toccoa. Continue through the town of Toccoa on this route, which becomes Broad Street, and follow the signs for Toccoa Falls College, directly off Route 17N. Follow the signs to the Gate House and Toccoa Falls.

Traveler's Rest State Historic Site

Come Sit A Spell

George W. Featherstonhaugh stayed at Traveler's Rest stagecoach inn in 1837 and reported, ". . .I got an excellent breakfast of coffee, ham, chicken, good bread and butter, honey and plenty of good new milk for a quarter of a dollar. . .What a charming country this would be to travel in if one was sure of meeting with such nice clean quarters once a day."

Visitors are still impressed with Traveler's Rest. The history of this area goes back to prehistoric culture, when the Cherokees built a town in this vicinity. It was on the site of a mound erected by the Mississippian people. In 1785 when the Cherokees withdrew from the Tugaloo Valley, the land was granted to Revolutionary War veteran Major Jesse Walton. Before he could build a home on his land, Walton was killed by attacking Creek Indians. A dwelling was erected by his children, but it wasn't until the property was acquired by Walton's son-in-law, Joseph Martin, that the structure, which became known as Traveler's Rest, was begun.

The next owner, James R. Wyly, enlarged the house and turned it into an inn. As transportation commissioner for the Tugaloo River, Wyly realized the value of his location since both stagecoach and riverboat traffic were continuing to grow. Two main roads intersected at Traveler's Rest: the National Highway, from New York to St. Augustine and the Unicoi Turnpike, from Cherokee Territory to Chattanooga.

After fifteen years Wyly sold the property and inn to his neighbor Devereaux Jarrett. Traveler's Rest was his plantation house, and on his land Devereaux operated a country store, tavern, post office, blacksmithy, tanyard, cotton gin, sawmill, gristmill and toll bridge. In a very few years he was known as "the richest man in the Tugaloo Valley." During Jarrett's tenure, Traveler's Rest served both as his home and as an inn. Georgia's Confederate Governor Joseph E. Brown spent his wedding night at this inn. Throughout the Civil War, Jarrett's youngest son, Charles Kennedy, ran the inn. The inn remained in the Jarrett family until 1955 when the daughter of Charles Kennedy Jarrett sold the inn and nearly three acres to the state. In 1966 it was included on the list of National Historic Landmarks because of its distinctive architectural touches like the 90-foot porch, hand-numbered rafters and 20-inch-wide paneling.

A guided tour of the inn reveals that almost all the furniture in the downstairs family rooms is original. There's also a display case filled with original artifacts like old tools, hats, shoes and other items. There are two letters on display that were sent from this post office and one received here. In the 1840s, patrons paid ten cents for the first hundred miles, and the cost was paid by the person who picked up the letter.

Traveler's Rest is open year-round Tuesday through Saturday from 9:00 A.M. to 5:00 P.M. and Sunday 2:00 to 5:30 P.M. Closed on Mondays, Thanksgiving, Christmas Day, and New Year's Day. A nominal admission is charged.

Directions: From I-85 take Route 17 northwest to Toccoa and turn right and take Route 123 for six miles. Traveler's Rest will be on the left.

State Parks

Amicalola Falls State Park, Dawsonville (see selection)
Black Rock Mountain State Park, Mountain City (see selection)
Bobby Brown State Park, Elberton; lake and swimming pool, boat
ramp and dock, fishing, water skiing, camping and hiking,
(706)283-3313
Fort Yargo State Park, Winder; swimming beach, fishing, boat and
canoe rentals, nature trails, camping, picnicking and miniature golf,
(706)867-3489
Hart State Park, Hartwell (see selection)
Lake Richard B. Russell State Park, Elberton; swimming beach, water
skiing, boating, fishing and picnic facilities, (706)283-8184
Mocassin Creek State Park, Clarkesville; on shore of Lake Burton with
boating, water skiing, lake and stream fishing, camping, fish
hatchery and hiking, (706)947-3194
Tugaloo State Park, Lavonia; lake with beach, boat ramp and docks,
fishing, water skiing, camping, cottages, hiking trails, miniature golf
course and tennis, (706)356-4362
Unicoi State Park, Helen (see selection)
Victoria Bryant State Park, Royston; swimming pool, fishing,
camping, hiking, picnic facilities, playgrounds and nine-hole golf
course, (706)245-6270
Vogel State Park, Blairsville (see selection)
Watson Mill Bridge State Park, Comer; canoe and paddle boat rentals,
fishing, camping, picnic facilities and hiking trails, (706)783-5349

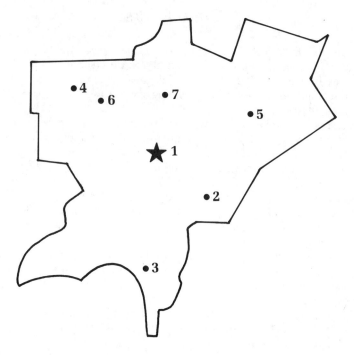

ATLANTA METRO AREA

1. **Atlanta**
   Botanical Garden
   CNN Studio
   Heritage Row and Underground
   Atlanta
   History Center
   GA State Capitol and Governor's
   Mansion
   Herndon House
   High Museum of Art
   Jimmy Carter Library Museum
   King Center
   Museums of Atlanta
   World of Coca-Cola
   Wren's Nest
   Zoo Atlanta and Cyclorama

2. **DeKalb County**
   Callanwolde Fine Arts Center
   and Your DeKalb Farmers
   Market
   Fernbank Museum of Natural
   History and Science Center

   Michael C. Carlos Museum
   Stone Mountain Park and
   Village

3. **Jonesboro**
   Stately Oaks Mansion

4. **Kennesaw**
   Big Shanty Museum
   Kennesaw Mountain National
   Battlefield Park

5. **Lilburn**
   Yellow River Wildlife Game
   Ranch

6. **Marietta/Cobb County**
   Six Flags Over Georgia
   Cannonball Trail

7. **Roswell**
   Bulloch Hall and Roswell
   Teaching Museum
   Chattahoochee Nature Center
   and Roswell Mill

═══Atlanta Metro═══

A geographically small sliver to the west of the Heartland holds an abundant array of options for the traveler. Atlanta combines northern razzle-dazzle with southern hospitality.

Those with an interest in the distant past can see the archaeological exhibits at the Michael C. Carlos Museum. Civil War buffs can take the Cannonball Trail, visiting Big Shanty Museum, the Atlanta Cyclorama, Kennesaw Battlefield and Jonesboro. Reflecting more recent history is the Museum of the Jimmy Carter Library and the King Center. The State Capitol and Governor's Mansion provide a glimpse of Georgia's legislative and executive branches of government.

The largest natural science museum built in the U.S. since the 1930s is Fernbank. SciTrek explores a battery of intellectual concepts in an innovative manner that makes learning fun. Nature enthusiasts will enjoy the trails at Chattahoochee and the floriferous grounds of the Atlanta Botanical Center. For beauty crafted by men not nature, there are the collections at the High Museum of Art.

Family fun is plentiful, from one of the South's premier theme parks, Six Flags over Georgia, to Stone Mountain Park with its popular laser show. Young children relish a visit to American Adventures/Whitewater Park in Marietta and the Yellow River Wildlife Game Ranch outside Stone Mountain. The World of Coca-Cola is fun for visitors of all ages. Zoo Atlanta, CNN Studio Tours and the Center for Puppetry Museum are also fascinating family options.

Atlanta Botanical Garden

Flowering Oasis

The Atlanta Botanical Garden is worlds away from the big city, though it is five minutes from the downtown area. Adjoining Piedmont Park, the Atlanta Botanical Garden includes the ver-

Exotic, rare plants from all over the world thrive in the 16,000-acre glass world of the Dorothy Chapman Fuqua Conservatory, Atlanta Botanical Garden.

dant Storza Woods, the Dorothy Chapman Fuqua Conservatory and the tranquility and beauty of the landscaped gardens.

Each season brings its own charm to the specialty outdoor gardens. Even in the winter months one experiences the harmony of the traditional Japanese garden. From the entranceway, which sets the mood, to the Moon Gate and teahouse there is a feeling of balance and symmetry that soothes the spirit.

Keep your eyes open because there are many subtle touches throughout the garden like the girl walking the tightrope, the mischievous Pan and other droll sculpture tucked amid the foliage. The tiled lily pond, with its design of fish, lilies and lotus, is particularly enchanting with three stone faces peering through the waterfall.

In the spring the rock garden and wildflower area are floriferous; then as the weather warms, the rose garden has its first burst of glory. After their first peak in late spring, roses are in flower all summer ending with another showy bloom in autumn. The perennial borders and annuals change with the seasons. There is also a southern crops vegetable garden and a herb garden.

In addition to the garden paths, nature trails wind through Storza Woods. This 15-acre reclaimed hardwood forest gives visitors a feeling of being out in the country, miles away from urban congestion. Along these paths native plants and wildflowers grow in their natural setting. The Upper Woodlands has a backyard wildlife habitat and a fern glade with a recycling stream.

Lush jungle vegetation and arid desert plants now grow year-round in the Botanical Garden's **Dorothy Chapman Fuqua Conservatory**. This 16,000-acre glass world contains delightful exotic plants. Unusual color combinations, brilliant shades, strange shapes, overgrown foliage and other noteworthy features capture the attention of visitors strolling through the mist-dampened conservatory. The focal point is the tropical rotunda's 14-foot waterfall surrounded by rare palms, exotic orchids, endangered ferns and brilliant bromeliads. Live birds add sound and vibrancy to the lush setting.

The Atlanta Botanical Garden is attempting to save a number of plants from extinction. Although many seedlings and plants of these endangered varieties are in greenhouses that are closed to the public, some of them can be seen in the carnivorous plant bog on the south side of the conservatory.

There are weekly classes, lectures, demonstrations and special events at the Atlanta Botanical Garden. A 24-hour recorded message gives up-to-date information on all activities; call (404)876-5858. On weekends from April through October at 10:00 A.M. and 2:00 P.M. guided walking tours of the garden are available. Show up five minutes before tour time in the Cox Courtyard. Annual events include spring and fall plant sales, camellia, daffodil, bonsai and rose shows plus a Country Christmas celebration.

If you have garden questions, call the Plant Hotline and a Master Gardener will answer your query; call 888-GROW (404-888-4769). To research a horticultural question, use the Sheffield Library's botanical collection of 2,000 volumes and 80 periodicals. The library is open from Tuesday through Sunday from 9:00

A.M. to 8:00 P.M. No material can be checked-out. There is also a gift shop with an impressive array of garden-related gifts and live plants. From April through October you can enjoy a light lunch on the Lanier Terrace overlooking the rose garden.

The Atlanta Botanical Garden is open Tuesday through Sunday from 9:00 A.M. to 8:00 P.M. during daylight-savings time; the rest of the year it closes at 6:00 P.M. Admission is charged. Camera tripods and strollers are not permitted in the Conservatory.

Directions: From I-75/85, which bisects downtown Atlanta, take the 14th Street exit east. If you are traveling north turn right; if heading south turn left. Continue on 14th Street until it dead ends at Piedmont Road. Turn left on Piedmont and the Garden entrance is at the next traffic light. Turn right into the Garden.

Atlanta Heritage Row and Underground Atlanta

Fun Upstairs and Down

The sights and sounds of new and old Atlanta come to life in a unique display—more an experience than an exhibit—that covers virtually every element of the city's past and present: settlement, strife, transportation, recreation, sports, fictional recreation, politics and personalities.

You walk into, not past, these creative presentations and often interact with them. You'll follow train tracks in the door and past the terminus of the Western and Atlantic Railroad, hear the whistle of the train and almost smell the pine trees standing by the early settlement. A basket of cotton sits beside the station, and visitors are welcome to pick up a fluffy cotton boll. Here is Atlanta before and after the Civil War. With the sounds of fierce fighting filling the air, you'll step through the ruins of a bombed Atlanta bank. In a bomb shelter you listen to excerpts from the diary of ten-year-old Carrie Berry during the 44 days Atlanta was under attack.

A time line runs along the wall, chronicling events at each stage of Atlanta's history. You'll hear voices from the past: *Atlanta-Constitution* editor Henry Grady's stirring 1886 New South speech and Dr. Martin Luther King, Jr.'s poignant 1964 account of the black struggle. Visitors can stand behind Dr. King's pulpit and listen to his dramatic address.

Video monitors show newsreels from Atlanta's past including sports highlights and scenes from the 1939 premier of *Gone With the Wind*. The history of Atlanta's transportation is covered from a turn-of-the-century trolley car that you can board to the cockpit of a jetliner where you can sit at the controls and listen to pilots converse with the tower at Atlanta's Hartsfield International Airport. The economic growth of this city is also celebrated, and its major companies like Coca-Cola, CNN and Delta Air Lines are showcased.

Your stroll through Atlanta's past ends with an innovative and visually stunning video production called, "People, The Spirit of Atlanta." This "environmental experience" was shot in high definition television, seen in only one other site in America, Atlanta's World of Coca-Cola (see selection). The wide-screen presentation, in which 12 community leaders and countless Atlanta citizens discuss their city, has twice the resolution and color density of ordinary television. The show also captures Atlanta's mystique through songs, stories and images.

Atlanta Heritage Row is open Tuesday through Saturday from 10:00 A.M. to 5:00 P.M. and from 1:00 to 5:00 P.M. on Sunday. Admission is charged. Besides the theater and six interactive exhibit halls there is a museum store with more than 500 books on Atlanta's history and people and a wide array of unique gifts, toys, games, educational material and regional crafts.

With all this above ground it's hard to imagine 12-acres of adventure awaiting beneath your feet, but that's what **Underground Atlanta** offers. This $142-million entertainment and shopping extravaganza opened in June 1989. This new "must see" landmark is the very heart of Atlanta, the historic birthplace of the city where the 1850 zero-mile post was placed to mark the terminus of Atlanta's first rail line. By 1900 more than a 100 trains a day traveled in and out of Atlanta. In the 1920s, permanent concrete viaducts elevated street traffic one level, improving the traffic flow. The original storefronts on the lower level survived and are now part of Underground Atlanta. Some of the "new" Underground (it first opened in 1969 and enjoyed slightly more than a decade before closing in 1981) is now above ground including the **Peachtree Fountains Plaza**, whose 138-foot-high light tower is the Underground's landmark, and **Depot Plaza**.

Underground Atlanta has 16 restaurants and nightclubs clustered around Kenny's Alley. You can buy gourmet food items at Packinghouse Row, where meat packers and food wholesalers operated in the 1800s. Reminiscent of the old street markets is nearby Humbug Square Market, selling an equally wide array of merchandise from wagons, pushcarts and vintage trucks that date back to the early 1900s.

Near the zero-mile post marker at the eastern entrance to Underground Atlanta is the boarding point for the New Georgia Railroad. Here a restored 1926 locomotive with 1920–1960 vintage passenger cars now accommodate weekend trips and excursion runs including an 18-mile trip around the central city and one to Stone Mountain and the mountains. A dinner train runs on Thursday, Friday and Saturday nights. Call (404) 656-0768 or 656-9769 for more information and reservations.

Directions: Traveling south on I-75/85 take Exit 93, Martin Luther King, Jr. Drive; make a right on Central Avenue or continue straight for underground parking. Going north on I-75/85 take Exit 90, Georgia Avenue/Capital Avenue; use the left lane over bridge to Central Avenue. From I-20 East use Exit 22, Windsor Street, and turn left on Central Avenue. From I-20 west take Exit 21, Capital Avenue, and make a left on MLK Jr. Drive. Continue straight for the underground parking or make a right on Central Avenue.

Atlanta History Center

Where's Tara

One of the first questions visitors ask at the Atlanta History Center is "Where's Tara?" Tara was a fictional creation of Margaret Mitchell and never existed, but her description in *Gone With the Wind* is far closer to the Center's Tullie Smith Farm than to David Selznick's columned showplace. As described in Mitchell's book: "It was built by slave labor, a clumsy sprawling building that crowned the rise of ground overlooking the green incline of pasture land running down to the river...."

The **Tullie Smith House** is an 1840s plantation house that survived the near-total destruction wrought by Federal General William T. Sherman in 1864. The Plantation Plain farmhouse, separate open-hearth kitchen, barn and other outbuildings were moved here from east of Atlanta, just outside the city limits. Visitors can observe everyday activities typical of 19th-century Georgia, including open-hearth cooking, blacksmithing, basket-weaving, candle-making, quilting, spinning, weaving, and craft demonstrations. Farm animals—chickens, sheep, a goat, and rabbits—fill the pens and barnyard. The house is filled with simple furnishings and household objects of the period. Outside the farmhouse there is a flower and herb garden.

The Tullie Smith House, on the National Register of Historic Places, is open for tours Monday from 10:30 A.M. to 4:30 P.M. On Tuesday through Saturday it opens an hour earlier, and Sunday and holidays it is open from 12:30 to 4:30 P.M. From November through February, the house closes a half-hour earlier. A Folklife Festival in October, a Civil War Encampment in July and Candlelight Tours in December are held at the farm.

Exhibit at Atlanta History Center tells the story of the city from Reconstruction to the present with special sections on the Civil Rights Movement.   CREDIT: WILLIAM F. HULL

A more elaborate lifestyle is depicted at the lovely **Swan House**. This well-known Atlanta landmark was built in 1928 by banker Edward H. Inman. The classically styled house is situated on a rise above its oak-shaded grounds. A series of terraces and fountains reach towards the front entrance. The swan motif is seen both inside and outside; there are wooden swans on the table legs, painted swans on the wallpaper and plaster swans over the door. The chandelier even throws the shadow of a swan on the wall.

In 1966, the Atlanta Historical Society, which operates the Center, purchased the house and most of its original furniture plus 22 acres of surrounding woodland. The Society subsequently purchased ten more acres. In 1982, Philip Trammell Shutze, the Atlanta architect who built Swan House, bequeathed to the Center his research library and personal collection of decorative arts. Items from this collection are displayed in several of the second floor rooms on a rotating basis. Shutze amassed an outstanding collection of antique Chinese export porcelain; English and European ceramics; Chinese, English, and American silver; plus furniture, paintings and sculpture.

Visitors may tour Swan House on Monday 10:30 A.M. to 4:30 P.M. Tuesday through Saturday tours begin an hour earlier and

Visitors observe typical 19th-century activities at the Tullie Smith House. The 1840s Plantation-Plain dwelling survived Atlanta's near total destruction wrought by General Sherman.

Sunday from 12:30 to 4:30 P.M. Here too the house closes a half-hour earlier from November through February. Tours focus on the house's architecture, landscaping, interior design, furnishings, historical context and on the Inman family. You will gain an insight into the lifestyles of prominent Atlantans of the 1930s.

The grounds of the Atlanta History Center are well maintained, and the gardens are designed to show the landscape and history of the area. Plantings include native and, in one garden, Asian species. The labeled trails give both botanical and historical information. Specialty areas include the Garden for Peace, the Swan Woods Trail, the Cherry-Sims Asian-American Garden, the Frank A. Smith Memorial Rhododendron Garden, the Mary Howard Gilbert Memorial Quarry Garden, Swan House's formal gardens and the Tullie Smith Farm's kitchen and herb garden.

In October 1993 the Center opened the **Museum of Atlanta History**, the largest freestanding structure in Georgia devoted exclusively to interpretations of history and one of the largest museums devoted to urban and suburban history in the United States. The central exhibit, "Metropolitan Frontiers: Atlanta, 1835-2000," tells the story of Atlanta using artifacts, mixed media, historical environments and interactive displays. The ex-

An Atlanta landmark, the classically styled Swan House reflects the lifestyle of wealthy Altantans in the late 1920s.

hibit covers Atlanta as a rural frontier, its importance as a transportation and commercial center and the city as a suburban metropolis. The exhibit's Now Gallery offers news broadcasts and Atlanta statistics that are updated daily.

The Center's noted Civil War collection, one of the best in the country, has weapons, uniforms, medical instruments, photographs and personal memorabilia. Highlights of the collection include a Federal "war wagon" that followed troops along Sherman's March to the Sea, the chair Confederate President Jefferson Davis was using when he dissolved the Confederacy and two camp scenes showing the equipment used by Union and Confederate troops.

The museum also houses the John A. Burrison Folklife Collection and offers a series of changing exhibits highlighting various aspects of Atlanta's culture and history—from the Civil War through Civil Rights—and current ethnic diversity. The galleries are open Monday through Saturday from 9:00 A.M. to 5:30 P.M. On Sunday the museum opens at NOON. Closed on major holidays. Admission is charged.

The Atlanta History Center has an extensive research library and a 3.5-million-item archives that's popular with Civil War enthusiasts, genealogical researchers, history buffs and scholars.

The library is open Monday through Friday from 9:00 A.M. to 5:30 P.M.; on Saturday it closes a half-hour earlier. There is no charge to use this facility. There's a shop in the new Museum of Atlanta History, also open without charge; hours are Monday through Saturday from 10:00 A.M. to 5:00 P.M. and Sunday 1:00 to 5:00 P.M. The shop carries regional handicrafts, *Gone With the Wind* collectibles, Civil War-related items, books and more. The Swan Coach House Restaurant is open for lunch Monday through Saturday from 11:30 A.M. to 2:30 P.M.; call (404)261-0636 for reservations for parties of ten or more. This former garage and servants' quarters also has a gift shop and art gallery that are open Monday through Saturday 10:00 A.M. to 4:00 P.M. For more information on the Atlanta History Center, call (404)814-4000.

You also can visit the **Atlanta History Center Downtown**, 140 Peachtree Street, N.W., where you can see videos on Atlanta's history as well as special exhibits. This is an official Georgia Welcome Center where you can pick up literature on all the things to do and see around Atlanta and the state.

After getting the background on Atlanta's past and present, you may want to take a walking tour of the city. The Atlanta Preservation Center offers tours of eight distinct districts. The Fox Theatre District Tour is the only one that is given year-round. Other tours include the West End: Hammonds House and Wren's Nest Tour, Historic Downtown, Walking Miss Daisy's Druid Hills, Inman Park Tour, Underground and Capitol Area Tour, Sweet Auburn Tour and the new Ansley Park Tour. To get information on these walks call (404)876-2040.

Directions: From I-75 going north from downtown, take the West Paces Ferry exit 107. Turn left at the end of the ramp onto Northside Parkway. Then turn right at the next intersection onto West Paces Ferry Road. Go two-and-a-half miles, and the entrance to the Atlanta History Center will be on your right, three blocks from Peachtree Road in the Buckhead District.

Big Shanty Museum

The Great Train Race

Buster Keaton's silent classic *The General* and Disney's *The Great Locomotive Chase* were based on one of the most unusual episodes of the Civil War. James J. Andrews, spy and contraband merchant, organized a group of Union soldiers who seized the **General**, a locomotive, and three cars and steamed north towards Chattanooga—a ride that excited the imagination of the country. Andrews Raiders, as they came to be known, were the first to be awarded the Congressional Medal of Honor. What happened to earn them this honor? The action began on April 12, 1862, exactly one year after the Civil War began. The purpose of the raid was to destroy the bridges along the Western & Atlanta Railroad, thereby isolating Confederate troops in Chattanooga from supplies and reinforcements in Atlanta.

Most of the 22 raiders were Ohio troops from Colonel Joshua W. Sill's brigade. The men dressed in civilian clothes, split into small groups and made their way behind enemy lines rendezvousing in Chattanooga where they caught the train for Marietta. Once they reached this Georgia terminus most of the raiders (two had been forced to enlist in a Confederate unit and two overslept) boarded the General. When the locomotive stopped at Big Shanty for breakfast, the raider seized the train despite the fact that the station sat beside the newly established Camp McDonald, a Confederate military instruction camp.

Andrews pulled off the heist beneath the nose of the guards and recruits at the camp as well as the conductor, engineer and regular passengers aboard the General. Conductor Fuller happened to glance out of the window of the Lacy Hotel where he was enjoying his 25-cent breakfast of grits, ham with red gravy, eggs, hot biscuits, flapjacks and coffee. He watched in horror as his train chugged out of the depot. "Someone who has no right to has gone off with our train!" he yelled and started off on foot in pursuit of his locomotive.

Big Shanty was chosen as the site of the raid because it did not have a telegraph office. Once the raiders traveled into the countryside they stopped and cut the telegraph wire and placed obstructions on the track to delay pursuit. The chase was on— it would eventually cover 87 miles and write a new page in the history books. The General passed uneventfully through Moon's Station, Acworth and Allatoona, then stopped again for the men to cut the telegraph wire, pry up and carry off another rail, thus further impeding any Confederate train following them.

Fuller, who ran all the way to Moon's Station, was able to obtain a crew's platform car there that he could pole down the track. When they reached a spur line, the Yonah, an engine used in switching box cars at Major Mark Cooper's Iron Works, was all steamed up and ready to go, and the men on Andrews's trail commandeered the old engine.

Meanwhile the raiders were delayed in Kingston by heavy traffic. In fact, the Yonah pulled into the depot just four minutes after the General pulled out. Unable to clear the tracks for the Yonah to continue in pursuit, Fuller and the men he had enlisted to help him took another train that was standing under steam and ready to roll. Now aboard the William R. Smith, the anxious Confederates continued their race with the abducted locomotive until they came to another missing section of track just north of

Kingston. Again they found themselves running after their quarry until they came abreast of the southbound Texas. They boarded and, with the Texas running backwards, continued the chase.

As the raiders neared the Oostanaula bridge south of Resaca they tried to achieve their mission objective by burning the bridge, but the rain had soaked all the wood they were carrying, and they were not able to get a roaring fire going. As they dispiritedly pulled away, they looked back and watched the rapidly advancing Texas push the smoking box car from the bridge.

The raiders resorted to dropping cross ties on the track in hopes of slowing the progress of their pursuers, but the distance between the engines was narrowing. Once past Dalton, the General again stopped for the men to cut the telegraph wire, but all but a few lines of Fuller's warning about the train theft had already gotten through to General Leadbetter in Chattanooga.

The two trains were in such close proximity that the raiders did not have time to take any action against the Texas. Even worse for the raiders was that they needed fuel and water but had no time to stop. As the train started slowing down two miles north of Ringgold, Andrews told the men, "Jump off and scatter! Every man for himself!"

Again fate was against the raiders, for it was muster day at Ringgold and hundreds of mounted and armed farmers were in town. They quickly hunted down the raiders, and within days all had been captured and imprisoned in Chattanooga. Ironically when the raiders were moved to Atlanta and then to Madison (because of fears of demonstrations), the train they traveled in was pulled by the General. After only a few days the raiders were returned to Chattanooga. Then 12 members of the group were taken to Knoxville for trial. Andrews, having already been court martialed and sentenced to hang, was placed in solitary confinement. The ten remaining plotters, who were still in Chattanooga, attempted to escape, but only John Wollam succeeded. He was only able to evade capture for two weeks; then he was retaken and jailed with his comrades in Atlanta. Andrews and seven other raiders were hanged. On October 16, 1862, the 14 surviving raiders, once again together in the Fulton County Jail in Atlanta, staged a daring jailbreak and this time eight men made it to the Federal lines. Six were recaptured but later exchanged. The Congressional Medal of Honor was awarded to all but two of the raiders who were in the Union army. It is not entirely clear why two were not honored, although some think it is because their families did not actively pursue the tribute.

In August 1888, the surviving raiders held a reunion as part of the Grand Army of the Republic's encampment at Columbus, Ohio, and the guest speaker was William Fuller, who spoke of the dramatic chase. Also in attendance was the General, which today is enshrined at Big Shanty just 100 yards from where it was stolen.

At the Big Shanty Museum you can watch a narrated slide film on the raid, but if you know you are going it is more fun and more significant to watch the Disney film that presents an accurate account of the chase. Visitors do not have to be railroad buffs to be thrilled by a close-up look at this historic locomotive.

The Big Shanty Museum is open Monday through Saturday from 9:30 A.M. to 5:30 P.M. and on Sundays NOON to 5:30 P.M. During December, January and February the hours are 10:00 A.M. to 4:00 P.M. Admission is charged.

Directions: From I-75 take Exit 118 and turn left. The museum is just two-and-a-half miles down Cherokee Street on the right, next to the railroad tracks.

Bulloch Hall and Roswell Teaching Museum

Old South on Outskirts of New South

The town Roswell King and his son Barrington founded in 1838 was, by the time of the Civil War, a comfortable New England-style village with gracious homes, a picture-book-pretty church and a full complement of businesses and public buildings. When Sherman's army swept through Georgia, only the mill—a leading supplier of cotton and woolen goods to the Confederate army—was burned.

The headquarters for the Roswell Historical Society is the **Smith Plantation**. Visitors coming into Roswell can stop at the Smith Plantation, 935 Alpharetta Street, which is open daily except Sunday. This plantation home belonged to Archibald Smith, who, along with Roswell King, helped found the town. It's Roswell's best preserved, unaltered landmark and still has its original out-buildings. The Smith Plantation furnished with period pieces can be seen during the tours given at 11:00 A.M. and 2:00 P.M. on weekdays and hourly from 11:00 A.M. until 2:00 P.M. on Saturdays.

Most of the historic homes in Roswell are privately owned, but visitors can also tour **Bulloch Hall**, the ancestral home of President Theodore Roosevelt's mother, Mittie Bulloch. The house was built in 1840 by one of the town's first settlers, Major James Stephens Bulloch, the grandson of Georgia's Revolutionary Governor Archibald Bulloch.

The Greek Revival home is one of the South's only examples of true temple-form architecture with full pedimented portico.

In recognition of its significance, it is on the National Register of Historic Places. The wedding of Major Bulloch's daughter, Mittie, to Theodore Roosevelt of New York took place here on December 22, 1853. Their son became President Theodore Roosevelt, and they were the grandparents of Eleanor Roosevelt, who married Franklin Delano Roosevelt.

After the death of her husband, Mrs. Bulloch moved north to live with her daughter and rented out the house in Roswell. During the Civil War, Thomas E. King, co-owner of the woolen mills, lived here with his family. In 1978, the house and 16 acres were purchased by the city of Roswell.

Tours are given Monday through Friday on the hour from 10:00 A.M. to 2:00 P.M. An admission is charged. The house serves as a cultural center, and there is gallery space, a few rooms furnished with period pieces, a reference library, museum rooms and an antebellum garden. The house can be rented for private functions, and you can get married standing on the same spot in the dining room where Mittie Bulloch stood during her Christmas wedding. A recreation of this event is just one of the annual festivities hosted at Bulloch Hall.

You'll discover more of Roswell's history at the **Teaching Museum–North** in the city's former elementary school. Four former Fulton County principals serve as docents, leading tours of the facility. The Roswell Room is a reception area for the auditorium where musical, dramatic and educational programs are held. The reception area has a replica of the antebellum homes and buildings left after the Civil War and a mural emphasizing the importance of home, church and school.

In the writer's corner, Georgia authors are honored with quotes from their work and first editions of their books. Noted natives include Sidney Lanier, Flannery O'Conner, Carson McCullers, Eugenia Price, James Dickey, Erskine Caldwell, Anne Rivers Siddons, Alice Walker and Pat Conroy to name just a few. There are also three Georgia writers who won Pulitzer Prizes: Conrad Aikin, Margaret Mitchell and Caroline Miller. The Teaching Museum holds lectures and discussions on creative thinking and writing.

The corridors are filled with exhibits that continue to tell the story of Roswell, including a diorama of the once thriving mills. A mural traces the history of the region from the days of the Indians to the present. In a typical Georgia courtroom from the turn of the century, students have the opportunity to conduct mock trials from famous Georgia cases reviewed by the U.S. Supreme Court.

Children also can learn a great deal in the storyteller's corner, located in a rustic 1880 house with spartan furnishings. Young visitors put on bonnets or suspenders and join a costumed docent who tells stories about life after the Civil War.

Another room showcases the economic, political and social history of Georgia. Oral history brings back the tragedy of the Depression, while photographs also capture those grim days. The brighter side of the 1930s is recalled with photographs of noted athletes like Babe Ruth, Lou Gehrig, Bobby Jones and Jessie Owens. Exhibits also show how cartoons like Dick Tracy and movies like *Robin Hood* and *The Wizard of Oz* helped people escape their problems. It's fascinating to discover the eight most-read books in the 1930s were Hemingway's *A Farewell to Arms*, S. Lewis's *It Can't Happen Here*, Faulkner's *The Sound and the Fury*, Fitzgerald's *Tender is the Night*, O'Neill's *The Iceman Cometh*, Buck's *The Good Earth*, Wolfe's *Look Homeward, Angel*, and Steinbeck's *The Grapes of Wrath*. Other exhibits cover the Civil Rights Movement and the Women's Movement.

The Teaching Museum–North, at 791 Mimosa Boulevard, is open from 8:00 A.M. to 4:00 P.M. daily. For more information about special programs and events call (404)552-6339.

A delightful, delicious and historical spot to eat in Roswell is **The Public House** on Historic Roswell Square. The building dates back to 1854 when it was a mill store. The mill was directly behind The Public House. The loft area, now a piano bar, was once the Roswell Funeral Home. The restaurant faces Roswell Park, whose focal point is the picturesque bandstand built in 1905 for President Teddy Roosevelt when he visited his mother's home, Bulloch Hall. The restaurant serves what it calls creative American cuisine for lunch, dinner and Sunday brunch. For more information call (404)992-4646.

The Public House is next to Old City Hall, newly renovated to serve as the city's visitors center. This is the place to pick up information on all the attractions in and around Roswell. If you have time you can watch a video on the town. There is also a gift shop for visitors.

Directions: For Bulloch Hall, from I-75 take I-285 and Roswell Road to Roswell where you will bear left at the park just before the town square (Route 120), and then make a right on Mimosa Blvd. and another left on Bulloch Avenue. For the Teaching Museum-North just stay on Mimosa. The Roswell Visitor Center is at 617 North Atlanta Street on the Square, and the Public House is right next door.

Callanwolde Fine Arts Center and Your DeKalb Farmers Market

Feed the Mind, Feed the Body

The Callanwolde Fine Arts Center serves visitors, students and artists through a variety of performances, art education programs and workshops. Classical and contemporary concerts, recitals, dance performances, poetry readings and dramatic productions are held throughout the year. Classes are offered in painting and drawing, textiles and writing. Pottery making is taught in the southeast's largest pottery department outside of a university setting. There are roughly 100 classes given on a quarterly basis.

The setting for this creativity is the imposing Gothic-Tudor style home of the Charles Howard Candler family. The estate was built in 1920 by the eldest son of Asa Candler, who founded the Coca-Cola Company. The house's unusual name is taken from the ancestral home, Callan Castle in Kilkenny, Ireland. Callan is the Irish name for Candler, and wold means wood or forest. The Candler family was granted Callan Castle for their service to Oliver Cromwell in 1655. In the late 18th century, Daniel Candler was the first of the family to come to America. He, his wife and 28 servants settled first in Virginia, then moved to Georgia.

The **Callanwolde** estate was designed by Henry Hornbostle, a Pittsburgh architect who designed Emory University's campus. Originally Callanwolde encompassed 27 acres with a gardener's cottage, four-car garage, large swimming pool and two-storied clubhouse. There was also a tennis court, conservatory, greenhouse, outbuildings for the livestock, vegetable and flower gardens and formal gardens.

After 39 years the estate was bequeathed by the Candler family to Emory University, who later sold it to The First Christian Church. In 1972 Callanwolde was purchased by the Druid Hills Civic Association and DeKalb County, who maintain the property. It is now listed on the National Register of Historic Places.

Restoration projects are funded in part from Christmas at Callanwolde, the first two weeks in December. Each room is decorated by interior and floral arts designers according to the theme selected for that year. Entertainment is offered and lunch, dinner and desserts are served in the Courtyard Cafe. Unusual gifts and seasonal decorations are available in the Art Shop, Holiday Shop and Boutique. This popular event has been voted by the Southeast Tourism Society as one of the "Top Twenty Events in the Southeast."

Money from this event was used to help restore the 3,752-pipe

Aeolian organ in the Great Hall. This is the largest organ of its kind that is in playable condition. Its outlets extend from the main hall to every major room in the house.

After wandering around inside, spend some time in the garden. Twelve acres of the original grounds remain, and the sculptured lawns and formal gardens have been restored. Callanwolde is in the Druid Hills section of Atlanta, a residential area planned by Frederick Law Olmsted, who designed New York's Central Park. This famed landscape designer personally developed a master plan for the neighborhood with Ponce de Leon Avenue and its shaded parks as the core.

Callanwolde's administration offices are open Monday through Friday from 9:00 A.M. to 5:00 P.M. The gallery is open Monday through Saturday from 10:00 A.M. to 3:00 P.M. Art shop hours are Tuesday through Saturday from 10:30 A.M. to 2:30 P.M. and the conservatory is open Monday through Friday from 10:00 A.M. to 4:00 P.M. Historical tours of Callanwolde are given by the Callanwolde Guild. To arrange a tour call (404)872-5338. There is a nominal charge for these guided tours but no charge to explore on your own during regular operating hours.

Not far from Callanwolde is **Your DeKalb Farmers Market**, where in a facility the size of two football fields food from around the world is sold. Employees from 44 countries sell over 450 varieties of fresh seafood, 500 kinds of cheeses, an amazing array of 300 vegetables and 150 fruits, plus 110 varieties of fresh flowers and 4,000 kinds of international dry goods. There are also 700 different wines and 300 beers. No wonder this market, one of the largest indoor markets in the country, is called the "U.N. of Fresh Food." It is open Monday through Friday from 10:00 A.M. to 9:00 P.M. and weekends from 9:00 A.M. to 9:00 P.M.

Directions: From I-85 take the North Druid Hills Road exit and head east. Make a right turn on Briarcliff Road and in roughly four miles you will soon see Callanwolde on your right. Callanwolde is at 980 Briarcliff Road. From I-20 head north on Moreland Avenue, which will become Briarcliff, and Callanwolde will be on your left.

For Your DeKalb Farmers Market going north on I-85 take I-285 east to Exit 31, turn right off the exit ramp on to East Ponce De Leon Avenue and go approximately two miles, and Your DeKalb Farmers Market is on the right.

Chattahoochee Nature Center and Roswell Mill

By the River Side

The Roswell Manufacturing Company's mills opened in 1838 and operated until 1975. Water power generated by five dams on Vickery Creek, an offshoot of the Chattahoochee River, provided the power for the company's four mills. In the 1890s more than 600 people worked in the mills, and it was these workers that sparked the growth of the city of Roswell.

But the growth of Roswell has not been at the cost of the natural environment. At the **Chattahoochee Nature Center**, along the quiet banks of the river, you get a sense of nature undisturbed by man's intrusion. On the trails that wind through wooded uplands and past fresh water ponds and marshes you glimpse wildlife and indigenous plants. You might see otters swimming in the rippling pool, kingfishers foraging in the marshy waters, turtles and frogs basking in the sun, beavers diligently building their dams and red and gray foxes beginning their nightly hunt.

It takes about 45 minutes to hike the woodland trail. Markers will guide you and provide background on points of interest along the way. You'll skirt the pond, then cross a small stream and travel along the ridge before returning through the forest to the nature center. Wildlife abounds in the spring-fed lake, herons and belted kingfishers, the symbol of Chattahoochee Nature Center, feed on the small fish. Ducks and geese search for their food among the lake's aquatic plants. Notice the moss, lichen and fern as you hike the woodland trail. As the small stream empties into the pond a bog is formed. Its spongy ground supports a wide variety of wildflowers. Denizens of the forest include squirrels, raccoons, opossums, rabbits and foxes. Each season brings a new look along this wooded trail.

The trail ends in a cluster of hardwoods where you will find the rustic nature center overlooking one of the ponds. Inside this environmental education facility you'll find live animal displays including turtles, snakes and fish. There are also activity rooms for children's story hours, nature workshops and classes, most of which include field work or trips. There's also a nature store with books, art, educational and ecological items as well as some that are just for fun.

Outside the center, injured birds are caged, and there is a bald eagle exhibit. A backyard habitat provides examples of plants that can be grown by visitors in their own gardens to encourage wildlife to visit. There is also a butterfly and bog garden in the native plant area.

Across Willeo Road from the nature center is the wetland trail that takes about 35 minutes to cover. Be sure to stay on the boardwalk. The paths you see through the vegetation are made by marsh rabbits, muskrats and beavers and are not for human use. As you stroll along the wooden walkway (if it is wet be extra careful as it gets very slippery) you will see the marsh on your left and the swamp on your right. Native trees of the swamp include black willow, silky dogwood, alder and river birch. The marsh area has grasses and cattails. From June through early fall you will notice a stringy orange parasitic vine, called dodder, draped over much of the dense vegetation.

The marsh platform overlook is a good birding area, as a large number of Canada geese, mallards and wood ducks are permanent residents here. Nesting in the area during the summer months are red-winged blackbirds, catbirds, ducks, wrens and prothonotary warblers. A little farther along the trail you'll come to the levee platform that offers a glimpse across Bull Sluice Lake, formed by the construction of Morgan Falls Dam, two miles downstream.

The Chattahoochee Nature Center is open 9:00 A.M. to 5:00 P.M. daily. Guided walks are given on weekends at 1:00 and 3:00 P.M. On Tuesday evenings from May to September from 6:30 to 8:30 P.M. the center's staff lead **float trips** on the Chattahoochee River. The program begins with basic instruction on canoe paddling and safety; then the group ventures out on the river in hopes of spotting herons, waterfowl, beaver and other wildlife. Reservations must be made one week before the float trip, and a fee is charged; call (404)992-2055.

After enjoying the Chattahoochee in its natural state, continue to Roswell Square and visit **Roswell Mill** overlooking Vickery Creek. Here you'll see the changes the mill brought to the area and how the mill has now been changed and renovated.

Roswell King rode through this part of Georgia in 1828 on his way to seek gold in the mountains of North Georgia. Seeing Vickery Creek he realized this would be an ideal location for a cotton mill, as at the time there was only one cotton mill in the entire state of Georgia. Ten years later he purchased vast expanses of land in the area, and with the help of his son, Barrington King, he built the Roswell Cotton Mill. From 1840 to 1860 the Roswell Manufacturing Company, as it was soon named, prospered and the mill and the town grew. During the Civil War, the mill, a leading supplier of goods for the Confederacy, was destroyed by Union troops under General Kenner Garrard. The approximately 400 women and children working in the mill were sent to Tennessee, Kentucky and Indiana. Most were never heard from again.

The mill was rebuilt and ran until 1975. Now it's once more filled with life and activity, but it is of a different sort. Today the Roswell Mill is an entertainment complex with an array of shops, art studios, six restaurants and an evening concert series on the deck overlooking Vickery Creek. An entire building is set aside as the Arts Pavilion with galleries and studios for working artists who demonstrate, sell and in some cases teach their craft. There are painters, woodcarvers, a furniture maker, puppeteer and glass blowers. There are also craftsmen and specialty shops in the main building where the restaurants are located. Currently there are restaurants featuring German, Mexican, traditional Southern and Continental cuisine, as well as a classic 1950s diner. Several spots offer entertainment and the mill hosts several special events each year. The Concert Series offers a wide array of artists in a picturesque setting; call (404)642-6140 for current schedule and prices.

Just down from Roswell Mill off of Sloan Street is Vickery Creek Park. A trail leads from the parking area to a scenic waterfalls. You will have to descend a number of steps to get to the trail along the creek. This park is across from Founder's Cemetery.

Directions: From I-75 north of Atlanta take I-285, then exit on Roswell Road and proceed north to Azalea Drive and turn left. Continue on Azalea to the intersection with Willeo Road and bear left. The Chattahoochee Nature Center will be on your right at 9135 Willeo Road. For Roswell Mill take Roswell Road/Route 9, Atlanta Road, to Roswell Square. As you approach the Square, where Route 120 goes to the left, you will take a right into the entrance to the mill.

CNN Studio Tour

New View of News Network

In a sprawling complex in downtown Atlanta you can watch writers, editors, technicians, directors and on-air personalities as they cover the latest world events. It's a behind-the-scenes look at journalism in action at Turner's three 24-hour news networks—CNN, Headline News and CNN International—that have revolutionized television journalism.

CNN beams the news to over 60 million U.S. cable households (that's an increase from 1.7 million in 1980, CNN's first year) and broadcasts in more than 130 countries. The 45-minute state-of-the-art tour lets you observe the heart of the Turner Broadcasting System. After passing through a security gate similar to those at airports, you'll watch programs shown on CNN, Headline News, TBS, TNT and CNN International. Then you ride up on

In *CNN's* newsroom, a highlight of their *Studio Tour, over 1,000 TVs and 500 computer terminals monitor news-in-the-making.*

one of the world's longest free-standing escalators to the first stop at the TBS exhibit area.

As you exit the escalator there is a life-size cut-out of the charismatic Ted Turner and an artist's sketch of him at the helm of *Courageous*, the sailing ship which successfully defended the America's Cup in 1977 against the Australian challenge. Turner was nicknamed "Captain Outrageous" because of his publicity-oriented style. Proudly displayed is the January 16, 1992, issue of *Time* magazine that named Turner the 1991 "Man of the Year."

Sports memorabilia such as jerseys and bats also figure prominently in the collection displayed, especially from Turner's baseball team, the Atlanta Braves, that in 1991 went from last place to almost first, only failing to win the World Series. There are also photographs from the 1990 Goodwill Games and the Olympic Games.

Photographs are displayed from the 1991 War in the Gulf, in which CNN reporting gained world-wide attention. During the first week of fighting in the Persian Gulf, the ratings for CNN's live broadcasts from Baghdad were higher than those of ABC, NBC and CBS in households with cable. A map pinpoints the nine domestic CNN bureaus and the 19 international bureaus. Turner purchased MGM/UA Entertainment Co. in 1986, and you'll see posters from some of the well-loved movies he now controls like *Gone With the Wind*, *Ben Hur*, *Night at the Opera*, *Grand Hotel*, and *North by Northwest*.

Specially constructed walkways provide a bird's-eye view of the newsroom through walls of glass. The news floors are connected by 600,000 feet of coaxial cable and 90 miles of telephone and computer cable. By a rough count the newsroom has roughly 1,000 television monitors and about 500 computer terminals. As you look down at the journalists who work here, you'll see the script desks, the terminals of the copy editors, the control room, the in-use set and the on-camera anchors reading the day's fast-breaking news on TelePrompTers.

Next the tour moves on to the glass-windowed booth of CNN's international desk. The broadcast originates here but is shown overseas through three satellite feeds (a Hughes Galaxy I satellite used in these transmissions is in the exhibit area). The last stop is the weather set where visitors not only watch a demonstration of the chroma-key weather broadcast but can try delivering a televised weather report. Volunteers stand in front of a blank, blue wall, watch their images on the monitor, and point, coordinating their gestures with the weather map on the monitor. Try it; it's a lot harder than it looks, and it will give you an appreciation for the skill required in the next weather forecast you watch.

CNN Studio Tours are given daily every half hour from 9:00 A.M. to 5:30 P.M. except on major holidays. Admission is charged, and tickets must be used on the date of purchase. These tours are popular, and if you have a limited amount of time stop by early. Tickets for each day's tours go on sale at 8:30 A.M., and it's first-come, first-served. Tours sell out between 11:00 A.M. and 2:00 P.M. for the entire day. For additional information call (404)827-2300.

Directions: CNN is located in downtown Atlanta at the intersection of Techwood Drive and Marietta Street. CNN Center is part of a complex that includes the Omni Hotel, the Omni Sports Arena and CNN Cinema 6, as well as a shopping arcade and restaurant area. One of the stops is The Turner Store with film and television related memorabilia. There's also a Turner Store at Lenox Square.

Fernbank Museum of Natural History

Experience Past/Encounter Future

The next time you're in a science museum, look around at all the people sharing your experience. A startling statistic indicates that in a given year more people visit museums than attend all professional baseball, football and basketball games combined. Almost half of those who visit museums—and several years ago that was in excess of 500 million people—choose a science museum.

All that suggests a built-in audience for Atlanta's latest and largest museum—the Fernbank Museum of Natural History—which opened in October 1992. It's actually the largest museum of the natural sciences south of the Smithsonian in Washington, D.C., and the largest to be built in the country since the 1930s.

Over the last fifty years the concept of museum design has changed considerably. Museums today are interactive, drawing the visitor into the experience with animated sight-and-sound exhibits that challenge the imagination. The Fernbank Museum of Natural History reflects these trends. The museum's theme is "A Walk Through Time in Georgia." Using the state as a microcosm, exhibits tell the story of the earth's development covering science from A (astronomy) to Z (zoology).

Georgia's natural history covers each of the six major periods in the earth's geological calendar, and representatives of the flora and fauna of every historic epoch are found in the state. The five landform regions are: the Piedmont Plateau, the Blue Ridge Mountains, the Ridge and Valley, the Cumberland Plateau, and the Atlantic and Gulf Coastal Plains. Twelve paired galleries, off a soaring, skylit Great Hall, match a geological epoch in the earth's development with each of these regions in Georgia.

Besides this permanent centerpiece exhibit, there is the **Harris Naturalist Center**, where visitors of all ages can use sophisticated laboratory equipment. Under the guidance of trained professionals, visitors can identify and categorize their own fossils, shells or plant samples.

Young visitors have two special areas geared specifically to them. For the three-to-five-year-old child there is Fantasy Forest. There kids can put on plush, honeybee gloves and pick up golf ball-size "pollen" puffs as they investigate a large, velcro-coated beehive; or climb a large "tree" to feed mechanical baby birds, who warble birdsongs as the toy worms are dropped in their open beaks. In the Georgia Adventure, children six-to-ten-years old are given explorer backpacks as they set out to discover how cats see at night, how a water strider walks on water and what it is like for a raccoon to pick up a persimmon with its paws. Youngsters feel the spongy earth shift under their feet as they enter the Okefenokee Swamp. Kids get to stand on the deck of a shrimp boat, haul in the net then sort through their catch. These rooms succeed in getting children excited about science.

The museum has the state's first IMAX theater, with a concave three-story screen measuring 52 by 70 feet. This gives visitors the "big picture" of natural history.

The museum sits on the edge of the **Fernbank Forest**, a 65-acre hardwood preserve. An 85-foot-tall glass atrium seems to bring the outdoors inside. The floor of this great hall has real fossils embedded in the tile. The museum is open Monday through Saturday from 9:00 A.M. to 6:00 P.M. On Sunday the museum does not open until NOON. It is closed on Christmas Day and New Year's Day. Admission is charged.

Not far away, is the **Fernbank Science Center**, a far-older, associated facility. A museum and an educational center, it has both a planetarium and an observatory. In the center's exhibition hall there are traditional exhibit cases filled with taxidermy specimens and hand-fabricated plants and animals set against sculptured terrain and painted scenery suggesting Georgia's diverse terrain. There's even a depiction of prehistoric Atlanta that includes a saber-toothed tiger as well as dinosaurs. There are exhibits on minerals, gems and butterflies.

Planetarium shows are presented in the 70-foot-diameter projection dome. Seasonal and holiday shows are popular favorites, and if you call in advance, on your birthday they will show you what the sky looked like the day you were born. Planetarium performances are on Tuesday through Saturday at 8:00 P.M. and Wednesday, Friday, Saturday and Sunday at 11:00 A.M. and 3:00 P.M. Admission is charged.

Fernbank's observatory houses the largest telescope in the world that is used specifically for public education. The 36-inch reflecting telescope is available to the public for scanning the skies. The observatory is open Thursday and Friday evenings when the sky is clear from 8:00 to 10:30 P.M.

You can hike the self-guided trails in the Fernbank Forest on Sunday through Friday from 2:00 to 5:00 P.M. and on Saturday from 10:00 A.M. to 5:00 P.M. There are two miles of hard-surfaced trails. Seasonal guidesheets identify native flora and fauna. An Easy Effort Trail has been laid out for handicapped visitors.

Directions: From I-75/85 from the north take the North Avenue exit and go three blocks to Peachtree Street. Then go left one block to Ponce de Leon Avenue and turn right. From the south, take the Peachtree Street North exit, and go left (or north) on Peachtree Street. Travel four blocks, then make a right on Ponce de Leon Avenue. Take this for three miles before turning left on Clifton Road. Once you are on Clifton, you will see the museum on your immediate right. For the Science Center, continue on Ponce de Leon approximately one more mile to Artwood Road. Turn left, continue one block and turn right onto Heaton Park Drive. The Science Center is immediately on the left.

Georgia State Capitol and Governor's Mansion

Legislative and Executive Branch

Make civics fun by watching government in action on a tour of the Georgia State Capitol and the Governor's Mansion. Atlanta was not the state's first capital. The first one was Savannah, then respectively Augusta, Heard's Fort in Wilkes County, Louisville, Milledgeville and Macon.

The Georgia Legislature first met in Atlanta in 1868, but it was not until 1883 that one million dollars was allocated to build the Capitol. Construction began in October 1884, and the dedication on July 4, 1889, left $118.43 in the building fund. Costly Georgia marble was used on the interior, while the exterior of the Classic Renaissance building was of Indiana oolitic limestone. On the Capitol's west front a wide concrete plaza leads to the four-story portico, with a stone pediment supported by six Corinthian columns. The Great Seal is engraved on the pediment.

The Georgia Capitol looks like a small-scale version of the Capitol in Washington, D.C. The interior cross-shaped open rotunda extends from the second floor through the upper stories to a height of 237 feet, 4 inches. A gilded dome, 75 feet in diameter, was redone in 1956 with 43 ounces of native gold donated by Dahlonega and Lumpkin County. A fresh application of gold was put on in 1981. A cupola sits atop the dome, and crowning the building is a Greek-inspired statue commemorating the war dead.

Originally the Capitol consisted of three main floors with stables in a section of the basement. The state adjutant general lived with his family on the top floor. Over the years the basement was converted to offices and the floors renumbered. The second floor is now the main entrance where the offices for the governor, lieutenant governor and secretary of state are located.

Also on the main floor, inside and around the rotunda, are marble busts of members of the Georgia Hall of Fame and other famous Georgians, as well as portraits of noted Americans. On the second floor are portraits of Georgia's governors. The second floor north wing houses a portrait of Martin Luther King, Jr., and a statue of Georgia orator Benjamin Hill. Flags from each state hang from the fourth floor balustrades, and to the north of the rotunda in the Hall of Flags are all the flags that have flown over Georgia.

The legislative chambers are on the third floor. On the west side is the red-carpeted House of Representatives, where delegates sit at hand-carved cherry wood desks. In the blue-carpeted Senate on the east side, each senator has a carved oak desk. Visitors' galleries are entered from the fourth floor. The State Museum of Science and Industry exhibits part of its collection on the first and fourth floors of the Capitol. On the lower level exhibits carry out the theme "A Walk Through Georgia" with wildlife dioramas. Flags from Georgia regiments in the Civil War, the Spanish-American War and World War I are displayed, and four cases are filled with model airplanes. On the fourth floor, exhibits cover Georgia's natural history with cases displaying mounted specimens of reptiles, birds and fish. Dioramas show indigenous birds and animals in their natural habitat.

Tours of the Capitol are given at no charge Monday through Friday at 10:00 and 11:00 A.M. and 1:00 and 2:00 P.M. The Capitol is closed on weekends. Visitors also should take the time to explore the grounds. Within the stone-walled area are monuments, statues, markers and a replica of the Liberty Bell set among a variety of trees and flowers.

Georgia's governor has his office in the Capitol, but his **official residence** is in Atlanta's Buckhead neighborhood. This Greek Revival mansion was dedicated in January of 1968. Visitors are welcome to tour the first floor rooms filled with 19th-century furnishings, paintings and porcelain. Most of the furniture, which belongs to the people of Georgia and not to the governor personally, is by American designers, and much of it is from the Federal period.

At the entrance there is an oversized inlaid bronze seal of the state of Georgia. The entry hall has bronze busts of George Washington and Benjamin Franklin made in 1778 by Jean Antoine Houdon. Each visitor is given a pamphlet that provides details on each of the public rooms, and docents are located throughout the house.

To the left of the entryway is the cherry wood-paneled library filled with first editions of noted Georgia authors. An engraved portrait of Georgia founder General James Oglethorpe sits on a Pembroke table near the antique scroll-arm sofa. One of the finest pieces in the room is the 1875 Persian Tabriz carpet.

Across the hall is the state drawing room with its brilliant Aubusson tapestry carpet. The room features exquisite examples of the cabinetmakers art, from the large English breakfront to the matching Duncan Phyfe card tables and the New York City-made mahogany Pembroke tables and square-back Grecian scroll-arm sofas. Be sure to notice the Darby porcelain.

The state dining room seats 18 (large formal dinners are held in the lower level ballroom) at the mahogany accordion-style extension table. The Empire sideboard is filled with elegant serving pieces, and there is a tea service by New York silversmith

Garrett Eoff. More informal, family dining quarters are accessible to the kitchen. The huntboard was made in Georgia in 1810; it's the only regional piece in the public rooms. There is also a comfortable family living room. One final room visitors can view is the first floor guest bedroom with its 1815 alcove bed and English needlepoint carpet.

The private living quarters are on the second floor. After touring the ground floor, visitors can stroll around the porch, from which there is a view of the formal gardens on the west side of the mansion and the family's swimming pool.

The Governor's Mansion is open for self-guided tours Tuesday, Wednesday and Thursday from 10:00 A.M. to 11:30 P.M. Advance reservations are not required.

Directions: From I-75/85 south to reach the Georgia State Capitol take Capitol Avenue, Exit 91. Traveling from the north, take Martin Luther King, Jr. Drive, Exit 93. If you are traveling on I-20 east take Capitol Avenue, Exit 24, and if you are coming from the west take Windsor/Spring Exit 22 to Central Avenue. For the Governor's Mansion take the Peachtree Road exit off I-85 and head north to West Paces Ferry Road. The mansion will be on your right past the Atlanta History Center.

Herndon Home

Elegant Symbol of Black Achievement

When you speak of an American success story it would be hard to top that of Alonzo F. Herndon. Born a slave in 1858 in Social Circle, with only one year of schooling, he became one of America's foremost African-American businessmen.

At age 13 he was working as a farm laborer for his former master. By age 23 he was cutting hair on weekends and eventually opened a barbershop in Jonesboro. By the 1880s he moved to Atlanta and began investing in real estate while still working as a barber. Over the years he opened several barbershops in Atlanta. In 1905 Herndon purchased three benevolent and protective associations and combined them to form what eventually became the Atlanta Life Insurance Company, one of the largest black-owned businesses in the country.

Herndon was active in his church, First Congregational. While not politically involved, in 1905 he did attend the founding meeting of the Niagara Movement, the forerunner of the NAACP, and in 1907, he signed a petition opposing disfranchisement of blacks in Georgia.

Alonzo Herndon considered himself a builder, and he and his wife Adrienne designed the Herndon home and managed its construction after acquiring ideas and art on a trip to Europe in 1900. Thus there is the Renaissance Revival reception hall and dining room and the rococo detailing of the music room. The 15-room Beaux Arts Classical mansion was built by skilled black craftsmen in 1910.

Adrienne taught elocution and inaugurated Shakespearean productions at Atlanta University. She had a son, Norris Bumstead. When Norris was in his early teens, Adrienne was stricken with Addison's disease and died the very week the house was completed. Two years later, Alonzo Herndon married Jessie Gillespie, a successful hairdresser in Chicago, Illinois.

Norris continued to live at the Herndon house until his death in 1977. Much of the antique furniture and fine art you'll see were part of his collection; other pieces were acquired by his parents. A series of paintings on the ceiling of the living room tell the story of Alonzo Herndon's life. Upstairs are cases filled with Norris's collection, exquisite Venetian and Roman glass and delicate decorative pottery. Before Norris died, he established a charitable trust that operates the house museum.

The Herndon Home, listed on the National Register of Historic Places, is significant because it is one of the few historic residences available to the public that interprets an upper middle-class African-American lifestyle. Free guided tours are given hourly from 10:00 A.M. to 4:00 P.M. Tuesday through Saturday. Before beginning the house tour there is a 12-minute video tape about Alonzo Herndon and the Herndon Home.

Directions: From the north travel south on I-75/85 and take the Martin Luther King Jr. Drive exit, go west (right) on MLK. Travel three blocks past the intersection of MLK and Northside Drive and then turn right on Vine Street. Take Vine for one block to University Place and turn right. The Herndon Home is on the left at the end of the street. If you are traveling from the south, go north on I-75/85 and take Central Avenue exit. Go north on Central Avenue, make a left onto MLK and follow directions above. From the east, take I-20 west and follow the Spring Street exit, turning right on Spring Street. Turn left on MLK Drive and follow above directions.

High Museum of Art

Masterpieces in a Masterful Setting

The centerpiece of Atlanta's Midtown arts district, the High Museum of Art, opened in October 1983. The dazzling white building designed by Richard Meier tripled the space of the museum's former home. The High's innovative design garnered interna-

The dazzling, award-winning High Museum of Art houses an important collection of 19th-century American paintings.

tional acclaim and prestigious awards, including the American Institute of Architects' 1984 Honor Award. That same year Meier won the coveted Pritzker Architecture Prize.

Figuring prominently among the 9,200 objects of the High Museum's permanent collection are a significant number of American paintings of the 19th century and work by major contemporary artists. The museum also has the critically acclaimed Virginia Carroll Crawford Collection of American Decorative Arts, nearly 200 pieces that document styles from 1825 to 1917.

There are five floors. Visitors enter on the main floor with its well-stocked museum shop and auditorium. On the lower level is "**Spectacles**," the junior gallery installation where children can explore art through hands-on activities. Tours of the junior gallery exhibition are available throughout the year; call (404)898-1145 for details. Workshops for children and families are also offered; call (404)892-3600 for workshop information.

On the second floor there's the American Decorative Arts exhibit and the Cocke and Scott-Allen Collections of English, French and German porcelain and ceramics dating from the

1630s to the 1840s. There is also a display of China Trade Porcelain made between 1500 and 1800 for the European and American markets. The museum's collection of Sub-Saharan African art is also on the second floor. The museum is now a regional center for the study of African art and artifacts, including a striking collection of masks and ceremonial figures.

The third floor galleries showcase the museum's collection of European art from the 14th through the 19th centuries. This exhibit integrates painting, sculpture and miniatures to give an overview of the history of Western art. The Samuel H. Kress Foundation has contributed works by major Italian painters and sculptors. Included in this exhibit are works by Italian artists Tiepolo, Ricci and di Giorgio; French paintings by Monet, Girodet and Tournier; Dutch and Flemish works by Jan Brueghel the Elder and Reineir Nooms; and sculptures by Rodin, Riemenschneider and Barye. On this level there are additional galleries devoted to a variety of traveling exhibitions on view throughout the year. The fourth floor is devoted to special exhibitions and works by 20th-century artists such as Ernst, Gorky, Guston, Lawrence, Rauschenberg and Murray.

The High Museum of Art, located at 1280 Peachtree Street, N.E., is open Tuesday through Saturday from 10:00 A.M. to 5:00 P.M. On Friday night the museum remains open until 9:00 P.M. and Sunday NOON to 5:00 P.M. Admission is charged, except on Thursdays from 1:00 to 5:00 P.M. For information about museum programs call (404)892-HIGH. The museum presents films, gallery talks, workshops, lectures, monthly highlight tours and docent-led tours. These 45-minute tours are included in the admission fee.

The High Museum also operates a branch facility at 133 Peachtree Street, N.E., one block south of Peachtree Center. The High Museum of Art at Georgia-Pacific Center displays major works from the High Museum as well as traveling exhibitions. Gallery talks, lectures and special programs are held at this satellite as well. Hours are Monday through Friday from 11:00 A.M. to 5:00 P.M. For more information call (404)577-6940.

Directions: From the south take I-75/85N to the 10th Street exit. Go right on 10th, and turn left on Peachtree Street. Or, from the north take I-75 south to 10th/14th Street exit. Go left on 14th Street and left again on Peachtree Street. Then, proceed to the intersection of Peachtree and 16th Street. The High Museum of Art is in the Woodruff Arts Center.

Kennesaw Mountain National Battlefield Park

Friendly Fire

Action at the Kennesaw Mountain National Battlefield Park was part of General William T. Sherman's Atlanta Campaign that began in the spring of 1864. The action started in Chattanooga, Tennessee, with orders from General Ulysses S. Grant for Sherman to attack the Confederate army in Georgia and "break it up, and go into the interior of the enemy's country as far as you can, inflicting all the damage you can upon their war resources."

In the first week of May 1864 Sherman began his march with 100,000 men and 254 pieces of artillery. Waiting for them in the northwest mountains of Georgia was General Joseph E. Johnston with 65,000 men and 187 cannons. The prize was Atlanta, the railroad hub and war manufacturing center of the Confederacy.

As he moved south, Sherman attempted to hold the main body of Johnston's force in place while he moved part of his army behind their flank. Sherman's objective was to cut the Confederacy's Western & Atlantic Railroad supply line.

By June, Sherman was southwest of Marietta facing a well-entrenched Confederate position anchored by Kennesaw Mountain. When Sherman saw the lofty ridge and twin peaks of the mountain he described the scene as too beautiful to be disturbed by the horrors of war—but disturbed it was. On June 22, Johnston shifted 11,000 men under General John Bell Hood to the south to meet Sherman's flanking motion. The two armies engaged around **Kolb Farm**, and though Hood failed to drive the Union army back, he did temporarily halt their southward thrust.

The Kolb farm house, built in 1836 by Peter Valentine Kolb with the help of neighboring Cherokees, is a stop on the battlefield tour. The house was damaged by gunfire but has been restored to its appearance before the battle. After the fight the wounded of both armies were treated in the house. The interior is not open for tours.

Unable to move forward and hampered by muddy roads, Sherman decided to attempt a strong attack at the center of Johnston's line while staging a diversionary movement against the Confederate left flank. Sherman's men moved into position at dawn on June 27. After an 8:00 A.M. artillery bombardment, the Union army attacked. Three Union brigades, roughly 5,500 men, marched across the swampy, heavily wooded terrain under a steady barrage of fire. Their attack was a bloody failure. They never reached their objective, Pigeon Hill (now stop 2 on the battlefield tour).

As part of Sherman's two-pronged attack, 8,000 Union infantrymen, five brigades, attacked Johnston's two best divisions commanded by Generals Patrick R. Cleburne and Benjamin Franklin Cheatham. To protect the hill, now called Cheatham Hill and stop 3 on the tour, the Confederates created a projecting angle. It was along this salient that the fiercest fighting of the battle occurred with hand-to-hand combat taking place on top of the defender's earthworks. This part of the battlefield was called the Dead Angle because the Union army lost 3,000 men while the Confederates lost 800.

Along the short trail to the Illinois Monument on Cheatham Hill, the Confederate earthworks are visible. Near the base of the monument you can see the entrance to a tunnel dug by the Union troops with the intention of blowing up the Confederate line, a plan never realized. Also in the vicinity are the Union entrenchments that were dug under enemy fire and held for six days.

During one of the periods of intense artillery fire, the forest in which the Union troops were positioned caught on fire, and the wounded Yankee soldiers were in danger of being burned alive. Lieutenant Colonel William H. Martin, commanding the First and Fifteenth Arkansas Infantry Regiments, called a truce, and the Confederates helped the Union soldiers put out the fire and move the wounded. The Federal officers presented Lt. Col. Martin with a matched set of pistols in appreciation of his humanitarian action.

On July 2nd, the Confederate force abandoned their position on Kennesaw Mountain, and Sherman continued his drive to Atlanta, the action that preceded his March to the Sea. To gain a perspective on the action at Kennesaw and the Atlanta campaign, stop at the **Kennesaw Mountain Visitor Center**: There are exhibits, a map of the battle and a ten-minute slide program. Hours are 8:30 A.M. to 5:00 P.M. Just a short distance from the center is an observation overlook that gives you a sweeping panoramic view of the city of Atlanta. The trail to this overlook is moderately steep, but the view is worth the effort.

There's an ironic footnote to this campaign. General Johnston admired Sherman's tactics in their many confrontations, and when Sherman died Johnston attended his funeral. The day was rainy and and Johnston caught a cold that became pneumonia. He died within a week.

Directions: From I-75 take Exit 116, Barrett Parkway, until it intersects with U.S. Route 41. Make a right and travel north on Route 41. When Old Route 41 breaks off to the left, follow that for about two miles to the park entrance off Stilesboro Road. There are signs from the interstate exit.

King Center, Sweet Auburn and Freedom Walk

The Dream is Alive

In 1968, Coretta Scott King established the King Center as a living memorial to her slain husband. The Center stands on a 23-acre National Historic Site that includes the birthplace and final resting place of Martin Luther King, Jr.

The Martin Luther King, Jr. Center for Nonviolent Social Change recognizes and continues Dr. King's work in the human rights movement. The crypt of this noted humanitarian, surrounded by the quiet waters of the Reflecting Pool, bears his famous words, "Free at last; Free at last. Thank God Almighty, I'm free at last."

The King Center operates independently from the National Park Service historic site. The Center focuses on education and training programs in nonviolent philosophy and strategy for bringing about social change, community service program development and leadership training. The Center also serves as a research facility. Its vast archives include Dr. King's papers, documents from the Civil Rights Movement and personal papers of individual leaders in the movement plus the records of nine major civil rights organizations.

Visitors at the King Center are welcome to view the photographs and memorabilia from Dr. King's public and private life in the Exhibition Hall. There is also a Chapel of all Faiths and the Eternal Flame at Dr. King's grave site. The King Center is open daily 9:00 A.M. to 5:30 P.M. During the summer months the Center closes later.

After exploring The King Center, you can join one of the National Park Service tours of Dr. King's birthplace a block away. Tours begin at the **Bryant-Graves House** at 522 Auburn Avenue. Formerly the home of two prominent blacks, the house is now a visitor information center. Before touring the birthplace, watch the 15-minute video on Dr. King's life, shown every half hour from 10:00 A.M. to 5:00 P.M. There is no charge for the tour.

Martin Luther King, Jr., was born in his grandfather's house at noon on January 15, 1929. M.L., as he was called in the neighborhood, grew up in was a close-knit black residential community. Auburn Avenue, formerly Wheat Street, was an area that symbolized achievement for the black citizens of Atlanta. After the Civil War, former slaves purchased property east of the city's central business district. As they prospered they improved their community. By 1929, more than 100 black-owned or black-operated businesses could be found on Auburn Avenue. The opportunities for blacks were so wide, even with Atlanta's segregation laws, that political leader John Wesley Dobbs nicknamed the area "Sweet Auburn."

The nine-room, two-story Queen Anne style house where Martin Luther King, Jr., was born was built in 1895. Fourteen years later the Reverend A.D. Williams bought the house for $3,500, and the Williams-King family called it home for the next 32 years. When M.L. was growing up he lived here with his parents, grandparents, brother and sister. When he was 12, after the death of both grandparents, his parents moved with their children a few blocks from this house.

Much of the furniture in the birthplace home is original. Those pieces that are not are carefully duplicated. The front parlor was the family study and game room, and visitors see a Monopoly game still set up on the table. The small table in the kitchen is still set for two. M.L. got a quarter each week for shoveling coal into the basement furnace. Young Martin not only shared a bedroom, he shared a bed with his brother A.D., and their Uncle Joe, who was just 13 years older, also shared their room. The boys' toys still fill the room: Lincoln logs, Tinkertoys, puzzles and a baseball bat, glove and ball.

Just down the street is the **Ebenezer Baptist Church**, another site that has been carefully restored to re-create M.L.'s childhood environment. Reverend A.D. Williams was the pastor at this Gothic Revival church built in 1922. At his death, his son-in-law Martin Luther King, Sr., became pastor and served here until he retired in 1975. At different times both A.D. and M.L. served as co-pastors. For more than 80 years the ministers of Ebenezer were members of the same family. If the church is associated with great pride, it also has played a role in great family tragedies. In April 1968, thousands of mourners viewed Martin Luther King, Jr.'s body as it lay in state in this church. In 1974, Dr. King's mother was killed by an assassin as she sat at her regular place at the church organ.

At the Bryant-Graves House, visitors can pick up a walking tour map of Sweet Auburn that highlights other points of interest. The walk takes you past the Atlanta Life Insurance Co. Building and the Herndon Building. A visit to Herndon Home (see selection) is an interesting comparison with the King family home, the King home being a comfortable middle class home while the Herndon Home is a more elaborate estate. The Sweet Auburn preservation district includes private homes, businesses, public buildings and churches.

When you reach the Atlanta Life Insurance Co. Building you will be picking up yet another walking tour route, that of the **Freedom Walk**. This walk traces the origins of the Civil Rights Movement. The 1.2-mile walk actually begins at the Information

Center in Underground Atlanta (see selection) and ends at the Martin Luther King, Jr. Center for Nonviolent Social Change. This walk includes part of Sweet Auburn that is included in the National Historic Park area. There are 24 points of interest on the Freedom Walk, and walking tour maps are available at Underground Atlanta or in the Bryant-Graves House.

Directions: From I-75/85 southbound take the Butler Street exit. Go straight for one block on Butler Street to Auburn Avenue and turn left on Auburn Avenue. Traveling northbound on I-75/85, take the Edgewood/Auburn Avenue exit, and go straight for one block to Auburn Avenue; turn right on Auburn.

Marietta

Antebellum Resort

Fifteen miles north of the capital, Marietta and its mild summers have attracted vacationers since it was established in 1834 on former Cherokee Indian land. Although much of the city was left in ashes after the Civil War Battle of Kennesaw Mountain, there are still antebellum homes in the four National Register Historic Districts.

The place to begin exploring Marietta is in the **Welcome Center**, located in a renovated train station on Depot Street, on the west side of Marietta Square. This site is singularly appropriate since the town's development was hastened by the construction of the Western & Atlantic Railroad, which put Marietta in touch with the rest of the country. One of the businesses that developed near the tracks was John H. Glover's tannery. In 1852 as mayor of the city, Glover established a park. Within this Victorian wonderland is a sculptured fountain and landscaped gardens surrounded by a decorative wrought-iron fence. The park has recently been restored and now serves as the focal point of Marietta Square with a band shell where festivals and music programs are often performed. The turn-of-the-century feeling is heightened by a copper-roofed gazebo and Victorian benches. The playground has a scaled-down replica of the famous steam train, the General, which children can climb on and pretend they've joined Andrews Raiders (see Big Shanty selection). Around the square you'll find a collection of quaint restaurants and shops.

Before you leave the Welcome Center (open weekdays 9:00 A.M. to 5:00 P.M., Saturdays 10:00 A.M. to 3:00 P.M. and Sunday 1:00 to 4:00 P.M.), pick up an historic walking/driving tour brochure. A 90-minute rental cassette tour is also available, highlighting 52 points of historic interest in and around Marietta.

Next door to the Welcome Center is the three-story **Kennesaw**

House Hotel, which was called Fletcher House when it was built around John H. Glover's Breakfast House in 1855. Andrews Raiders rendezvoused here in 1862 before hijacking the General. Union General Sherman made his headquarters at Kennesaw House, while Confederate General Joseph Johnston made his headquarters at Fair Oaks, now the Marietta Educational Garden Center. The house and gardens have been restored and are open for tours Monday, Wednesday and Friday from 10:00 A.M. to 2:00 P.M. The tour also includes the National and Confederate cemeteries (see Cannonball Trail selection).

Restoration work is underway on the 1840 Root House, and when it is completed, this too will be open for tours. William Root, one of the city's pioneer businessmen, built this simple Virginia Plantation Plain farm house in 1840. Root was instrumental in the founding of the St. James Episcopal Church in 1843. The church was commandeered by the Union army during the Civil War, and local lore claims that the Yankees put molasses in the organ and stabled their horses in the church. Twenty years later when the elderly church organist was asked to play at a wedding ceremony uniting a local Southern belle and a Northerner, she reputedly played the funeral dirge. Though the Yankees didn't burn the church, it did burn in 1964, and only a small portion of the original structure survived.

Bushy Park, a Greek Revival Mansion built in 1848 by John H. Glover, is now listed on the National Register Of Historic Places as the Glover-McLeod-Garrison House, recognizing subsequent owners. This gracious white-pillared antebellum plantation is now also an elegant restaurant called **The 1848 House at Bushy Park Plantation** that sits amid 13 acres of what was once a 3,000-acre spread. Cotton and corn grown here were sent by the Glovers to be sold in Savannah, Mobile and New Orleans.

Mrs. Glover felt the house was too far out of town, and in 1851 it was acquired by the McLeods. During the Civil War a battle was fought on the estate grounds. A bullet from that skirmish is still embedded in the wooden door frame of one of the restaurant's dining rooms. The house survived Sherman's March to the Sea. It was a private residence until it was acquired in 1979 by Calvin G. Adams who established the noted restaurant that has garnered nation-wide acclaim. Dining on the glassed-in portico or amid the splendor of period antiques is a true taste of the gracious hospitality of the Old South. (Reservations are required; call 404-427-4646.)

Although not part of the historic tour, there are several other spots of interest to include on a day trip to Marietta. Just south of Marietta Square is the **Marietta/Cobb Museum of Art** that features traveling exhibits and monthly art shows. Some may question its artistic value, but the **Big Chicken** is also one of Marietta's most well-known landmarks. This 56-foot-tall red chicken on Route 41, Georgia's first four-lane highway, is known throughout the metro-Atlanta area. Originally the location of the Chick, Chuck and Shake Restaurant, it is now a Kentucky Fried Chicken franchise.

In addition to this fowl landmark, children enjoy **American Adventures** entertainment complex with its amusement rides, miniature golf, penny arcade and adjacent 35-acre Whitewater Park. There is no general admission to American Adventures, which is open year-round. Whitewater Park is open weekends in May and daily from Memorial Day through Labor Day.

For information on all the Marietta attractions call the Welcome Center at (404)429-1115. Throughout the year festivals and celebrations add to the fun beginning with the Atlanta Dogwood Festival Concerts in April, the Old-Fashioned Fourth of July Celebration, Art in the Park over Labor Day weekend, the Marietta Arts & Crafts Festival the first weekend in October and Christmas in the Square in early December. Perhaps the best-loved celebration is the Marietta Pilgrimage; a Christmas Home Tour that is held the first weekend in December.

Directions: Take Exit 111 off I-75 just 20 miles north of Atlanta. For the 1848 House at Bushy Plantation take Exit 111, the Lockheed Dobbins exit. Be in the left exit lane that curves around and goes back over I-75. Take Delk Road for 4.3 miles and turn right at Pearl Street. Almost immediately on your left you will see the main gate of the restaurant.

Michael C. Carlos Museum

Art and Archaeology of Ancient Cultures

When you see a flawless gemstone, you might think it needs no setting to enhance its beauty—yet seeing that same stone in an exquisite piece of jewelry does add to its singular charm. The same might be said of the Michael C. Carlos Museum. The art pieces on display have an enduring beauty, yet seen in the jewelbox setting of this new award-winning museum, they are even more breathtaking.

The museum is located on the main quadrangle of Emory University. The original section is in one of the oldest buildings on campus, a Beaux-Arts design by Henry Hornbostel, that is included on the National Register of Historic Places. After an interior renovation in 1985 by Post-Modernist architect Michael Graves, the museum was given an Honor Award from the American Institute of Architects. In the spring of 1993, a major expansion, also designed by Graves, increased the museum's size by 350 percent.

The museum has benefited from the generosity of its benefactors. Atlanta businessman Michael Carlos, for whom the museum was renamed in 1991, donated his nationally recognized collection of Ancient Greek art. William C. and Carol W. Thibadeau gave the museum their 1,301-piece, pre-Colombian art collection. For three decades the Thibadeaus built their spectacular collection, buying from art dealers and other collectors. One of the collection's greatest strengths is the more than 600 pieces from Costa Rica, making this museum one of the six top American museums in terms of antiquities from this Central American country. Major works from the Thibadeau collection fill the galleries on the first floor of the old section of the museum. Other highlights of the museum include material from the Kathleen Kenyo excavations of Jericho in the 1950s and Egyptian coffins and mummies from Professor W. A. Shelton's 1920 expedition to Egypt. There is also a collection from native cultures of North America, especially the southeastern United States, as well as work from Asia, Africa and Oceania.

On long-term loan from The Metropolitan Museum of Art in New York are roughly 210 plaster casts taken from original master works of art and architecture. These replicas represent the best of Classical, Near Eastern, Islamic, Egyptian and Medieval architectural sculpture. Casts are made of friezes, reliefs, column capitals and decorated elements from famous monuments, temples and buildings from antiquity to the Renaissance.

The Michael C. Carlos Museum is open Monday through Saturday from 10:00 A.M. to 5:00 P.M. (Friday until 8:45 P.M.) and Sunday from NOON to 5:00 P.M. There is no set admission fee but rather a suggested donation. A gift shop—well worth visiting—is one of the most profitable museum gift shops in the country. There is also a cafe overlooking a wooded ravine south of the museum.

Directions: From I-75/85 exit on Ponce de Leon Avenue east. Make a left turn on Briarcliff Road and then right on N. Decatur Road. Make a left on Dowman Drive, at the main gate of Emory University. Take the second right onto Kilgo Street, the museum is at 571 South Kilgo Street.

Museums of Atlanta

Special Interest Groups

Amid the towering commercial buildings of downtown Atlanta, tucked beside international banks and corporate headquarters, are a selection of off-beat museums that focus on economics, technology, science, entertainment and sports.

The **Monetary Museum**, on the third floor of the Federal Reserve Bank of Atlanta, welcomes visitors at no charge Monday through Friday from 9:00 A.M. to 4:00 P.M. Twenty-seven glass-enclosed cases tell the story of money as a medium of exchange. An illustrated narrative begins with bartered items, jade money and gold. One crowd-pleaser is a 27-pound gold bar, on loan to the museum from the U.S. Treasury, worth approximately $148,500. Gradually coin money was introduced as a uniform method of exchange. One of the oldest pieces is a silver tetradrachm that dates back to between 430 and 490 B.C. Visitors discover that China issued the world's first paper money. The story of banking is also explained, starting with the 15th-century De Medici Bank in Florence, Italy, one of the first great private banking houses. The Bank of England, the "Old Lady of Threadneedle Street," is one of the first great charter banks. One surprising fact visitors learn is that paper money is not made from paper but from a blend of cotton and linen.

There are extensive examples of American and international coins, as well as uncut sheets of currency in denominations that range from $1.00 notes to $100,000 Gold Certificates. The most valuable single item is the 1794 U.S. silver dollar. These were the first silver dollars minted by the government, and less than a hundred have survived. Interested visitors can leave the museum with $125 in shredded currency because, as is explained in the 28-minute video tour of the Federal Reserve Bank, they don't make money here, they shred it. The Atlanta Fed is one of 12 regional Reserve Banks, which along with the 25 branch offices and 11 regional check-processing centers form the Federal Reserve System.

Organized group tours of the Federal Reserve Bank of Atlanta can be arranged by contacting the Public Affairs Department at (404)521-8747. Individuals can explore the Monetary Museum on a walk-in basis. The Federal Reserve Bank of Atlanta, located at 104 Marietta Street, N.W., is half-way between CNN and Underground Atlanta (see selections). For a recorded message giving directions to the Bank call (404)521-8337.

The Federal Reserve Bank is also a few blocks away from the **Georgia Dome**. Walk-in visitors can join tours of the world's largest cable-supported domed stadium. The Dome, home to the Atlanta Falcons and host for numerous other events including the Super Bowl XXVII in 1994 and the 1966 Summer Olympics, opened in August 1992.

Tours of the Georgia Dome take visitors out on the playing field, into the visitor's locker room and to the press box. Located at One Georgia Dome Drive in downtown Atlanta, the impressive structure is as tall as a 27-story building, rising 275 feet from the center of the playing field to the center of the roof. The Teflon-coated Fiberglas fabric roof weighs 68 tons and covers 8.6 acres. The 110,000 cubic yards of concrete used to build the dome could form a sidewalk from Atlanta to Cincinnati, Ohio. For additional information on tours call (404)223-TOUR.

At the Southern Bell Center, 675 W. Peachtree Street, visitors learn about America's first century of telecommunications at **The Telephone Museum** (located off the retail mall on the Plaza Level).

The story of the telephone begins with its invention by Alexander Graham Bell. Visitors learn that the first call was an emergency call, and Bell's first words into his prototype telephone were: "Mr. Watson, come here, I want you. . . ." Bell may have intended his first words to be more historic, but he spilled sulphuric acid on his clothes and needed quick attention. Among the first to have a telephone was Mark Twain who remarked, "If Bell had invented a muffler or a gag, he would have done a real service. Here we have been hollering 'shut up' to our neighbors for centuries, and now this fellow comes along and seeks to complicate matters."

Museum exhibits trace the evolution of telephones from the earliest models to switchboards and switching systems and on to the modern area of cable satellites and other types of communication systems. The popularity of telephones can be gauged from the following statistics: In 1876 there were 3,000 phones or 0.1 per 1,000 Americans; in 1880 there were 48,000 or 0.9 per 1,000; by 1890 the number had increased to 228,000 phones or 3.6 per 1,000, and by 1919 there were 7,635,000 phones or 82.0 per 1,000 Americans. In 1930 the numbers had jumped to 20,103,000 phones or 162.6 per 1,000, and in 1940 it was 21,928,000 or 165.1 per 1,000 Americans.

One of the Telephone Museum's most popular exhibits is an early 20th-century street scene with a 1925 Model "T" telephone truck parked in front of a drug store. A mini-theater shows a ten-minute multi-image program about the telephone industry. The museum is open at no charge Monday through Friday from 11:00 A.M. to 1:00 P.M.

Several blocks away at 395 Piedmont Avenue, NE, is **SciTrek**, Atlanta's Science and Technology Museum. This interactive sci-

Screw Balls, an exhibit at SciTrek, demonstrates the use of a screw to lift objects, such as balls.

ence center has more than 100 permanent exhibits designed to illustrate basic scientific principles and show their importance in everyday terms. SciTrek ranks as one of the top ten science centers in the country.

Permanent exhibits in the Hall of Electricity and Magnetism, one of four halls, demonstrate phenomena like spectacular electric discharges, natural magnets, lines of force, magnetic repulsion and a magnemaze. Mathematica, a permanent exhibit, makes numbers interesting to inveterate math-phobics. Inventors are remembered in exhibits like Ohm's Law where the relationship between voltage across a circuit and the circuit's resistance are investigated. Watt's the Difference demonstrates the concept of electrical power through voltage and currents. The Hall of Light and Perception has a kinetic light sculpture, a flying mirror, kaleidoscope and the popular distorted room—a full-size funhouse of illusions. The third hall focuses on Simple Machines like pulleys, levers, chain hoists, screw balls, a bicycle wheel gyro and others. Finally, in Kidspace there are bubble carts, a crystal cave, a ball ramp, a sound studio, a giant hot-air balloon, puppets and a TV theater and much more.

SciTrek is open Tuesday through Saturday from 10:00 A.M. to 5:00 P.M. and Sunday NOON to 5:00 P.M. Call ahead (404)522-5500 to check on extended summer hours. Admission is charged. The museum has traveling exhibits, live demonstrations, workshops, lectures, films, summer camps and other special events. Within the museum is a shop with a wide array of science-oriented items that are both educational and entertaining. You can spend an afternoon or a day in this engaging museum.

One final downtown museum, high on children's lists of where to go in Atlanta, is the **Puppetry Museum** at the Center for Puppetry Arts, 1404 Spring Street at 18th. This delightfully droll museum has puppets from around the world. Visitors see pre-Columbian articulated clay figures, Chinese hand puppets, ritualistic African figures, Javanese shadow puppets and well-known Punch and Judy characters. Some of these highly stylized figures are sumptuously dressed like the rod puppets from Japan and Java and the Italian puppets. Young visitors are attracted to the puppets they recognize from the Muppet movies. There's Fishface from *Labyrinth* and Link Hogthrob and Dr. Strangeport from *The Muppet Movie*.

Kermit the Frog, accompanied by his creator, the late Jim Henson, cut the ceremonial ribbon opening the **Center for Puppetry Arts** on September 23, 1978. The Center, the only one of its kind in the country, has three thrusts: museum exhibits, education and performance.

The Center for Puppetry Arts annually presents five shows for adults in their New Directions Series. Guest puppeteers from around the world have taken part in these performances. The Family Series presents classic stories for all ages. The Xperimental Puppetry Theatre and the Family Theatre Workshop showcase new talent, often presenting works in progress. The Center offers classes for children and adults.

The Center for Puppetry Arts is open Monday through Saturday from 9:00 A.M. to 5:00 P.M. Closed on major holidays. The museum closes one hour earlier. There is an admission charge. Children ages four and up can participate in a Create a Puppet Workshop. Call ahead (404)873-3391 to check the exact time of this program and to reserve a spot. Puppetry performances are also presented daily. Call ahead and obtain the schedule for these shows. The Center's 24-hour information line is (404)874-0398.

Directions: All museums are in downtown Atlanta. To reach the Federal Reserve Bank from I-75/85 south, exit right at Williams Street, then turn right onto International Boulevard. Take a left onto Techwood Street and left again on Marietta Street. The Bank is located one block south at the intersection of Marietta and Spring streets. From I-75/85 north, exit at Central Avenue, then turn left on Martin Luther King Jr. Drive and merge into the right lane. Turn right on Spring Street and continue to Marietta Street. Turn right on Marietta and the bank is the first building on the right.

For SciTrek, traveling southbound on I-75/85 take Exit 97, Courtland Avenue/ Georgia State University. Turn left at the second light onto Harris Street. Turn left at the first light onto Piedmont Avenue. If you are on I-75/85 northbound take Exit 98, Pine Street/Peachtree Street. Turn right onto Piedmont Avenue. SciTrek is at 395 Piedmont Avenue.

For the Center for Puppetry Arts, driving northbound on I-75/85, take the 10/14th Street exit. Cross 10th Street and turn right on to 14th Street. At second traffic light turn left onto West Peachtree Street. Turn left onto 18th Street (it's the second street on left, marked by yellow pilings). Cross Spring Street and the parking lot will be in the rear of the Center. If you are on I/75 southbound, take 14th/10th street exit. Turn left on 14th Street, crossing over I-75, then follow directions above.

Museum of the Jimmy Carter Library

Presidential Time Capsule

Franklin Delano Roosevelt established the first presidential library in 1939. Each successive chief executive has followed that tradition. The Jimmy Carter Library is the eighth facility to be established and administered by the National Archives and Records Administration. Former President Richard M. Nixon has a library in Yorba Linda, California, but it is not designated as a presidential library.

These are not typical libraries but are repositories for the papers, photographs, campaign material, memorabilia and other items of historical interest associated with each president's administration. These libraries give visitors a better understanding of the American political system, the office of president, the individual presidents and the times in which they lived. The nine presidential libraries are: Herbert Hoover in West Branch, Iowa; Franklin D. Roosevelt in Hyde Park, New York; Harry S Truman in Independence, Missouri; Dwight D. Eisenhower in Abilene, Kansas; John F. Kennedy in Boston, Massachusetts; Lyndon B. Johnson in Austin, Texas; Gerald R. Ford in Ann Arbor, Michigan (actually the Gerald R. Ford research facility is on the University of Michigan campus at Ann Arbor and the museum is in Grand Rapids); Jimmy Carter in Atlanta, Georgia; and Ronald Reagan in Simi Valley, California.

Shortly after taking office, Jimmy Carter indicated that he wanted to establish a presidential library "someplace in Georgia." A site was found outside Atlanta and the facility built. The museum opened to the public October 1, 1986, with the research room opening the following year.

Jimmy Carter's **Oval Office** has been recreated at the Museum of the Jimmy Carter Library. Here visitors will gain insights into what is was like to be President. As you look around this historic White House nerve center, you will hear Jimmy Carter talk about the first time he visited the Oval Office and what is was like working in this awe-inspiring environment. The primary concerns of the Carter presidency are addressed in exhibits and interactive videos. Issues addressed include the Camp David Accords and the Middle East peace process, arms control, normalization of relations with China, the hostage crisis in Iran and the need to protect the future.

One of the most fascinating aspects of the museum is the **Town Meeting** section where visitors can ask President Carter questions through an interactive video. You select from a series of questions, and the next question Carter answers on the screen is the one you picked. These queries range from "Why did you choose to go to Camp David with Sadat and Begin?" to "What did Amy do all day at the White House?"

Other exhibits also involve the visitor. For example, in the area devoted to the hostage crisis in Iran there is an interactive video. You choose among responses to a terrorist crisis. Options include: attack with military force, negotiate, apply sanctions or try all options. Once you have made a selection, Carter comes on the screen discussing the pros and cons of that choice.

The museum has continual showings of a 30-minute movie narrated by Cliff Robertson on the powers of the President. Another video features young children talking about what they would do if they were President.

The museum also showcases Jimmy Carter's life from his early years through his campaign for the presidency. Over 27 million pages of material from the Carter White House are stored in the stacks, plus more than 40,000 objects, 1.5 million photographs and hundreds of hours of motion picture film, videotape and audiotape, as well as gifts to the President from American citizens and foreign dignitaries.

The Museum of the Jimmy Carter Library is open 9:00 A.M. to 4:45 P.M. Monday through Saturday and NOON to 4:45 P.M. on Sunday. The Carter Center is closed on Thanksgiving, Christmas and New Year's Day. Admission is charged. The museum is just part of the **Carter Presidential Center** that also includes the offices of public policy programs in conflict resolution, human rights, child survival, disease eradication and urban social problems.

The Carter Center grounds are lovely. A Japanese garden, the gift of Tadao Yoshida, has two waterfalls that symbolize President Carter and Mrs. Carter. The falls merge and flow into a quiet pond. Stone lanterns in the heart of the garden represent the hope that the activities of the Carter Center will bring peace and happiness throughout the world.

Directions: If you are heading south from I-75/85 in Atlanta, take Exit 96A, Boulevard/Glen Iris and turn left at the dead end. Make a right turn when you reach the intersection with Highland Avenue, continue a half mile to Cleburne Avenue and turn left into the Carter Center parking lot. If you are traveling down I-75/85 from the north take Exit 100, North Avenue, and turn left. When you reach North Highland Avenue turn right and continue one block to Cleburne Avenue. Make a right turn into the Carter Center parking lot. The Museum of the Jimmy Carter Library is at One Copenhill Avenue. There is a restaurant at the Carter Center.

Six Flags Over Georgia and American Adventures/White Water Park

Twice the Thrills, Chills and Excitement

There are seven Six Flags theme parks, six larger in size than Disneyland. The first Six Flags was built by a wealthy Texan, Angus G. Wynne, Jr., after a visit to Disneyland. He wanted a similar park closer to home, so he built one between Dallas and Fort Worth. Six Flags parks were the first to create a log flume ride, a tubular steel roller coaster, manmade whitewater rafting rides and freefall rides. Over the last quarter century the Georgia park, which opened in 1967, has grown to include these and other rides. In fact there are over 100 rides and roughly ten shows at the park.

The world's first roller coaster was built in St. Petersburg, Russia, in the 16th century. Thrill-seekers rode sleds down a 70-foot wooden-frame ice slide. Since those prototype roller coasters, rides have become high-tech, and in 1992 Six Flags inaugurated **Ninja**, a one-of-a-kind, steel roller coaster that turns riders upside down five times during its breathtaking ride. The coaster rises 122-feet, has corkscrew dives and a speed in excess of 52 mph. The park also has the Mind Bender, the world's only true triple-loop coaster. The Great American Scream Machine is noted for plunging dips and sharp turns; it climbs more than 100 feet and has nearly 3,800 feet of track. There's also the Georgia Cyclone with 11 drops, the first of which is a 53-degree drop. For the less adventurous, there's the slower paced Dahlonega Mine Train.

Six Flags offers something for all ages. Visitors too young for the thrill rides, find their thrills in meeting Looney Tune characters like Bugs Bunny, Daffy Duck and Sylvester. These popular cartoon characters circulate through the park and perform in some of the shows.

There are eateries throughout the park where you can enjoy anything from a snack to a meal. In an average season, roughly 163 days, visitors at Six Flags Over Georgia consume 176,000 pounds of hamburger, 480,000 pounds of french fries, 3.6 million soft drinks, 51,000 chocolate chip cookies and 439,000 novelty ice creams.

The park's Southern Star Amphitheatre features top name entertainers. Country, rap, pop, contemporary Christian and other musical groups perform in concert and as part of special park events. Many of the performances are included in the admission price.

The park schedule changes seasonally running from March through October. Other than during spring break the park operates on weekends only until late May and resumes a weekend schedule in September. For detailed times call (404)948-9290. Admission is charged.

North of Atlanta in Marietta, there is an amusement park for children under 12 called **American Adventures**. Outdoors are 14 rides for kids, an 18-hole miniature golf course and two-seat go-carts. The 40,000-square-foot indoor section, Imagination Station, has a new interactive play area—that includes Storybook

One of several roller coasters at Six Flags Over Georgia, the Great American Scream Machine thrills riders with plunging dips and sharp turns.

Theatre, Bubble Works and Construction Junction—where children create their own adventures. The indoor area also has a huge penny arcade, a restored antique carousel and a theme restaurant.

American Adventures is open year-round, but times change seasonally. Call for current hours (404)424-9283. There is no general admission. You pay as you play or purchase an economical pass for all-day fun.

Right next door is **White Water Park**, the largest water theme park in the region with more than 40 water adventures for visitors to enjoy on 35 tree-shaded acres. For children 12 and under there are over 100 activities in Captain Kid's Cove and the neighboring Little Squirt's Island. Older family members may want to relax in a lounge chair on the sand at the Atlanta Ocean, a wave pool that has everything the ocean offers but salt and fish.

USA Today said White Water Park was the most scenic water theme park in the nation. For the adventurous, there are steep water slides like the Banzai Pipeline, Gulf Coast Screamer, Cyclone, Twister and Sidewinder that send riders careening around curves and hurtling though long tunnel-like tubes. You can also spend hours floating calmly on the winding Little Hooch and Suwanee River rides.

White Water Park is open weekends in May and daily from Memorial Day through August, plus Labor Day weekend. Admission is charged. You can call (404)424-WAVE for current schedule.

Directions: Take I-20 west of Atlanta to the Six Flags exit. For American Adventures/White Water Park take I-75 north to Exit 113, North Marietta Parkway, and follow the well-marked route.

Stately Oaks and Jonesboro

Home of Gone With The Wind

Throughout the early 1900s, Peggy made frequent trips by carriage with her mother to visit her great aunts, Mary and Sarah Fitzgerald, who lived southwest of Jonesboro. The elderly sisters sat on the porch of the house they called their "rural home" and reminisced about the War Between the States, passing on their tales to young Peggy. Driving past burned homes, the girl's mother taught her that what was left to the South was what you could do with your hands and what you had in your head. Peggy, whose given name was Margaret Mitchell, used these stories when she wrote her Pulitzer Prize winning Gone With the Wind.

Mitchell did not have any particular plantation home in mind when she wrote of Tara. She did use Clayton County as the background area for her book and the setting for her fictional home. None of the movie was filmed in Georgia, and all the sets were built on MGM's back lot.

During the Civil War, Clayton County saw heavy fighting and much of the county was in ruins by the end of the war. The Battle of Jonesboro was one of the last confrontations of the Atlanta Campaign. Union soldiers cut the railroad lines at Jonesboro providing a clear passage to Sherman on his devastating March to the Sea. There are more than 600 Confederates and a few Federals buried in the Confederate Cemetery at Jonesboro.

A driving tour of **Historic Jonesboro** includes the cemetery, on the north side of town at Johnson Street, as well at the 1867 Depot, 104 N. Main Street, which replaced the wooden one burned by the Northern troops in 1864. Plans are underway to establish a railroad museum in the depot. The business district was also torched by the Union soldiers. At the time of the Civil War there were 13 saloons in the basements of buildings along Main Street, which explains in part why Jonesboro was known as a rowdy town.

The residential in-town plantation homes were stately and elegant, and some remain for you to see on your driving tour.

Built in the 1850s by Dr. Francis Gayden, the privately owned Gayden-Sims-Webb House, 158 Church Street, was the town's only brick house before the war. Another antebellum property is the Waldrop-Brown-Edwards House, 158 S. Main Street, whose back portion was destroyed during the Battle of Jonesboro.

The gracious Ashley Oaks Mansion, 144 College Street, is open by appointment for tours. Built between 1879 and 1880 for Leander Carruth Hutcheson, its interior and exterior brick walls were kilned at Hutcheson's nearby plantation on the Flint River. Lunch and dinner can be arranged at Ashley Oaks for groups of 20 or more, call (404)478-8986.

The place to tour is **Stately Oaks Plantation Community**, 100 Carriage Drive. Whitmel Allen built his Jonesboro home in the Greek Revival style using heart-of-pine lumber. He liked to sit in the white-columned veranda and shoot deer as they crossed his 404-acre plantation. In 1858, when he felt the area was growing too populous, he sold the plantation to Robert McCord for $3,700. McCord left his wife and six children on the estate while he served in the Confederate army. The Union troops camped in the fields below the house and drew water from the property's well during the Battle of Jonesboro. Although the family packed the wagon to leave in the face of the oncoming Yankees, they decided against abandoning their home, unpacked the wagon, locked the doors and stayed. Federal soldiers did break into the cellar, stole some food and clothes, but though they made a mess they didn't damage the furniture or the house. A day after the house was broken into, a Union officer posted guards to protect the family while the troops camped on the grounds. Family stories claim the officers "certainly were gentlemen even if they were Yankees."

In 1879, the house was sold again, and two years later Mr. Wallace purchased it. Wallace's church was on the other side of the Flint River, while a Mr. Orr who had property on that side of the river crossed it to attend church not far from Stately Oaks. Being practical gentlemen, the two swapped houses. Since it wasn't an even trade, Stately Oaks being grander, Mr. Orr threw in two teams of mules and a hundred dollars. The house had been called The Oaks, but Mrs. Orr renamed it Stately Oaks. In 1972, Emily Orr Haynie donated the house to Historic Jonesboro.

The guides who escort you around Stately Oaks are dressed in the styles popular in the 1800s. You'll discover some interesting things about the clothes they wear. For example, it wasn't until 1830, the year metal eyelets were invented, that Southern belles could corset themselves tightly. Before then, pulling the fabric tight tore the garment. You'll see that day dresses fastened in front so that they could easily be put on, while ball gowns required help to lace, or hook, up the back. The fainting couch on the second floor was useful for ladies who were too tightly laced, as the exertion of climbing the stairs would leave them out of breath. The expression "loose women," derives from women of lower social station who did not practice the custom of wearing tight corsets, hence they were loose.

One last fashion note: When you see the stiff horsehair upholstered furniture, remember that horsehair was the derivation of the crinoline. Southern ladies added horsehair to their petticoats to stiffen them. The French word for horsehair is "crin," hence the term crinoline.

The interior of Stately Oaks has been repainted downstairs to look as it did in 1839. Upstairs the colors are original. The base of the paint used when Stately Oaks was first painted was buttermilk and contained arsenic. The furniture you see is not original but spans the hundred years the house was occupied. The only item owned by a resident is a chair you will see in the upstairs hall. One intriguing item is the courting candle that could be adjusted to allow a wide range of time for visiting. If the father approved of the suitor he could allow him the full time.

There are several additional outbuildings surrounding Stately Oaks, including the original log cabin kitchen. Constructed in 1839 of hand-hewn logs and wooden pegs, it has a large open fireplace for cooking. Old utensils, pots and dishes recreate a bygone era. One of the other dependencies is the well house. A third may well have been a slave cabin. You also can tour the 1893 Bethel Church School. Badly fire-damaged in 1900, it was rebuilt and used until 1941. Also on the grounds is the restored Juddy's Country Store built in 1894 and operational until 1978. Stately Oaks is open from 11:00 A.M. to 3:00 P.M. Thursday and Friday. A nominal admission is charged. Lunch and dinner can be arranged for groups; call (404)473-0197.

At nearby Clayton State College in Morrow in January 1991 a striking new 405-seat concert hall opened. **Spivey Hall**, donated by Emilie Parmalee Spivey and Dr. Walter Boon Spivey, is an architectural and cultural gem. If you are in the area when there is a performance scheduled be sure to attend. The hall's near-perfect acoustics make it a favorite with performers. It's worth a visit even if the stage is dark. Even the lobby glitters with marble pillars, gold leaf pilasters, crystal chandeliers and a grand staircase.

Directions: From I-75 take Route 41/19 south to Jonesboro. Morrow is north of I-75 at the Route 41/19 exit.

Stone Mountain Park

Eighth Wonder of the World

If you arrive at Stone Mountain Park when the gates open at 6:00 A.M. and stay until they close at midnight, you would still be hard put to cover all the park's attractions, and you certainly couldn't do them justice. This is a park you'll want to return to, not only as seasons change but as years pass.

The 3,200-acre super-park has a skylift, laser show, 19th-century plantation, gristmill, scenic train, paddlewheel riverboat, wildlife habitat, museums, craft shops, fishing lake, beach, tennis courts, golf course, ice rink, plus hiking and biking trails.

The park's success is literally carved in stone; riding across the north face of the world's largest exposed granite mountain is a triumvirate of heroes, the **Confederate Memorial Carving**. Over 50 years to complete, the equestrian figures measure 90 feet by 190 feet in a frame that is over 360 feet square, or three acres. This depiction of Confederate President Jefferson Davis and Generals Robert E. Lee and Stonewall Jackson is the world's largest high-relief sculpture.

The granite monolith on which the sculpture is carved rises dramatically 825 feet above the surrounding plateau. The mountain is seven miles in circumference and covers 523 acres. A skylift takes visitors to the mountain's summit from 10:00 A.M. to 8:30 P.M. (5:30 P.M. in the fall and winter months). The view from the top is far reaching; the view on the way up is also inspiring. The Swiss cable cars provide an up-close look that gives you an appreciation for the sheer size of the memorial. The depth of the carving is such that you could actually drive a car along the back of Lee's horse. Once the skylift reaches the top, you can walk around the summit. Imagine while you are there the days when Spanish explorer Hernado De Soto built a fortification on this rocky perch or when Indians met here for powwows. You can watch a free film in the Theater in the Sky, a 20-minute movie about the legendary gnomes who reputedly live on the mountain. The mountaintop also has a gift shop and snack bar.

The idea of creating a sculpture on the monolith was proposed around 1915. Gutzon Borglum, who had just completed an impressive bust of Lincoln, was asked by the United Daughters of the Confederacy (UDC) to carve the head of Robert E. Lee on the mountain's face. On seeing his massive granite canvas, Borglum had a grander vision, arguing that the original proposal would look like a postage stamp on a barn. He suggested instead a depiction of Confederate leaders on horseback and on foot moving across the face of the mountain.

The world's largest stone carving, the Confederate Memorial at Stone Mountain Park, depicts equestrians Jefferson Davis, Robert E. Lee and Thomas J. "Stonewall" Jackson.

Borglum was charged with the task of bringing his vision to life and given three years to do the job. World War I interrupted his work, but by mid-January 1924 he had completed the head of General Robert E. Lee—interestingly enough the only thing he had originally been asked to do. During the next year there were misunderstandings and problems between Borglum and the UDC, and in February 1925, Borglum was discharged. He destroyed his models and left the state. Years later Borglum used the knowledge he gleaned at Stone Mountain when he began carving the faces on Mount Rushmore.

Finding a replacement was not easy. Reports say that eight sculptors considered for the job developed vertigo when they attempted to inspect the steep mountain face. When Augustus Lukeman obtained the commission, his first step was to blast off Borglum's work. By 1928 he had completed his own rendition of General Lee's head, plus a rough outline of Lee's horse and the mounted outlines of the remaining two Confederates.

A hiatus occurred from 1929 to 1958 because the UDC ran out of funds. The project wasn't reborn until 1957 when Governor

Griffin spearheaded a move to create a public park at the base of the mountain and money was generated to finish the sculpture.

Walter Hancock was hired to finish the carving and develop the memorial area. Roy Faulkner, the foreman of the working crew and chief carver, spent 3,140 days, or roughly 8½ years, finishing the job. The carving was dedicated on May 9, 1970, but finishing touches continued until March 3, 1972.

Memorial Hall sits at the base of the mountain, and telescopes on the porch provide another opportunity for a close look at the carving. Within the hall you can listen to a 7-minute narrated tape of the history of Stone Mountain and the carving. There are fascinating photographs of sculptors at work and pictures of VIPs picnicking within the sheltering depths of the carved figures. The hall also has a Civil War museum: open daily 9:30 A.M. to 9:00 P.M., 5:30 P.M. during the fall and winter months.

Each evening during the summer months the lawn in front of the hall is filled with visitors jostling for a choice spot from which to view the **laser show**. With the mountain face serving as a screen, a combination of laser images and music makes for an entertaining 50-minute performance. The traditional finale is to "Dixie," and the mounted figures seem to be galloping off to the strains of this show stopper. The laser shows start at 9:30 P.M. and run daily from weekends in May through Labor Day weekend, at 9:00 P.M. on September weekends, and October weekends at 8:30 P.M.

Stone Mountain Park has a strong historical focus. The park's **Antebellum Plantation** has 19 authentically restored and completely furnished 18th- and 19th-century buildings that have been moved here from locations throughout the state. A pre-Civil War plantation is recreated. The 14-room Dickey House, formerly in the Albany area, was built in 1840 in a Neo-Classical style with twin outside stairways representing "welcoming arms." Surrounding dependencies include a barn, corncribs, smoke house, slave cabins, coach house, well, necessary, cook house, kitchen garden and formal garden with a tea house. There is also a plantation office, now used as the office for the Georgia Chapter of the United Daughters of the Confederacy, the organization that began the work on the face of Stone Mountain. Another office was used by one of DeKalb County's first doctors. The overseer's house is from the Allen Plantation in Kingston. The complex also boasts the oldest restored house in the state: The Thornton House dates back to 1783 and is typical of the cottage architecture popular in the Piedmont region.

The Antebellum Plantation is open 10:00 A.M. until 9:00 P.M., though no visitors are admitted after 8:00 P.M.; this also closes at 5:30 P.M. in the fall and winter. Outside the complex are the

Country Store, with a wide choice of regional crafts and gourmet items, and the Clayton House, another craft shop. Behind that is the Christmas Shop.

If this complex represents the agrarian South, the gristmill and covered bridge are part of the Old South industries. The railroad was important to the businesses of the South, and the park has its own trains that make a five-mile journey around the base of the mountain. The park's excursion trains, full-sized replicas of the famous Civil War steam engines the General and the Texas (see Big Shanty Museum selection and Atlanta Cyclorama selection), make two stops: One is at **Confederate Hall**, where from 10:00 A.M. to 7:30 P.M. (5:30 P.M. seasonally) you can see the Civil War artifacts, a lighted battlefield map and a diorama on "The War in Georgia." **Wildlife Trails**, the second stop, take you past wildlife habitats to see animals once indigenous to Georgia including cougar, elk and bison. The trails, which take at least 45 minutes to explore, are laid out in a 20-acre natural woodland section of the park. Young children enjoy spending time at Traders Camp Petting Farm.

An ideal way to make a **circuit** of the park is to start at Memorial Hall to gain an understanding of the background of the sculpture, then take the skylift to the summit. Next, hike the 1³⁄₁₀-mile trail down the mountain, board the train at the base and stop at both the Confederation Hall museum and Wildlife Trails.

Another museum within Stone Mountain Park features hot rods and juke boxes. The **Antique Auto & Music Museum** has over 40 restored antique automobiles, old nickelodeons, vintage motor bikes, antique carousel horses, Wurlitzers and memorabilia related to cars and music.

During the summer months, water-related activities are popular. There is a beach area with a water slide that is open from 10:00 A.M. to 6:00 P.M. You can take a cruise on Stone Mountain Lake aboard an authentic paddlewheel riverboat. Cruises depart every half hour from 10:00 A.M. to 8:30 P.M. and at 5:30 P.M. at other times of the year. Another way to enjoy the lake is to rent a canoe, pedalboat, rowboat or pontoon. It's lovely to be out on the water when the the carillon concerts are given. You also can walk to the lakeside carillon concerts on weekdays and Saturdays at NOON and 4:00 P.M. and on Sundays at 1:00, 3:00 and 5:00 P.M. Performances are live except on Mondays and Tuesdays, when a tape is played. A fishing hut on the lake is open daily 7:00 A.M. to 8:00 P.M. in the spring and summer months.

Recreational opportunities abound. There are paved walks for joggers and bikers, and *Golf Digest* ranks the park's 36-hole **golf course** as one of the top 25 in the country. A sports complex includes tennis, mini-golf, batting cages and bicycle rentals. Down the road is the ice rink, open daily from 1:00 to 4:00 P.M.

and Monday through Saturday from 7:30 to 9:30 P.M. On Friday and Saturday nights the rink reopens from 10:00 P.M. to midnight. The park also has carriage rides (Friday 4:30 to 8:30 P.M. and weekends 11:00 A.M. to 6:00 P.M.), pony rides (Monday through Sunday 11:00 A.M. to 6:00 P.M.) and hayrides by reservation only from February through May and from September though November.

In addition, the park hosts a series of annual festivals and events. In early May there is a Springfest and BBQ Cookoff. Later in the year in August, there's a Chicken Wing Cookoff and in October a Chili Cookoff. In September they hold the Yellow Daisy Festival; then in October there's the annual Scottish Festival and Highland Games. Holidays like July 4th, Memorial Day, Halloween and Christmas are also celebrated at the park. The latter prompts a month-long holiday party.

There are several restaurants at Stone Mountain plus snack bars located throughout the park: Memorial Depot Chicken Restaurant is a favorite with locals; Whistle Stop Barbecue also has its fans. The Stone Mountain Inn and The Waterside Restaurant are a little more up-scale, while the Memorial Plaza Deli is casual. Visitors can overnight at Stone Mountain Inn or at the Evergreen Conference Center Resort. The park has campgrounds with over 400 sites. For additional park information call (404)498-5600. You can purchase an all-attractions ticket to the park that includes the six major attractions or you can buy individual admission tickets to the park's points of interest.

Directions: From I-285 take the Stone Mountain Freeway Exit 30B; that will lead directly to the East Gate. If you take the Memorial Drive exit, Route 78, off I-285, you will enter the park's West Gate. The park is 16 miles from Atlanta.

The World of Coca-Cola

Refreshing Stop

Over 7,500 Coca-Cola soft drinks are served every second of every day in more than 185 countries around the world. If 6½-ounce bottles were filled with all the Coca-Cola ever produced and placed end-to-end, the bottles would stretch to the moon and back 1,045 times.

The World of Coca-Cola stretches to the remotest points of the globe, as you'll see during the scenically splendid 13-minute HDV, high-definition video, "Every Day of Your Life." Filmed in 17 countries on six continents and shown on the first permanent large-screen HDV theater in the country, this is a not-to-be-missed visual treat. One shares the amazement of the camel-riding Egyptians as the Coca-Cola truck drives past the Pyramids to restock a dispenser—the driver is singing Italian opera at full voice. The film travels from the Imperial Palace of Thailand to the Masai Steppe in Africa.

This is just one of the popular features of Coca-Cola's three-story pavilion, whose revolving neon sign is a beacon for downtown visitors heading for adjacent Underground Atlanta (see selection). In the World of Coca-Cola visitors are taken on a journey through more than 100 years of company history.

The exhibit space is divided into quadrants starting with a **bottling fantasy**, a kinetic sculpture representing a fanciful bottling plant. But the liquid that fills the 1,100 familiar bottles is not really Coca-Cola. After you pass this fantasy, you'll see more than 1,000 objects with some Coca-Cola association, the largest collection of Coca-Cola memorabilia in the world.

Exhibits and videos trace the company's development and expansion from its earliest days to the present. They start with the hand-written formula book of Coca-Cola creator Dr. John Pemberton (see Heritage Corner selection) and then move to the marketing strategies of Asa Griggs Chandler, who made Coca-Cola a household name. "First Things First," a short film shown in this exhibit area, gives a brief history of the world. . .the world of Coca-Cola, that is.

Visitors could spend a lot of time just reading the advertisements, like the 1911 boast that "a charming lady doesn't really need her fan, with a glass of Coca-Cola in her hand." The 1916 ads feature Pearl White the star of *Perils of Pauline* with a Coca-Cola.

The first floor exhibit area has giant Coca-Cola cans that visitors can step inside to experience interactive videos. The "Take Five" videos show five-year segments, beginning in 1886, of world events and lifestyles interwoven with the development of Coca-Cola.

In the second quadrant you'll find the **Barnes Soda Fountain**, a replica of a 1930s' soda fountain. The jukebox plays songs from the 1930s and 1940s written about Coca-Cola and excerpts from radio programs the company sponsored from 1906 to the early 1950s. Few people today remember the songs it plays like Shirley Temple's rendition of "Sweet Coca-Cola Bush" or Andre Kostelanetz's "Coca-Cola Waltz." You'll learn that a sundae evolved because soda fountain drinks couldn't be sold on Sunday, so the "soda jerks" left out the soda water and added ice cream. The only bad news is that the soda fountain doesn't serve samples—that comes later.

The third quadrant offers the **HDV film**. The theater doors open every fifteen minutes on the quarter hour. After the show you'll head down to the second floor and explore the contemporary gallery with its multi-media effects tracing the growth of Coca-Cola from the 1950s to the present. Vintage radio and television commercials are replayed, and you can watch a video of the shooting of the commercial in 1971 that introduced the refrain "I'd like to teach the world to sing. . . ." A video shot 20 years later shows all the original participants on the same hilltop in Italy, joined by their children.

By this time the average visitor is ready to enjoy a pause that refreshes, and the futuristic soda fountain is dazzling. It's called **Club Coca-Cola**, and the production involved in getting your cup filled is state-of-the-art. Infrared sensors trigger spotlights when a visitor steps up to the soft drink station. Liquid streams arch more than 20 feet across the room in a long, tight flow. The streams that fill each cup are colored by a process of fiber optics and overhead spotlights—a crowd pleaser that has to be seen to be believed. Adjacent to this high-tech fountain is the international sampler, **Taste of the World**, where you can try Coca-Cola products marketed around the world. Be sure to try the Fanta Peach made in Botswana and Mesa Mix, a German orange and cola favorite.

Visitors exit through the Coca-Cola TradeMart store, where international visitors and locals enjoy the wide array of company products. The World of Coca-Cola is open Monday through Saturday from 10:00 A.M. to 9:30 P.M. and Sunday from NOON to 6:00 P.M.; closed on major holidays. A nominal admission is charged. Ticket sales stop an hour before closing. In the busy summer months reservations are recommended. You can make reservations by calling (404)676-5151.

Directions: From I-75/85 take Martin Luther King Jr. Drive into downtown Atlanta. The World of Coca-Cola is at 55 Martin Luther King, Jr. Drive across Central Avenue from Underground Atlanta.

The Wren's Nest

Folk Writer's Lair

Joel Chandler Harris feared the dangers of the 1876 yellow-fever epidemic in Savannah. Seeking safety, he moved his family to Atlanta. Signing in at his Atlanta hotel, he wrote: "J.C. Harris, one wife, two bow-legged children and a bilious nurse."

Reading this, one is not surprised that he was hired by the *Atlanta Constitution* to write "pithy and philosophical sayings." One day, roughly a year after he started working, inspiration failed. Seeking a source for his column, Harris recalled the boyhood tales he had heard from slaves, like Uncle George Terrell, on a large, middle-Georgia plantation outside Eatonton (see Uncle Remus Museum selection). Harris wrote up one of these stories, inventing the character of **Uncle Remus** to tell the tale of Br'er Fox and Br'er Rabbit.

This story brought a flood of letters requesting more, and for four years Harris wrote these stories for the newspapers. In 1880 they were published in book form. Over a 25-year period, Harris wrote nine volumes telling roughly 185 Uncle Remus tales. (He actually wrote 30 books in all on a number of topics.) His success enabled Harris to move to the home he called Wren's Nest because of the family of birds who set up housekeeping in the Harris mailbox. The Harrises rented first, then bought the house in 1883 from Colonel Clark Howell, who owned the *Atlanta Constitution.*

The Wren's Nest is a charming, magnolia and oak-shaded Queen Anne Victorian house in the West End, Atlanta's oldest neighborhood. Joel Chandler Harris added the Queen Anne look in 1884 when he enlarged the house. The Harrises also added electricity, indoor plumbing and a central coal furnace. When he added electricity, he kept the gas fixtures because Harris was a country boy at heart, and he considered electricity nothing but a fad. He also refused to use the indoor plumbing, preferring the outhouse in the back. Harris lived here until his death in 1908, and his wife remained until she sold the house in 1913 to the Uncle Remus Memorial Association, a group of Harris admirers. The association, reorganized as the Joel Chandler Harris Association in 1983, has undertaken a massive renovation of the Wren's Nest.

When you tour the Wren's Nest, you see the home much as it was when Joel Chandler Harris lived here. The tour starts with a 12-minute slide presentation on the life and work of the author. In the parlor where the slide program is shown is Harris's newspaper desk and the original mail box that prompted the home's name. There is also a diorama on the side porch with critters from his stories. The tour continues into the other eight rooms of the house, including his bedroom that was never changed after his death. Be sure to note the photograph of Harris sitting on the Wren's Nest bric-a-brac decorated wrap-around porch.

There are mementoes from friends and admirers like the stuffed great horned owl given to Mr. Harris by Teddy Roosevelt and a tooth from Clio the elephant, a gift from the school children of Atlanta because they knew that Clio was one of Mr. Harris's favorite animals at the Atlanta Zoo. There are also first editions of his own books and copies of writings by his contemporaries including Mark Twain and James Whitcomb Riley. His personal book collection including titles such as *How To Remain Happy Though Married* demonstrates Mr. Harris's impish nature.

In his children's bedroom (there were nine children, three of whom died in childhood) are old photographs. One picture shows his daughter Lillian, whom he called Billie, picking vegetables in the Wren's Nest garden. Another shot is of Mildred, called Tommy by her father, playing tennis in a long skirt and fancy hat. The room has a collection of toys including a doll's tea set and the girls' porcelain dolls.

There are special story-telling sessions at the Wren's Nest, during which the Uncle Remus tales are recounted. The Wren's Nest emphasizes Harris's role as one of the first to record the folktales of black Americans; roughly two-thirds of the stories can be traced to African folklore. During the summer months story-telling sessions are given on Tuesdays through Saturdays at 11:30 A.M., 12:30 and 1:30 P.M. During the winter, stories are told every Saturday at 2:00 P.M. Visitors can purchase books and memorabilia at the museum shop.

Harris once wrote the following which was later selected by his family as the epitaph for his tombstone: "I seem to see before me the smiling faces of thousands of children—some young and fresh—and some wearing the friendly marks of age, but all children at heart, and not an unfriendly face among them. And while I am trying hard to speak the right word, I seem to hear a voice lifted above the rest saying, 'You have made some of us happy.' And so I feel my heart fluttering and my lips trembling and I have to bow silently and turn away and hurry into the obscurity that fits me best." Mr. Harris is buried at Westview Cemetery less than two miles from the Wren's Nest.

The Wren's Nest, a National Historic Landmark, is open Tuesday through Saturday from 10:00 A.M. to 5:00 P.M. and Sunday from 1:00 to 5:00 P.M. The last tour is at 4:00 P.M. Closed on major holidays. Admission is charged. For additional information call (404)753-8535.

Directions: From I-20 in Atlanta, take Exit 19, Ashby Street/West End. Head south on Ashby Street and make a right on R. D. Abernathy Blvd., S.W. The Wren's Nest is at 1050 R.D. Abernathy Blvd.

Yellow River Wildlife Game Ranch and Stone Mountain Village

Animal, Mineral and Vegetable

The Yellow River Wildlife Game Ranch seems homey—homey, that is, for the more than 600 animals that live at this 24-acre spread along the Yellow River. Art Rilling and his family have been nurturing native Georgia animals for more than 20 years, first at Stone Mountain Park and now in this wooded setting in Gwinnett County.

Visitors stroll along a winding path through the reserve. While some of the animals are caged others roam free, and there are deer everywhere. The best time to see young fawns is around Easter time. Many of the animals enjoy being fed; some even consider food their due. If you pass the barnyard area without feeding Scarlett and Rhett, two of the ranch's burros, they'll kick the gate to remind you. Then there's Tara. Few visitors can resist this appealing donkey; she's learned that if she cocks her head sideways and opens her drooling lips she can entice visitors to feed her. Across the path is the goat yard, and an elevated bridge over the path has a sign reading "Billy Goat Gruff Memorial Bridge."

There are areas set aside for bear, fox, raccoon, hawks, coyote, mountain lion, bobcat and the largest herd of buffalo east of the Mississippi River. The bunny burrow is a favorite of young children because they can enter the fenced area and feed the small, furry rabbits. The Yellow River Wildlife Game Ranch is a family outing that young children will especially enjoy.

The Yellow River Wildlife Game Ranch is open daily from 9:30 A.M. to 6:00 P.M. During the summer the ranch stays open until dusk. Admission is charged. Groups can schedule parties and hayrides at the ranch. Call (404)972-6643 for additional information.

The game ranch is only 15 minutes from **Historic Stone Mountain Village** a collection of more than 90 shops, galleries, and restaurants at the base of Stone Mountain Park (see selection). This 19th-century village is not a theme village, but a real community that developed around the mountain quarries. The visitors information center is in the newly renovated Red Caboose, located on Poole and Main Street. The village is a great place to window shop and browse. Many of the shops feature unique handcrafted items from pottery to nationally known Stone Mountain handbags. There are roughly a dozen eateries, from the Mountain Pharmacy where locals enjoy tasty, old-fashioned milk shakes to the newly opened Continental Park Cafe, which has a charming porch overlooking the main street where you can enjoy cappuccino and delectable desserts.

The village hosts special events including a St. Patrick's celebration in March, an arts and crafts festival in June, a patriotic extravaganza on the 4th of July, a holiday open house in November and special candlelight shopping in November and December. The main celebration however is the Sugarplum Festival in December with Santa Claus arriving on a fire truck to begin the holiday parade. The village is filled with holiday carolers and festive decorations adorn the shops.

Directions: From I-285 east of Atlanta take Exit 30-B, Route 78 East for ten miles. The ranch is at 4525 Highway 78, near Snellville, past the turn-off for Stone Mountain Village. If you are heading directly for Stone Mountain Village from I-285, take Memorial Drive east for four miles then turn right on West Mountain. That will take you to Main Street in Stone Mountain Village.

Zoo Atlanta and the Atlanta Cyclorama

Fun Inside and Out

Zoo Atlanta, one of the ten oldest zoos in continuous operation in the country, is in the midst of a multi-million dollar redevelopment. Like so many zoos, it is changing from traditional animal confinement to naturalized habitats. Zoo Atlanta's collection includes more than 250 species and approximately 1,000 animals and birds.

The zoo was started in March 1889 with a traveling circus's exotic animal collection purchased by Atlanta merchant G.V. Gress. In 1935, this original collection was augmented by the private animal collection of Asa Candler Jr., one of the heirs of the Coca-Cola fortune. In 1951, new exhibit buildings were funded by the state legislature. In the 1980s, the 37-acre zoo began operating under the auspices of a private, nonprofit corporation.

This new corporation undertook needed renovations and an extensive redevelopment project, elements of which are already evident. In place is the **Ford African Rain Forest** featuring four gorilla families from the Yerkes Regional Primate Research Center of Emory University. Also open is the exhibit on the orangutans of Ketambe, the Sheba Sumatran Tiger Forest, the monkeys of Makokou display and the Masai Mara. Still in the planning stage is the Okefenokee Swamp, Coastal Lagoon, Koala Station and Conservation Village.

The $4.5-million Ford African Rain Forest is the home of zoo favorite Willie B., a western lowland gorilla who was caught in Africa when he was about three. Willie B. was named after former Atlanta mayor William B. Hartsfield. When Willie B. moved to his new home in 1988, he had his first chance to interact physically with other gorillas. He has now successfully socialized with two females who live with him in his grassy habitat that simulates the gorillas' native West African environment. There are four habitats separated by moats, and four adult male gorillas head the groups in each. Holding areas behind the habitat provide the gorillas with a place to sleep at night and socialize that is not open to the public. Nearby the rain forests of West Africa are recreated in the Monkeys of Makokou exhibit with colorful mandrill baboons and playful mona monkeys. There is also a walk-though aviary with West African birds.

The **Sheba Sumatran Tiger Forest** simulates an Indonesian forest glade complete with waterfalls, rivers and rocky crevices for these rare and endangered tigers. There are only 300 of these tigers in the wild. The zoo has had two tiger births, one in 1991 that did not survive and another in 1992 that now lives in Seattle.

The five-acre **Masai Mara** exhibit simulates the plains of East Africa with lions, giraffes, rhinos, zebras, gazelles, impala, ostriches, crowned cranes, white storks and other animals and birds. The **Mzima Springs** habitat has three elephants. A sign beside this exhibit explains why the elephants are red: they wallow in mud and spray themselves with the dust of the red soil. Throughout the zoo the signs provide enlightening, entertaining and educational information.

Another way to discover more about the animals in the zoo is to attend the daily shows. These include elephant demonstrations, gorilla and sea lion feeding, a program in the OK-to-Touch Corral and Wild Encounters on weekends at the Elder's Tree. There is also a zoo train that runs daily in the summer months. Other seasonal activities include a 20-minute NatureQuest show in the **Kroger Wildlife Theater** and a puppet show.

Zoo Atlanta is open Monday through Friday from 10:00 A.M. to 4:30 (grounds close at 5:30) P.M. On weekends the zoo closes at 5:30 and the grounds at 6:30 P.M. It is closed on major holidays. Admission is charged.

Just outside the gates of the zoo is the **Atlanta Cyclorama** where 15 times a day a recounting of the Battle of Atlanta is presented. A massive painting and three-dimensional diorama moves circularly around the seated audience, while the story of what happened on July 22, 1864, is dramatically told. The painting depicts the beginning of the successful Union attack led by Major General William T. Sherman on the troops of Confederate General John B. Hood. By nightfall there were over 12,000 soldiers killed, wounded or missing.

The painting measures 42 feet in height, 358 feet in circumference and weighs over 9,334 pounds. It was commissioned by U.S. Major General John A. Logan, who fought with Sherman, to promote Logan's campaign for the vice presidency in 1884. The painting toured for years before being brought to Atlanta in 1892. The diorama was added in 1935–1936 as part of a Works Projects Administration project. The diorama includes 128 figures (be sure to notice Clark Gable's features on one of the fallen soldiers), cannon, trees and railroad tracks. The painting was restored and the 200-seat theater added in 1979.

The Cyclorama also has Civil War artifacts and exhibits, the highlight being the steam locomotive Texas used in the great locomotive chase in April 1862 (see Big Shanty selection). A display tells the story of how Andrews Raiders seized the General at Kennesaw and how the Confederates pursued the raiders on the Texas, finally causing them to abandon the stolen locomotive near Ringgold. The General is displayed at the Big Shanty Museum, where a movie brings this exciting chase to life.

The Cyclorama Book Store has an extensive selection of Civil War books and memorabilia. The Cyclorama is open daily from 9:30 A.M. to 5:30 P.M. from June through September; the rest of the year it closes at 4:30 P.M. It is closed on major holidays. Admission is charged.

Directions: From I-75/85 take I-20 east from downtown to Exit 26, Boulevard. Zoo Atlanta is one-half mile south on the right at 800 Cherokee Avenue in Grant Park. The Atlanta Cyclorama is adjacent to the zoo.

Regional Trail

Cannonball Trail

Length: 17 miles
Gateway: Via I-75 at Marietta
Theme: Marietta's Civil War Sites
Background: The lore of the Blue and the Gray comes alive at locations associated with heroic deed and furious battles
Highlights: (see individual selections where starred *)
Western and Atlantic Passenger Depot: on site of depot briefly used in July 1864 as Sherman's HQ while pursuing Johnston, then burnt by Sherman's troops later that year.
Kennesaw House: Andrews Raiders met here the night before they stole the General (see Big Shanty selection).
Marietta Confederate Cemetery: 3,000 Confederate soldiers are buried here. Of those 1,000 are unknown.
Brumby-Trezevant-Little House: home of Colonel Arnoldus V. Brumby first superintendent of the Georgia Military Institute and Civil War officer of 14th Georgia Regiment.
Georgia Military Institute Site: entire cadet corps of 200 joined Confederate forces in 1864.
*Kolb Farm: Hood's troops attacked strong Federal forces on this 600-acre farmhouse now restored by National Park service (see Kennesaw selection).

*Cheatham Hill/Illinois Monument: Five Union brigades attacked Confederates on this hill, called the "Dead Angle" because of the 480 Illinois soldiers who died here (see Kennesaw selection).
*Pigeon Hill: Hiking trails lead through the battle area where McPherson's brigades attacked (see Kennesaw selection).
*Kennesaw Mountain National Battlefield Park Visitors Center.
Oakton: HQ of Confederate General W. W. Loring in summer of 1864.
*Fair Oaks: HQ of General Joseph E. Johnston during Battle of Kennesaw Mountain, open to public.
Tranquilla: General Andrew J. Hansell, adjutant of Georgia, Federal troops occupied house during Civil War.
Archibald Howell House: HQ Union General H.M. Judah.
First Presbyterian Church: used as Federal hospital in 1864.
St. James Episcopal Church: used by Federal forces in Civil War, suffered fire damage in 1964.
Glover Park/Historic Marietta Square: Confederate troops mustered and drilled on this square. Sherman burned a courthouse that stood on the square when he began his March to the Sea.
Marietta National Cemetery: More than 10,000 Union soldiers are buried here; 3,000 are unknown.

With Braves baseball, Hawks basketball and Falcons football, professional sports abound in Atlanta.

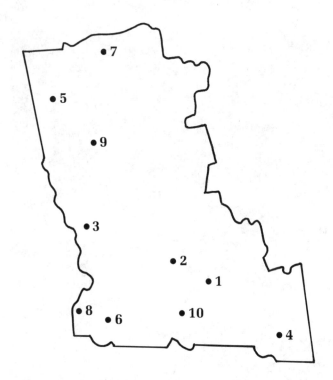

PRESIDENTIAL PATHWAYS

1. *Andersonville*
    Andersonville and Trebor
       Plantation
    Andersonville National Historic
       Site

2. *Buena Vista*
    Passaquan

3. *Columbus*
    Columbus Museum
    Confederate Naval Museum
    Heritage Corner
    Industrial District
    National Infantry Museum

4. *Cordele*
    Georgia Veterans Memorial State
       Park

5. *LaGrange*
    Bellevue

6. *Lumpkin*
    Providence Canyon State
       Conservation Park

7. *Newnan*
    Antebellum Newnan and
       Windemere Plantation

8. *Omaha*
    Florence Marina State Park and
       Rood Creek Indian Mounds

9. *Pine Mountain*
    Callaway Gardens
    Cecil B. Day Butterfly Center
       and John B. Sibley
       Horticultural Center
    F.D. Roosevelt State Park and
       Pine Mountain Trail
    Little White House and Warm
       Springs
    Wild Animal Farm

10. *Plains*
    Jimmy Carter National Historic
       Site

—Presidential Pathways—

Unexpected delights beckon at every turn in this middle-western region of the state. Pathways lead to historical figures and events, natural wonders and man-made curiosities.

American history through the ages unfolds across this region; the Rood Creek Indian Mounds at Florence Marina State Park extend back to before recorded time. Westville's 25 homes, businesses, schools and other buildings gathered from more than a dozen communities bring back the 1850s. The years before war cut a swath through Georgia. The war years are tragically brought to mind at Andersonville and the adjacent National Historic Site. Military buffs, students of the past and the curious are apt to discover some fascinating facts when they visit the Confederate Naval Museum in Columbus and the National Infantry Museum on nearby Fort Benning.

Inspiration is evoked at Franklin Delano Roosevelt's Little White House in Warm Springs. The private side of this popular president is revealed at his beloved retreat. The personal side of another president is also discovered when you visit Jimmy Carter's home town, Plains.

Customarily, great natural wonders are ageless. They are formed by the earth's movements in distant epochs, but Providence Canyon State Conservation Park, which clearly qualifies as a natural wonder, began to be formed in the early 1800s as a result of poor irrigation methods. The colorful walls of the park's 16 canyons are striking, and the trails that lead into them provide the opportunity to see abundant wildflowers and the world's largest stand of rare plumleaf azalea. This unique Georgia bush is responsible for the establishment of a man-made wonder, Callaway Gardens, that lures travelers to this area. In addition to a myriad of recreational options available at this resort, there are splendid gardens and a horticultural center. Callaway also boasts one of the country's most outstanding butterfly centers.

Another man-made attraction that concentrates on nature is the Pine Mountain Wild Animal Park where you drive among throngs of wild animals. The chance to feed these undomesticated beasts from your car window makes you feel like the Pied Piper, with a furry following.

Quite a different man-made attraction can be found outside Buena Vista, where Eddie Owens Martin created Passaquan, his phantasmagorical compound—a spot that has to be seen to be believed.

Andersonville and Trebor Plantation

City of Peace

In 1854 the town of Andersonville, named after railroad superintendent John W. Anderson, developed around a Georgia Southwestern Railroad depot. A decade later the town was the terminal from which 45,000 Federal prisoners of war entered Camp Sumter prison camp, now called the Andersonville Civil War Prison. The foul conditions in this camp led to the death of 13,000 prisoners, and the name Andersonville was forever tainted by association.

The village was the supply center for Camp Sumter, and Union officers had homes and offices in Andersonville. Brigadier General Winder, who was directly responsible for the welfare of the prisoners, used the old Scott Place as his home while he was commandant of the camp. He also had his headquarters in the village. Captain Wirz had an office in town as well as his headquarters, which were just outside the stockade prison wall near Star Fort. All of these sites are marked on a walking tour map of Andersonville along with a picturesque old log church and several other community buildings.

The original depot is no longer standing, but the **Andersonville Welcome Station** and museum is located in a 19th century railroad depot with pitched roof and abbreviated watch tower. The museum features Civil War artifacts, many of which relate to the nearby camp.

Andersonville had virtually disappeared by 1973, but a concerted effort by concerned townspeople succeeded in restoring the village to its Civil War appearance. Today many of the old stores are antique and craft shops. Among them is the **Drummer Boy Museum**, which the editor of Blue and Gray Magazine calls the finest Civil War museum in the country. Crammed into one room in a former shop is an impressive array of memorabilia dominated by an eight-by-ten-foot diorama of Andersonville Prison Camp and the town. Surrounding this impressive layout are 15 mannequins in a variety of Civil War uniforms.

The museum takes its name from the uniforms of two young drummer boys, one from each army. John Lincoln Clem, the Union drummer boy, ran away from his home in Newark, Ohio when he was nine. He shot a Confederate colonel when he was only 12. Clem served in the army for 47 years before retiring with the rank of general. His uniform looks small, but even as an adult Clem reached only five feet. Legend claims that one time when young Clem was riding beside General Grant he called to the men, "Johnny Shiloh won't run. Are you going to let a boy and his general stand here and fight alone?" The Zouave drummer boy's uniform is from the First Carolina Infantry.

There are Mathew Brady pictures of the prison camp, shots taken at the hanging of the six Union raiders who preyed on their fellow prisoners, as well as photographs of the hanging of Captain Wirz at the end of the war. Also exhibited is the bonnet taken from Mary Surratt as she was led to the gallows to become the first woman executed in the United States. Mary Surratt was convicted of participating in the plot to kill Lincoln.

The Drummer Boy Museum is open Monday through Saturday from 10:00 A.M. to 5:00 P.M. and on Sunday from 1:00 to 5:00 P.M. A nominal admission is charged.

Just outside the museum at the center of the village is the **Wirz Monument**. Feelings still run high regarding Captain Henry Wirz, Commandant of Andersonville Prison. His commanding officer, General Winder, died two months before the Civil War ended and Wirz was convicted and hanged for his role in the inhumane conditions at Andersonville. Many Southerners and historians dispute that judgment, and in 1909 the Georgia Division of the United Daughters of the Confederacy erected this monument in his honor.

Behind the Post Office on Main Street is a recreated seven-acre farm evoking life as it was on a Georgia farm in the mid-1800s. There is a furnished log cabin and log barns, a water-powered gristmill and a mule-powered sugar cane mill. Farm animals fill the pens and pastures.

Andersonville's biggest annual event, the Historic Fair, takes place on the farm grounds the first weekend in October. Visitors can see craft exhibits and watch the makers at work—blacksmiths, glassblowers, potters, quilters, chair caners and basket weavers. Both mills are operational, and there is country music and dancing, a parade, historic encampments and a flea market. On Memorial Day weekend there is another flea market at the antique, arts and crafts show and sale.

Andersonville's pioneer farm depicts a one-man operation, but at nearby **Trebor Plantation** you can glimpse the lifestyle of the landed gentry. According to family legend, Robert Hodges won his land grant in a poker game. He soon developed it into one of the region's most prosperous plantations. Trebor Plantation, one of five houses Hodges built (and the only one still standing) was first called Cedar Ridge, then Tudor Hall.

Trebor Plantation is a Greek Revival mansion with Edwardian adaptations. The original hand-planed virgin pine boards remain on the front of the house and in the two front parlors. Judge Robert Hodges's great-granddaughter, Ruth Hodges Frick, has restored the main house to its Civil War appearance. It looks much as it did when the Hodgeses invited Union officers from Andersonville prison to dinner. They had 60 acres set aside for growing vegetables, primarily sweet potatoes and corn, for the prison camp.

Trebor Plantation has remained in the Hodges family and is still a private home so parts are off limits to visitors. Escorted tours of the first floor are given, and visitors are free to explore the outbuildings and grounds. Be sure to peek in the Doll House directly behind the main house to see Mrs. Frick's extensive doll collection.

Trebor Plantation is open Wednesday through Monday from 10:00 A.M. to 5:00 P.M. Admission is charged. For additional information write to the Andersonville Welcome Center, P.O. Box 6, Andersonville, GA 31711. The phone is (912)924-2558.

Directions: From I-75 take Route 27 to Americus, then head north on Route 49 to Andersonville. Trebor Plantation is eight miles north of Americus on Route 49. Andersonville is two miles farther north.

Andersonville National Historic Site

An American Tragedy

Almost a third of the 45,000 Federal prisoners sent to the prison camp at Andersonville died there. Camp Sumter, as it was officially called, was the largest Confederate military prison. It operated from February 25, 1864, to May 7, 1865, but though it existed only briefly, it remains to this day a blot on the pages of American history. It wasn't inhumanity that led to the outrageous loss of life; it was instead the South's inability to meet the most basic needs of the prisoners. The Confederacy was unable to provide housing, food, clothing, water or medical care to their prisoners, leaving them to die of malnutrition, exposure and disease.

There was no prison building at Andersonville. Union captives marched from the railroad station to a stockade where they fended for themselves without shelter or supplies.

The 17-foot-high pine stockade originally enclosed 16½ acres, but was enlarged to 26½. That created a roughly four-by-six-foot living space for each man. The prisoners often established groups to share their crudely made "shebangs," some examples of which can be seen by visitors. Sentry boxes, or pigeon-roosts, stood every 30-yards around the parallelogram-shaped prison yard.

The guards for the most part were old men and young boys, some barely past 12. The prison area was built to contain 10,000 men, but the numbers swelled to a peak of roughly 33,000 in August 1864. For the unskilled and nervous guards to control that many men there had to be stringent rules, and there was a dead-line beyond which the prisoners could not trespass on penalty of death.

There was no prison building at Andersonville. The Union prisoners marched from the railroad station to a stockade where they were left to fend for themselves without shelter or supplies. They were allotted one meal a day, most often a pint of bug-infested peas and a pint of cornmeal and occasionally three or four ounces of bacon (a piece roughly the size of two fingers). The small stream of swampy water that ran through the center of the camp became contaminated early on. It was used for drinking, laundry, washing and as a latrine. The guards used the water before it entered the camp so it was already contaminated. The prisoners knew the water made them sick, but they had no other source. It was said that "drinking from Stockade Creek is drinking a cup of one's own death." The area around the creek became a gigantic sewer, and the stench could be smelled for ten miles when a breeze was blowing. Even able-bodied prisoners would die if they got creek water in a cut. The summer of 1864 was particularly dry, and during the drought the prisoners prayed for water. Their prayers were answered on August 13 when a violent rainstorm flushed out the creek. Legend has it that a bolt of lighting hit the ground, and out bubbled clear spring water. **Providence Spring**, as it is called, has flowed continuously.

For most of those who survived the pestilence, their days at Andersonville ended in September 1864 when General Sherman occupied Atlanta. Confederate high command moved the prisoners from the camp because it was vulnerable to the Federal cavalry. Prisoners were interred at camps in Florence, South Carolina, and Millen, Georgia. Some P.O.W.s were returned to Andersonville after Sherman occupied Savannah.

After the war Captain Henry Wirz, the only Confederate officer with whom the prisoners had come in frequent contact, was arrested and charged with conspiring with other Confederate officials to "impair and injure the health and destroy the lives...of Federal prisoners" and "murder, in violation of the laws of war." No conspiracy was ever proved, nor did one exist, but the temper of the times allowed no reasonable explanations, and Wirz was found guilty and was hanged in Washington, D.C., on November 10, 1865. A monument to Wirz was erected in the village of Andersonville by the United Daughters of the Confederacy (see Andersonville Village selection).

At the end of the war in July and August of 1865, Clara Barton joined with Dorence Atwater, a former Andersonville prisoner, and a detachment of laborers and soldiers to identify and mark the graves of Union dead. Atwater prepared a list of 12,918 men interred at Andersonville. Their efforts left only 460 of those as unidentified graves in **Andersonville National Cemetery**. When you tour the cemetery take note of the separate graves of the raiders. They were gang members who were tried and hanged by their fellow prisoners. During May 1864, at least one prisoner was murdered each day; many more were robbed or beaten by the raiders. The Andersonville National Cemetery is still a functioning cemetery open to military personnel and their immediate families.

In 1875 the land on which the prison stood reverted to private ownership. In 1890 the Georgia Department of the Grand Army of the Republic purchased it. Unable to finance improvements the Department sold it for one dollar to the Woman's Relief Corps. After improvements were made and the Providence Spring Memorial was added, the site was turned over to the United States government. It became a national historic site in 1970.

Andersonville is now more than a memorial to those who lost their lives as prisoners during the Civil War. At the Prisoner of War Museum exhibits memorialize American soldiers who have become prisoners of war from the American Revolution through all of the nation's armed conflicts. This museum traces the experiences of soldiers unlucky enough to be captured. It reveals the conditions under which they were held, the mistreatment they suffered, and the political indoctrination they endured.

The best place to begin your tour of Andersonville National Historic Site is from the **Visitor Center**. Here you can watch a 12-minute slide program that orients you to the events that happened here. There are exhibits and photographs on Andersonville, the National Cemetery and Civil War prisoners in general. If you want to find out more about any of these topics the center has an extensive collection of books that cover these issues. For a nominal fee you can rent a tape tour for your drive around the site. You will have to leave your drivers license as security.

The tour route takes you past 13 monuments erected by states who had citizens imprisoned here. The location of the stockade fence is marked by white posts, while the inner white stakes indicate the dead-line that ran 19 feet inside the fence. It had to be that far away since it was necessary to permit the prisoners to light fires, and had they got close to the fence they could have set it on fire. One of the most prevalent activities inside the compound was digging tunnels, and the locations of almost 60 escape tunnels are marked by concrete blocks. Locations of well sites dug by the men in their unsuccessful efforts to find water are also marked. The north gate and sentry post have been reconstructed, and the location of the south gate is marked with a stone block. The earthen embankments of Star Fort, headquarters for the Confederate defense of the prison camp, can still be seen.

On weekends park rangers present guided walks on a variety of topics. A ranger may address you as if you were a "fresh fish," the name given new prisoners, telling you what to expect and how to survive. You may be led by a ranger acting in the guise of a Women's Relief Corp member who tells about the efforts to save this historic site. There is a talk on the artifacts associated with Andersonville and one on prison life. There are also ranger-led cemetery walks.

Andersonville National Historic Site is open daily from 8:30 A.M. to 5:00 P.M. On Memorial Day it stays open until 7:00 P.M. There is no charge.

Directions: From I-75 take Route 27 west to the intersection with Route 195 and head north to Andersonville. You also can exit I-75 at Perry and head south on Route 224 to Montezuma, then continue south on Route 49 to the historic site.

Antebellum Newnan and Windemere Plantation

City of Homes

Newnan was founded in 1828 under the Land Lottery Act, passed after the Creek Indians ceded their land to the state in 1826. One of the houses on the city's driving tour, the Terrell-Jones-Hobbs House at 167 LaGrange Street, dates from that first year. It is one of 22 homes whose history and architectural details are related on the self-guided drive that encompasses the city's five historic districts. Two of the homes you'll pass, the Storey-Buchanan-Glover and the Storey-Hollis, appear in Medora Perkerson's attractive coffee table book White Columns in Georgia. The antebellum homes of Newnan were spared by General Sherman on his March to the Sea because during the war the wounded of both armies were treated in the city's hospitals.

Although not listed with the antebellum homes on the tour, the Parott-Camp-Soucy House at 155 Greenville Street, is a Victorian delight. It was built by one of the first settlers but was enlarged and remodeled in 1885 to its present Stick-Eastlake/French Mansard style. It has been honored with numerous awards and is now an elegant bed-and-breakfast (706)253-4846.

End your driving tour at the center of Newnan and take a short walking tour of historic downtown. The walking tour guide provides a building-by-building map of all four sides of the Court Square. The diverse architectural styles include Classical Revival, Victorian, Italianate, Romanesque and Tapestry Brick. Coweta County Courthouse, also noteworthy, adds an excellent example of Neo-Greek Revival architecture; it is included on the National Register of Historic Places. Each of the four sides of its copper-covered dome has a clock, rather like the old timepiece in *Back to the Future.*

To discover more about the history and people of Newnan stop at the **Male Academy Museum**, 30 Temple Avenue. The name derives from the 1883 seminary for boys that has been restored and now serves as headquarters for the Newnan-Coweta Historical Society. One of the Society's projects, the museum, features permanent exhibits such as a typical classroom from the 1800s and furniture from the same in the Zeke Smith Room. Civil War memorabilia include *Gone With the Wind* collectibles. Indian history, period clothing and local records are also covered. The museum is open Tuesday, Wednesday, and Thursday 10:00 A.M. to NOON and 1:00 to 3:00 P.M. Weekend hours are 2:00 to 5:00 P.M. This is a good spot to pick up the walking and driving guides.

Crowds gather each year over Labor Day weekends just outside of Newnan at the annual **Powers' Crossroads Country Fair & Art Festival**. The crafts and traditions of early settlers are showcased through the work of over 300 artisans selected from across the country. The fair brings back the rhythm of bluegrass music, the energetic steps of mountain clog dancers and the tastes and aroma of country cooking. Blacksmiths make the sparks fly, corn and wheat are ground at the gristmill, and cane, at the sorghum mill. The only spot that doesn't operate quite the way it once did is the moonshine still. Regional travel and tourism organizations list the fair as one of the top 100 events in North America and also as one of the top 20 in the nine southeastern states.

Another place you can easily include in a visit to Newnan is **Windemere Plantation** in nearby Palmetto. If you are traveling between these two spots around mealtime, stop at Sprayberry's for their deservedly famous barbecue. This unassuming family restaurant is known throughout the state for its barbecue and Brunswick stew.

The manor house at Windemere Plantation is quite different from most Greek Revival antebellum homes because it is designed in a modified Z-shape. Its name means "windy hill" probably because it sits on one of the highest elevations in the county. It was built by a local builder-architect, William Yarbrough, and his trademark, a Greek key motif, is seen in the decorative exterior carving.

Legend has it that the house escaped burning during the Civil

War because Union General Edward M. McCook who led the troops was a Mason; he mistook one of the carvings on the stairwell for a Masonic emblem and spared the house. Another story claims that during the war food was hidden in the hollow portion of the huge Doric columns to keep it from both armies. With 63 people to feed—51 slaves and 10 children—plantation owners had to save all they could.

In 1979 Windemere was purchased by Robert and Vivian Harrison. The furnishings are primarily post-Civil War Victorian though there are pieces from other periods. House tours are given by appointment only. Call (706)463-0940.

Directions: For Newnan from I-85 take Exit 9, and take a right on Route 34 to Route 29. Turn left on Route 29 to downtown Newnan. If you want to get to the Powers' Crossroads County Fair & Art Festival, continue on Route 34 west for 12 miles. Sprayberry's is on Route 29. Windemere Plantation lies four miles east of Palmetto on Collinsworth Road, or one mile east of I-85, Exit 11, on Collinsworth Road.

Bellevue and LaGrange

City of Elms and Roses

In 1824 the Marquis de Lafayette paid a 14-month visit to the country he helped establish. While traveling with Georgia Governor George M. Troup through the western part of the state, Lafayette remarked that the countryside reminded him of the land around his home, the Chateau de LaGrange. Four years later Troup County named its county seat LaGrange.

Decades later, the president of LaGrange College, Dr. Waights G. Henry, Jr., obtained permission from LePuy, France, to reproduce the exceptional statue of the Marquis de LaFayette sculpted by Ernest-Eugene Hiolle. It shows LaFayette holding his tricorn hat in one hand and in the other his cockade, a colorful ribbon that was worn on a hat as a symbol of liberty. The statue stands in the place of honor on one of the most beautiful town squares in the South, glorified by an oversized round fountain ringed with flowers.

Lafayette is not the only Revolutionary War hero commemorated in LaGrange. The town has the distinction of being the only one on this continent to commission a military company of women soldiers. During the Civil War the women of the community, seeking to protect their homes, formed a group they called the Nancy Harts, after Georgia's Revolutionary heroine. Nancy Hart was six feet tall, with fiery red hair and crossed eyes.

Members of the LaGrange Symphony Orchestra and LaGrange Ballet entertain by the fountains in LaFayette Square.

Whenever the British stopped at her cabin for a meal, she made them keep their rifles outside. Legend has it that she caught one of the British trying to steal a chicken and shot him. When she pulled a gun on the British, it was said, they couldn't tell whom she was looking at. Some reports have it that Nancy and Daniel Boone were first cousins.

LaGrange boasts one of Georgia's finest Greek Revival houses. **Bellevue**. The stately antebellum home of Benjamin Harvey Hill was built in the early 1850s. Now a National Historic Landmark the house has imposing Ionic columns across the wide porticoes and an upstairs balcony with a classic balustrade.

Bellevue was built after Mr. Hill married Caroline Holt of Athens and established his law practice in LaGrange. He was elected to the state legislature in 1851, ran unsuccessfully for governor in 1857 and became a United States congressman in 1875. Known as "the silver-tongued orator," Hill developed cancer of the tongue and died at the age of 59.

Bellevue's interior woodwork is exceptional; if you look carefully you will notice that the carving is subtly different. For example, the waves carved over the windows in the four main downstairs rooms flow in different directions. Don't miss the ornate plaster ceiling medallions, the black carrara marble mantels in the double parlor and the custom-made wallpaper in the entrance hall. Though most of the furnishings are of the period, the piano is original.

Bellevue is open for guided tours Tuesday through Saturday from 10:00 A.M. to NOON and from 2:00 to 5:00 P.M. Admission is charged. The house, operated by the LaGrange Woman's Club Charitable Trust, is rented out for various functions.

Special events are often scheduled at the **Chattahoochee Valley Art Museum**, nearby on Hines Street in the innovatively remodeled Victorian building that was once the community jail and for a time a newspaper office. The exhibits change often and much of the art work is for sale. There is no admission and the galleries are open Tuesday through Saturday from 9:00 A.M. to 5:00 P.M. and Sunday 1:00 to 5:00 P.M.

The Lamar Dodd Art Center on the campus of LaGrange College also features monthly exhibits of art and photography. The center has an impressive permanent collection of paintings by Lamar Dodd, who took his first formal art lessons at this college. The center is open weekdays 10:00 A.M. to NOON and 1:00 to 4:00 P.M. and weekends 1:00 to 4:00 P.M.

The 26,000-acre lake that borders LaGrange offers townsfolk and visitors a variety of recreational options. Along 500 miles of shoreline of West Point Lake you can take your pick of sandy beaches, picnic areas, campgrounds, boat rentals, fishing areas, playgrounds and tennis courts. Cottages and a lakeside restaurant are located at Highland Marina.

For award winning cuisine enjoy lunch or dinner at LaGrange's most noted restaurant, In Clover (706-882-0883). The decor is classic Queen Anne Victorian and the menu is continental, but diners' dress may be casual. Prices are reasonable.

Directions: From I-85 take Exit 4, The LaFayette Parkway, Route 109 west. The Chattahoochee Valley Art Museum will be on the left as LaFayette Parkway becomes Hines Street. The museum's address is 112 Hines Street. For Bellevue, proceed one block to the Square, turn right at the southeast corner, turn left at the northeast corner. Take Broad Street to Ben Hill Street, turn right. The estate is #205. The restaurant In Clover is at 205 Broad Street. For the Lamar Dodd Art Center go past the College on Broad, turn left on Forrest Avenue, and in two blocks you will see the Art Center on a hill on the right. Just about any highway that leads north or west out of town takes you to West Point Lake.

Callaway Gardens

A Blooming Treasure

Callaway Gardens defies the maxim that it's impossible to be everything to everybody. There truly is something for everybody at this 12,000-acre, four-star resort with its 13 man-made lakes and nearly ten miles of scenic trails.

Cason Callaway and his wife, Virginia, began building the gardens in the late 1940s on what were primarily worn-out cotton fields. It's amazing to gaze at the luxuriant wooded backdrop to the gardens and realize that they were added so recently. Cason Callaway did more than preserve the area's natural beauty; he brought it back to life.

Callaway believed, "Every child ought to see something beautiful before he's six years old—something he would remember the rest of his life." At Callaway Gardens he said "All I've done is to fix it so that anybody. . .would see something beautiful wherever he might look."

One of Georgia's unique beauties is the **Prunifolia** azalea, or plumleaf azalea, a plant that grows natively only within a hundred miles of Callaway. Once Cason Callaway discovered the prunifolia he was determined to save it, and it became the emblem for Callaway Gardens. Its delicate red-orange, honeysuckle-shaped flowers bloom in late July.

The **Azalea Trail** is one of eight walking paths at Callaway. From late March to May the 700 varieties of cultivated azaleas bloom along this trail. An overlook pavilion provides an excellent vantage point from which to treat your eyes to the beauty. The pastel and bright pink flowers are multiplied by their mirror images in the still waters of Whippoorwill Lake. Planted with these colorful spring bushes are rhododendrons, dogwoods and wildflowers. In late July look for the plumleaf azalea blooms.

The Meadowlark Gardens area has three trails. Spring is the best time to walk the **Wildflower Trail** (allow 25 minutes for the short portion, 40 minutes for the entire trail). In addition to wildflowers you see flowering quince and Oriental magnolias. Just off the Wildflower Trail sits the Pioneer Log Cabin which was moved here in 1959. Made largely of heart-of-yellow pine, the cabin was built in 1800 and used until 1936. As many as 13 children lived with their parents at one time in this small house. Today volunteer caretakers prepare food and demonstrate such crafts as making corn-husk dolls and pine-needle baskets.

The **Rhododendron Trail**, at the height of its color in late spring, has ornamental shrubs, ground covers and ferns that make it attractive year-round. In winter take the nearby 40-minute Holly Trail for cheery color. In early spring its daffodils and camellias are splendid, and in mid-summer you find prunifolia azaleas.

A paved walkway extends along the shoreline of Robin Lake. There is also a seven-mile paved **bike trail** through the gardens. You may bring your own or rent a bike. Should you tire, you can bike the trail for four miles and catch a ferry back across Mountain Creek Lake. Biking is one of the best ways to see the garden. There is also a five-mile scenic auto drive that takes you past all the major points of interest.

You can rent canoes, sailboats and paddleboats at the Boat Dock on Mountain Creek Lake. A three-hour **walking trail** takes you along the southern edge of the lake. Along this trail you'll spot a variety of waterfowl, like colorful mallards and great herons as well as turtles and squirrels. Native rhododendron, azaleas and wildflowers line the path. A scenic serpentine bridge and an arched bridge cross this lake.

The **Chapel Trail** meanders along Falls Creek Lake starting at the Ida Cason Callaway Memorial Chapel. A garden sign quotes an unknown poet: "We are nearer God's heart in a garden than anywhere else on earth." At the heart of Callaway Gardens rises the lovely English Gothic chapel of native fieldstone dedicated to Cason Callaway's mother. Organ recitals on Sunday afternoons from 3:00 to 5:00 P.M. are open to the public. The six stained-glass windows represent the four seasons, the hardwood and the evergreen forests.

Cason Callaway believed that "the best fertilizer that soil can have is the footprints of the owner." His mark is felt throughout the garden, and one special area called Mr. Cason's **Vegetable Garden**, is the last major project he developed. This seven-and-a-half-acre seasonal demonstration garden has three large terrace gardens and grows over 400 varieties of vegetables, herbs and fruits. Information displays provide take-home hints for gardeners. The television show "Victory Garden South" is taped in the Home Demonstration Garden here.

No tour of the garden area would be complete without a stop at the John A. Sibley Horticultural Center and the Cecil B. Day Butterfly Center (see selection).

The natural wonders are the draw, and the recreational options keep visitors staying on. Callaway has 63 holes of golf; there's the original 18-hole Lake View course, a quick 9-hole Sky View no-cart course, plus the 18-hole Gardens View course and the Mountain View championship course where the PGA Tour held the Buick Southern Open.

Tennis enthusiasts can choose from 17 lighted courts on what *Tennis Magazine* ranks as a "Top 50" facility. Callaway claims Robin Lake Beach is the largest white-sand, man-made inland beach in the world. There's also swimming in Callaway's pools. During summer, the "Flying High" Circus from Florida State University performs at the beach area. Water ski shows are regularly performed and there are trips on the riverboat. Games include miniature golf, volleyball and badminton adjacent to the mile-long beach.

If hunting is your sport, Callaway's 1,000-acre preserve should prove tempting. The fields and woodlands abound with quail, white-tail deer and wild turkey. There's a skeet and trap range if you prefer shooting clay pigeons. Fishermen angle for bass and bream in the 175-acre Mountain Creek Lake.

There's also 23 miles of paths for joggers and bicyclists. If you need to tone up, stop at the DP "Fit For Life" Fitness Center where you'll find state-of-the-art equipment and a sauna.

Overnight accommodations are available at the Inn, in the Mountain Creek Villas or in one of 155 country cottages; food and drink, at seven restaurants and two cocktail spots. The Country Store lets you take a little of Callaway home with you, their own brand of speckled heart grits, jam, jelly and preserves as well as other regional products.

Throughout the year there are many special events at Callaway. May traditionally finds Callaway hosting the prestigious Masters Water Ski Championship. In November the resort hosts the Beaujolais Nouveau/Steeplechase Weekend. The Christmas season is dependably festive. For information call 1(800)282-8181.

Directions: From the Atlanta area take I-85 south to I-185.

Continue south to Exit 14, turn left on Route 27 and go 11 miles
to Callaway Gardens.

Cecil B. Day Butterfly Center and
John A. Sibley Horticultural Center
at Callaway Gardens

Georgia's Garden of Eden

Enchantment fills the air at the Cecil B. Day Butterfly Center. In
a range of shades and hues that puts most palettes to shame,
butterflies glide and swoop from flower to flower and from
branch to branch. If you're wearing a bright color, these winged
flowers, as they are whimsically called, are apt to alight on your
shoulder.

Watching visitors wander through this crystal palace with wide
smiles and even wider eyes, it's hard to believe that the idea of
a butterfly center was a hard sell, but it was. The widow of Days
Inns founder Cecil B. Day, now Mrs. Deen Day Smith, conceived
the idea after visiting butterfly centers in England and Scotland.
She felt Callaway Gardens was the ideal spot for a butterfly conservatory, but Hal Northrop, then CEO and president, wasn't
convinced that spending millions of dollars for butterflies was
justified. Mrs. Smith arranged for him to visit the European centers she had seen. Northrop returned to Georgia enthusiastic
about the project. Deen Day Smith made a substantial contribution to the center that bears her first husband's name.

North America's largest free-flight, glass-enclosed conservatory did more than copy European butterfly houses; it improved
on them. Most of the centers throughout the world are commercial showcases with live butterflies in a screened-in room. There
are slightly over 50 centers and most are in effect butterfly farms.
At Callaway Gardens the conservatory was designed specifically
to duplicate the butterflies' natural environment. Visitors experience the butterflies as they would in the wild, except they
can enjoy a profusion of species unlikely to be matched anywhere
in the world.

The 8,000-square-foot conservatory holds 800 to 1,000 tropical
butterflies, encompassing roughly 50 species. They flit among
60 species of tropical plants. The air is moistened from a 12-foot
cascading waterfall that flows into a pool. The butterflies are not
released into the conservatory until they take wing. As ravenous
caterpillars they would quickly denude the tropical plants, so in
this early stage they live behind the scenes in production facil-

At Callaway Gardens, year-round floral displays enchant visitors to the Sibley Horticulture Center, the most advanced greenhouse/garden complex in the world.

ities. Caterpillars go on display in the conservatory's anteroom once they become chrysalises. You can peer into their glass-front incubators that look like small refrigerators. The chrysalises resemble tiny mummies. About 65 percent of the butterflies at Callaway are raised right here; other exotic specimens are shipped in from around the world.

Butterflies are artistically captured in the Center's lobby where a copper chandelier designed by Ivan Bailey is shaped like the passionflower, a butterfly host plant. Georgia's state butterfly, the Eastern tiger swallowtail, is featured in the specially made rug beneath the chandelier. On the walls is a collection of butterfly watercolors done by Chevalier de Freminville, a 19th-century artist, and by John Abbot, a pioneer naturalist who painted in Georgia from 1776 to 1840.

To fully appreciate the butterflies you will see, watch the 12-minute orientation film on the life of these "world-class eating machines," elegantly known as "flying gemstones."

Be sure not to rush through the conservatory, take the time to sit and watch the butterflies. When you leave the glass-enclosed world, you can stroll through the gardens outside designed to show you what plants to grow in your own garden to attract butterflies. More than 70 native species of butterflies fly around this garden. Also, though it is better appreciated from an aerial photo, take note of the brick work and landscaping around the conservatory formed in the shape of a butterfly.

The cupola crowning the conservatory's main entrance once graced Highland Villa, the Pelham home of Virginia Hand, who grew up to marry Cason Callaway. In 1971 when her home was scheduled to be demolished, Virginia brought the cupola to Callaway and restored it as a gazebo. When it was moved yet again and placed atop the conservatory, workers removed countless layers of thick paint and uncovered ornate brass engravings of flowers, hummingbirds, and—you guessed it—butterflies! Perhaps the Victorian cupola has finally reached the home for which it was intended.

The Cecil B. Day Butterfly Center is open daily; call (706)663-2281 for current schedule. Admission is part of the general gate pass to all the attractions within Callaway Gardens.

There is one more wonder to discover at Callaway Gardens (see selection) and that is the **John A. Sibley Horticultural Center**. It's the most advanced greenhouse/garden complex in the world, flowing as it does from an indoor to an outdoor setting in a seamless sweep. Visitors hardly realize they have made the transition.

Within the controlled environment of the conservatory you pass through a tropical garden filled with plants from the warm, wet climates of the world. After stopping at the overlook patio for a view of the exterior grounds, you move through a rock wall garden with seasonal floral plants, ferns and camellias. Just outside this area is a sculpture garden dedicated to James M. Sibley, son of John A. Sibley.

Behind the conservatory's 22-foot waterfall is a grotto filled with ferns and bromeliads. The floral conservatory features 18 main floral themes during the year. Through the huge half-doors that stand open during pleasant weather you'll have a view of the five-acre outdoor garden. Depending on the season, flower beds of spring bulbs, summer annuals and autumn chrysanthemums are surrounded by shrubs and perennial borders.

The John A. Sibley Horticultural Center is named for a close friend of the Callaway family. Mr. Sibley, a Georgia banker, lawyer and civic leader, shared the Callaway's interest in horticulture and land conservation. He was a trustee of the Ida Cason Callaway Foundation from 1964 until his death.

Directions: Take I-85 south to I-185 south. From I-185 take the Pine Mountain exit and follow Route 27 north to Callaway Gardens.

Columbus's Industrial District

An Artistic Eye for Business

It's rare to see an industrial complex—ironworks, gristmills, and cotton warehouses—artistically renovated. The Riverfront Industrial District of Columbus, now a National Historic Landmark, features once thriving businesses that have been transformed into public-oriented facilities.

The **Columbus Iron Works**, built in 1853 near the city's steamboat landing, operated into the early 1970s. By that time the company had outgrown the facility and moved to more modern quarters. Today the Iron Works is a bustling and exciting convention and trade center. Housed here is the Columbus Convention and Visitors Bureau where you can pick up information on all of the city's major attractions. The center's innovative use of the old brick walls, huge timbers and exposed ceilings of the foundry won a 1981 National Trust for Historic Preservation Honors Award.

Foundries were first built in Columbus in the 1840s. William R. Brown's Columbus Iron Works hastened the city's transformation from frontier town into one of the South's leading industrial centers. During the Civil War the Iron Works supplied cannons to the Confederates, including the "Ladies' Defender," made from brass collected by the women of Columbus. In 1862 the Confederate navy leased the foundry and converted it into the largest naval machinery factory in the South. Engines and broilers made here powered at least half of the steam-powered vessels built for the Confederate navy.

Using war-developed technology, the Iron Works expanded after the Civil War and became one of the leading businesses in the city. Surprisingly, the most profitable product the factory ever made was a commercial ice-making machine. In 1902 a fire destroyed everything but the 1890s foundry. A new facility was built and used for the next 65 years. Photographs of the 1902 fire and of the rebuilt factory are displayed in the convention center along with Civil War cannons and parts from ships built here.

Across the street from the convention and trade center is the **Columbus Hilton Hotel**, which incorporates the former Empire Mills into its design. Originally, this site was the location of William Waters Garrard's cotton warehouse; there, in 1847, E.T. Taylor began operating his Cotton Gin Company. In 1861 G. W. Woodruff began operating Empire Mills, and from 1875 to 1890 this was Columbus's largest gristmill with a capacity of 600 barrels of flour per day. The older portion of the hotel has rooms that retain Empire Mills's original wooden beams and 100-year-old bricks.

Just down Front Avenue, between 10th and 12th Streets, is the **W. C. Bradley Company**, a diversified company that is still a major cotton dealer. In April 1865, Union troops burned the original cotton warehouses, but they were rebuilt and expanded in the 1860s, and in 1883 they were acquired by the W. C. Bradley Company.

A unique art exhibit is displayed in the Bradley Company museum. More than 20 noted painters were commissioned to represent diverse aspects of the company's activities. It is intriguing to see through the eyes of these artists; some chose to portray the faces of the workers, while others captured scenes of the cotton warehouses along the river. Several painters left letters and remarks explaining their work. Adjacent to the gallery is a small chapel, a Centennial gift from the workers to the company. The museum is open to the public without charge Monday through Friday during business hours.

As Columbus became a major industrial center, the arts flourished. In 1871 Francis J. Springer built an **opera house**, and over the years a glittering list of renowned artists performed on its stage. Familiar names include Buffalo Bill Cody (1875), Edwin Booth (1876), Oscar Wilde (1882), Lily Langtry (1888), Will Rogers (1906), Irene Dunne (1922), Martha Graham (1970) and Burt Reynolds (1991). This Victorian theater, with its curving double balconies, delicate tulip lights and high proscenium arch, became the State Theater of Georgia in 1971. Tours of the historical public areas and the behind-the-scenes working areas are given by appointment, and arranged by calling (706)324-5714. On the first and second floors there are museum areas with photographs, programs, posters and theater memorabilia. The Glesca Marshall Library of Theater Arts has a large collection of programs, press clippings and reference books available to researchers. The library has the designs of internationally-known stage lighting expert Abe Feder and the career memorabilia of stage and silent film star Alla Nazimova. The Springer Opera House is a National Historic Landmark, a repository for theatrical history as well as a still-active theater.

While in the uptown business district of Columbus you don't want to miss Rankin Square in the 1000 block of Broadway and First Avenue. This is considered the most outstanding concentration of Victorian commercial buildings in the district. Try lunch at the popular Rankin Quarter. Another lunch or dinner spot favored by locals is Country's on Broad, 1329 Broadway, noted for its delicious barbecue.

Directions: Traveling south on I-185 take Exit 7 onto the J.R. Allen Parkway. Go to Exit 1, which is the 2nd Avenue exit. Take 2nd Avenue to 9th Street. Turn right onto 8th Street to approach the Riverfront Industrial District.

Columbus Museum

Indian Legacy

The Chattahoochee River forms Georgia's western boundary. Life along this important waterway is captured in an award-winning film *Chattahoochee Legacy* shown at the Columbus Museum. This state-of-the-art film, shown four times a day in the Heritage Theater, is a sensory treat. In the darkened theater you are transported slowly into a rainy summer evening along the river. You hear the sounds of crickets, owls and other birds. As a storm develops there comes the sound of rain and the sharp crack of lighting. Suddenly the screen bursts into life with a view of the North Georgia mountains in a driving rain storm. The water racing down the mountainside pours into the mist-shrouded Chattahoochee River. It's all so real you almost feel the mist.

Life along the river is covered in all its dimensions, starting with the natural world of marsh birds, waterfowl, amphibious animals and insects, then moving to the inroads made by man. The story of man along the river is traced back to the prehistoric people who built impressive mounds overlooking its banks like

A surrealistic film at the Columbus Museum shares life past and present along the Chattahoochee River.

those at Rood Creek. From such frontier towns as Westville to the foundries of Columbus, man's interaction with the river is charted.

The film is but one part of the museum's continuing effort to present the history of the region. A prototype of an archaeological dig at a burial mound begins the exhibit on man's existence in this region. It is followed by a series of life-size recreated period settings depicting various aspects of existence in and around Columbus. There is a 1860 urban slave house, a 1900 one-room school and a 1925 shotgun house where old-time music is still played on the phonograph.

The Columbus Museum is the second largest museum in Georgia, and history is just one of its domains. The museum houses one of the southeast's finest collections of 19th- and 20th-century American art. Its permanent collection includes works by John Singer Sargent, Robert Henri, Alma Thomas, Reginald Marsh, Lamar Dodd and Albert Bierstadt.

Pablo Picasso said, "Every child is an artist. The problem is how to remain an artist once he grows up." The participatory exhibit "Transformations" helps children of all ages interact with art through activities like line bends, shape wall, surface sensations and a block-building area. Expanding on this participation the museum offers a continuing schedule of films, demonstrations, classes, tours and symposia.

The Columbus Museum is one of the region's premier cultural and educational facilities. In 1989 the museum expanded into a $10-million addition built around the W.C. Bradley home that had housed its collections from the time of its opening in 1953. The Italian style of the Bradley home was blended into the new design. The highlight of the new museum is the **Turner Galleria** that rises three levels with gallery space off each. The Mediterranean influence is seen in the Tuscan colonnades, monolithic arches and decorative grillwork. From the galleria visitors have an excellent view of the newly restored Olmsted garden.

The Columbus Museum, at 1251 Wynnton Road, is open Tuesday through Saturday from 10:00 A.M. to 5:00 P.M. and Sunday 1:00 to 5:00 P.M. There is no admission but donations are gratefully accepted. The museum has an excellent gift shop.

Directions: From I-185 take Columbus Exit 4 and go west on Wynnton/Macon Road. The museum will be on your right just after you cross Buena Vista Road.

Confederate Naval Museum

Little Known Facts

Did you know that the Confederate Naval Academy was a single ship, the CSS *Patrick Henry*, that sailed the James River in Virginia? Did you know the Confederate navy got about two dozen ironclads into operation? Did you know that submarine and torpedo warfare began during the Civil War? The Confederate Naval Museum in Columbus provides interesting background on these little-known parts of naval history.

At this museum you discover how the Confederacy improvised a navy. With few shipyards, little money, virtually no heavy industries or naval mechanics and hardly any trained personnel, the Confederate States Navy was established on February 21, 1861. The South attempted to overcome these obvious disadvantages by developing new weapons and new-fangled sailing vessels like the ironclads.

The museum focuses on the salvaged remains of the ironclad ram *Jackson*. Construction of the *Jackson* began in December 1862 at the Confederate States Navy Yard in Columbus, and the *Muscogee*, as it was first called, was built as a center paddle-wheel-powered ironclad. A launch attempt in 1864 failed and the propulsion system was changed to a twin screw arrangement. Other minor changes were made, and the ironclad was successfully launched on December 22, 1864. The vessel was renamed in honor of the capital of Mississippi. While awaiting delivery of armor plating needed to finish the vessel, Columbus fell to Union forces and the *Jackson* was set afire. Union troops cut her loose and she drifted downriver for 30 miles before running aground on a sandbar. The *Jackson* burned to the waterline. The remains of the hull you see at the museum were salvaged in the early 1960s.

In 1964 a 30-foot stern section of the gunboat *Chattahoochee* was salvaged and presented to the Confederate Naval Museum. These two salvaged remains are among only a handful of Confederate vessels on exhibit anywhere in the country. The *Chattahoochee* was a conventional wooden sail/steam gunboat commissioned on January 1, 1863. It sank in Florida after a boiler explosion. The ship was raised and taken to Columbus for repairs, but the Confederates scuttled it in April 1865 so that it wouldn't fall into Union hands.

These two oversized exhibits are outside; the smaller artifacts from them and from other Confederate ships can be seen inside the museum. Models help visitors visualize what the two salvaged ships originally looked like and show other vessels in the Confederate navy as well.

The CSS *Hunley* was the first submarine to sink an enemy vessel in conflict. She rammed her spar torpedo, an example of which is on exhibit, into the U.S. *Housatonic* off Charleston Harbor. The *Hunley* failed to return, and all hands aboard were lost at sea. The Confederates built the first torpedo boat, the CSS *David* in 1863. It too used a spar torpedo. The Confederates also used keg torpedoes, examples of which are displayed. The USS *Cairo* sank when it ran into five-gallon glass jugs filled with black powder, considered to be the first successful torpedo.

The Confederate Naval Museum is open Tuesday through Friday from 10:00 A.M. to 5:00 P.M. and on weekends from 1:00 to 5:00 P.M. Donations are encouraged.

Directions: From I-85 take the Columbus exit for Route 280/80, Victory Drive. The Museum is on the corner of Victory Drive and 2nd Avenue.

F. D. Roosevelt State Park and Pine Mountain Trail

Presidential Inspiration

For many years Pine Mountain, at the southern end of the Appalachian Mountains, was farmed under the provisions of the Homestead Act. Franklin Delano Roosevelt, who played such a significant role in the reclaiming of the mountain, owned a farm on Pine Mountain (near the present site of WJSP-TV). The land's transformation into a park took place during the Roosevelt administration. The park was one of the first Depression era Civilian Conservation Corps projects. All the trees you see across the valley were planted by the CCC. Roosevelt conceived the idea for the Liberty Bell swimming pool, which became well known far beyond the boundaries of Georgia. He also instigated the scenic highway over the mountain.

Roosevelt's favorite spot on Pine Mountain was **Dowdell's Knob**. At 1,395 feet this rocky pinnacle is the highest spot on the mountain, offering a breathtaking view of the valley. FDR often picnicked at Dowdell's Knob. Though the charcoal grill he used has been bricked over to protect it for posterity, there are others nearby that can still be used. Roosevelt's idea of a picnic was a bit more formal than most; he insisted on linen-draped tables, silverware and hot dishes. He never sat on a blanket but instead had the automobile seat from the car carried over to the bluff. Between 1924 and 1945 FDR made 41 trips to Warm Springs (see Little White House selection). He visited Dowdell's Knob as a private citizen, while governor of New York and as the 32nd president. The last time Roosevelt sat at Dowdell's Knob, in April 1945, he undoubtedly pondered the formation of the United Nations and lamented the loss of American lives on Okinawa. You can visit Dowdell's Knob April to September from 8:00 A.M. to 8:00 P.M. and from October to March from 8:00 A.M. to 5:00 P.M.

Dowdell's Knob, above Kings Gap, is just one of the scenic spots along the 23-mile blue-blazed **Pine Mountain Trail**. Early trails over Kings Gap were used by the Indians. Indeed, the original park acreage was given to the United States by the Creek Indians under the Indian Springs Treaty of 1825. The trail used today was organized in 1975, and it's considered one of the most popular in the southeast. Other scenic spots along the trail include Cascade Falls, Buzzard Roost, Sunset Rock and Beech Bottom. Springtime in Pine Mountains, with its abundance of native azalea, flowering dogwood, mountain laurel, rhododendron and wildflowers, is a genuine delight. The Pine Mountain Trail begins at the F.D. Roosevelt State Park entrance near the Callaway Gardens Country Store and ends at the WJSP-TV tower near Warm Springs. There are nine designated campsites along the trail.

Visitors also can camp in the F.D. Roosevelt State Park near the park office. There are 140 recreational vehicle campsites and 21 rental cabins. Recreational options include the bell-shaped pool, two lakes—Lake Delano and Lake Franklin—and horseback riding.

Just down the road from the Mountain Top Inn (which offers

scenic accommodations, call (800)533-6376 for information) is a popular fishing hole. The 15-acre Lake Delano is stocked with bass and bream, and fishermen can rent boats at the park. The F.D.R. Riding Stables, (706)628-4533, are just a mile off Route 354 on King's Gap Road. There are five miles of horseback trails in the park; however, no horseback riding is permitted on the Pine Mountain Trail. The stables offer guided trail rides and overnight rides plus hayrides and cookouts beside an old covered wagon.

If you want to see more of the Pine Mountain area, then join the Pine Mountain Trolley tours that run from the town of Pine Mountain over to Warm Springs and around Callaway Gardens. If you are in Pine Mountain at dinner time, you can't go wrong at any of the restaurants in the Callaway Resort, or you might want to try a little spot in town called Bon Cuisine (706)663-2019. This store-front restaurant on Main Street features a selection of wild game items that can't be beat (among the offerings are nilgai antelope, wild boar, snapping turtle, alligator, white-tail deer and blackbuck). This regular fare is prepared with a mixture of herbs and spices that make even familiar items seem deliciously exotic. You also can enjoy continental cuisine at the Mountain Top Inn, where the Sunday buffet is a popular local treat.

Directions: From I-85 take Exit 13, Route 18 east to Pine Mountain. Then take Route 190 east towards Warm Springs, and you will see the park entrance on your right.

Florence Marina State Park and Rood Creek Indian Mounds

Prehistoric Reminders au Natural

Recreation and historical interpretation are dual draws at Florence Marina State Park at the northern end of Lake Walter F. George (and the Eufaula National Wildlife Refuge) in Stewart County. Formerly a private recreational area for the W. C. Bradley Company (see Columbus's Industrial District selection for information about this cotton manufacturer), the 150-acre park is now open to the public. Park facilites include a marina, lighted fishing pier, aluminum johnboats for rent, swimming pool, tennis courts, miniature golf course, rental cottages and recreational vehicle campsites.

At the park's **Kirbo Interpretive Center** you can learn about the city of Florence that once stood where the park is today. In 1836 roughly 1,500 people lived in Florence, and steamboats

docked here in their travels up and down the Chattah
River. A victim of economic changes and natural disaste,
town was virtually gone by 1958 when the Corps of Engi
created the lake. Displays at the Kirbo Center also tell abou
flora and fauna of the area and the Indians—Mound Peo
Mississippian and Creek. Just south of the park are the **R**
Creek Indian Mounds, and park personnel give free 1½-hc
tours on Saturday at 10:00 A.M. For information on the tours ca
(912)838-4706 or 838-4244.

Dating from 900 A.D. to 1540 A.D., this site has eight earthen
mounds making it the largest Indian settlement in the Chattahoochee River basin. At its height between 3,000 and 4,000 Indians lived here. The prehistoric Mound People built five ceremonial mounds on a large flat bluff overlooking the river.
Originally this settlement was surrounded by two moats roughly
ten feet deep and six to eight feet across. Part of the original moat
is pointed out during the tour. The largest mound is a five-sided
pyramid 25 feet high, the smallest, a mere three-foot-high circular
mound. Two of the mounds were dramatically altered in shape
by years of farming.

When the Rood Creek Site was excavated in the 1950s, it was
discovered that it had served as a business, political and religious
center and not a burial center (although the remains of two children were found). Unlike the mounds at Kolomoki and Etowah
(see selections), these have not been cleared. It makes an interesting comparison to see mounds covered with trees and brush.

As you travel from the park headquarters to the mound site
you will pass Shepherd Plantation, where one of the last battles
of the Creek War took place. Three hundred Indians attacked a
group of Georgia volunteers at this plantation, just shortly after
burning the town of Roanoke down the river.

Florence Marina State Park is open from 7:00 A.M. to 10:00 P.M.
daily. The office is open only from 8:00 A.M. to 5:00 P.M.

Directions: From I-185 take Exit 1, Route 27, east to Lumpkin.
At Lumpkin take Route 39C west for 16 miles to the park.

Heritage Corner

City on the Chattahoochee

Columbus was founded in 1828 on land strategically located on
the Chattahoochee River. Harnessing the power of the river's
waterfalls, the city fathers quickly created a major manufacturing
and trading center.

Columbus's 1976 Bicentennial project was a reclamation of the
Chattahoochee Promenade, a greenbelt along the river included

in the original layout of the city. The restored walkway has historic markers that highlight the development of the city and its role in the Civil War. The 430-seat River Front Amphitheater, built at the corner of Front Avenue and 6th Street where Confederate warships were once constructed and launched, now offers free outdoor shows. Call (706)571-4895 for schedule.

A block away is the Promenade Center, a renovated Victorian cottage built in the 1860s. Here you find an exhibit on the growth of Columbus. Adjacent to the center is a gazebo housing Columbus's Liberty Bell, one of 100 cast by Whitechapel Bell Foundry in London, creators of the original bell in Philadelphia.

To the east of the promenade lies the 26-block **Columbus Historic District**. At the heart of the district, included on the National Register of Historic Places, are five homes that comprise Heritage Corner. The best place to start is in the Historic Columbus Foundation headquarters at 700 Broadway. This gracious two-story Italianate townhouse built in 1870 is one of the few 19th-century brick houses remaining within the boundaries of the original city. It has four decorated museum rooms on the first floor. Tours are given twice a day at 11:00 A.M. and 3:00 P.M. and on weekends at 2:00 P.M. There is a nominal fee for the tours.

Next door at 708 Broadway is **Period Pieces**, a museum and gift shop, that was moved to this site. A cottage from the 1840s, formerly the Woodruff farm house, is open Monday through Friday from 10:00 A.M. to 4:00 P.M. Behind the gift shop is a log cabin representing the lifestyle of traders and settlers who preceded the establishment of Columbus.

Adjacent to the log cabin is the 1828 **Walker-Peters-Langdon House**, the oldest house in the original city of Columbus. The land was purchased for $105 by Colonel Virgil Walker the year that the city was founded. The cottage is an early prefabricated house with four rooms furnished with early to mid-19th century pieces. One of the few items original to the house is a rocker made by a member of the third family to live here. There are several Georgia-made pieces including the 1810 sideboard. Behind the house there is a Victorian garden as well as a slave cabin (also furnished), the drying house, necessary and a dovecote.

The fifth and last house on Heritage Corner is actually around the corner at 11 Seventh Street. From 1855 to 1860 the **Pemberton House** was the home of Dr. John Stith Pemberton, a Columbus druggist who invented the formula for Coca-Cola. There are those who claim that the "French Wine of Coca" that he served patrons in the Eagle Drug and Chemical Company in Columbus was the forerunner of the Coca-Cola he eventually created while living in Atlanta in the 1870s and 1880s. Pemberton sold the formula shortly before his death in 1888 and made only $1,750 from his invention. (You'll learn that if all the Coca-Cola ever produced

were placed in 6½-ounce bottles and placed end to end, they would wrap around the equator 21,161 times!)

Dr. Pemberton's house, a Greek Revival cottage, is furnished with period pieces that include a few family heirlooms. The parlor table belonged to the family, and the rolling pin in the kitchen was made by Mrs. Pemberton's father. An oil portrait of John Pemberton hangs in the parlor; daguerreotypes (early photographs) of the family appear throughout the house. Behind the house, in what was once the kitchen, is the Pemberton Apothecary Shop that houses a substantial array of Coca-Cola memorabilia. There are two soda fountains and a collection of apothecary jars.

After touring these five properties pick up a map of the historic district and drive around the tree-lined streets. One unusual spot you should look for is "**The Folly**," a private home at 527 First Avenue. Columbus's first National Historic Landmark, it bears the distinction of being the only historic double-octagon house in the country. This antebellum structure was converted to its present neo-Gothic shape in 1861.

A second historic district called **High Uptown** is also worth exploring. Columbus's wealthiest and most influential citizens made their homes in this area between 1850 and 1920. Most of the homes now serve as headquarters for civic organizations and as commercial properties.

The **Rankin House**, owned and operated by the Historic Columbus Foundation, is one of the few homes in the High Uptown district that is open for tours. Hours are Monday, Tuesday and Thursday from 9:00 A.M. to 1:00 P.M. Although the French Empire style house was started before the Civil War it was not finished until 1870. The elaborate iron grillwork on the house is reminiscent of Natchez and New Orleans. The lower floor has been restored as an 1850–1879 house museum and is filled with Victorian furniture and decorative pieces.

Other homes of note in the Uptown district are the Swift-Kyle House, 303 Twelfth Street, a Greek Revival house with 11 Corinthian columns on its U-shaped porch; the Lion House, 1316 Third Avenue, which has six Greek "Tower-of-the-Winds" columns and a flying balcony; and the Illges House, 1428 Second Avenue, an antebellum mansion that has been called a textbook example of Southern Greek Revival style.

One of the most exceptional antebellum homes in the Columbus Historic District is the **Goetchius House** at 405 Broadway. Now an elegant restaurant, this 1839 house was designed in the popular Second Era of New Orleans style with a wide front veranda and ornamental iron lacework. Goetchius, a member of a New York Dutch family, was an architect and builder, and he supervised the construction of his home which stood originally at 11th Street and 2nd Avenue. The interior has been restored in Victorian and Empire periods, and the cuisine is continental.

Directions: Traveling south on I-85 take I-185 at LaGrange to Columbus. Take Exit 7 when approaching Columbus. Take Exit 7 to Exit 1 which is 2nd Avenue. Take 2nd Avenue to 9th Street. Turn right onto 9th Street to Broadway. Take a left onto Broadway and you will be in the Historic District.

Jimmy Carter National Historic Site

Georgia Roots

Think of the homes of our recent presidents:the Truman House in Independence, Missouri; the Eisenhower family home in Abilene, Kansas; Kennedy's birthplace in Brookline, Massachusetts; the LBJ ranch in Stonewall, Texas, and Nixon's birthplace in Yorba Linda, California. Each seems to stand apart from its environment. Jimmy Carter, the 39th president, is so much a man of the people, most particularly the people of communities like **Plains**, that visiting his hometown tells you almost as much about him as reading can. This town shaped the boy and supported the man, and it was to Plains that Jimmy Carter returned after his tenure in Washington.

The story of Jimmy Carter's life unfolds as you drive around this rural community. There are three self-touring options: a free self-guided walking/driving tour supplied at the Visitor Center, a booklet on sale at most of the stores that outlines a 30-minute driving tour, or a cassette driving-tour tape, also available at the Visitor Center on which the former President and Mrs. Carter guide you and tell about growing up in Plains.

At **B.J.'s Pitt Stop**, formerly Billy Carter's Service Station, you can join an escorted tour of the area. Tours run Monday through Saturday beginning at 9:00 A.M. and continuing as long as people request them. They last an hour and cost $5 per person. When folks in Plains talk about the Carters, they are talking about people they know. As you listen to them you sense the pride they take in their famous neighbor, the only Georgian ever elected president, and the first from the Deep South since the Civil War.

Tours start at the railroad depot, now the Visitor Center for the Jimmy Carter National Historic Site, open daily 9:00 A.M. to 5:00 P.M., except for Christmas and New Year's Day. When the renovation of the Plains school is completed the Visitor Center will be housed there. In 1976 the old **Seaboard Railroad Depot** was the headquarters of the Carter Presidential Campaign. It currently houses a small photographic exhibit and shows an intro-

Where it all began: Jimmy Carter's boyhood home in Plains.

ductory film about the Carters. Unlike the slick professional films at most historic attractions, this one has the charm of a home movie. Jimmy and Rosalynn give a relaxed tour of the house they still call home. He points out the furniture he made, and she notes gifts they received from world leaders. You'll learn what they eat, how they spend their time, and by the time the film ends you'll feel you've come to know the Carters personally.

On the escorted driving tour of Plains, the driver usually takes visitors into the Carter compound to give them a close look at the Carters' home. When he left the White House the presidential staff gave Carter a complete set of woodworking tools, and he, with Rosalynn, built the split-rail cedar fence that lines his property.

As you drive around Plains you begin to feel that everybody is related to one or the other of the Carters, but not quite all of the 680 residents are extended family. You'll see the **Wellons Home** where Jimmy Carter's parents, Miss Lillian and Earl Carter, had an apartment after they married. This Victorian home is now the Plains Bed-and-Breakfast Inn (912)824-7252. You'll also see the Lillian G. Carter Nursing Center, formerly the Wise Sanitarium, where on October 1, 1924, Jimmy Carter was born, the first U.S. president to be born in a hospital. When Jimmy was four, the family moved to a farm four miles southwest of Plains; it too is on the tour. He lived here until he was 18, attending school, helping with the chores and hunting and fishing with his friends.

Young Jimmy walked the four miles into town to attend Plains High School, where he attended grades one through 11 (at the time he graduated, the school did not go to the 12th grade). Rosalynn also attended school here, making them the only presidential couple to have attended the same school throughout the years preceding their high school graduation. Carter was greatly influenced by Miss Julia Coleman, one of his teachers, whose house is also noted on the tour. He quoted her in his inaugural address: She told her students, "Any schoolboy, even one of ours, might grow up to be president of the United States." Another of her quotes that Carter took to heart was the message that "we must adjust to changing times and still hold to unchanging principles." Once the high school is restored it will be the main Visitors Center for the National Park Service's National Historic Site and will highlight four themes of importance to Plains and other small towns across the country: family, agriculture, education and religion.

Both of the Carters are closely associated with the churches of Plains. While growing up Jimmy Carter attended the Plains Baptist Church and eventually served as teacher and deacon. Rosalynn attended the Plains United Methodist Church, and Jimmy proposed to her on the steps leading into the church. They were married here in 1946. When the Carters returned from Washington they began attending the Marantha Baptist Church, and when he is in town Jimmy Carter teaches its 10:00 A.M. Sunday school class. A sign is posted in Hugh Carter's antique store on Main Street informing when Jimmy will be teaching.

All the tours take you past the homes of brothers, cousins and in-laws. The family's former peanut business is now the Golden Peanut Company. Peanuts are still big business in this part of the South. It is said that roughly one ton of peanuts are shelled every 15 minutes. Most of the stores in town have them for sale.

For more information, write the Jimmy Carter National Historic Site, P.O. Box 392, Plains, GA 31780. Or call (912)824-3514 or 824-3413.

Directions: From I-75 take Route 280 west past Americus to Plains.

Little White House and Warm Springs

Personal Side of Public Man

Franklin Delano Roosevelt came from a wealthy, influential family. But the only home he built to his personal specifications, the Little White House, was far more modest than his ancestral home at Hyde Park, New York, or the rambling Campobello estate in Maine.

Three years after Roosevelt, a young New York attorney, was stricken with polio, he heard about the partial recovery of another young victim, Louis Joseph. The Joseph family had a summer home near Pine Mountain, and the warm spring water helped Louis's paralyzed muscles. Roosevelt, on the verge of despair over his own condition, headed for the Georgia resort and immediately became a familiar pool-side figure. Roosevelt, too, noticed an improvement in his condition. Once he began regaining some feeling in his legs his mood improved, as did his languishing political career. He had been the 1920 vice presidential candidate, but he wasn't elected to office until 1928 when he became governor of New York. In 1932 he was overwhelmingly elected president of the United States.

The concern and empathy Roosevelt felt for the suffering and the underprivileged influenced the programs he inaugurated to cope with the Great Depression. Techniques for improving livestock breeding, crop rotation and reforestation grew out of work done around Roosevelt's Georgia retreat. Many other New Deal programs had their roots in the experiences Roosevelt had at Warm Springs.

The first eight years Roosevelt visited **Warm Springs** he stayed in various summer cottages, but while still governor he decided to build his own retreat. He picked a site on the north slope of Pine Mountain overlooking a deep wooded ravine. The natural setting was preserved at Roosevelt's request, and only essential landscaping around the house was undertaken. His six-room cottage cost $8,738.14. Roosevelt moved into the Little White House on May 1, 1932, and before the week was out gave a big party (at a cost of $31 for supplies) "for the residents of the village of Warm Springs—also the Foundation patients, guests, employees and cottagers."

Although the waters of Warm Springs did not cure Roosevelt, they were highly beneficial. Roosevelt wanted to make the healthy waters more widely available, so with associates he created the Georgia Warm Springs Foundation. Each year on his birthday the Foundation sponsored a ball to raise funds for its work and for polio research. **The March of Dimes** evolved from these early fund raising efforts. Near the Little White House you can still see pools of 88-degree spring water. The Foundation, now called the Roosevelt Warm Springs Institute for Rehabilitation, provides help to more than 3,000 people each year.

If you drive through the grounds you pass the McCarthy cottage where Roosevelt often stayed. The back view closely resembles that of the Little White House. Pine Mountain Trolley Tours, originating in Pine Mountain and at Callaway Gardens, offer a great deal of information about former residents and the community of Warm Springs. Call (706)663-4000.

The Little White House looks the way it did when Roosevelt died here on April 12, 1945. When you visit make sure you stop first at the **Franklin D. Roosevelt Museum** housed in Miss Georgia Wilkins's former home. Roosevelt's neighbor was noted for her thriftiness (reputedly she used paper napkins twice), yet she gave her two-million-dollar estate, Mustian Place, to the Foundation. Within this museum you'll see photographs and memorabilia such as carved canes, an old fishing hat, wheelchairs, gifts Roosevelt received while president and candid snapshots as well as dated newspapers. It's interesting to see what a good looking boy and handsome young man Roosevelt was. A not-to-be-missed 12-minute film has rare home movies of Roosevelt enjoying the therapeutic waters, picnicking at Dowdell's Knob and relaxing at the Little White House.

The path from the museum to the house leads down the Walk of States lined with flags and stones from each state. On entering the fenced grounds, you pass the bump gate Roosevelt added. It opened with pressure from car bumpers. There's also a sentry house at the gate, one of eight built when Roosevelt became president. A detachment of 65 Marines guarded the compound when he was in residence. In the garage sit his 1940 Willys roadster and a 1938 Ford convertible with a license plate that reads: "1945, FDR 1, Georgia." The president drove the specially hand-levered Ford for six years. In the book, *Splendid Deception*, Hugh Gallagher tells about Roosevelt's driving and how the media protected him by not disclosing the extent of his disabilities. Many Americans never realized that the president could not walk. The servants' quarters are upstairs in the garage, and opposite is a small rustic cottage used for guests.

Though you tour the Little White House on your own you get recorded messages in each room describing the major features. Visitors enter through the kitchen. Be sure to look for the penciled note by the pantry door. It reads: "Daisy Bonner cook (sic) the first meal and the last one in this cottage for the President Roosevelt." In the combination living and dining room you see the famous unfinished portrait. The president was sitting in his favorite chair posing for artist Elizabeth Shoumatoff when he suffered his fatal stroke. The portrait stands on the easel just as she left it that tragic day. The room also has several ship models that reflect Roosevelt's great love of the sea. In fact, the sundeck off the room is shaped like the fantail of a ship. Roosevelt enjoyed many of his meals out on this deck overlooking the ravine.

Two bedrooms open onto the sundeck. On one side of the

house is his secretary's bedroom, while on the other side of the deck is the President's bedroom, the simplest room in the cottage. A small hooked rug, a tufted coverlet on the three-quarter size bed, a sea chest and a Storm-o-guide on the wall—these and a few utilitarian pieces of furniture are all that Roosevelt added to his room. This is the way he lived and this is where he died. Off the president's bedroom was Mrs. Roosevelt's room, although she joined him in Warm Springs only infrequently. In the entry hall through which you exit, look for Fala's dog chain and the scratch marks the Scottie made on the front door.

The Little White House State Historic Site is open daily from 9:00 A.M. to 5:00 P.M., though the last full tour begins at 4:15 P.M. A nominal admission is charged.

When you visit the Little White House you should stop in the town that Roosevelt took to his heart. Warm Springs has recently undergone a major face lift, and boutiques, eateries and the restored Hotel Warm Springs, now a bed-and-breakfast, grace Main Street. Handicrafts, gourmet food items, antiques, old-fashioned dolls and doll houses, books and clothes are available in profusion. There are also some dining spots. The Victorian Tea Room, (706) 655-2319, is located in an old general merchandise store that has been renovated and filled with delightful handicraft items. The food is popular with locals and a treat for daytrippers. Another charming spot is the Bulloch House Restaurant, (706) 655-9068, in an old Victorian home built in 1892. The Tuscawilla Soda Co. & Restaurant, where Roosevelt occasionally dined, is now part of the Hotel Warm Springs, (706) 655-2114.

Avid fishermen and young children will enjoy a stop at the Warm Springs National Fish Hatchery just outside of town. The hatchery raises striped bass in outdoor pools and includes them among other fish in the exhibits in their indoor aquarium. This hatchery, established in 1905, has 40 production ponds raising striped bass to stock Gulf Coast waters. The aquarium is open 7:30 A.M. to 4:00 P.M.

Directions: From I-85 take I-185 south, and at Exit 14 take Route 27 south to the town of Pine Mountain, continue south of the town of Pine Mountain and turn left on Route 190, which takes you through F.D. Roosevelt State Park (see selection). At the intersection with Route 85W make a left, and the Little White House Historic Site will be on your left. If you want to visit the natural warm springs Roosevelt enjoyed and see the community pool (plans are under way to reopen this pool), take Route 27A for a quarter of a mile west from the Warm Springs traffic light.

National Infantry Museum

Home of the Infantry and Mother-in-law of the Army

The fighting in World War I underscored the need for good infantry training. In the spring of 1918 a search began to select a site for an infantry school. The Columbus area was picked, and on October 1, 1921, the first troops arrived at **Fort Benning**. The Columbus Rotary Club requested that the post be named for the town's most honored military leader, Confederate General Henry Lewis Benning.

Today the fort is the largest infantry training center in the world. The 182,000-acre installation, called the "Home of the Infantry," trains 67,000 infantry students a year. Fort Benning also trains the all-volunteer Ranger and Airborne troops. It is the base for the U.S. Forces Command units (comprised of the 3rd Brigade, 24th Infantry Division, the 36th Engineer Group). The 75th Ranger Regiment Headquarters are here as well and, finally, the home of the School of Americas.

Fort Benning acquired the nickname the "mother-in-law of the army" at the beginning of World War II when four out of five of the commanding general's staff officers had wives from Columbus. They still like to tell about General Patton's World War II tenure at Fort Benning. The general became concerned because too many of his men were being arrested across the river in Phoenix City, on charges he felt were overly harsh. Patton lined up tanks along the river bank and told the city fathers to let his soldiers go—and they did! Thereafter, Patton had the men paid in silver dollars so that the locals would be visually reminded of the military's contribution to their economy.

When you visit the **National Infantry Museum**, on the base's Baltzell Road, be sure to allow ample time. History and military buffs could easily spend a day and not see all of the 30,000 plus items. It takes several hours just to get an overview of the three floors of exhibits.

The main floor has a gallery of military art, a collection of military documents with the signatures of all the U.S. presidents, an exhibit of military band instruments, an array of silver presentation pieces and weapons. Some of the arms date from the 16th century including a double-handed espadon from Switzerland, a Danish infantry spontoon and a French halberd. The halberd was a symbol of authority for non-commissioned officers. British army sergeants of infantry and artillery carried a halberd, using it to keep men in a straight line during drills. In the British army the officers never spoke directly to regular soldiers but spoke to the non-commissioned officers who issued orders to their troops. British soldiers who did not wear wigs often used flour and tallow in their hair to create the same effect. The problem with that method was that it attracted head lice and other bugs.

The infantry is America's oldest branch of service. Ten companies of riflemen were authorized by the Continental Congress on June 14, 1775. But the real father of the U.S. Infantry was the Prussian **Baron Friedrich Wilhelm von Steuben**, as the museum display shows. Von Steuben drilled the Continental army at Valley Forge during the winter of 1778 and wrote a manual for drill that was used by the army for the next 33 years.

On the second floor the American collection begins with pieces from 1750 and extends to the Pacific portion of World War II, following the steps of the foot soldiers across two centuries. Details of the conflicts involving American soldiers start with the Revolutionary War and continue through the Persian Gulf crisis of 1991.

Only historians and military buffs are likely to know that our 14th president, Franklin Pierce, went from private to general in a matter of months during the Mexican War. His duffel bag is on exhibit. Pierce, a dark-horse candidate for president, had his horse shot from under him during the war with Mexico.

Visitors will discover the derivation of the term "leathernecks" when they see an example of the leather collars infantrymen and Marines once wore to protect them from sabre wounds. The exhibits on the Civil War reveal a wealth of little-known information. One learns, for example, that for every day in battle, the men spent roughly 50 days in camp. At the start of the war infantrymen on both sides wore gray uniforms; the resulting confusion prompted the Union troops to switch to dark blue. The second floor also has special exhibits on Fort Benning and on America's Medal of Honor winners.

In addition to in-depth displays on the American soldiers in World War II, the museum's third floor has an extensive array of captured military paraphernalia—uniforms, medals, flags and weapons from Nazi Germany, Imperial Japan and Fascist Italy. From the more recent past there are General Manual Noriega's flag and helmet and Iraqi guns and uniforms obtained during Operation Desert Storm. Altogether this is a fascinating repository of America's military past.

The National Infantry Museum is open at no charge Monday through Friday from 8:00 A.M. to 4:30 P.M. and on weekends from 12:30 to 4:30 P.M. Tours can be arranged by calling (706)545-2958.

Directions: From I-185, exit right onto Dixie Road, then right on 1st Divison Road. Make another right on Baltzell Road. The museum will be on your right.

Pasaquan

Passing Belief

It would be hard to imagine a more incongruous sight than Eddie Owens Martin's Pasaquan. St. EOM, as he styled himself, was a visionary artist and a unique character. When he was 14, he left his home, a Georgia sharecropper's farm where he was born, and headed for New York City. During the 1920s he worked in the theater district at a variety of jobs. In the Depression he rode freight trains and spent a year in prison on a narcotics charge. After an illness in 1935, he felt he was reborn as St. EOM. To fashion the symbols of his new faith he borrowed a little from the religious art he had studied at New York's Metropolitan Museum.

When he inherited the family farm from his mother in 1957, he proceeded to create a phantasmagorical compound, painting and decorating virtually every square foot of the farm both inside and out, including the outbuildings, walls and fences. Even the doghouse bears his distinctive touch. Pasaquan, as he called it, means "where the past meets the future." Part temple, part fortress and part dance platform, it borrowed symbols and imagery from Oriental, African and American Indian mythologies.

Speaking of his enclave, Martin said, "I built this place to have something to identify with. Here I can be in my own world, with my temples and designs and the spirit of God. I can have my own spirits and my own thoughts." He was the High Priest of his own one-man religion and created his own house of worship.

As your attention shifts from one colorful mural to another, the eyes, large and small, in his creations seem to be watching you. Giant faces and figures march across the stone fence, some drawn with great attention to anatomical details, others merely sketched. All are colorful and riveting. Geometric shapes, bright flowers and brilliant borders bedazzle the eye. This is folk art carried to its zenith. If you had to compare it with other places, you might think of the mysterious sculpture on Easter Island or the Pre-Columbian ruins in Mexico, but these lack the riotous colors of Martin's creations.

To help finance his efforts, St. EOM told fortunes. A steady stream of visitors showed up to share in his view of the future. He also sold beadwork that he created with the help of apprentices.

On April 16, 1986, by then in failing health, Eddie Martin took his revolver and fired one shot into his temple. He died at Pasaquan. If you are intrigued by your visit to Pasaquan, you should have a look at an excellent book by Tom Patterson called *St. EOM in the Land of Pasaquan*, published by the Jargon Society. It is available at In Season on the Square in Buena Vista. Tours of Pasaquan can be arranged at this store as well or from the Marion County Historical Society by calling (912)649-9444. At present, the grounds are open Saturday from 10:00 A.M. to 6:00 P.M. and Sunday from 1:00 to 6:00 P.M. The interior rooms will be open following restoration.

Just outside Buena Vista is Yesteryear Inn (912)649-7307. This old house built in 1866 is filled with antiques and unusual mementos from the town doctor and his family who once lived here. Staying here is like being at your grandmother's, adrift in quilts and feather beds.

Directions: From I-75 take Route 26 to Buena Vista. From there head north on Route 137. After .9 miles the road forks; veer left and continue on Route 137. When you cross Big Sandy Creek bridge watch for Road 78, a paved county road. Turn right on Route 78 and continue for .6 miles, and Pasaquan will be on your right.

Pine Mountain Wild Animal Park

Drive in the Wild

Up close and personal. That's the way you experience the animals at the Pine Mountain Wild Animal Park. You can look deeply into the limpid eyes of a gaur, wildebeest or zebra. They are but three of the 300 species that roam the park's more than 500 acres.

The park owes its existence to the Snider family. When Ron Snider sold his ambulance company in the mid-1980s, he and his wife, Vivian, spent three years traveling the world to see animals in the wild. They took small planes to isolated spots, camped and trekked to see magnificent beasts in their natural environments. They also visited game parks. At the end of their travels they wanted nothing more than to share this adventure with others. They also wanted to give young children an appreciation of the wonders of nature. Thus the idea of a game park was born. The Sniders incorporated all the things they had observed in their travels, copying no one particular park but adding the best parts of many. Their main concern was to allow the animals to roam free.

Remarkably, it took Ron Snider only one year to realize his dream. After consulting with designers, he decided to lay out the park on his own. With six assistants he walked the woods laying out the road and marking every single tree for cutting or saving. He left most of the trees and the underbrush so that

Tourists are not the only rubbernecks at Pine Mountain Wild Animal Park.

spotting the animals would be as much of a challenge as it is in the wild.

Pine Mountain Wild Animal Park opened in June 1991, and before the end of the first year there were more than 3,000 animals in residence. Since the United States leads the world in raising exotic animals for restocking, it was not difficult to obtain the animals. Specimens include spotted axis deer, muntjac, addax, water buffalo, camels, llamas, elands, gnu, elk, Himalayan tahr, mouflon, antelope, Watusi aoudad and still more. The park does not have predators like lions, tigers and bears because of the danger they pose, though special shows are planned featuring these carnivorous beasts.

In the drive-through area all the animals roam free except for the giraffe and the white rhino. The giraffe are penned because they have to be housed when the temperature drops below 40 degrees, and it would be quite a task to try to gather them if they were roaming free. In the last wild game park the rhino called home, it was not penned. Visitors became unnerved when this mammoth creature came up to their car window to get food. They often dropped the food right outside the window, and the rhino frequently pushed the car out of the way with its giant horn to get the food. Fearing any repeat, Ron Snider decided in favor of penning.

There are several suggestions that will increase your enjoyment of the park. You can travel through the game preserve as many times as you want on your own, so it's best to take the bus tour first. The guide will identify the species and point out the areas where you're likely to see various animals. Before you drive through on your own, purchase one or two buckets of food. The real thrill of visiting Pine Mountain Wild Game Park comes from actually feeding these incredible specimens. You may feel like the Pied Piper as the animals follow your car along the drive. The speed limit is only five miles per hour and should be strictly followed. You'll want to go slow in order to see the animals, but you also need to go slow to protect creatures who may dart across the road or be sunning in the middle of it. If you want to stop for pictures, pull off to the side so that other cars can pass. Never get out of the car! Remember these are wild animals. Even though they eat out of your hand, they are not domesticated and should be treated warily.

After driving through the park, visit the farm area. **Old McDonald's Farm** is directly behind the gift and snack shop. At this working farm, cows are milked, eggs are gathered and the animals fed. There is a petting area where children can pet the deer, sheep, pigs and goats. Nearby is the strictly hands-off alligator pit where you'll see a 13-foot gator, one of the largest in captivity, and the serpentorium with boa constrictors, pythons and other exotic snakes. More playful are the inhabitants of the monkey house.

Before leaving, you might want to take one more drive through the park to see if you spot any previously hidden beasts. The animals are more active in the early morning and the late afternoon hours. If you are going to be in the area in the evening you might want to sign up for a hayride. During the rides attendants will shine spotlights on the animals. Dinner is prepared on the outdoor grills, and the evening winds up with story-telling and sing-alongs. There are picnic tables and grills for use by visitors at any time of day.

Pine Mountain Wild Animal Park is open daily, except Christmas, at 9:30 A.M. The admission is high, but the visit is definitely a once-in-a-lifetime experience, totally unlike most drive-through parks and worlds away from a day at the zoo.

Directions: From I-185 south take Exit 5. This will put you on I-185 south, which you take to Exit 14, where you turn left and cross over the interstate. Now you will be on Route 27 south. Take this for 6.8 miles and turn right on Oak Grove Road. The park is two miles on your left. From the Columbus area, take I-185 north to Exit 13, turn right and you will be on Route 18. Take this to the first traffic light (you will be in Pine Mountain), and turn left onto Route 27 north. Take Route 27 for roughly three miles and turn right on Oak Grove Road. The park is two miles beyond on your left.

Providence Canyon State Conservation Park

Georgia's Little Grand Canyon

Providence Canyon is one of the seven natural wonders of Georgia, and its scenic beauty fully warrants such a distinction. Its appeal, however, extends far beyond the state's borders. It could justifiably be considered one of the country's scenic wonders. If the breathtaking vistas are the first thing to overwhelm visitors, the second thing is learning that these canyons were formed less than 150 years ago.

The 16 canyons within the 1,108-acre park were formed in the early 1800s when settlers began clearing trees in order to farm the land. Cultivation caused the loose grained, easily eroded soil to wash away. By 1850 there were ditches between three and five feet deep. Over the years the ditches became canyons that are now 150 feet deep. Some of these canyons are over a half mile long and 300 feet across. Within the canyons, striking rock formations jut out and up from the canyon floor. Folklorists of the region claim that the canyons were formed when one of the women settlers continually threw out her dish water over her back porch, each day eroding the soil a little more.

The erosion caused by the poor farming practices gradually eliminated the upper-layer of red sandy clay, called the Clayton Foundation. It is iron ore in the soil that gives this roughly 25-foot-thick layer its color. Beneath that is the colorful sandy soil geologists call the Providence Foundation, roughly 150 feet thick. More than 80 million years ago the ocean coastline receded leaving sandy deposits in this region. The presence of a wide range of mineral deposits creates the colorful hues—tan, buff, pink, salmon, orange, red, lavender and snowy white—that make the canyon so visually exciting. A system of cross bedding gives the layered look to the canyon walls. At the lowest level—the Perote—fossils are embedded in the sand and clay. Underlying this is the Ripley Foundation, the floor of the ancient ocean. Its erosion-resistant clay-like soil prevents the canyons from being cut deeper, but the canyons do continue to get wider.

Once the erosion began it proved impossible to halt, although in the 1930s the Civilian Conservation Corps planted trees and built impediments to try to stop the run-off. It was not until 1971 that the area was designated as a state park in order to protect and preserve its scenic splendor.

The park interpretive center, open 8:00 A.M. to 5:00 P.M. daily, has a ten-minute narrated slide show that provides a great deal of background information about the canyon, its wild denizens and its unique wildflowers. Abundant and rare wildflowers grow in the deep canyons; spring and fall give hikers the biggest variety of blossoms. Providence Canyon has the largest wild stand of the rare plumleaf azalea in the world. Blooming from late July to September, these azaleas come in a wide range of colors, from light orange to salmon and brilliant shades of red. You may spot the yellow-fringed orchid, big leaf magnolia, Cherokee rose, false foxglove, lupine, dwarf iris and cardinal flower to name just a few of the more than 150 varieties that have been identified.

The best way to get a panoramic view is from one of the several overlooks that rim the canyon, but if you have time the park has seven miles of hiking trails, including the three-mile **Rim Trail**. These trails give you an altogether different perspective. It's only a quarter of a mile down to the canyon floor, but keep in mind when it comes time to climb back up it seems more like two miles. Nine of the canyons can be explored on the day-use trails. The rest of the 16 canyons are on the back side and can be explored only on the seven-mile back-packing trail, which also leads to overnight camping areas. Hikers who frequent the park particularly recommend exploring canyon four and five for their striking beauty.

There are 65 picnic tables in the park and two picnic shelters. If you are visiting with young children be sure to allow time for them to create a unique souvenir at the center. For a nominal fee, visitors can fill a glass bottle with colorful sand from the canyon.

Providence Canyon State Conservation Park is open from 7:00 A.M. to 6:00 P.M. from mid-September through mid-April. The rest of the year it stays open until 9:00 P.M.

Directions: From I-185 take Exit 1 and head east on Route 27 toward Lumpkin. At Lumpkin, take Route 39C west and the park will be on your left.

Westville

A Georgia Williamsburg

The crowds are not as thick and the era depicted is not as early, but there are definite parallels between Williamsburg and Westville. Williamsburg brings to life Colonial Virginia: the homes, shops, government buildings, taverns, churches and even hospitals. Westville brings pre-industrial West Georgia to life.

This was the time after the land lottery dispersed the Indian holdings to the settlers and before the Civil War turned the soil red with their blood. In the 1850s the economy in many parts of Georgia changed from agricultural to industrial.

Westville was never a real town. The buildings you see here are from Stewart and surrounding counties. They were relocated, restored and furnished with period pieces. Life is depicted as it once was lived. Craftsmen are busy in their shops, teachers in the schoolrooms and women in the homes. Smells of gingerbread and biscuits waft through the kitchens and household chores still fill the day.

More than 25 historic homes, shops and public buildings dot the 58-acre landscaped streets of Westville. Visitors who want to settle into the slow pace of this earlier era can ride in mule-drawn carriages that clip-clop along the village's dirt roads. You'll pass the village "residents" going about their daily chores. The village map includes 33 points of interest, including nine private homes. The oldest was built before 1827 by a Yuchi Indian family. After the Indians lost their land, the house was home to several generations of the Wells family. The homes range from the gracious, columned McDonald House (where you can purchase delicious gingerbread and lemonade) to Patterson-Marrett Farmhouse, a typical log house with a dogtrot running through the center. The West House was the home of the grandparents of Colonel John W. West, for whom the village is named.

West, a president of North Georgia College at Dahlonega, collected 19th-century furnishings, tools, carriages and other memorabilia. His will expressed the wish that his collection be used to recreate "a functioning Georgia village of 1850." The first house was moved to Westville in 1968, seven years after West died. Gardens and fields were planted, farm animals were added and Westville opened to the public in 1970.

The village soon acquired its requisite share of public buildings including the two-story frame Chattahoochee County Courthouse, the 1845 Doctor's Office, the Stewart County Academy, the Climax Presbyterian Church, the 1840s Bagley (Cotton) Gin House, the Adams (General) Store, the Yellow Creek Camp Meeting Arbor, plus pottery, blacksmith, cabinet and shoemaker shops. The village entrance is marked by a replica of the triple gates to the old state Capitol grounds at Milledgeville, one of Georgia's most well-known landmarks.

Celebrations in the village also bring back a bygone era, like the Fair of 1850 held annually in late October. The harvest-time festivities include cane grinding and syrup making. The traditions of West Georgia settlers' European homelands are joyfully incorporated into the Christmas season. Music of the era sets feet to tapping during the spring festival in April, and the patriotism of the new country is celebrated on the Fourth of July.

Westville is open Tuesday through Saturday from 10:00 A.M. to 5:00 P.M. and on Sunday from 1:00 to 5:00 P.M. Closed on major holidays. The nominal fee covers admission to all the exhibit buildings.

Before leaving Lumpkin you may want to include a stop at the **Bedingfield Inn**. This stagecoach hotel from the 1840s is furnished to represent its use by a prosperous family of the era. It was both the family residence of the Bedingfields and a rest stop for travelers on the stagecoach that passed its doors. Dr. Bedingfield was the first physician in the county, and his son, who also became a doctor, was the first white male child born in the county.

The inn's public room where men gathered to smoke and drink and exchange news of crops and politics has been recreated. A ladies' parlor is also furnished, as are two private family rooms. The family bedrooms and guest accommodations are upstairs. The Bedingfield Inn is open Tuesday through Sunday from 1:00 to 5:00 P.M. An admission is charged.

A **Stagecoach Trail** around Lumpkin routes you past private homes from the 1830s and 1840s. This drive-by tour takes you past 22 architecturally interesting houses. You can pick up a map either at Westville or at the Bedingfield Inn.

On the town square in Lumpkin stop at the Hatchett Drug Store and see a collection of old medicines, nostrums and sundries. During the summer months ice cream is sold in this old store. It is open concurrently with the inn, and one fee covers admission to both.

Also on the square is **The Singer Company**, Georgia's oldest hardware store. It was opened in 1838 by a German immigrant as a boot and shoemaking shop but expanded over the years. The shop still has its original showcases, rolling ladders, bolt cabinets and other fixtures. Today you can purchase Depression glass, local jams and jellies, wooden and cast toys and other giftware and hardware.

Directions: From I-85 take I-185 south to Columbus, then continue south on Route 27 to Lumpkin (at the intersection of U.S. 27 and Georgia 27). Follow the signs in Lumpkin. From I-75 head west on Route 280 to Richland. Continue west in Richland on Georgia Route 27 for nine miles to Lumpkin. Bedingfield Inn is on Route 27 on the courthouse square.

Regional Trail and State Parks

Andersonville Trail

Length: 75 miles

Gateways: You can access the trail via I-75 south at Perry and at Warner Robins, via I-75 north at Cordele and via Highway 280 east at Plains

Theme: Civil War Sites and U.S. Presidents' Sites

Background: Within Central Georgia this trail combines the charm of antebellum and Victorian towns with significant historical sites

Highlights: (sites marked by asterick * are described in individual selections)

*Andersonville National Historic Site with Andersonville National Cemetery and the Prisoner of War Museum

*Andersonville Village

*Jimmy Carter National Historic Site and Plains

Americus: Home of the Carter Library at Georgia Southwestern College and the Historic Hotel Windsor

Veterans Memorial State Park: 8,500-acre Lake Blackshear with boating, fishing, picnicking, golf course, WW I & WW II museum and cabins

Perry Historic District

Whitewater Creek Park: camping, picnicking and fishing

*National Headquarters of the American Camellia Society with Massee Lane Gardens, greenhouse, research library and collection of Boehm porcelain birds

Museum of of Aviation at Robins Air Force Base

State Parks

Florence Marina State Park, Omaha (see selection)
Franklin D. Roosevelt State Park, Pine Mountain (see selection)
Georgia Veterans Memorial State Park, Cordele; offers swimming pool
   and beach, boat ramp and dock, fishing, pioneer camping, water
   skiing, 18-hole golf course, 10 cottages, 85 tent and trailer sites,
   park museum (see Andersonville Trail)
Providence Canyon State Conservation Park, Lumpkin (see selection)

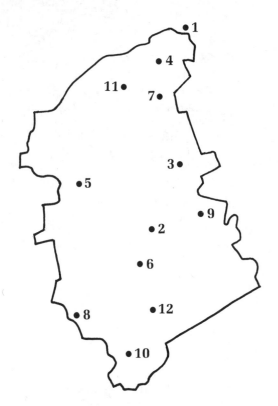

HISTORIC HEARTLAND

1. **Athens**
   Historic District
   Museums
   State Botanical Garden

2. **Clinton**
   Old Clinton and Jarrell
     Plantation State Historic Site

3. **Eatonton**
   Rock Eagle Mounds
   Uncle Remus Museum

4. **Farmington**
   Happy Valley Pottery

5. **Jackson/Indian Springs**
   High Falls State Park
   Noah's Ark

6. **Macon**
   Black Heritage Tour
   Hay House
   Historic Macon
   Ocmulgee National Monument

7. **Madison**
   Madison-Morgan Cultural
     Center and Heritage Hall

8. **Marshallville**
   Massee Lane Gardens

9. **Milledgeville**
   Flannery O'Connor Collection
   Lockerly Arboretum and Woods
     Museum
   Trolley Tours and Old
     Governors' Mansion

10. **Perry**
    Georgia National Fairgrounds
      and Agricenter

11. **Rutledge**
    Hard Labor Creek State Park

12. **Warner Robins**
    Robins Air Force Base Museum
      of Aviation

──Historic Heartland──

The Antebellum Trail winding through this central region takes visitors to the heart of the Old South. This is the South Hollywood brought to the screen in *Gone With the Wind*. Macon, Madison, Milledgeville and Athens are blessed with graceful homes and a rich history.

Heartfelt stories from the blacks who worked the land were captured by Joel Chandler Harris, a legacy explored at Eatonton's Uncle Remus Museum. Other reminders of African-American contributions to the South are found at the Harriet Tubman Museum in Macon.

One can almost feel the quickened heartbeat of the ancient people who sat in the earthlodge at Ocmulgee National Monument. This recreated ceremonial mound, built over the original floor of a mound dating back a thousand years or more, was used for special ceremonies. Also serving a ceremonial purpose are the two huge Rock Eagles near Eagleton.

Feelings from the heart are often shaped by the hands, and this region is rich in skilled craftsmen whose studios can be found here and whose work is exhibited at the Mossy Creek Barnyard and at events at the Georgia National Fairgrounds. Flannery O'Conner's stories captured the South; her work is collected at the library in Milledgeville.

One of the heart-wrenching stories to come out of World War II was Robert L. Scott's *God is My Co-Pilot*. His experiences are just one part of the exhibits covering all aspects of aviation at the Museum of Aviation at Robins Air Force Base.

This richly rewarding region has yet another trail to focus travelers: The Peach Blossom Trail offers a flower-bedecked landscape in spring and a summer-long harvest of sweet, juicy peaches.

Athens Historic District

Three Decades of Antebellum Opulence

In 1801, 633 acres of land on the banks of the Oconee River, amid the rolling foothills of the North Georgia mountains, were purchased by John Milledge, who was then a member of Congress though he returned to Georgia in 1802 to serve as Governor. Milledge gave the land to the board of trustees of the University of Georgia to build the campus for America's first state chartered college, incorporated on January 27, 1785. The view from the hill, where the chapel now stands, reminded Milledge of the Acropolis in Athens, Greece. The new campus community was named after this classical Greek center of learning. The location was considered ideal as it was "far from the sins of city life and the harmful vapors of the coast."

The university's most enduring and recognizable symbol, other than the bulldog, is the arch, which appears on the state's Great Seal. Forged of cast iron in 1857, its three columns represent "Wisdom, Justice, and Moderation."

The Athens Welcome Center is located in a Federal period house built in 1820 that was home to two presidents of the University of Georgia: Alonzo Church and Dr. Moses Waddel. The **Church-Waddel-Brumby House** is the oldest surviving residence in the city. You can tour the house and pick up brochures on the attractions in and around Athens. Be sure to get a walking tour guide to the Athens Historic District, which is listed on the National Register of Historic Places. For three decades the college attracted wealthy residents who built impressive Greek Revival homes along the shaded streets. Athens also has one of the first Main Street programs in the country.

Many of the lovely white-columned mansions are now used by sororities and fraternities; others are used for academic or commercial use. Only one Athens estate is open as a house museum and that is the **Taylor-Grady House**. This Greek Revival house was built in the mid-1840s by General Robert Taylor, who moved to Athens when his sons attended the University of Georgia. In 1863, the house was purchased by Major William S. Grady. His son Henry W. Grady lived here from 1865 to 1868 while attending journalism school at the University. Henry Grady, called the "young Georgia Cicero," became managing editor of the *Atlanta Constitution* and the spokesman for the New South. He wrote of the need for post-war reconciliation between the North and South. Because of its link with Grady, the house is designated as a National Historic Landmark and is furnished with period pieces.

Athens has one of the most unusual relics preserved from the Civil War era. In fact, this is the only **double-barreled cannon** in the world. It was designed by John Gilleland of Athens and forged at a local foundry in 1863. The premise was that this cannon could be loaded with two balls connected by several feet of chain. When the cannon was fired the chain would whirl out and cut down any Northern soldiers in its path. Reports of a test firing revealed that the projectile "had a kind of circular motion, plowed up an acre of ground, tore up a cornfield, mowed down saplings, and the chain broke, the two balls going in opposite directions. One of the balls killed a cow in a distant field, while the other knocked down the chimney from a log cabin. The observers scattered as though the entire Yankee Army had been turned loose in that vicinity." The cannon was presented to the city and has only been fired for ceremonial purposes. It sits today on the lawn of City Hall—pointing North!

Dining options abound but the best of the up-scale spots is **Trumps** at the Georgian, 247 E. Washington Street. In this elegantly restored building, once a historic Athens hotel, you can sample mouth-watering contemporary cuisine and delicious chocolate specialty desserts. For down-scale noshing you can't beat Guthrie's of Athens, 795 Baxter Street, where they have some of the best fried chicken you'll find anywhere in the South. Chocaholics should stop at the Chocolate Shoppe, 216 E. Clayton Street, where they have hand-dipped and imported chocolate as well as luncheon specials.

Athens is gaining a high profile because of its music scene. Popular local groups include the B-52's and R.E.M. Country music star T. Graham Brown started here, and one of his old bands, Rack of Spam, still occasionally plays in town. Check at the Welcome Center for a listing of the various clubs.

The Athens Welcome Center, 280 E. Dougherty Street, is open Monday through Saturday 10:00 A.M. to 5:00 P.M. and Sunday 2:00 to 5:00 P.M. The Taylor-Grady House, 634 Prince Avenue, is open Monday through Friday from 10:00 A.M. to 3:30 P.M., but you should call in advance because the house is occasionally booked for private functions. Call (706)549-8688. A nominal admission is charged for tours.

Directions: From Atlanta take I-85 north, then take Route 316 to its temporary end (it is still under construction), then pick up Route 29 to Athens. Ignore the perimeter by-pass and continue into town on Route 29, which becomes Broad Street. Turn left on Milledge Avenue and then right on Prince Avenue, which becomes Dougherty Street. The Welcome Center will be on your right.

Flannery O'Connor Collection

Brilliant Writer, Gallant Woman

The Savannah-born Flannery O'Connor lived most of her life, from age 13 until her death in 1964, in Milledgeville. After completing college, she lived in New England with poet Robert Fitzgerald and his wife Sally for two years, one of the most fruitful and satisfying periods of her life. Like Flannery, the Fitzgeralds were committed Catholics, and she felt a great affinity for them.

This halcyon period ended in 1950 when Flannery was stricken with lupus, the same illness that had killed her father when she was 15. She recovered from her first attack, and with the help of steroid drugs (debilitating as they were) she was able to move to Andalusia, a farm outside Milledgeville. Her mother, Regina Cline O'Connor, had inherited the 500-acre farm from her brother, who used it as a hunting lodge. Regina turned it into a cattle farm and hired tenant farmers and other laborers to help her. Flannery wrote every day. One of her short stories, "The Displaced Person," was about a Polish tenant family at the farm. For as long as she was able, Flannery attended daily mass. Every Wednesday evening, a group of teachers, clergy and other members of the Milledgeville community met with her at the farm to discuss literature and philosophy.

Shortly after the 1946 publication of O'Connor's first short story, "The Geranium," the Ina Dillard Russell Library staff at Milledgeville's Georgia College set up the Flannery O'Connor Collection. Newspaper reviews, articles, published stories and memorabilia from Flannery's early schooling in town quickly formed the nucleus of the collection. At the end of 1970, Flannery's mother gave the library some of Flannery's manuscripts. Currently there are more than 6,000 pages of manuscripts, including an early draft of her first novel, *Wise Blood*.

The Flannery O'Connor Room at the library is filled with furnishings from Andalusia. Regina O'Connor gave the library Flannery's personal library of more than 700 books and journals. Fiction, critical studies of the major literary figures of her day and theology were her main areas of interest. Many of the volumes are annotated, giving scholars an opportunity to determine various influences on Flannery's own writing.

Flannery's self-portrait, one of several paintings in the room that she did, helps visitors imagine her curled up on her old settee or in the matching armchair, sitting beside the oval table with one of her books or working at her library table. Flannery's love of birds is suggested by the brilliantly colored peacock on the colorful French hand-loomed carpet.

The Flannery O'Connor Collection includes many editions and translations of her work, critical writings about it as well as photographs, tape recordings and a film on Flannery O'Connor. The Flannery O'Connor Room is open weekdays 9:00 A.M. to 5:00 P.M. when the college is in session. Scholars who want to do research must prearrange it with the library staff (call (912)453-5573). Flannery O'Connor T-shirts are available at the Georgia College book store.

Flannery O'Connor is buried at **Memory Hill Cemetery** on Franklin Street between Clark and Wilkinson streets. This is the oldest burial ground in Milledgeville, dating back to Revolutionary War days. When you enter its main gates, turn left and walk to a point about midway down the length of the cemetery, and you'll see on the left the O'Connor plot surrounded by a low stone wall. Flannery is buried beside the father she dearly loved.

While you are exploring Memory Hill Cemetery note the graves of slaves. Their plots are marked by one, two or three rings, any one of which signified that the person buried was born into slavery. Three rings tell that the person died in slavery. Two rings indicate the individual was freed before dying. One ring shows that the person lived most of his/her life in freedom.

Directions: Take I-75 to Macon, then travel northeast on Route 40 to Milledgeville where you will pick-up Route 441 Business that becomes Columbia Street in Milledgeville. From Columbia Street turn left at McIntosh Street, and you will see the Georgia College Campus directly in front of you.

Georgia National Fairgrounds and Agricenter

Old-Fashioned Fairs and Festivals

The state-of-the-art, state-built agricultural center in Perry is a year-round facility. Livestock and horse shows are held here, as well as circuses, concerts, meetings, trade shows, fairs, sporting events, antique exhibits, folk festivals and a host of other events.

One of the biggest events of the year, the **Georgia National Fair**, a state-sponsored, nine-day, old-fashioned fair takes place every October. There is something for everyone at this event that brings together rural and urban Georgia, young and old, professional and amateur. During the fair the Georgia Living Center has exhibits of antiques, fine arts, textiles, food, flowers and other horticultural products. Heritage Hall hosts livestock and horse shows, and in Reaves Arena you find Wild West shows, clowns, marionettes and musical groups. This is all part of the free daily marionettes and musical groups. This is all part of the free daily entertainment. There are also featured artists whose concerts are charged for. A midway has carnival games, rides and nightly fireworks.

The 628-acre complex with three man-made lakes includes a 480-stall horse barn; a beef and dairy barn with show arena; a sheep, swine and goat barn connected by a walkway to the New South Arena. The layout of the fairgrounds is such that even in bad weather visitors can get around without getting wet or muddy. The last weekend in February, or early in March, the annual five-day **Georgia National Stock Show and Rodeo**, one of the largest in the nation, is held here. The rodeo is one of the three largest rodeos east of the Mississippi. Another big event is the mid-March **Georgia Folk Festival** celebrating "Georgiana," with storytelling, dancing, music, arts and crafts.

Three miles from Perry on the third weekend of April and October artisans and craftspeople gather at the Mossy Creek Barnyard to celebrate "The Way it Was. . ." at the **Mossy Creek Arts and Crafts Festival**. In a wide open tree-shaded space there are craft demonstrations, country cooking, old-time music and dancing, storytelling and mule and wagon rides.

The town of Perry annually holds a **Dogwood Festival** in early April. A citywide merchants sidewalk sale draws crowds to Main Street, recently refurbished with a Williamsburg look. Antique hunters can pick up a guide to ten shops in the Perry area at the Welcome Center just off I-75 at Exit 42. The center is open Monday through Saturday from 8:30 A.M. to 5:30 P.M.

Beautiful blossoming peach trees line the streets of Perry by mid-March, and from mid-May through mid-August roadside stands overflow with fresh peaches. Another floriferous spot, from May through June, is **Cranshaw's One Horse Farm and Day Lily Garden**. More than 400 varieties of day lilies are shipped from here all over the world. The garden is located six miles north of Perry on Sandefur Road off Route 41. Visitors are welcome to picnic on the grounds.

Since 1870, when the railroad line arrived in Perry, a popular spot to eat has been the Perry Hotel located at an old stagecoach stop. In 1924 the first hotel was razed and replaced by the New Perry Hotel. Generous portions of tasty food have kept travelers coming back over the decades. The dining room overlooks the hotel's garden, and flowers grace each table year-round. Call (912)987-1000 for reservations.

Directions: From I-75 take Exit 42, and the Welcome Center is right off the interstate.

Happy Valley Pottery and Area Arts and Crafts

Pots and Plans

It's one thing to have a dream come true, but when you have imagined every single detail of it, and reality conforms totally with your imagination, it can be downright eerie. That's the experience Jerry Chappelle had when he received a phone call from his real estate agent after moving from Minnesota to teach art at the University of Georgia.

Chappelle had dreamed of finding an old farm surrounded by stately trees and roomy outbuildings and had described to the agent the buildings, trees, small pond and even the chicken coops he envisioned. What the agent found fit the vision so perfectly that Chappelle named his studio "Happy Valley" after a Mickey Mouse update of "Jack and the Beanstalk."

In the more than 20 years since Jerry Chappelle and his wife Kathy began their commercial pottery enterprise, it has grown to include a blown-glass artist and another potter. Their studios occupy the old chicken coops. In the gift shop the Chappelles sell their own work and that of other regional artists. Bargain lovers relish the chance to purchase seconds.

Happy Valley Pottery in Watkinsville is open 9:00 A.M. to 5:00 P.M. Monday through Saturday. You can arrange a Sunday visit by calling (706)769-5922. On the first weekend in June and from the Friday after Thanksgiving until Christmas the studios have Open House with guest artists demonstrating and selling their works.

If you drive through Watkinsville, stop at the **Eagle Tavern Welcome Center & Museum** on Route 441. Built in 1790 when this was a frontier settlement on the edge of Creek and Cherokee territory, the tavern was a stagecoach stop from 1801 until the late 1820s and served as a tavern for another century. The two upstairs bedrooms were reserved for stage passengers, but wagon drivers and those who walked from town to town could spread their bedrolls in the two downstairs public rooms. The tavern is open Tuesday through Friday from 9:00 A.M. to 5:00 P.M. and Sunday from 1:30 to 5:00 P.M.

You also may want to visit nearby **Mockingbird Forge** just five miles south of Watkinsville in Farmington. Jeff Mohr operates this forge in an old railroad depot. Visitors are welcome to watch Mohr, a 15-year master of his craft, and his assistants mold the hot slabs of metal into ornamental shapes. Most of the work done is by commission, but some pieces are for sale in the small gift shop. Mockingbird Forge is listed as being open weekdays 9:00

A.M. to 5:00 P.M., but it is advisable to call and check before making a special trip. Call (706)769-7147.

If your interest runs to quilts and/or hand-crafted furniture then head over to Rutledge and visit the **Barn Raising**, on Fairplay Road. Master craftsman Paul Jones, who has been designing and building furniture since 1976, opened his own workshop and showroom in 1980. You may custom-order or select from his finished pieces. Paul's wife, Pam Jones, is an award-winning quilter. Although she has been quilting for more than 14 years, she was the youngest artist featured in the art exhibit "Patterns: A Celebration of Georgia's Quilting" that toured the state's art museums.

Pam had no formal instruction in quilting but sewed under her grandmother's tutelage since she was a girl. When Pam starts a quilt she says she already "sees" the finished product. She met Paul when they had side-by-side booths at a crafts' show. Now both display their artistic creations together in their own shop, the Barn Raising, along with handcrafted items from other artists. The shop is open Monday through Saturday from 10:00 A.M. to 5:00 P.M.

Next to the Barn Raising is **The Yesterday Cafe** featuring "Modern Country" cooking. Located in a turn-of-the-century drug store with walls filled with regional photographs that date back to the Civil War, this cafe serves breakfast (until 11:00 A.M.), lunch (11:00 A.M. to 2:00 P.M.) and supper (Thursday, Friday and Saturday 5:30 to 9:30 P.M.).

Two miles north of Rutledge on Fairplay Road is **Hard Labor State Park**. This 5,805-acre park has a challenging 18-hole golf course, 15 miles of horseback trails (no horse rentals), boat rentals, fishing on the park's two lakes, a swimming beach, two-and-a-half miles of hiking trails, cottages, camping sites and picnicking facilities. The park is open 7:00 A.M. to 10:00 P.M. but the office is open only from 8:00 A.M. to 5:00 P.M.

Directions: From I-20 take Exit 51, Route 441, north to Farmington. Make a right on Salem Road and continue to the first road on the left, Mayne Mill Road. Make a left on Mayne Mill Road and proceed to the stop sign, make a right on Colham-Ferry Road and follow that (stay to the right as the road forks) to a gravel road on your right, Carson Graves Road. Take this gravel road to the first mailbox and follow drive for Happy Valley Pottery. For Eagle Tavern return to Colham-Ferry Road and make a left. Continue on Colham-Ferry Road for approximately nine miles, the road deadends at Route 441. Make a right on Route 441 and continue into Watkinsville. The tavern is on your right. Mockingbird Forge is approximately five miles south of Watkinsville on U.S. 441, and is visible from the highway, just across the railroad tracks that run parallel to U.S. 441. The quickest way to reach Rutledge is to return to I-20 and head east; then take Exit 49, Newborn Road, for three miles to Rutledge. The Barn Raising and Yesterday Cafe are in Rutledge on Fairplay Street and Hard Labor Creek State Park is just outside town.

Hay House

Avant-Garde Antebellum

It sounds like an oxymoron—can you have an avant-garde antebellum mansion? Well, Hay House in Macon proves you can. In its day, Hay House was one of the most innovative and technologically advanced mansions in the South, if not the country. It took five years (1855 to 1859) to build this 24-room Italian Renaissance Revival masterpiece.

After returning with his bride from their European honeymoon, Macon entrepreneur, William Butler Johnston, traveled to New York to find an architect to build his dream house. He selected Thomas Thomas who, as Johnston wrote his wife, was ". . .the most accomplished and tasty architect in New York. . ."

The house that the firm of Thomas & Son designed included three bathrooms with hot and cold running water, central heat, walk-in closets, a 15-room speaker tube system, a large in-house kitchen and an elaborate ventilation system. An article in the local newspaper in 1857 claimed, "This will probably be the finest house in the state if not in the South." The story priced the house at $100,000, comparing that to $6,000 to $12,000 for lesser mansions of the day. Upon completion the house was called, "the palace of the South."

Details that inspired this princely description included exquisite stained-glass windows, *trompe l'oeil* walls in the main hallway, elaborate plaster embellishments and massive 500-pound faux metal doors.

During the Civil War, after the depository in Richmond became endangered by advancing Federal troops, the Confederate government established a second depository at Macon and appointed William Johnston Depositary of the Treasury. Because of Johnston's position a story grew that he hid the Confederate gold reserves in a secret room of his house that was accessed by a hinged panel on the stair landing. Though there is such a room, the story of the Confederate treasure being hidden there is only a myth.

The real treasure is the house itself and second to that, the imported art and furnishings collected by the Johnstons and by the subsequent owner, Parks Lee Hay. To the complete surprise

In the ballroom of the Hay House, an Italian marble statue rotates on ball bearings for optimum viewing. The six-foot-high chandeliers contain thousands of crystals.

of his wife, and without a single discussion, P.L. Hay bought the Johnston House in December 1926.

The Hays made significant changes to the house. They rehabilitated the electrical system, added a gas-fired furnace and updated the bathrooms and kitchen. The priceless antiques and ornate furnishings you see on your 40-minute guided tour of the house date from the Hay era.

Although the ground floor, or basement level, was the primary living space for the Johnstons, it was used for storage by the Hays. Today it is used for office space and for the gift shop.

Visitors pass through the huge doors into the entrance hall with its ornate plasterwork ceiling and unbelievably realistic walls considered by many authorities to be the finest *trompe l'oeil* work in the country. Eyes are immediately drawn to the rosewood pocket doors and the walnut staircase. Off the hallway are the reception room, library, dining room, double parlor and music room. The last room is probably the most splendid of all: 1,200 square feet under an ornately decorated clerestory hung with chandeliers. Built as a "picture gallery," and used as a music room, the gallery was hung with paintings collected in Europe by William Butler Johnston. "Ruth's Room," off the gallery, was named for Randolph Rogers' 1857 statue entitled *Ruth Gleaning*. The statue is bathed in natural light from an overhead skylight.

The four main bedrooms are on the second floor. The master bedroom survives as the Hays left it with original furnishings, prints, bric-a-brac, draperies and rugs. The children's suite has a bedroom, nanny's room and bath. Visitors do not have access to the third floor, attic or cupola level.

This remarkable house, now a National Historic Landmark, is a not-to-be-missed visual treat. It is open Monday through Saturday 10:00 A.M. to 4:30 P.M. and Sundays 1:00 to 4:30 P.M. Admission is charged. Guided tours start on the hour and half hour.

The most glorious time to visit Macon is during the city's **Cherry Blossom Festival** starting in the third week of March. Timed to coincide with the blooming of the city's Yoshino cherry trees, the festival offers about 250 activities over a ten-day period. Even the streets are painted with pink lines and delicate blossoms. A special Cherry Blossom Riding Tour takes you past rows and rows of flowering trees, 170,000 of which were given to Macon by the Fickling family. Other events include a parade, art show, continual entertainment, athletic competitions, fashion shows, craft exhibits, and plenty to eat. Write to the Cherry Blossom Festival, 794 Cherry Street, Macon, GA 31201 for dates and other details of the festival.

Directions: From I-75 take I-16 east. Exit at Spring Street, turn right and go 2½ blocks to Georgia Avenue, and Hay House will be on the your immediate left.

High Falls State Park

Tumbling Water

For most travelers, the scenic falls are the draw but for fishermen it's the record of the park's lake for having the state's highest density of crappie. The lake in High Falls State Park is known as the best public trophy bass water in Georgia. One fisherman pulled a 57-pound flathead catfish from the 650-acre lake. You can rent flat bottom boats and canoes if you want to try your luck.

Fishing is only one of the recreational options at this park. Visitors may hike, swim, play miniature golf, camp and picnic. High Falls has a good bit of history to impart, some of which can be seen on the trails. This area was once Creek Indian territory, and stories are told about a raid in the 1800s. It was July and the Creeks attacked and massacred white settlers. By the time they returned to their encampment beside the river, the scalps they had taken as trophies had begun to spoil. The Indians tried drying or smoking the scalps, and ever since the river has been called Towaliga (pronounced Ti-Laggi), which means "roasted scalp."

Despite the fate of early settlers, those who came later certainly prospered. By the late 1880s, the 100-foot drop in the river was a power source for businesses like the gristmill and sawmill. In its heyday from 1883 to 1899 the town of High Falls had a population of about 200. In the late 1890s the railroad bypassed the town in favor of Jackson, eight miles to the east. Most of the residents moved and High Falls became a ghost town. During the Civil War, Confederates from Wheeler's Cavalry burned the gristmill to keep Union soldiers from getting at the supplies stored in it. The mill was rebuilt in 1866 and operated until 1960 when it was torn down. Now only remnants mark where it once stood.

In 1890 the Towaliga Falls Power Company was formed and started work on a dam and power plant on the river to provide energy for the cotton mills in nearby Griffin. Eight years later the Georgia Hydro-Electric Company bought the still uncompleted project, finished the job and began generating power. The dam, finished in 1904, was made of local stone cut from the stream bed. The **Historic Ruins Trail** takes you to the remains of the old powerhouse and transformer house. In 1930 the facility was transferred to the Georgia Power Company who closed it in 1958. Eight years later a 995-acre portion of the northwestern corner of Monroe County became High Falls State Park. The park office is open 8:00 A.M. to 5:00 P.M. daily.

In addition to the Historic Ruins Trail there is a Nature Trail. Both pass the tumbling cataracts of the river. There's also a two-mile Non-Game Trail where you spot creatures like chipmunks and butterflies. There is a platform overlooking the falls area. You may see people wading in the river, but be forewarned before joining them. The mossy rocks are extremely slippery and require great caution to navigate. A better way to cool off is in the park's pool, open weekends in May and six days a week from June through Labor Day. Hours are 11:00 A.M. to 6:00 P.M. Tuesday through Thursday and 11:00 A.M. to until 7:00 P.M. Friday through Sunday. It is open on Monday only if it is a legal holiday. There is no swimming in the lake because the water is too dark to see swimmers if they go under.

For information about camping or fishing call the park office (912)994-5080. There are 142 campsites in the park, including several picturesque sites along the river and on the lake.

The steel bridge you cross over the Towaliga River was built in 1902 as part of one of the first roads in central and western Georgia. The Old Alabama Road started at the Seven Islands of the Ocmulgee in Jasper County, now part of the Jackson Lake Dam, and went through Indian Springs (see selection) and continued west to what is now Columbus.

Directions: From I-75 take Exit 65, High Falls Road north. The park is 1.5 miles away on the left.

Historic Macon

Quintessentially Old South

Macon is a picture-book city where the romantically inclined find ghosts of the antebellum South. The streets seem to sing with voices from the past, from that of the old blind street singer, Rev. Pearly Brown, who performed at Carnegie Hall and was the first black performer to appear on the Grand Ole Opry (see Macon's Black Heritage Tour selection) to the voices of the internationally famous opera stars who have performed at the city's Grand Opera House.

When it was built in 1883-1884, at a cost of $75,000, the **Grand Opera House**, then called the Academy of Music, had one of the largest stages in the country. With a stage almost seven stories high, it still ranks as one of the nation's largest. An 1884 newspaper report called it ". . .a model of elegance and a triumph of good taste; the prettiest amusement house in the south. . . ."

Renowned stars like Sarah Bernhardt, Lillian Russell, Will Rogers, George Burns and Gracie Allen, the Gish sisters, Rosa Ponselle, Dorothy Lamour, Bob Hope and a host of others have performed here. A backstage tour gives you a chance to see trap doors in the stage floor installed for the Great Houdini, the magician, as well as dressing rooms and rehearsal halls of the stars.

Tours of the Grand Opera House, 651 Mulberry Street, are given 10:00 A.M., NOON, 2:00 and 3:00 P.M. Monday through Friday except during performances or rehearsals. If you want to make sure tours are being given, call (912) 749-6580. Admission is charged.

Native-son Sidney Clopton Lanier, one of the South's most illustrious poets, died two years before the opera house was built.

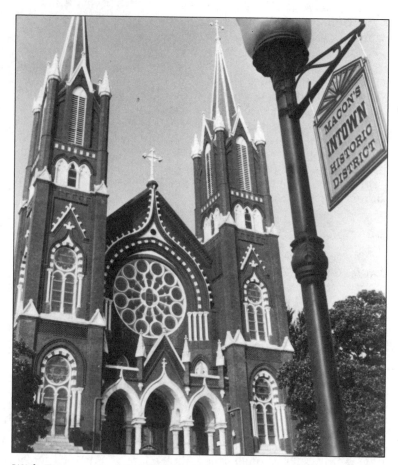

With Romanesque flair, twin cross-topped spires of Macon's St. Joseph's Catholic Church rise 200 feet, framing Bavarian stained-glass windows and a triple arch facade.

"Music," he wrote, "is Love in search of a word." The cottage where he was born on February 3, 1842, was built two years earlier by his grandparents. Originally just four rooms, it has been enlarged twice. Today it is the headquarters of the Middle Georgia Historical Society and is open as a museum house. It holds a few pieces of furniture linked to Sidney Lanier, some personal effects and his portrait as a young man. Behind the house is an old-fashioned garden.

The **Sidney Lanier Cottage**, 935 High Street, is open Monday through Friday from 9:00 A.M. to 1:00 P.M. and from 2:00 to 4:00 P.M. On Saturday hours are 9:30 A.M. to 12:30 P.M. Guided tours are given and admission is charged.

Another Macon landmark is the **Old Cannonball House**, the only house in the city that suffered a direct hit during the Civil War. On July 30, 1864, Union troops under General George Stoneman were firing on the city, and Judge Asa Holt's Greek Revival mansion was hit. The cannonball "struck the sand sidewalk, passed through the second column from the left on the gallery and entered the parlor over a window, landing unexploded in the hall."

One hundred years after the house was built, in 1963, the Sidney Lanier Chapter, United Daughters of the Confederacy, purchased the house and restored it as a museum and chapter house. Period furniture and antique crystal and china from other Macon homes fill the rooms.

Two furnished parlors recreate the Wesleyan Female College sorority rooms of the Adelphean Society, the first secret society for college women. The Adelphean Society was the mother of the Alpha Delta Pi Sorority, formed in 1851 and the Philomathean Society, established a year later, that developed into the Phi Mu Fraternity. These historically authentic rooms for many years were housed in the Conservatory building at Wesleyan College. When the building was demolished in 1962, the rooms were moved to the Cannonball House.

Behind the house, in what was once a four-room servants quarters, is the **Macon-Confederate Museum**. Old photographs, uniforms, weapons, mortuary art and other memorabilia fill the museum's display cases. The house and museum, at 856 Mulberry Street, are open Tuesday through Friday from 10:00 A.M. to 1:00 P.M. and from 2:00 until 4:00 P.M. Weekend hours are 1:30 to 4:30 P.M. Admission is charged.

One of the Greek Revival houses in the Historic District is now a bed-and-breakfast. The **1842 Inn**, 353 College Avenue, built by the organizer and first president of Macon Manufacturing Co. (now the Bibb Company), is elegantly furnished. Some of the rooms have working fireplaces and others have whirlpool baths. Adjoining the inn is a Victorian cottage that also houses guests. Just down College Street is Beall's 1860 Restaurant (315 College Street), once a two-story frame house but remodeled into a Greek Revival Mansion in 1901.

There are three walking tours of Macon: Victorian, White Columns, and Historic Downtown. Information and maps for the three tours are available at the **Macon-Bibb County Convention and Visitors Bureau** in the Macon Terminal Station, a location that is also worth a visit. This formal Roman Classical style terminal at the foot of Cherry Street was once the railroad center of the Southeast. In its heyday, roughly 100 passenger trains stopped here daily.

The **Victorian Tour** includes the Lanier Cottage; Washington Memorial Library, 510 College Street, that has a bust of the Georgia poet and an extensive genealogy department; and the Garden Club Center, 730 College Street, in an English Tudor home designed by Neel Reid. The Victorian Tour also has a number of historic churches.

The 200-feet-high twin-cross spires of the Romanesque Neo-Gothic St. Joseph's Catholic Church, 830 Poplar Street, have been an important part of the Macon skyline since the church was completed in 1892. There are over 60 stained-glass windows. The medallion-shaped rose window in the front is particularly striking.

Also worth seeing is the First Baptist Church, 511 High Place. Built in a High Victorian Gothic style, it still has its origianl pews and a unique sanctuary, shaped like an inverted ship's hull. The Washington Avenue Presbyterian Church, at 939, is the oldest black Presbyterian Church in Georgia. The Romanesque Gothic St. Paul's Episcopal Church, 753 College Street, has memorial Tiffany stained-glass windows in the chancel.

The **White Columns Walking Tour** includes the Hay House (see selection), the Old Cannonball House, the 1842 Inn and Beall's 1860 Restaurant. This walk takes you past the Woodruff House at 988 Bond Street, a Greek Revival plantation style house built in 1836 for a railroad financier and banker. During the Civil War it was occupied by Union General Wilson. Winnie Davis, daughter of Jefferson Davis, President of the Confederacy, had her 16th birthday ball here. The house is open by appointment. Call (912)752-2715.

The **Historic Downtown Walking Tour** includes City Hall, the Grand Opera House and numerous government and commercial establishments.

To quickly grasp the flavor of Macon, it's hard to beat an escorted tour. Sidney's Old South Historic Tours starts from the historic Macon Terminal Station, departing daily, except Sunday and some holidays, at 10:00 A.M. and 2:00 P.M. Snippets from Lanier's best-loved poems, fascinating legends from the past and historic background from the guides enrich the ride. For details about these two-hour tours, call (912)743-3401.

Another option is Colonel Bond's Carriage Tours that start at the Green Jacket Restaurant, 325 5th Street. These 25-minute surrey rides, that run from 7:30 to 10:30 P.M., also impart some of the legend and lore of Macon. For additional details call (912)477-4748, 746-4680, or 749-7267.

Directions: From I-75, take Exit 53 to I-16 east, then Exit 4, (Coliseum Drive/Martin Luther King Jr. Blvd.), and turn right off the ramp and cross the Ocmulgee River. At the third light, make a left at Fifth and Mulberry Street. The Macon Terminal Station appears immediately on your left. If you are traveling I-75 south-bound, stop at the Macon Welcome Center just before the I-475 bypass and ask for information and directions.

Lockerly Arboretum and Woods Museum

Botanical Treasures of Middle Georgia

On 47 acres of rolling Piedmont country, just south of Milledge-ville, discover Lockerly Arboretum's expansive array of flora and fauna. This facility is a horticultural laboratory, not a showplace garden; but visitors are interested in the 22 growing areas, with plants from Georgia's mountains, coast and center.

The arboretum sits on the grounds of Lockerly Hall, a Greek Revival temple house, built in the mid-1800s. The house is owned by the English China Clay Company and is not open to the public. The grounds, however, are criss-crossed by walking trails and driving lanes. There is no charge to explore the grounds planted by gifts from the late Edward J. Grassman, a New Jersey businessman who developed the local kaolin industry. He es-tablished the arboretum in appreciation of the support he re-ceived from Milledgeville and Central Georgia.

Lockerly has several collections of note. From February through December large showy flowers bloom on more than 300 rhododendrons. The woodland walking trail is at its best in late March and early April when the azaleas bloom. There are also Southern Indica azaleas whose large blooms appear in mid-April. The fragrant blossoms of the lily-of-the-valley bushes, also known as pieris, appear in March and April. From October through April more than 300 camellias are in bloom.

Among the arboretum's prized collections are the guest iris on loan from gardens located throughout the country. Nearly 200 of the known species of iris are represented as part of the col-lection of 600 different hybrids. Iris bloom from April through July. From June through September, 15 species of day lilies bloom.

Other garden areas include the shore and aquatic plants, haw-thorn collection, hostas, ferns, holly, viburnum, lantana, coni-fers, herbs and climbing shrubs and vines. Over 600 species of tropical and desert plants grow in the greenhouses next to the headquarters building. Visitors will find a substantial collection of horticultural and botanical books in the headquarters library.

Nearby there is a restored servant's cabin that is now the **Woods Museum**. The shelves are filled with cut wood sections from different Georgia trees. Represented are such diverse grains as the cucumber tree, shagbark hickory, red maple, black cherry, pecan, loblolly pine and sycamore.

If you want to arrange a guided tour of the arboretum, call (912)452-2112 during the arboretum's visiting hours, weekdays from 8:30 A.M. to 4:30 P.M. and Saturday from 1:00 to 5:00 P.M.

There is an annual blossoming of crafts in the Milledgeville area. For more than 20 years the Brown's Crossing Craftsmen Fair has lured visitors to the region. Crafts and skills are demonstrated at this celebration of Americana. Among the crafts demonstrated and sold are weaving, pottery, woodworking, bobbin lacemaking, basketry, leatherwork, quilting, handcrafted furniture making, sculpting and jewelry making.

Milledgeville area also has several craft shops: The Flower Pot at Hatcher Square Mall; the Sugar Tree at 1045 N. Jefferson Street; Miss Sara E. Finney at 150 Coopers Road; the Country Storehouse on Route 441 north; and The Craft Shoppe at 1631 N. Columbia Street.

Directions: Take I-75 to Macon, then travel northeast on Route 49 to Milledgeville where you will pick up Route 441-Business. Proceed south on Business 441 to the arboretum entrance on the left just beyond Milledgeville.

Macon's Black Heritage Tour

"A Past to Cherish, A Future to Fulfill"

Macon has a rich African-American heritage felt in the culture, education, religion and business of the city. A Black Heritage Tour map encompasses more than 20 spots around Macon that reveal aspects of black Americans' influence on this Southern city.

The best place to start is the **Harriet Tubman Historical and Cultural Museum** at 340 Walnut Street. Local artist Wilfred Stroud's wall-length mural *From Africa to America* starts with African tribal princes and includes many noted black inventors, educators and political leaders in the U.S. The mural's final panel has noted entertainment figures like Lena Horne, Otis Redding and Little Richard. Not all the figures depicted are associated with Macon, but the last three have their musical roots here. Other local black artists have their work on display in the center along with exhibits of African art.

In his mural From Africa to America *at the Harriet Tubman Historical and Cultural Museum, Macon artist Wilfred Stroud traces important African American contributions.*

This cultural center was created by a white Catholic priest who wanted to instill racial pride in his congregation. He wanted his young parishioners to have role models both from the past and the present. Accordingly, one section has photographs of black leaders in Macon. Art workshops are conducted at the center, and it has a dance studio. The Harriet Tubman Museum is open weekdays from 10:00 A.M. to 5:00 P.M. and Saturday from 2:00 to 5:00 P.M.

One of the primary arteries into town crosses the Otis Redding Memorial Bridge, named for one of the city's most famous musical sons. For 40 years, the blind street singer Reverend Pearly Brown performed along the streets. Trained at Macon's Academy for the Blind, he was the first African American to play the Grand Old Opry; he also performed at Carnegie Hall. Visitors are welcome to stop at WIBB Radio, 369 Second Street, the first black radio station in Macon and Middle Georgia, where another Brown, the noted performer James Brown, got his first big recording break with this station. Restoration efforts are underway at the Douglass Theatre, Broadway at M.L. King, Jr. Blvd., where the top black entertainers performed for more than 60 years.

The **Ruth Hartley Mosley Memorial Women's Center**, established by the country's first licensed female mortician, gives young women a chance to study a wide range of vocations. The late Mrs. Mosely set up a trust so that her home at 626 Spring Street could be used to help women realize their potential. At the Washington Memorial Library, 510 College Street, there is an extensive African-American heritage collection. It is one of the best resources in the southeast with rare genealogical, archival and biographical information.

Religion is an important element in the heritage of Macon's black population, and the tour route takes you to six city churches. St. Peter Claver Catholic Church is in the Pleasant Hill Historic District, one of the first black neighborhoods in the country to be included on the National Register of Historic Places. Many of these churches are not open during the week, but you are welcome to attend Sunday services, or you can call ahead and arrange a mid-week visit. The churches are: First Baptist Church at 595 New Street, Tremont Temple Baptist at 1860 Forsyth Street, Steward Chapel African Methodist Episcopal Church at 887 Forsyth Street, Washington Avenue Presbyterian Church at 939, and the Hosley Temple Christian Methodist Episcopal Church at 1011 Washington Avenue.

Cotton Avenue, once an Indian trail and one of Georgia's earliest Federal roads, is one of the main centers of black business. Along this street, visitors will find some of the best soul food in the South. Jefferson Long, the first black man elected to the U.S. House of Representatives, in 1871, had a tailoring business on Cotton Avenue. Along this street you'll also see a monument to Macon's only Medal of Honor recipient, Sgt. Rodney M. Davis. In 1967 this young Marine threw himself on a hand grenade to protect his platoon in Vietnam.

To obtain a copy of the Black Heritage guide, call the Macon-Bibb County Convention and Visitors Bureau at (912) 743-3401. Or write them at 200 Cherry Street, P.O. Box 6354, Macon, GA 31208-6354.

Directions: From I-75 take Exit 53 to I-16 east, then Exit 4, Coliseum Drive/Martin Luther King Jr. Boulevard. Turn right off ramp and cross the Ocmulgee River. Then turn left at the third light, Fifth and Mulberry Street. The Terminal Station Welcome Center will be immediately on your left. If you want to make the Harriet Tubman Museum your first stop, turn right at the second light onto Walnut Street, and the museum will be immediately on your left.

Madison-Morgan Cultural Center
and Heritage Hall

Passing the Torch

In 1809, the new community of Madison became the county seat of Morgan County. For six decades the town grew, with roomy colonnaded homes being built along its tree-lined streets. Towards the end of the Civil War, all were nearly lost. Native son and U.S. Senator Joshua Hill, who had been friends with General Sherman's brother at West Point, saved the town by leading a delegation to ask Sherman to spare Madison from the torch.

You can have a look at Senator Hill's uniform coat, along with other Civil War and regional memorabilia, at the Madison-Morgan Cultural Center located in one of the South's first brick grade schools. Built in the Romanesque Revival style in 1895, the school has an attractive 400-seat auditorium that still serves the community. The old wooden seats, however, are now padded. The cultural center has history exhibits, a restored schoolroom and galleries for rotating art exhibits.

The Madison-Morgan Cultural Center, 434 South Main Street, is open Tuesday through Saturday from 10:00 A.M. to 4:30 P.M. and Sunday 2:00 to 5:00 P.M. A nominal admission is charged.

Down the street is **Heritage Hall**, a house museum owned and restored by the Morgan County Historical Society. This Greek Revival house was built in 1833 by Dr. Elijah Evans Jones. Several members of the Jones family left messages inscribed on the windowpanes, including personal avowals like "Stewart and Jennie" and "I Love Will."

The house is open for tours and can be rented for private and community functions. Furnishings are from the 1830s. Tours are given Monday through Saturday 10:00 A.M. to 4:30 P.M. and Sunday 1:30 to 4:30 P.M. A nominal admission is charged.

One way to enjoy Madison is to pick up a walking tour guide at the Madison-Morgan Cultural Center and stroll through the community. The map includes 32 points of interest including the county courthouse and jail, numerous churches and scores of charming antebellum homes in a range of styles that include Federal, Greek Revival and Victorian. If you want a glimpse inside some of these old homes, visit during the Spring Tour of Homes in May or December's Christmas Tour of Homes.

Four of these homes are now bed-and-breakfasts. **The Burnett Place**, dating from 1830, is on the National Register of Historic Places. It seems appropriate that this Federal-style inn offers high tea to its guests. Burnett Place is at 317 Old Post Road; for more information call (706)342-4034. The Brady Inn, 250 N. Second

Street, is an 1800s' Victorian cottage in the center of Historic Madison (706)342-4400. You can also stay at the Victorian Bed & Breakfast at 450 Pine Street, (706)342-1890. Sea Captain Nelson Dexter built the Boat House, 383 Porter Street, in 1850. Now filled with antiques, it offers accommodations, for non-smokers only, and tours on the weekends (706)342-3061.

If you want to maintain the mood, dine at Katy's On Main. Southern gourmet dining is offered in this antebellum house at 270 S. Main Street. Everything is made from scratch, including breads, ice-cream and a mouth-watering array of other desserts. One of the specialties is Derby Pie, and repeat customers agree you won't taste a better pie anywhere in the state. It's open Tuesday through Saturday 11:30 A.M. to 2:00 P.M. and on Friday and Saturday evenings when special events are held in Madison. Reservations are recommended for dinner; call (706)342-1020.

Directions: From I-20, Madison is just off the interstate on Route 441 north. When you enter town, Route 441 becomes Main Street.

Massee Lane Gardens

Home of the American Camellia Society

Only true aficionados realize that there are as many as 1,200 varieties of camellias. You'll actually find all 1,200 growing at Massee Lane, the headquarters and gardens of the American Camellia Society.

The height of the camellia season runs from November through March, which explains why the blossom is sometimes called the rose of winter. Each February, when other flowers are dormant, the Society hosts a Camellia Festival, an event that includes an arts show, entertainment, house tour, a fashion show and a constant spotlight on camellias. A large greenhouse, open to the public year-round, showcases approximately 200 varieties.

Brick pathways wind through Massee Lane's nine acres. Beginning in early September the camellia japonicas flower, peaking in January and February. The camellia sasanquas, which belong to the Asiatic tea family, bloom from late August into November.

Camellias are the stars, but the gardens at Massee Lane also have abundant spring blossoms: azaleas, dogwoods, narcissus and iris. During the summer day lilies predominate and roses bloom in a garden that opened in 1985. The next year, the Society added a Japanese Garden centering on a pond stocked with Koi— colorful, oversize goldfish.

In the **Annabelle Lundy Fetterman Education Museum**, named for the Society's first woman president, visitors can watch a 15-minute slide program on camellias and the American Camellia Society.

The museum also displays some of the Society's 234 Boehm sculptures and four Boehm porcelain paintings. The majority of the collection is displayed in the Stevens-Taylor Gallery, beside the rose garden. Boehm porcelain is America's most famous and expensive porcelain, and the Society has the world's largest and most important Boehm collection open to the public. Several of these Boehm pieces depict camellias, and it seems singularly appropriate to house them here.

Another strong theme in Boehm's work is birds. His sculpture of the great white egret seems ready to rise in flight; the feathers on the egret's wings are incredibly life-like. One of only two life-size California condors that Boehm created is displayed here. The size is not the only staggering element to this piece; the exact duplication of feathers rivals nature in their complexity. The nucleus of the collection was donated to the Society by Macon-native Mildred Taylor Stevens. Other porcelain artists represented include Royal Copenhagen, Connesseir, Worcester and Cybris.

Massee Lane is open November through March, Monday through Saturday 9:00 A.M. to 5:00 P.M. and Sunday 1:00 to 5:00 P.M. Off-season the hours are Monday through Friday 9:00 A.M. to 4:00 P.M. Admission is charged. To schedule a tour, or for information, call (912)967-2358 or 967-2722. The museum's gift shop offers lovely camellia-related items. The headquarters building, open for research purposes, houses the world's largest collection of books about camellias.

Directions: From I-75, south of Macon, take Route 49 south, Exit 46, to Fort Valley, then continue straight on Route 49 towards Marshallville. Massee Lane Gardens will be on your left, approximately five miles south of Fort Valley.

Milledgeville's Trolley Tours and Old Governor's Mansion

Planned Prominence

Milledgeville is one of the few cities in the country established to be a capital city; another city that has that distinction is Washington, D.C. The National Trust for Historical Preservation considers Milledgeville the only surviving example of a complete Federal Period city since that architectural era covers the years from 1780 to 1825, and the city was essentially completed in the years from 1803 to 1825.

The Milledgeville Trolley Tours take you along streets laid out in the master plan for the city. All but two of the 19 original streets bear the name of patriots from the American Revolutionary era, two exceptions being Liberty and Columbia streets.

There were four official governor's residences in the old capital, and all but one still stands. The first three executive mansions were smaller, but in 1838 the official governor's mansion was completed at a cost of $50,000. Ten Georgia governors would make their home in this imposing Greek Revival mansion, patterned after Palladio's Villa Rotunda and Villa Foscari. There is a pink tint to the stucco covering the exterior masonry walls. Four towering Ionic columns on the portico have caps and bases of New England granite.

The two-hour trolley tour includes a stop at the **Old Governor's Mansion**, or you can tour on your own. You will be escorted through the ground floor service rooms. The kitchen still has its original fireplace and hearth. This ground floor area was an architectural departure from the clapboard houses usually built in Milledgeville. These rooms now contain furniture that belonged to the various governors who lived in the mansion. Exhibit cases contain Cherokee and Creek Indian artifacts as well as reminders of the Civil War period.

The mansion's most commanding feature is the 50-foot-high central rotunda. The domed ceiling has gold leaf on the ornamental moldings around the recessed plaster panels. It was on the rotunda balcony that Confederate Governor Joseph Brown was arrested by Union soldiers. At the time, in 1865, there were 30,000 troops occupying the town. It was in Milledgeville that the Georgia Ordinance of Secession was adopted on January 19, 1861. That fateful night Governor Brown's wife burned a candle in each pane of every window in the mansion.

The tour of the Old Governor's Mansion includes the public rooms on the first floor—parlor, dining room, library and drawing room. The furniture is primarily English Regency, which was popular in the 1830s when the mansion was completed. Other styles represented are French Empire and American Federal as well as a collection of Georgia-made pieces.

One can imagine even the Marquis de LaFayette, on his visit in May, 1825, being impressed with the 50-foot-long drawing room with its two black Italian marble mantels. An invitation to the LaFayette Ball is on display. The State House and Mansion came close to being destroyed by Sherman during the Civil War, but after consulting with his officers, Sherman decided not to burn the city, although he did burn the state penitentiary. In 1868 the capital was moved from Milledgeville to Atlanta.

A gracious Milledgeville mansion in the Historic District of Georgia's antebellum capital.

The Old Governor's Mansion can be toured Tuesday through Saturday from 10:00 A.M. to 5:00 P.M. and Sundays 2:00 to 5:00 P.M. Admission is charged.

Another spot you can tour on your own, if you make an advance appointment, (or see as part of the Trolley Tour) is the **Stetson-Sanford House**, at the corner of Jackson and West Hancock Streets. This two-story clapboard Federal style mansion with a Palladian double portico was built in 1825. The house, now the headquarters of the Old Capital Historical Society, is furnished with period pieces and open by request; call (912)452-4687.

A drive through the historic district is a must, and the anecdotes you'll hear from the guide on the trolley tour make that the preferable way to see the old homes and churches. More than 20 architectural landmarks are pointed out during the tour. You can explore on your own after you pick up a tour map at the Tourism and Trade Office at 200 W. Hancock Street. It's open Monday through Friday 8:30 A.M. to 5:00 P.M. and Saturday 10:00 A.M. to 2:00 P.M. The office is closed on holidays.

One of the architectural special points of interest is the **Old State Capitol** at 201 East Greene Street. It is likely this is the oldest government building in the country built in the Gothic style. The crenelated gates look positively Medieval. This was Georgia's seat of government from 1803 to 1868. Today the Georgia Military College holds classes in this complex. It's also the site of the Old State Capitol Museum open weekdays by request from 9:00 A.M. to 5:00 P.M.

Trolley Tours leave the Trade and Tourism Office at 10:00 A.M. Tuesday through Friday. The tickets include the admission fees at the Old Governor's Mansion and the Stetson-Sanford House. For more information call (921)452-4687 or (800)653-1804.

Directions: From the Atlanta area take I-20 east towards Augusta. In about an hour, leave at Exit 51, and take Route 441 south and follow the signs to the Milledgeville Information Center. From the Macon area take I-16 and follow Route 129/22 east to Milledgeville. At traffic signal for Route 441 By-Pass follow signs to Route 49, Hancock Street, for the Tourist Information Center.

Museums of Athens

City of Classics

Outstanding performance in diverse fields is celebrated at an eclectic mix of museums in Athens. The **Heritage Museum** at the Butts-Mehre Heritage Hall focuses on Georgia's sports history, while a specialized approach is taken at the Collegiate Tennis Hall of Fame. An outstanding collection of American paintings is exhibited at the Georgia Museum of Art, and the Navy Supply Corps School presents a look at provisioning the military.

The Georgia Athletic Association has its headquarters at **Butts-Mehre Heritage Hall**. The Georgia Bulldog staff and team operate out of the building's first two floors. The third and fourth floors showcase Georgia's football legends and triumphs and outstanding male and female stars of baseball, basketball, tennis, track and field and other sports. Collegiate championships and participation in the Olympic Games are featured.

The hall is named for Wally Butts and Harry Mehre, two outstanding Georgia football coaches. Video displays give game highlights, trophy cases attest to the continuing excellence of the home team and retired jerseys, photographs and equipment remind visitors of some of the best of the best, like Charley Trippi, Vernon Catfish Smith, Bill Harkin, Fran Tarkenton, Herschel Walker, Frankie Sinkwich and Dan Magill.

Heritage Museum is open Monday through Friday from 8:00 A.M. to 5:00 P.M. and weekends from 2:00 to 5:00 P.M. Fans can purchase tickets for most Georgia athletic events at the third floor ticket office. If you call ahead, (706)542-1622, you can tour the NCAA Tennis Hall of Fame and see the photographic collection of college tennis legends. The museum has murals of outstanding collegiate tennis events, trophies and tennis memorabilia.

On the University of Georgia's historic North Campus quadrangle you'll find the **Georgia Museum of Art**. This venerable museum was created in 1945 when Alfred H. Holbrook donated his collection of 100 American paintings to the university. Holbrook was an art dealer in New York, and towards the end of his life he began searching for an institution to exhibit his collection. He remembered studying art with Lamar Dodd at the University of Georgia and so deeded his art to the Athens college.

Over the years the museum's collection has grown to more than 5,000 works of art, including pieces by European and Oriental artists and an outstanding array of works on paper. Traveling exhibitions are scheduled throughout the year. The museum is open at no charge Monday through Saturday from 9:00 A.M. to 5:00 P.M. and Sunday 1:00 to 5:00 P.M. It is closed during university holidays. While on the North Campus, take the time to note the Greek Revivial architecture of several buildings near the art museum, including the Phi Kappa Hall and the University Chapel. This is also where you will find the Founders Memorial Gardens (see selection).

Athens is so closely linked with the University of Georgia that most visitors do not realize that the campus of the Navy Supply Corps School is also located here. Since 1954 officers responsible for supplying, feeding, clothing and paying Navy personnel have been trained at this facility. At the **Navy Supply Corps Museum** exhibits commemorate these "business managers of the U.S. Navy." Uniforms, personal memorabilia, ship models, mess and galley gear and navigational instruments are on display. Visitors can consult the extensive archives that contain photographs, Navy cookbooks, directories, newsletters and yearbooks. The museum is in the 1910 Carnegie Library building that recently was restored to its original ornate classical appearance. Hours are Monday through Friday from 8:30 A.M. to 5:00 P.M.

Directions: From Atlanta, take I-20 east and exit at Route 138 in Conyers; follow Route 138 left towards Athens, intersecting Route 78 and continuing into Athens. Ignore the perimeter by-pass and continue into town on the Atlanta Highway, which becomes Broad Street. Follow the signs to the University of Georgia campus. Butts-Mehre Heritage Hall is at Pinecrest Drive and Rutherford Street just off Lumpkin Street. The Georgia Museum of Art entrance is on the south side of Broad Street in downtown Athens. Access is off the North Campus quadrangle. The U.S. Navy Supply Corps School is at Prince and Oglethorpe avenues. (For an alternative route see directions for Athens Historic District selection.)

Museum of Aviation

"Keep 'Em Flying"

Robins Air Force Base has the fastest growing military aviation museum in the Southeast. Since 1982 a dedicated band of volunteers, aircraft experts and staff have created an exciting museum that transforms virtually all their visitors into aviation enthusiasts.

Starting with two airplanes and a bank balance of $20, the museum's collection has grown to include 80 historical aircraft, a staggering array of aviation memorabilia dating back to World War I, a vistascope theatre and a technical/historical/educational research center. Eventually, 70,000 square feet of hangar space will be added to the existing 80,000 square feet of indoor exhibit area.

The basic thrust of the museum is preserving and exhibiting historical aircraft, artifacts and archives relating to the role of Robins Air Force Base in supporting the U.S. Air Force. Retired Brigadier General Robert L. Scott is a technical adviser to the museum. Exhibits tell about his years with General Clair Chennault's Flying Tigers and the Hump Pilots. These pilots flew over the Himalaya Mountains to provide logistical support to China, Burma and India in World War II. General Scott's personal reminiscences and stories, many of which are included in his well-known book *God is My Co-Pilot*, bring these heroics to life. It is quite common to see Scott, still spry in his 80s, checking around the museum.

The **Robert L. Scott Vistascope Theater** shows films premiered at the Smithsonian's National Air and Space Museum like *Flyers* and *To Fly*. The Rotunda History Theater gives a visual program on the aircraft and weapon systems that have been important to Robins for the past 50 years. A real F-15, and real maintenance equipment, loom large in the Rotunda surrounded by a life size photomural that creates the illusion of maintenance hangars with civilian and military mannequins servicing various aircraft. Overhead, a World War II PT-17 and TG-4 Glider are suspended from the ceiling in simulated flight.

One of Robins Air Force Base's major missions during World War II was training personnel to establish maintenance and logistics depots in all theaters of combat. One of the first was an English airfield. A museum exhibit highlights one of the foremost fighters from this English base, the North American P-51 Mustang. The plane is shown being prepared for a mission against the Nazi forces.

Bomber Row traces the planes used from the early days of the war through the dropping of the first atomic bomb. The B-29, exhibited here, was cocooned at Robins after the war, then de-cocooned and reserviced for the Korean War.

The jet age began during the Korean War, as you see in the diorama focusing on this combat. The museum shows an F-84 in a revetment (a sandbagged protected embankment) undergoing field maintenance during a winter campaign in Korea. A "Huskie" helicopter and U-10 "Super Courier" represent the Vietnam conflict. The story of Operation Desert Shield and Desert Storm is told with video and photographs.

From exhibits visitors learn about the evolution of the cockpit, the development of electronic countermeasure weapons and systems, the mechanics of flight, the basic principles of aerodynamics and how to fly. For this last lesson, visitors can actually sit in a simulator and practice.

The history of flight in Georgia and the establishment of Robins Air Force Base are also reviewed. The Georgia Aviation Hall of Fame honors individuals who have made significant contributions to aviation. The first inductees were Ben T. Epps, Eugene Jacques Bullard, Guy Orlando Stone, Frank O'Driscoll Hunter, Hazel Raines, Hamilton McWhorter III and Robert Lee Scott, Jr. Additional members are added annually. A 15-minute video *Georgia Takes Flight* moves from a 1909 monoplane to the modern jet era.

Among the noted aircraft on display are the world record breaker SR-71 Blackbird, the last operational Lockheed U-2C

"Dragon Lady" that broke 16 world records in its last two weeks of operation, the only WW II British Aerospace Lightning on exhibit in the U.S. and a camouflaged painted C-60 Lockheed "Lodestar."

The Museum of Aviation is open at no charge 10:00 A.M. to 5:00 P.M. daily. The Home Front Gift Shop has plane models, leather flight jackets, aviation books (including autographed copies of Scott's book), WW II patches and other related items. Sandwiches, soup and beverages are available in the cafe.

Directions: From I-75 take Exit 45, Route 247 Conn-Watson Boulevard, make a right on Route 247, and the museum entrance is just past the Russell Parkway underpass.

Noah's Ark and Indian Spring

Creatures are Teachers

Animal lovers should put Noah's Ark on their list of must see spots. There's nothing fancy about this farm; the layout is crowded and chaotic (when they complete their new Welcome and Educational Center they will be able to spread out), but what's important is the feeling imparted by the staff and their interaction with the more than 600 animals at this outstanding educational rehabilitation facility.

You sense you've stumbled into a special place when you see bear cubs rolling on the floor with a miniature pig, while a baby lamb tries to get into the game. There's always a variety of cats and dogs underfoot. Many of the animals are like children, soliciting affection from visitors.

Noah's Ark is not a zoo, and it was not established to collect a wide variety of animals, although it does have quite a menagerie. Noah's Ark has one of the largest variety of species of any rehabilitation or educational facility, and it has animals such as binturongs that are no longer found in zoos. Founded by animal-trainer and breeder of miniature pigs, Jama Hedgecoth, this farm rehabilitates injured and orphaned wildlife. The mostly volunteer staff, many related to Jama, treat and care for the animals until they can be released back to the wild. If the injury is such that the animals could not defend themselves or forage for food, they become permanent residents at Noah's Ark. Exotic and domestic farm animals are also treated and often become permanent residents.

The goal of Noah's Ark is to bring animals and people together. The animals are used in pet therapy at nursing homes, children's homes, schools and other institutions. This is a true labor of love and the donations of visitors pay only a small percentage of the roughly $6,000 a month it costs to buy food and medical supplies. The center has been in this location since the early 1990s; before that it was located for 13 years in the small town of Ellenwood. Noah's Ark is open on Saturday NOON to 5:00 P.M. and Tuesday through Friday by appointment. It's always a good idea to call before visiting to check the current schedule (706)957-0888.

Not far away you'll find **Indian Spring State Park**, the first park in the United States. The sulphur spring water was prized for its curative and restorative power by the Creek Indians, whose land this once was. Locals still stop daily to collect the aromatic medicinal spring waters.

In 1800, about eight years after the first white settlers came to the area, Chief William McIntosh built a cabin beside the sulphur springs. In 1823 McIntosh and a partner built a tavern and inn that proved so popular they added a two-story addition two years later.

McIntosh, born in 1778 of an English father and Creek Indian mother, was a dashing and enigmatic figure. He rose to the rank of Brigadier General in the U.S. Army, fighting in the War of 1812 and under Andrew Jackson in the Florida campaign. He also had great stature among the Creeks, becoming the Chief of the Coweta or Lower Creeks. In this capacity, in 1825, he signed the second Treaty of Indian Springs, ceding all remaining Creek lands to the state of Georgia.

Apologists for the beleaguered McIntosh maintain that Georgia was determined to possess the Creek lands and that treaty eliminated unnecessary bloodshed. But this was not the prevailing view, and three months after he signed the treaty, McIntosh was killed by a group of braves, selected for the mission in Council. They burned the home of the "pale-face Chief," scalped him and then displayed their trophy on a pole in their village.

Your tour of the **Indian Spring Hotel** includes the treaty room where McIntosh signed the fatal document. The hotel is significant architecturally as well as historically. It is the only known antebellum mineral springs hotel in Georgia that is still standing. The hand-planed boards, wooden pegs and handmade bricks of this Federal style inn are remarkably intact. The rooms are painted with the same marbleizing and bright colors that were originally used. The heyday of the hotel was from 1840 to 1860.

Restoration of the Indian Spring Hotel is an on-going project. The rooms, still unfurnished, are used for civic and community functions. The gardens have also been restored and are among the few authentic 17th-century flower, rose and herb gardens in the Southeast. The Indian Spring Hotel is open for tours on Sundays from 1:00 to 5:00 P.M. from May through October. There is also an Indian Museum at Indian Spring State Park along with such recreational options as swimming, boating and fishing in the 105-acre lake, hiking trails and picnic and camping facilities. To arrange accommodations call (706)775-7241.

Even if you don't hit this area around meal time, eat anyway because **Fresh Air Bar-B-Que**, (706)775-3182, between Indian Spring and Jackson is one of the state's best barbecue spots. This sprawling wooden establishment first started serving in 1929, and it has changed very little over the years. It is also famous for its Brunswick stew. The pork barbecue is cooked over hickory and oak coals while you watch. Fresh Air-B-Que is open Monday through Thursday 7:00 A.M. to 7:30 P.M. and stays open on Friday and Saturday until 9:30 P.M. You might find it open as much an an hour later on a summer evening when the folks just keep stopping by.

Directions: From I-75 south of Atlanta, take Exit 68, Locust Grove/Hampton/Jackson. Turn left off the exit ramp onto Hampton Road and take that until it ends. Turn right onto Route 23/42, and take it past the small town of Locust Grove. Keep your eyes open and you will see a road sign for Griffin Road/Locust Grove Road; turn right and continue 2.5 miles to Noah's Ark on the left. Noah's Ark is at 1425 Locust Grove Road. Return to Route 23 and continue south past Jackson to Fresh Air Bar-B-Que and Indian Spring.

Ocmulgee National Monument

10,000 Years of Human Habitation

Nomadic Ice Age hunters once tracked giant mastodons across the great land bridge connecting North America and Asia. Clovis point spears testify to the presence of these Paleo-Indian hunters on the Macon Plateau before 9000 B.C. When the climate warmed, the glaciers receded and Ice Age mammals became extinct.

Indians crisscrossed the continent in search of food and shelter. Some **Archaic Indians** established themselves along the Ocmulgee River, the first of numerous groups to inhabit this plateau over the course of a hundred centuries. The Ocmulgee settlers made knives, scrapers and axes of stone. By the time of Christ the first crude clay bowls were being augmented by jars and basins with decorative designs, and the Indians were planting seeds and harvesting small crops. During the **Woodland Period**, usually dated from 1000 B.C. to 900 A.D., the earliest mounds were built.

Around 900 A.D. a more advanced people, the **Early Mississippians**, moved into the region, living side by side with the

Woodland tribes. They eventually numbered more than 2000 and built a town of wooden homes on the Macon Plateau overlooking the Ocmulgee River. These were the people who created the huge, flat-topped earthen temple mounds and at least one burial mound. Their ceremonies and meetings were conducted in earthlodges.

Each mound is actually a series of mounds built on top of the other, each succeeding mound filled with earth and capped with clay. More than 100 burials were uncovered in the seven layers of the Funeral Mound at Ocmulgee. Its present height corresponds to the third stage; a large portion was destroyed when a railroad line was cut through the side of the mound in the 1870s. Early railroad work in the 1840s also destroyed part of the Lesser Temple Mound. The largest Mississippian mound on the Macon Plateau is the Great Temple Mound. At one time it was topped by rectangular wooden structures, and religious ceremonies were held there. The 50-foot-high summit was reached by a stepped ramp up the side of the mound.

There were several ceremonial earthlodges at Ocmulgee, and the best preserved has been reconstructed. Only the clay floor is original, dating back a thousand years. The lodge is 42-feet in diameter with a firepit in the center. Opposite the entrance is a clay platform shaped like an eagle with a forked eye. The platform has three seats, and around the wall is a bench with 47 seats. This could have been a year-round council house or a winter temple.

At one time the earthlodge was surrounded by a village of clay-plastered huts and other mounds. On the east side of the village are two lines of prehistoric trenches that may have been defensive or perhaps just borrow pits, where dirt was obtained to construct or fill the mounds. Over the years the mounds grew larger rising 20, 30, 40, 50 feet above the plateau and extending as much as 300 feet across. Then in 1200 A.D. the Mississippians abandoned the Macon Plateau. Nothing is known about their departure. They may simply have migrated elsewhere, been assimilated with other people, or perhaps even have died out. Their culture continued to thrive at other sites in the region.

About three miles south of the Macon Plateau, a new village was built by a people whose culture combined elements of both the Mississippians and the Woodland people. It was Indians from this **Lamar Culture** who were encountered by the Spanish explorer Hernando De Soto in 1540. The Lamar village's spiral mound is different from all others found in North America. The ramp to its summit circles counterclockwise in four complete traverses around the mound. Across a central plaza there was a second mound. A log stockade enclosed the village of rectangular houses grouped around the plaza.

The Lamar site is closed to the public, but special permits are issued at Ocmulgee National Monument for those who have a strong interest in seeing it. It is reached by a two-mile round-trip hike through a floodplain river swamp. Hazards include mud, water, mosquitoes, snakes, and thick vegetation. Another Lamar Culture site that is open to the public and is far more accessible, is Etowah Mounds in Cartersville (see selection).

The Indians' encounters with the Spanish introduced diseases that became epidemic and wiped out three-fourths of the original Native American population. Some of the survivors became known to the Europeans as **Muscogee Creeks**. At Ocmulgee, an English trading post was built about 1690 to serve English traders from Charleston who were eager to obtain furs and deerskins from the Creeks.

The film *People of the Macon Plateau*, is shown every 30 minutes in the Visitor Center. The movie traces the story of these ancient people and helps visitors orient themselves before exploring the site. The Visitor Center also has an archaeological museum with artifacts from the early people. Exhibits deal with farming, hunting, fishing and the development of weapons, tools and pottery.

The park has four-and-a-half miles of walking trails, one of which connects the seven major points of interest. If the weather is bad, you can take the Temple Mound Drive to the large mounds. If the weather is good, save time for the Opelofa Nature Trail that branches off the main walking trail and winds through the lowlands of Walnut Creek.

If Ocmulgee has a message, it is perhaps best expressed in Chief Seattle's remarks: "All things are connected. Whatever befalls the earth befalls the sons of the earth. Even the white man cannot be exempt from the common destiny. We may be brothers after all; we shall see. This we know: the earth does not belong to man, man belongs to the earth."

Ocmulgee National Monument is open daily except Christmas and New Year's from 9:00 A.M. to 5:00 P.M. You may picnic on the grounds.

Directions: From I-75 exit on I-16 east. Take Exit 4, turn left on U.S. 80, Coliseum Drive, then turn right and follow U.S. 80, Emery Drive, for one mile to Ocmulgee National Monument.

Old Clinton and Jarrell Plantation State Historic Site

Time Passed Wayside Village

Like Rip Van Winkle, Old Clinton, to the north of Macon, seems to have been asleep for well over a hundred years. The tree-shaded streets of what was once Georgia's western-most frontier settlement have not changed since the days when Andrew Jackson was president. Only a dozen homes and a few businesses are left from these bygone days. The town is a mile in diameter and a half mile in each direction from the courthouse square. It is hard to believe that this was once the fourth largest town in the state after Savannah, Augusta and Milledgeville. By 1830 land in Clinton was selling by the foot, and the density of population was greater than it is in Atlanta today.

Clinton's decline is attributed to several events. First and foremost was the lack of rail, river and road transportation. The railroad bypassed Clinton, running through Gray instead. The development of Macon, along the river south of here, also diminished Clinton's ascendancy. During the Civil War large parts of the town were destroyed by fire and they were never rebuilt.

Clinton is on the Antebellum Trail, but it has no plantations like Tara or Twelve Oaks. Instead it offers reminders of the first settlers who built their homes in the style popular in New England. The oldest of the dozen homes built between 1808 and 1830 is the **McCarthy-Pope House**, started a year after the town was settled in 1807. Restored by the Old Clinton Historical Society, it now serves as a museum and visitor center that is open by appointment. There are roughly 40 points of interest noted on the self-guided auto tour map of Old Clinton. Many of these spots simply note the locations of long-gone homes and businesses. Several law offices and the Methodist Church are still standing. The town's founding fathers are buried in the Old Clinton Cemetery enclosed in a wrought-iron fence.

The annual Old Clinton War Days, the first weekend in May, brings to life the skirmishes that occurred here during the Civil War. Confederate and Union encampments are open to the public, and there is a street dance, crafts and food of the era.

Only a short distance west of Clinton, nestled within the Piedmont National Wildlife Refuge is the **Jarrell Plantation State Historic Site.** Jarrell represents a later period than Old Clinton, reflecting a middle Georgia plantation between 1847 and 1945. Nineteen structures were built during this period, and for over 140 years the Jarrell family farmed the land.

The 1847 weathered Plantation Plain style main house is filled with artifacts, 90 percent of which belonged to the Jarrells. There are looms, spinning wheels, baby cradle, cobbler's bench and so many other items that this is considered the most complete collection of its kind in the state. Outbuildings include a three-story barn, smokehouses, wheathouses, sugar cane furnace, steam-powered gristmill, saw mill, shingle mill and syrup mill. Another house, visible from the trail but not on the tour is occupied by great-grandchildren of John Fitz Jarrell who built the first house.

When you arrive at **Jarrell Plantation's Visitor Center** the family home from 1895 until the 1920s, you will get a self-guided tour map that indicates 30 points of interest. The center also has exhibits on the history of the family and the farm. Many of the vegetables and flowers that grow in the garden now are the same as those planted when the garden was first laid out in the 1890s. Farm animals can be seen in the fields, pens and barns.

Throughout the year the plantation hosts a series of special events such as demonstrations by spinners, weavers, blacksmiths and woodstove cooks. Events include a May Sheep to Shawl day, a 4th of July Folklife Celebration, Family Farm Day in August, Storytelling in September, Syrup Making in November and Candlelight Tours in December. For details call (912)986-5172.

Jarrell Plantation is open year-round Tuesday through Saturday from 9:00 A.M. to 5:00 P.M. and Sunday 2:00 to 5:00 P.M. A nominal admission fee is charged. Down a gravel road a short bit from the plantation is the **Piedmont National Wildlife Refuge Visitor Center**. It has hiking trails and fishing in the Ocmulgee River.

On the other side of Route 23 is Lake Juliette with a 62-mile shoreline. The town of Juliette also has a gristmill built in 1927 that was at one time the world's largest water-powered gristmill.

Directions: From I-75 at Macon take Route 129 north to Old Clinton. If you are traveling to Old Clinton and Macon on the Antebellum Trail from Milledgeville, take Route 22. Then head west on Route 18 to Jarrell Plantation. If heading to the plantation first, take Exit 55B off I-75 and travel north on Route 23 for 18 miles.

Rock Eagle Mounds

Ah, Sweet Mystery

Georgia has two gigantic unsolved mysteries in the form of eagle effigies that puzzle scholars as much as visitors. The first, called the **Great Rock Eagle Mound**, is perched within a 4-H Club

Center about nine miles from Eatonton. As you approach the fence surrounding the mound, you see a marker that reads: "Tread softly here white man, for long ere you came strange races lived, fought and loved."

You wouldn't dare tread anything but softly when your eyes fall on this mound shaped like a great bird lying prone, its body rising ten feet into the air. Constructed entirely of milky quartz rocks, ranging in size from baseballs to boulders, the eagle measures 102 feet from head to tail and 120 feet from wing tip to wing tip.

The mystery is who built this massive bird and why? Scientists believe it was shaped by a prehistoric stone mound group that was known to have been in this area. The nearest dirt mound is 25 miles away in Greene County, but small stone mounds and cairns have been found not far from this Eatonton site. About 20 miles away at Lawrence Shoals on Lake Oconee is another Rock Eagle almost precisely the same size except for a 12-foot-wider wingspread.

Your perspective of Eatonton's Great Rock Eagle Mound is improved by climbing the granite observation tower built in 1937. This was also the year the first real archaeological work was done at the mound, although it had been measured and sketched in 1877 by a Georgia historian. The initial study was done by Dr. A.R. Kelly, who was doing a dig at an Indian village site three miles from the eagle. The area was inhabited by a branch of the lower Creek tribes, most likely the Hitchitis. Kelly dug several exploratory trenches on either side of the effigy, but discovered no potsherds, arrowheads or other artifacts. At the end of his study he reported that the rock effigy was a ceremonial mound used for tribal rituals by an ancient people who may have built it more than 6,000 years earlier. To put it in perspective, if the Rock Eagle was built 50 centuries ago, it may be twice as old as the Great Pyramids in Egypt, built around 2500 B.C.

Although no artifacts have been uncovered here, it has been found that the mound contained layers of soil. The top layer was humus and soil. Beneath that was an area of red clay, then yellow-brown clay loam, followed by another layer of red clay. But again, no information is available on why it was constructed in this manner. The six- to eight-inch-thick bottom, or floor, on which the bird mound was begun, consists of small head-sized stones imbedded in burned soil and burned organic matter.

Some conjectures have been offered. There are those who contend that the bird does not represent an eagle but rather a buzzard. Aboriginal people relied on buzzards to carry off carrion and waste that could cause disease. Eagles were considered destroyers. Other theories suggest that the effigy might have had significance as a totem of a great chief, who perhaps was buried beneath the mound. Whatever its ancient significance, it stands today as an amazing link with the far distant past.

The Rock Eagle Mound is located within a 4-H Club Center that can be reserved by groups by calling (706)485-2831. The center is on the shores of a 110-acre lake lined with public picnic areas, as well as boats and fishing facilities. The public can rent cabins and meeting space.

The second rock eagle is in the **Lawrence Shoals Recreation Area**, (706)485-5494. Here approximately 15 miles away, in addition to a museum that displays artifacts from the mound, you'll find a white, sandy beach with dressing rooms and nearby picnic tables and grills. There are also campsites, tent camping areas and playgrounds. Lake Oconee has two other recreation areas: Old Salem and Parks Ferry. At the latter, there is also a wildlife habitat.

Directions: From I-20, Exit 51, take Route 441 south towards Eatonton. Nine miles before you reach Eatonton you will see the entrance to the 4-H Club Center on your right. To reach the second rock eagle follow Route 441 into Eatonton, then turn left on State Route 16 east. Go approximately 12 miles and turn left when you see the sign for the Georgia Power Land Deptartment Field Office and the Lawrence Shoals Recreation Area.

Sporting Clay Shooting Ranges

Have a Blast!

The roots of sporting clay ranges go back to 18th-century English live-bird shooting. Pigeons were held beneath hats, and at the cry of "pull" the hats were knocked over and the birds released. Introduced in the United States in 1831, its popularity was influenced by protests from non-hunters, and by 1841, glass balls were substituted for live birds.

Various improvements were made with the glass-ball targets, but there were many problems associated with them. In the 1880s a flat disc target made of baked clay and pitch was invented, an innovation that virtually ended live-bird targets. The first clay target championship in the United States took place in New Orleans, Louisiana, in 1885. Today's clay targets are made of limestone and pitch because of their consistent hardness, but the name clay target remained unchanged.

The next advance was the development of a course that included "hunting shots." Thus skeet (a Norse word for shooter) courses were designed that introduced new angles and crossover double shots for flight patterns that duplicated that of live birds. By 1925 the English were enjoying a game called sporting, today the most popular shooting game in England. Introduced in this country less than a decade ago and now the fastest growing shooting sport in America, it combines the thrill of field shooting with the concentration value of target shooting.

Sporting clay courses simulate hunting in a more realistic manner than the traditional skeet and trap ranges. Most courses are laid out over 30 to 40 acres and designed much like golf courses. The sport has been dubbed "golf with a shotgun." Most enthusiasts prefer to shoot with the gun they hunt with, but non-hunters can rent guns at most shooting clubs. Low-brass, light-recoil shot shells in 7½, 8 or 9 shot are suggested. For many this has become a family outing with less experienced shooters getting pointers from the more skilled. It takes just a couple of hours to shoot a round of 50 to 100 targets. Most courses also have skeet, trap and other options for those with less time.

One of the finest, if not the finest, sporting clay facility in the country is **Cherokee Rose Shooting Resort** in Griffin. Dubbed "Disneyland for Shotgunners," this facility has a ten-field course (two more courses are in the planning stage) that can be shot as 50-or 100-shot rounds. The course is laid out in hunting-like settings, and great care was taken not to disturb the natural terrain. Several shooting stations are on steep hillsides, and the wooden platforms blend with the surroundings. A duck pond offers targets from three different machines.

Cherokee Rose has the only Starshot layout in the Southeast, a large fan-shaped target grid with sections numbered for degrees of difficulty. The shooter has to break the target as it flys through a section to get that score. The higher the number, the more difficult the shot. The club has a stimulating array of shooting games including skeet, a dove tower with five stations, bunker trap and three different flush games. There's also a one-of-a-kind shotgun game called Gatlin Guns. In this game when the shooter says "pull" the targets appear at random from a variety of different directions: the tower, the trap bunker or from one of the skeet houses.

Another area, Five Stand Sporting Clays, operates off the Bird Brain Computer, where the targets are thrown in combinations of singles and doubles. Up to five shooters can get the same program, but the targets are thrown in different order for each. Of the 24 courses in Georgia, Cherokee Rose offers the greatest variety of options and the most exciting layout.

Shooting Ranges in the Metro Atlanta Region

Bulletstop, Marietta, (404)425-3597
Cherokee Rose, Griffin, (800)421-2529, (404)228-CLAY

DeKalb Firing Range, Lithonia, (404)482-8965
Georgia Sport Shooting Association, (404)874-6805
Master Gunsman, Stone Mountain, (404)469-0933
On Target, Marietta, (404)952-7834
River Bend Gun Club, Dawson County, (706)893-3319
Shooters, Gwinnett Plaza, (404)623-6065
South River Gun Club, Newton County, (404)786-3752
Wolf Creek Trap & Skeet Range, Atlanta (404)346-8382
X-Caliber, Douglasville, (404)489-2797

Other Georgia Sporting Clay Association Members

Cat Creek, Valdosta, (912)686-7700
Little Pachitla, Newton, (912)294-7207
Meadows, Smarr, (912)994-9910
Millrock, Cummings, (706)889-2936
Pinetucky, Augusta, (706)592-4230
Pigeon Mountain, Chickamauga, (706)539-2287
South River, Conyers, (706)789-3752

State Botanical Garden of Georgia and Founders Memorial Garden

Research, Respite and Refuge

There was a botanical garden at the University of Georgia in Athens as early as 1832, and a short while later an arboretum was added. As the Athens campus expanded these horticultural areas were encroached upon and eventually eliminated. The suggestion was made in 1967 that the university once again provide a "living plant library." Two hundred and ninety-three acres were set aside in 1972 and planting began. In a little over ten years, the garden became the **State Botanical Garden of Georgia**. In 1990 a 20-acre wetland tract was added.

The garden encompasses three ecological areas common to the Georgia Piedmont: a scenic frontage along the Middle Oconee River, a hilly wooded area canopied by giant hardwoods and upland grass and wildflower plateaus. Some of the acreage still has 125-year-old beeches, while other parts of the garden are reclaimed cotton fields and cattle farms.

Along any of the five nature trails visitors are apt to see a wide variety of birds including the nearly extinct red-cockaded woodpecker. Hikers may spot white-tailed deer, rabbit, raccoon, opossum or fox. The longest of the color-coded trails, the White Trail, is the outermost loop. It covers a substantial portion of the western section of the garden and runs alongside the river for a while before heading into the hardwood forested upland plateau. The Red, Green and Blue Trails are short paths that loop in and around the first trail. The Orange Trail, also links with the White, and covers the eastern portion of the garden. It is especially good for birding because it is sponsored by the Georgia Ornithological Society. A short loop off the Orange Trail takes you to the site of ancient Indian mounds.

In addition to the natural growth, there are specialty gardens including native azaleas, shade and ornamental plants, roses, dahlias, daffodils, rhododendron, herbs, plus annuals and perennials. In 1992 work was begun for the three-acre International Garden. A winding stream connects the plant communities representing China and the Orient, Spanish America, the Mediterranean and Middle East, and the American South. Other specialty areas will be the Chinese Wilson Garden, the Bartram Garden, an Indian Garden, Threatened and Endangered Plants, Bog Garden, Herbs and a Physic Garden.

The focal point of the garden is the **Visitor Center/Conservatory**. A ten-minute audio-visual orientation program introduces the complex. Then visitors wander through a three-story gleaming glass-and-steel conservatory where tropical and semi-tropical plants grow along a clear stream. The center has a cafeteria and a well-stocked gift shop filled with items that will interest garden fanciers.

The State Botanical Garden of Georgia is open daily from 8:00 A.M. to dusk. The Visitor Center/Conservatory is open Monday through Saturday 9:00 A.M. to 4:30 P.M. and Sunday 11:30 A.M. to 4:30 P.M. No fee is charged but donations are solicited. For additional information call (706)542-1244.

The first garden club in the country was established in Athens in January 1891. The 12 ladies who founded the group are honored by **Founders Memorial Garden**, a series of living memorial gardens on the campus of the University of Georgia. The gardens are laid out on two-and-a-half acres surrounding the 1857 antebellum home that serves as the Headquarters for the Garden Club of Georgia. The design by Hubert Owens, founder and head of the university's Landscape Architecture Department in the 1940s, includes a formal boxwood garden and a perennial garden, an arboretum, two courtyards and a terraced area. In the estate's old smokehouse there is a museum of landscape design with photographs and mementos from the state's first club, including a painting of the historic first meeting. The house itself has been restored and furnished with period pieces. It can be toured Monday through Friday 9:00 A.M. to NOON and 1:00 to 4:00 P.M.

Athens has one additional spot of horticultural interest, and that is the tree that owns itself, certainly one of the most unusual property holders in the world. Even Ripley's "Believe It or Not" featured this stately oak. Actually the original blew down in a windstorm in 1942, and the one standing today was planted from one of its acorns. Legend claims that University of Georgia professor William H. Jackson deeded to the oak on his property "entire possession of itself and of the land within eight feet of it on all sides." It is not certain that this deed was actually filed, but the townspeople did recognize the tree's title to the land and nurtured the magnificent oak. You can see Jackson Oak, Jr. at the intersection of Dearing and Finley streets.

Directions: From I-85 north of Atlanta, take Route 129 southeast through Jefferson to Athens. The State Botanical Garden of Georgia is two miles south of the main campus in Athens at 2450 South Milledge Avenue.

Uncle Remus Museum and Eatonton

Oft-Told Tales

Georgia poet Frank L. Stanton said of Joel Chandler Harris, author of the Uncle Remus tales: "He made the lowly cabin-fires light the far windows of the world." Fittingly, the Uncle Remus Museum is a log cabin made from two original Putnam County slave cabins. Though neither black, nor a slave, Joel Chandler was born in an equally spartan cabin in Eatonton, on December 9, 1848.

Joel's mother was deserted by his father. She worked as a seamstress, and she and her son lived in a cabin that the people of the community let her use. Up to the age of 11, Joel had some schooling. Although shy, he was mischievous and he got into some trouble. There's a story about his letting hogs loose in the livery stable.

Young Harris had a keen mind, and his favorite spot in town was the Post Office where he was allowed to read the discarded newspapers and magazines. When he was 13 he saw the first issue of *The Countryman*, a newspaper published at Turnwold, a local plantation. This was the only weekly ever published at a Southern plantation. There was an advertisement in the paper: "Wanted. An active, intelligent white boy, 14 or 15 years of age, is wanted at this office, to learn the printing business." Joel was hired by publisher Joseph Addison Turner. This was to be a turning point in Harris's life.

It was at Turnwold that Harris became friends with "Uncle" George Terrell and "Uncle" Bob Capers, plantation Negroes whose stories Harris later captured in his renowned Uncle Remus tales. Under the tutelage of Turner, Joel began writing for the newspaper. This fruitful period ended in 1864 when Sherman's army invaded Putnam County. When publication of the paper ceased, Harris moved on, working on newspapers in several Southern cities. He ended up at the *Atlanta Constitution*, and it was under the guidance of Captain Evan P. Howell, his editor, that he began publishing his Uncle Remus stories. These were popular in both the North and South, and Harris's fame spread worldwide. Joel Chandler Harris died in 1908 at the "Wren's Nest," his Atlanta home (see selection).

At the Eatonton museum one corner of the cabin looks like Uncle Remus's fireplace where he told his stories to the Little Boy, who was Joseph Addison Turner's young son. Hanging on the cabin's wall is a large portrait of Uncle Remus and the Little Boy. Walt Disney gave the museum the original watercolor drawings that were used for the Uncle Remus movie. Also on display are woodcarvings of Harris creations like Br'er Rabbit and Br'er Fox and 12 dioramas based on his stories. The museum's second cabin contains Putnam County memorabilia.

The Uncle Remus Museum is open daily from 10:00 A.M. until NOON and from 1:00 to 5:00 P.M. On Sundays it is open from 2:00 to 5:00 P.M. Closed Tuesdays. A nominal admission is charged. Yes, the museum sells Uncle Remus books; it also has a prized collection of first editions.

It is obvious to anyone driving into the town that Eatonton is proud of its native son. Many Southern courthouses have Confederate statues on their grounds, but the Putnam County Courthouse Square has a statue of Br'er Rabbit. It's a definite photo opportunity for anyone passing through. Eatonton is the birthplace of yet another noted American writer, Alice Walker, the first black woman to win the Pulitzer Prize for fiction. There are plans for a riding tour that will encompass Alice Walker's birthplace, church and family cemetery.

It's worth the time to stray from Eatonton's main street on to North Madison Avenue, and have a look at the stately antebellum homes along the side streets. The cottage where Joel Chandler Harris lived with his mother stood behind the Greek Revival home at 114 N. Madison Avenue. One of the town's loveliest homes is the **Reid-Green-Lawrence-Wood House** at 205 N. LaFayette Street. Former owner, Mrs. Louise Lawrence, in speaking of the house said, "It represents the best of an era that was doomed from the start. But it represents a part of every Georgian's and every Southerner's heritage."

Directions: From I-20, Exit 51, take Route 441/129 south to Eatonton. You'll pass the Rock Eagle 4-H Club Center nine miles before you reach Eatonton (see selection).

Regional Trails and State Parks

Antebellum Trail

Length: 117 miles
Gateways: You can access the trail via I-75 south at Macon or via
  Route 441 south at Athens and 441 north at Milledgeville
Theme: Romance of the Old South
Background: Developed by a University of Georgia student to link
  Georgia communities that capture a feeling of the Old South
Highlights: (individual selections are starred *)
*Athens: three decades of antebellum opulence exemplified by
  massive-columned mansions and magnolia-shaded gardens, home
  of the University of Georgia
*Watkinsville: Eagle Tavern (see Happy Valley Pottery)
*Madison: 19th-century town considered "the most cultured and
  aristocratic town on the stage route from Charleston to New
  Orleans"
*Milledgeville: in 1803 Georgia's Capital City
*Old Clinton: in 1820 Georgia's fourth largest city
*Macon: In the 19th-century this city was the "Queen City of the
  South"

Peach Blossom Trail

Length: 90 miles
Gateways: You can access the trail via I-75 south at Jonesboro and
  McDonough, via I-75 north at Perry and Forsyth
Theme: Peaches, People and Places
Background: Each year along this trail the peach blossoms delight
  travelers. The trail was created to recognize the importance of the
  peach industry to the state of Georgia
Highlights: The places starred (*) are written up in the individual
  selections.
*Jonesboro: Clayton County is where Margaret Mitchell situated
  Scarlett O'Hara's "Tara"
McDonough's: Geranium Festival, 3rd Saturday in May
Hampton: Site of Atlanta International Raceway
Barnesville: Three presidents have visited Buggytown
Culloden: Site of intense Civil War Battle
Forsythe's Left Banque: Trendy restaurants and boutiques in restored
  area
Crawford County's Roberta/Knoxville: Where Texas's Lone Star flag
  was made
*Fort Valley/Byron: Peach industry center, Massee Lane Gardens

*Warner Robins: Georgia's Aviation Museum, the city hosts
   International City Festival every April
*Perry: Georgia's Crossroads City, site of Georgia Agricenter

State Parks

Hard Labor Creek State Park, Rutledge (see Happy Valley Pottery
   selection)
High Falls State Park, High Falls (see selection)
Indian Spring State Park, Indian Spring (see selection)

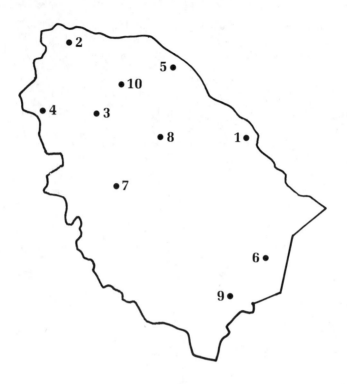

CLASSIC SOUTH

1. **Augusta**
   Cotton Exchange and Historic District
   Meadow Garden and Woodrow Wilson Boyhood Home
   National Golf Club and The Masters
   Riverwalk

2. **Comer**
   Watson Mill State Park

3. **Crawfordville**
   Alexander H. Stephens State Historic Park

4. **Greensboro**
   Jackson House and Lake Oconee

5. **Lincolnton**
   Clarks Hill Lake and Elijah Clark State Park

6. **Millen**
   Magnolia Springs State Park and Bo Ginn National Fish Hatchery

7. **Mitchell**
   Hamburg State Park

8. **Thomson**
   Belle Meade Hunt
   Upcountry Plantation Tour

9. **Twin City**
   George L. Smith State Park

10. **Washington**
    Callaway Plantation
    Kettle Creek Battlefield
    Robert Toombs House and Washington Historical Museum

———Classic South———

Legends—some were born here, some were invented and some just come to play in this mid-eastern region. George Washington visited Augusta in 1791. The state's largest ginkgo tree was planted where he stood to see where city fathers planned to build their Government House. Fifteen years later Parson Weems printed a fable in an Augusta shop, and the legend of Washington chopping down the cherry tree was born.

Two legendary Civil War characters had their homes in this region. Stories abound about good friends A.H. Stephens and Robert Toombs. Legend even suggests that the missing Confederate treasury lies buried in this region. More factual details on the final days of the Confederacy can be learned at The Washington Historical Museum. The early boyhood home of Woodrow Wilson, a towering world figure of a later age, is in Augusta.

Golfing legends make an annual pilgrimage to the Masters Tournament, a classic competition, on a course established by Bobby Jones. And finally, the pageantry of fox hunting as seen at Belle Meade is as colorful and enriching as the legends they inspire.

A. H. Stephens State Historic Park

Little Big Man

In August 1937, Margaret Mitchell received a copy of *The Sage of Liberty Hall*, a book about A. H. Stephens. In her letter expressing interest in both the man and the house, she wrote, "I frequently feel very apologetic when Northern visitors tell me indignantly (as though I had personally had a hand in it) that they cannot find any of the places I mentioned in *Gone With The Wind*. I always suggest that they visit Liberty Hall...How wonderful it is that it has been made possible for people to see Mr. Stephens's home as it was during his lifetime."

Alexander Hamilton Stephens was one of the most prominent and popular Georgians of the 19th century. Born outside Crawfordville in 1812, Little Aleck, as he was called throughout his life, was small of stature. He was five feet seven inches but seemed shorter because of his hunched posture. Frail of frame, he weighed under 100 pounds for most of his life.

Stephens's mother died when he was only three months old, and he lost his father at age 14. He lived with his uncle General Aaron Grier until 1832, when he received financial aid to attend the University of Georgia, then called Franklin College. His college roommate was Crawford Long. (It should be noted that these two Georgians, Long and Stephens, are represented in the Hall of Fame in the Capitol in Washington, D.C.)

After graduation Stephens taught for two years, then returned to Crawfordville to study law. After only three months he was admitted to the bar and began his practice in the county courthouse. Boarding with the Williamson Birds he grew fond of their house, and in 1845 he purchased it from their estate. Stephens call the Bird home his Bachelor's Quarters, adding a back wing and kitchen. In 1875 he demolished the main house and reconstructed the **Liberty Hall** visitors see today.

By the time he acquired the Bird House, Stephens was actively involved in the political career that would fill the remaining years of his life. He was a congressman for 16 years before the War Between the States and for ten years after the war. Once Georgia seceded from the Union, Stephens was chosen as the Vice President of the Confederacy and later during the last year of his life he served as Governor of Georgia.

Although frail, with a high-pitched shrill voice, Stephens was considered a skilled orator, who argued passionately for the causes he supported. His words swayed some and angered others. Abraham Lincoln, a fellow congressman from Illinois, wrote in 1848, "Mr. Stephens of Georgia, a little, slim, palefaced, consumptive man. . .has just completed the best speech of an hour's length I ever heard." But that same year Atlanta Judge Francis H. Cone thought so little of Stephens's words and actions he called him a traitor.

A heated correspondence between the two was filled with blistering words, and when they unexpectedly met in an Atlanta hotel, Cone drew a knife and chased Stephens around the lobby. Barely half the size of his opponent and unarmed, Stephens had only his umbrella to protect him and was soon on the floor. Cone stabbed him repeatedly and severed an artery in his hand before he was finally pulled off the bleeding Stephens. Though most of Stephens's wounds healed, he never fully regained use of his right hand. Ironically, Stephens and Cone had been friends before the harsh words led to blows, and their friendship was resumed after the fight. Cone went on to become a Judge of the State Superior Court.

Stephens's support of certain issues left many of his followers dismayed. He was not a secessionist and voted against Georgia leaving the Union in 1861. His was one of 89 "nays" against Georgia's 210 secession supporters. Had 16 additional delegates voted against leaving the Union, the Confederacy may well have foundered in its infancy. Georgia was the largest and most prosperous slave state, and only four states had seceded at the time the Georgia convention met.

Consideration was given to electing Stephens president of the Confederacy. Another more eager candidate was his best friend, Robert Toombs (see Toombs House selection). The two Georgians divided the state delegates' votes, and Jefferson Davis of Mississippi won the position with Stephens being chosen as vice president.

Robert Toombs was a frequent guest at Stephens's home Liberty Hall; in fact, a bedroom was designated as his room. Even these two friends occasionally argued. During one altercation, Toombs said, "You little squirt, I could pin back your ears and swallow you whole." To which Stephens retorted, "You'd have more brains in your stomach then, than you have in your head."

After the war, Stephens was arrested by Union soldiers and taken to Fort Wayne in Boston Harbor where he was imprisoned for four months. In 1869, shortly after Stephens returned to Liberty Hall, a heavy iron farm gate fell on him, crushing both hips and breaking both legs. From that time until his death, he had to use a crutch and wheelchair.

After his injury Stephens tore down the main house and rebuilt the house you'll see when you visit. He designed his new house putting his bedroom off the main hall at the front of the house. The bedroom has an adjoining sitting room. In 1990 a restoration was completed that took the house down to its heart pine walls and floors. The environment that Stephens enjoyed has been painstakingly recreated. Detailed descriptions from Stephens's days enabled restorers to redo the house and recover or reproduce the furnishings that once filled the rooms.

Stephens died in March 1883, just 119 days after his inauguration as Governor of Georgia. His body has been reinterred at Liberty Hall. A monument over the grave bears his words: "I am afraid of nothing on the earth, above the earth, or below the earth, except to do wrong."

During your tour of Stephens's home note the array of medicine on the table in his bedroom, his built-up shoes and three wheelchairs. After the accident Stephens wore built-up shoes and walked with a cane. Eventually he needed two canes, and in later years he used a rolling chair, but he was never a true invalid. You'll see his portrait done when he was 63.

After you tour the house, you should see several outbuildings including a servants' house used by Harry and Eliza. The pictures of their family on the wall and the religious tracts are worth noting. A nearby kitchen is filled with utensils and cookware and there is a wash house.

Adjacent to the house is the **Confederate Museum**. Cases are filled with articles typically found in Southern homes during Stephens's time, including some pieces that belonged to A.H. and his servant Dora. There are also artifacts from the war and from field hospitals. A 16-minute audiovisual show lets you hear Congressional arguments on secession and the war. There is also a camp scene depicting two soldiers in a wartime camp.

The A. H. Stephens State Historic Park has tent and trailer sites, picnic shelters, a nature trail and two lakes for fishing. The house and museum are open Wednesday through Saturday from 9:00 A.M. to 5:00 P.M. (closed for an hour at noon) and on Sunday from 2:00 to 5:00 P.M. The last tour starts an hour before the closing. The park itself is open daily 7:00 A.M. to 10:00 P.M. A nominal admission is charged at the historic site. A park pass fee is charged in the park.

Crawfordville has been the setting for several popular films and television shows including Hallmark Hall of Fame's "Home Fires Burning" with James Garner, numerous episodes of "I'll Fly Away," "Dukes of Hazzard" and the movie *Paris Trout*. The place to eat in town, actually it's the only restaurant, is Bonner's Cafe. Open since 1923, this spartan restaurant on the town square serves delicious Southern specialties. The crust on the fried chicken is worth a second visit. Mrs. Bonner has been running the cafe for 78 years.

At Christmas time, the Bennett family, who live in the Crawfordville area, put more than 200,000 lights around their 15-acre property. Hundreds of trees and seasonal decorations are illuminated from Thanksgiving through New Year's. The Historical Society sells crafts, baked goods, coffee and hot chocolate.

Directions: From I-20 take Exit 55, Crawfordville, and head north on Route 22 for two miles. Then take Route 278 east for one mile to Crawfordville. The park is located two blocks north of the county courthouse.

Augusta Cotton Exchange and Historic District

King Cotton

In 1793, Eli Whitney operated an experimental cotton gin near Augusta. He had perfected his invention at Mount Pleasant Plantation just east of Washington, Georgia. Whitney's cotton gin heralded a new age of prosperity for Augusta, a city established in 1736 on the banks of the Savannah River as an outpost for Indian trading.

During the 1800s, Augusta grew with the booming cotton industry. By the late 1800s, the city was the second largest (Memphis was first) inland cotton market in the world. The construction of the Augusta Canal in the 1840s provided waterpower for Augusta's textile mills. More than 100 mercantile firms were based here by mid-century.

The Cotton Exchange now serves only as a Welcome Center, but there are plenty of reminders of the boom days. You can still see the pulse of the exchange, the wall-size, 45-foot blackboard with notations that go back to the earliest days of trading. (They have survived because the blackboard was covered by a sheetrock wall.) In its heyday the Augusta Cotton Exchange had more than 200 members, including representatives from England, France, Germany, South America and India. The Cotton Exchange building was last used in 1964, but a few member companies are still brokering cotton. In 1990 three of them, S. M. Whitney Company, Jackson Company and Graniteville Mills, met for their 118th meeting to broker their cotton.

In 1886 the current Augusta Cotton Exchange building was erected after $9,000 in bonds were sold to finance the project. The building contained brokerage offices and the trading floor, where buyers and sellers watched the blackboard for the day-to-day prices of cotton and other commodities. You can still see old markings that indicate whether the cotton was "strict good middling" or just "fair middling."

Women and children were not admitted to the exchange because the men watching the trading activity whiled away the long hours playing checkers and cards. After the market closed the men enjoyed cock fights and bet on various other events.

The **Cotton Exchange Museum** has examples of tools used for planting and picking cotton. There is a photographic montage of cotton workers in the field. Exhibits tell about the boll weevil and the lien system. There's an old telephone booth used by the brokers for private transactions. A weather map was important to the cotton brokers because an untimely freeze or hale storm could damage the crop. The market aspects of the industry are highlighted as well, and there are antique adding and ticker-tape machines.

In 1978 the Augusta Cotton Exchange was listed on the National Register of Historic Places, and in 1988 through 1990 it underwent a full-scale restoration. Once again the architectural beauty of this Queen Anne and Second French Empire-styled building can be appreciated. The interior heart pine wood was painstakingly recovered after layers of paint were removed. Missing window frames were rebuilt using material to match the originals. It cost over 80 times more to restore the exchange than it did originally to build it.

The Historic Cotton Exchange Welcome Center is open Monday through Saturday from 9:00 A.M. to 5:00 P.M. and Sunday 1:00 to 5:00 P.M. The exchange is located at 32 Eighth Street at Riverwalk. For information call (800)726-0243 or (706)724-4067.

After you leave the Cotton Exchange if you stroll a short distance down the Riverwalk past the Shoppes of Port Royal, you will reach **St. Paul's Episcopal Church**. Markers on the church grounds indicate where Fort Augusta was built in 1739. One marker indicates that in 1763 roughly 700 Indians from five Indian nations met at Fort Augusta with the governors of Virginia, North and South Carolina and Georgia. The governors wanted the Indians to cede to the states land in north Georgia and North Carolina. Encounters with Indians had not always been so peacable. After James Oglethorpe had arranged for the first church in 1750, men attended services in the newly erected house of worship armed with two loaded pistols or a rifle.

The first Federal Marshall ever killed in the line of duty was a Georgian, Robert Forsyth who died at age 40 on January 11, 1794. He is buried in St. Paul's Cemetery. Forsyth and his deputy tried to arrest a Methodist minister for failing to pay his debts, and the minister shot Forsyth and escaped. During the Revolutionary era a battle took place near where the church stands. The British built the 30-foot Meyhem Tower out of logs approximately where the cotton exchange stands and fired a cannon from the tower top into Fort Augusta, capturing it and renaming it Fort Cornwallis. During the Revolutionary War, Augusta was the capital of Georgia.

The church you see today is the fourth to stand on this site and is a replica of the third church; the first two frame churches burned. St. Paul's does have the original 1751 baptismal font brought from England by the first rector, Reverend Jonathan Copp. The stained-glass windows in the church were done by Gorham, Geissler, Payne and Tiffany. The organ, with its 2,638 pipes, creates a splendid sound. From autumn through spring there are free Tuesday music programs in the church.

Another church you should visit in Augusta is the **Sacred Heart Cultural Center** at 1301 Greene Street. This building, reminiscent of great European cathedrals, first began services for the Catholics of the Augusta area in 1900 (the Sacred Heart congregation was established in 1873). This towering edifice with 15 distinctive styles of exterior brickwork, brilliant stained-glass windows and interior columns and arches was in danger of being razed when community action saved it and converted it to their use. Weddings, parties, lectures, concerts and a wide variety of other events are scheduled in the Great Hall. Church rooms are used for studios, offices, classrooms and a well-stocked gift shop that displays local artists' and authors' works. It is open Monday through Friday 10:00 A.M. to 4:00 P.M.

Also on Greene Street in the 500 block, in front of the Municipal Building, is the Signers' Monument. George Walton and Lyman Hall, two of Georgia's signers of the Declaration of Independence, are laid to rest beneath this monument. The Augusta historic district can be toured on your own; all you need is a map of the area, available at the Cotton Exchange Welcome Center. If you make reservations ahead of time you can join a guided tour of the city's historic sites. The hour-and-a-half tours leave the Welcome Center at 10:30 A.M. on Saturdays. Call Historic Augusta, Inc. (706-724-0436) by 3:00 P.M. on the preceding Friday. Admission is charged. There are also Civil War sites in and around the city that can be combined on a tour including the Confederate Powderworks Factory, Confederate Monument and Magnolia Cemetery. You can schedule a Black Heritage Tour that covers over 28 sites and attractions (not all associated with Black history), and includes a drive past the former home of poet and author Frank Yerby.

Perhaps the most curious story told in Augusta concerns a preacher. According to old-timers, a traveling minister was refused permission to preach in the Lower Market. The minister flew into a towering rage and bellowed that the entire market would be destroyed save for one post. There are those who claim that all subsequent attempts to remove the post resulted in injuries. Although it no longer stands on its original site, myths still abound about what some call the Haunted Pillar.

One of the spots most tours mention is **Ware's Folly**, so called because the $40,000 construction price was considered foolishly exorbitant in 1818 when this Federal style house was built. Unusual architectural touches include the exterior curved three-tiered central portico and the interior elliptic staircase ascending three stories. The building now houses the Gertrude Herbert Institute of Art, an independent art gallery and school. The gallery shows regional artists and southeastern contemporary art. The galleries are open Tuesday through Friday from 10:00 A.M. to 5:00 P.M. and Sunday 1:00 to 4:00 P.M.

Augusta boasts a wealth of alternative-use space, including the Sacred Heart Cultural Center, the Gertrude Herbert Institute, the Old Government House and the Telfair Inn. George Washington, during a visit to Augusta in 1791, was shown the site on which the Old Government House was to be built. A ginkgo tree was planted where Washington stood by those who wished to celebrate his visit. Now the tree is the largest ginkgo (86 feet tall and 13 feet, 6 inches in circumference) in the state, and in the fall this champion tree showers the grounds with golden, fan-shaped leaves. The seat of city government was not finished until 1801, and by 1821 it was sold to Samuel Hale who turned it into an elegant private home. Today Old Government House and grounds look much as they did in the 19th century. The house can be booked for private functions, and it is also open for tours by appointment.

Just down the street is Telfair Inn, which is comprised of 14 Victorian homes along Telfair Street. The furnishings may be old-fashioned, but the amenities are up-to-date including whirlpool baths. The inn has tennis courts, swimming pool and hot tub. For information call (800)241-2407 or (706)724-3315.

Elegant and historic accommodations are also available in the 105 oversize suites at the **Partridge Inn**, Augusta's landmark hotel. The inn was built in the early 20th century, incorporating an early 19th-century house, and over the years the service here has been refined into a fine art. Dining at The Partridge is a real treat. The inn is at 2110 Walton Way; for information call (800)476-6888 or (706)737-8888.

The Partridge is only one of Augusta's noted restaurants. Several others should not be missed. Barbecue fans flock to Sconyers Bar-B-Que, a place that boasts it has served the White House. This spot is only open Thursday through Saturday from 10:00 A.M. to 10:00 P.M. (404)790-5411. If you're in town during Masters week, you're apt to see a lot of the golfers at Luigi's, 590 Broad Street. Regulars will have dropped by the week before to satisfy their cravings for delicious Italian and Greek specialty items. The Ballast family has been serving customers for four decades.

Not all the architecture in Augusta is old. Three of the buildings were designed by I.M. Pei including the Chamber of Commerce building, the Civic Center and the Penthouse portion of the Lamar Building.

Directions: Take I-20 to Augusta. The Cotton Exchange Welcome Center is the place to pick up a map of the city and literature on Augusta's many attactions, restaurants and shops.

Augusta National Golf Club and
The Masters

Golf Capital of the World

The first golf course in Augusta was designed in 1897 by the Bon Air Golf Club, now the Augusta Country Club. Over the years this nine-hole course was expanded and other courses added. By the 1920s Augusta was a popular golfing destination that attracted one of the sport's best players, Bobby Jones. He and his friends traveled from their homes in Atlanta to play the courses of this riverside city.

In 1930 Bobby Jones became the first—and thus far, the only—golfer to win the Grand Slam. He won the Open and Amateur championships of the U.S. and Great Britain in a single year. Having achieved this pinnacle, he found himself surrounded by an admiring gallery wherever he played.

Bobby Jones solved his commuting problem and changed the world of golf when he found the land for his dream course. The idea of laying a course had long been a goal of his, and in 1930 he found the land he was seeking at a nursery in Augusta.

Fruitlands Nursery was established by a titled Belgian family, the Berckmans, in 1858 on what was originally an indigo plantation. Both father and son were enthusiastic horticulturists, and some of the most common southern shrubs and trees were developed at Fruitlands Nursery, the first commercial nursery in the South. Remnants of the Berckman's plantings remain on the golf course. Each hole of the course is named for the dominant shrub or nearby tree. Banks of azaleas, stands of large pines and clusters of camellias all date back to when the land was a nursery.

When Bobby Jones had his first look at the 365-acre nursery grounds, he exclaimed, "Perfect. . .and to think this ground has been lying here all these years waiting for someone to come along and lay a golf course on it." Jones invited Scottish architect Dr. Alister Mackenzie to help him design the course. The holes were not copies of other courses or classical golf holes. Instead they were designed as originals to complement the gently rolling Georgia terrain. Dr. MacKenzie claimed that a good golf hole depended to a large extent on its background and Augusta National's can't be beat. In the years since it was laid out perhaps 500 courses across the country have been remodeled or designed to include features of the Augusta National layout.

As soon as the course was ready for play, the U.S. Golf Association suggested they hold a tournament on Jones's course. But Bobby Jones and his business associate Clifford Roberts, who had arranged the purchase of the nursery for $70,000, decided

Home of the Masters Tournament and often called the Golf Capital of the World, Augusta boasts more than 20 golf courses, 12 of which are public.

to hold their own event. They had already formed a private club with membership drawn from across the country.

In 1934 Bobby Jones and his committee invited golfers to compete in the Augusta Invitation Tournament. The press immediately dubbed it the **Masters**. Bobby Jones resisted calling it that, thinking the soubriquet was presumptuous. But in 1938 Jones gave in, and the Invitational Tournament officially became the

Masters Tournament, one of the most renowned and esteemed sporting events in the world.

Horton Smith won two of the first three tournaments. During the 1935 Masters, Gene Sarazen (who went on to win in a playoff) hit one of the most dramatic strokes in tournament play, later called the "shot heard around the world." Sarazen's 220-yard four-wood shot on the 15th hole in the 4th round gave him a double eagle and set him up for the win. It also assured the Masters a preeminent position in the world of golf.

Golf legends Ben Hogan and Sam Snead dominated the Masters from 1949 to 1954, winning five out of six tournaments. The next titan on the scene was Arnold Palmer who won in all the even years from 1958 to 1964. Sharing the spotlight with Palmer was Jack Nicklaus. Between them they won seven Masters in nine years between 1958 and 1966, doing more than any other golfers to elevate the Masters to its position as one of golf's greatest events. There are those who say Nicklaus comes as close as any golfer since Bobby Jones to owning the course. Nicklaus has won six Masters, had four seconds and two thirds. His last tournament victory was in 1986.

The 1980s was the decade of the international golfer. South African Gary Player started the trend in 1978. It was his third win; others were 1961 and 1974. Then Seve Balesteros of Spain won in 1980 and 1983. West Germany's Bernhard Langer won the 1985 Masters. British golfers won in 1988 and 1989: Sandy Lyle and Nick Faldo, and Faldo won again in 1990. In 1991 Welsh golfer Ian Woosnan won the tournament.

Knowledgeable sports enthusiasts claim that the Masters is the toughest ticket in sports; it's almost impossible to obtain an entry. The only way the general public can ever get on Augusta National is to watch a practice round on one of the three days preceding the tournament. Tickets for the practice rounds are purchased the day of the event and gates open at 8:00 A.M. The enormous demand for tickets has prompted the tournament to limit the number of available tickets, so watching a practice round is likely to become more difficult. For information about practice round tickets write Masters Tournament, P.O. Box 2086, Augusta, GA 30913 or call (706)738-7761.

If you want to swing your club in the Masters' city, there are more than 20 courses in the area and 12 are public. Many of the city's hotels and motels offer golf packages. The **Georgia Golf Hall of Fame** was established in 1982, and eventually memorabilia will be exhibited in the Richmond County Museum scheduled to be built in Augusta in 1994. If you want information about golf in and around Augusta, call the Cotton Exchange Welcome Center at (800)726-0243 or (706)724-4067.

Directions: Take I-20 to Augusta. The Visitor Information Center where you can pick up maps showing the location of all the golf courses in and around Augusta is in the Historic Cotton Exchange at 32 Eighth Street at Riverwalk.

Augusta's Riverwalk

Beauty, Bustle and Bounty

The picture-perfect brick walkway along the Savannah River with its lavish banks of various flowering plants looks so absolutely right for the setting it's hard to imagine Augusta without it. Yet Riverwalk is still a new phenomenon, the early phases of which were finished as recently as 1987. Augusta residents and visitors alike flock to the riverbank. It's popular for picnics, midday walks, moonlit strolls, starlit concerts and excellent for watching action on the river.

Riverwalk's main access is the levee-break at Eighth and Reynolds streets. In front of the passageway stands a fountain that sends a geyser-like spray of water into the air. It's certainly refreshing on a hot summer day. As you walk through the levee, notice the lines indicating the water levels from Augusta's most devastating floods. In the flood of 1929 the water rose 149 feet above sea level, 144 feet in 1940, and 135 feet in 1964.

You can climb the steps to the brick esplanade on the upper level of the Riverwalk. It's lined with benches and there are historical markers that provide details about the river, about the cotton business and about Augusta's early history. Augusta was the second largest inland cotton market (Memphis was the first) in the world until the mid-20th century. You'll learn that during the peak cotton season, stacked bales were so numerous on Reynolds Street—Cotton Row—that a person could walk on top of bales from Fifth to Thirteenth Street without setting foot on the pavement. A flag terrace represents all the nations that played a role in the history of this city. There is also a lower path along the river. Besides the main entrance there is one at Tenth Street by the Radisson Hotel and Augusta Conference Center and one at Ninth Street that leads to the riverside amphitheater where evening concerts are presented. The streets that lead to these access points abound with quaint boutiques, local art galleries and diverse eateries, like the King George Pub at 10 Eighth Street.

At the opposite end of the four blocks that make up the original section of Riverwalk are the **Shoppes of Port Royal**, a French-developed retail center. This two-level complex at Seventh Street features unique stores. Jamaica Me Crazy offers Caribbean designs, music and frozen drinks. Georgiou has ladies' single-de-

Augusta Riverwalk, the cornerstone for riverfront development along the Savannah, is the place to meet for picnics, strolls, concerts, cruises and water sports.

signer fashions and Colette's offers internationally imported fashions and fragrances. The complex has several restaurants that overlook the river including Mesa Grill and Cantina, Patty Arbuckle's and Mikoto Garden as well as some informal eateries. The mall hours are Monday through Saturday 10:00 A.M. to 9:00 P.M. and Sunday NOON to 6:00 P.M. Restaurants stay open later.

New festivals and new traditions have come with Riverwalk. One that gained immediate community support is the Junior League's Festival of Trees held in late November at the Shoppes of Port Royal. Non-stop entertainment, a Christmas Tree Lane and Gingerbread Village are just part of the fun of this five-day event. Other holiday celebrations held along the river are St. Patrick's Day Weekend, an Easter Sunrise Service, Riverfront Fourth Celebration and Oktoberfest.

During the spring and summer Augusta hosts three world-class watersport competitions. The fun begins in late March with the Augusta Invitational Rowing Regatta when top rowing teams from around the country and the world test their skills on the 2,000-meter course. There are customarily about 35 collegiate teams competing. In mid-June the International Outboard Grand Prix Series holds a River Race. Formula One boats take hairpin turns at 140 mph in hopes of winning the largest purse in Amer-

Each spring top teams from all over the world compete on the Savannah River in the Augusta Invitational Rowing Regatta.

ican outboard motorboat racing. The following month Hardee's Augusta Southern National is held. This race is sanctioned by the U.S. Drag Boat Association and includes 150 hydroplane, or flatbottom, boats from across the country.

A much slower, calmer boat, the *Princess Augusta*, plies the Savannah River throughout the year offering sightseeing cruises, Sunday brunch, cookout cruises, a lock and dam trip, dinner dance cruises and special events. The 65-foot paddlewheel steamer is a replica of a 19th-century sternwheeler. The boat leaves from the Fifth Street dock, but reservations are advisable for most trips. Call (706)722-5020.

Directions: Take I-20 to Augusta and exit onto River Watch Parkway.

Belle Meade Hunt

The Glory Days

Fox hunting is a living reminder of an era passed—the traditional riding outfits, the thrill of the chase, the pageantry of the hunt itself. Watching, one yearns to be a part of the action. At Belle Meade hunts, visitors in tallyho wagons take to the field with the riders.

The Belle Meade Hunt was founded in 1966, 200 years after American fox hunting began in Philadelphia. George Washington's diary is filled with references to fox hunting. By the time of the Civil War, the landed gentry in Maryland, Virginia and Pennsylvania were fox hunting enthusiasts. Belle Meade is one of approximately 120 organized hunts in the United States and Canada. What surprises some visitors is that this is an egalitarian sport whose participants include men and women, young and old, as well as representatives of all economic levels.

Over the years, under the stewardship of founder and Hunt Master James E. Wilson, Jr., the Belle Meade Hunt has established a worldwide reputation for excellence. The members adhere to proper hunting attire, believing that part of the pleasure of hunting comes from the feeling of tradition and spectacle. Today the term fox hunting conveys the wrong impression; fox chasing would be more apt because the whole point of the activity is the thrill of the chase. All the foxes hunted are wild. The fox has much more to fear from highway traffic than from hounds. He is a sporting animal himself, leading the chase as long as he likes. When he's ready, the fox typically climbs a tree, goes into one of his many dens or swims down Maddox Creek to wash his scent away. Hounds are called up and the hunt moves on.

Carrying on the pageantry of fox hunting, the Belle Meade Hunt has established a worldwide reputation for excellence.

The hunt starts when the hunters, the members of the field, are joined by the foxhounds. The pack is disciplined and responds to the Huntsman's horn. Once the horn sounds, the hounds take off. A typical chase lasts 30 or 45 minutes. Throughout the day the hounds are cast numerous times, whenever a fresh scent is found. Of course, there are occasional days when no scent is found. The hounds can chase by scent or by sight; the latter producing more rapid pursuit. While the hunters jump fences and race through the woods, the tallyho wagon full of spectators tries to keep up with the action.

Twice a week, from November to March on most Wednesdays and Sundays, the Belle Meade Hunt usually takes to the fields from 1:00 P.M. until dark. The tallyho wagon goes out for several hours. The cost is roughly $10 and reservations need to be made a week in advance. (Call Mrs. Keith Green for current schedule at (706)855-7258.) You will be sitting on hard benches without any protection from the elements, so if the weather is cool be sure to dress warmly and bring a cushion or seat-rest. You also may bring snacks and coolers. The current Huntsman and Joint Master of the Fox Hounds is Epp Wilson, whose father founded the group. The elder Wilson continues as Senior Master of the Fox Hounds. The Wilson family owns and operates the Best Western White Columns Inn in Thomson, and you can call there for additional information, (800)528-9765 or (706)595-8000. Or call the County Tourism Bureau at (706)595-5584.

If you want to be part of a very special day, plan to watch the Opening Meet on the first Saturday in November. This is when the Belle Meade Hunt stages the **Official Blessing of Hounds** on the lawn of the white-columned Knox estate. The blessing takes place at 1:00 P.M. with the hounds moving off at 1:30 P.M. Close to 100 riders are usually on hand. Pageantry is never more keenly felt than at this annual opening ceremony.

Directions: From I-20 take Exit 59. Drive north on Route 78 to Knox-Rivers Road and make a left. Travel 1½ miles and make a right on Wrightsboro Road. Take that for two miles to the Belle Meade hunt barn on the left where the fox hunt begins and where you board the tallyho wagon. You can also watch the action from the nearby public roads.

Callaway Plantation and Kettle Creek Battlefield

Timeless Fields

Callaways settled in east central Georgia in the late 18th century, and the plantation they built can be seen today. The oldest building at Callaway Plantation is the 1785 settler's cabin and the newest, excepting the smokehouse, is the Greek Revival manor house built in 1869.

Callaway Plantation is a rich evocation of Southern antebellum life, as seen through successive generations of one family. The Callaways still own the land that surrounds the 56-acre core of the plantation. Most of the furniture and equipment you'll see in the various buildings belonged to Callaways.

The Callaways who settled the land lived in the rough-hewn functional **log cabin** for approximately five years. The kitchen, the cabin's single downstairs room, is fully stocked with crockery and pans. A bake oven is built into the masonry of the fireplace. Old tools hang on the walls, and there is an assortment of primitive furniture. Upstairs the sleeping loft now holds a collection of old tools.

In 1790 the Callaways built a Federal Plainstyle two-story, four-room **frame house**. They continued to use the cabin as an out-kitchen. Other dependencies include a smokehouse, pigeon house and barn. In the fields you'll see the kind of crops the Callaways planted in the 19th century: cotton, corn, cane and a variety of vegetables. Small herds of cattle are again raised here.

By 1869 when the plantation encompassed 3,000 acres, the family built a Greek Revival **manor house**. It looks much the same today as it did then: the doors, mantels, jib windows and most of the plasterwork are original. Legend has it that the reason Parker Callaway could build such a fine home after fours years of Reconstruction when so much of the South was suffering extreme economic hardship was that his had been the last boat load of cotton to leave the Savannah harbor when the Civil War broke out; it got out before the blockade was imposed. One of the last shipments to reach England, it commanded a high price. The money also gained interest in the Bank of England throughout the war, giving the Callaways a distinct edge when they finally could reclaim their fortune.

Some of the furnishings are original to the house, but all are from the 1890s. A number of the pieces were acquired in Europe. When a bidet arrived at this Georgia plantation, it was believed to be a baby's bathtub or foot bath. One of the upstairs bedrooms has a laundry basket similar to the one that was used to smuggle Acting Governor Stephen Heard out of jail during the Revolutionary War. Heard's family sent a black servant to the jail, ostensibly to get the laundry. But she succeeded in gaining Heard his freedom.

The Revolutionary years are also brought to mind eight miles east of town just off Route 44. A commemorative marker indicates the site of the 1799 **Kettle Creek Battle**. Led by Elijah Clark, Andrew Pickens and John Dooley the local Patriot force attacked the British troops under Colonel John Boyd. The British were caught unprepared, making a meal in their big cooking kettles. Legend claims they were cooking cattle they had stolen and butchered. During the first assault the Patriots swept past the pickets and took the high ground. Boyd tried to counter-attack but was mortally wounded; 40 other Tories died in the battle and 75 were captured. Colorful stories claim the jubilant Patriots threw the cooking kettles into the creek. After this rout, which occurred on St. Valentine's Day, the British troops withdrew from up-country Georgia for the duration of the war.

Callaway Plantation is open from March through mid-December Tuesday through Saturday 10:00 A.M. to 5:00 P.M. and Sunday 2:00 to 5:00 P.M. A nominal admission is charged. There's a Country Store on the complex that sells Callaway Garden merchandise besides an assortment of handcrafted and gourmet specialties.

Directions: On I-20 head east towards Augusta. Take Exit 53 to Greensboro. Continue through Greensboro on Route 44 past Union Point to Washington. Callaway Plantation is five miles west of Washington on Route 78 across from the Washington-Wilkes Airport.

Clarks Hill Lake and Elijah Clark State Park

No Clark Bar Here

Part of the southeastern border between Georgia and South Carolina is formed by a U.S. Army Corps of Engineers lake, the largest east of the Mississippi River. On the South Carolina side it's called Thurmond Lake and on the Georgia side, Clarks Hill Lake. This 70,000-acre lake is one of the largest inland bodies of water in the South with a total of 1,200 miles of shoreline. It is also one of the ten most visited Corps lakes in the country.

Recreational opportunities are plentiful on and around the lake. There are five Corps recreation areas in Georgia, and most have boat ramps, fish cleaning stations, piers, beach, playgrounds and picnic areas. The Lake Springs' area also has a hiking trail. Nine Corps campgrounds are located on Georgia's side of the lake plus three state parks, three county parks and the U.S. Army recreation area.

Boat rentals can be arranged at four commercial marinas: Mike's Marina in Appling (706)541-1358, Soap Creek Lodge in Lincolnton (706)359-3124, Raysville Bridge Marina in Thomson (706)595-5582 and Tradewinds Marina & Yacht Club in Appling (706)541-1380. All but the latter have campgrounds.

Fishing is one of the most popular sports in the area. The lake has white, striped and hybrid bass, but the largemouth bass is probably most plentiful. Other game fish include crappie, blue-gill and sauger. The lakeside woods abound with quail, dove and small game and are well-known hunting areas. Boating, water skiing and swimming are also recreational options.

On the western shores of Clarks Hill Lake is the 447-acre **Elijah Clark State Park**. It honors the Georgia Revolutionary War hero and frontiersman who led pioneers against the British. Clark's victory at Kettle Creek in the "Hornet's Nest" of Wilkes County was a turning point for the war in the South. It gave new hope to the cause of freedom and encouraged others in the area to continue the fight.

Clark died on December 15, 1799, and he and his wife Hannah are buried in the park. A replica of his log-cabin home is filled with furniture, utensils and tools from the 1780s. Two special events bring the pioneer years to life. The second weekend of October is the Fall Pioneer Rendezvous with cooking, Indian dancing, musket loading, blanket shoot and primitive weapon exhibits. On the first Saturday of December a Log Cabin Christmas is celebrated; this is a reenactment of the first Clark family Christmas.

The state park also has a beach, playground, miniature golf, four boat ramps, 165 tent and trailer sites, and 20 lakefront cottages. For more details, call (706)359-3458. One popular non-historical festival, the Lewis Family Homecoming and Bluegrass Festival, is held here the first weekend every May. The Lewis family, who are billed as "America's First Family of Bluegrass Gospel Music," are joined by other popular country, gospel and bluegrass groups. The park office is open 8:00 A.M. to 5:00 P.M. If you are hoping to rent one of the well-situated cottages, plan ahead; six months lead time is not excessive. These cottages and RV sites are among the most popular in the state.

While in the area you can stop and check the progress on the Lincoln County Historical Society Park, a work in progress. The Society is restoring the May House, home of one of the town's first doctors. Adjoining the house is the doctor's office, also being restored.

A little bit of the past that's still in use is **Price's Store**, not far from town. Now operated by the fourth generation, this is one of the state's oldest continuously operated country stores. It looks as though not many improvements have been made since it opened in 1897, but that's part of its charm. It has all the ingredients country store buffs seek: a pot-bellied stove surrounded by well-used chairs, a well-stocked penny candy case (this one has a wooden ledge so youngsters can see into the glass case), a huge wheel of cheese and homemade country ham biscuits. The store is open from 7:00 A.M. to 6:00 P.M. six days a week.

Directions: From I-20 head north on Route 47. To reach Price's Store travel four miles and turn right on Ashmore-Barden Road and take it to the end, then turn right on Doubles Branches Road following it one mile to the store on the right. To reach The Lincoln County Historical Park return to Route 47 and continue north into Lincolnton. For Elijah Clark State Park take Route 378 for seven miles northeast of Lincolnton.

Greensboro, Jackson House and Lake Oconee

The Greening of Georgia

In 1784 the Cherokee and Creek Indians abandoned their land north of the Oconee River. Scotch-Irish from the Carolinas and Virginia were among the settlers who headed into the region. Many of these settlers obtained the land under the "heads-right" grant, a reward of 250 acres of land with tax-free status for ten years to former Continental Army members and supporters of the Revolutionary cause.

Greene County was organized in February 1786 with Greensboro as the county seat. One year later the Creek Indians were back, raiding the town, burning it to the ground, killing 31 residents, wounding 21 others and taking some as prisoners. Within four years the town was rebuilt, and Greensboro was described in *A Gazetteer of Georgia* as having a dozen cabins built on the ruins of the first community.

The oldest building you'll see in Greensboro is the Old Gaol built on Main Street in 1807. It may well be the oldest jail in Georgia. Used until 1895, this fortress-like structure has granite walls two feet thick and a trap door in the second floor through which condemned prisoners were hanged. Patterned after the Bastille, the jail had two domed, dungeon-like cells that were wet, cold and impossible to heat.

Be sure to take the time to go into the **Post Office** on Main Street to have a look at two paintings done as part of the Works Progress Administration (WPA) program of the 1930s. The idea of decorating post office walls with mural art came from George Biddle, a schoolmate of President Franklin D. Roosevelt's. Biddle told Roosevelt that these murals would be "living monuments [to] the social ideals that you are struggling to achieve." The two Greensboro murals (most post offices got only one) were painted by Carson Davenport of Tennessee. One depicts both black and white cotton pickers from a time when the entire county was planted in cotton. The second depicts the burning of the town by the Creek Indians.

Many of the buildings on Main Street were used by the Confederate government as hospitals for the wounded. In the City Cemetery 45 unknown Confederate soldiers, wounded during the battle for Atlanta, are buried. The **Greene County Courthouse** on Main Street is one of the finest examples of Greek architecture in the entire state. The three-story building with four huge Doric columns is so highly regarded it was featured on the cover of a recent volume on courthouses across the country. This courthouse is unique because the upper floor is owned by the Masonic Lodge, an arrangement that has continued since 1848.

The Mary Leila Cotton Mill was Greensboro's most impressive industrial complex. Incorporated in 1899, the mill was named after the wives of the mill owners. Near the mill you can see approximately 75 millworkers' cottages, most still occupied, in a variety of styles: shotgun, bungalow and Victorian eclectic. For more details about the history of the town stop at the Greene County Historical Society Museum at the corner of East and Greene streets, open Monday through Friday, 2:00 to 5:00 P.M.. The Society displays a large photographic collection, Indian artifacts, as well as old clothes and memorabilia.

The area around Greensboro suffered economic decline after the Civil War. In 1883 William Reid Reynolds built the two-story Victorian Gothic **Jackson House** for his family here and various branches of the Reynolds family (not the tobacco Reynolds) acquired thousands of acres of land in Greene County for use in timber production and as a hunting and fishing retreat. On completion of the Wallace Dam in 1979, a sizeable portion of Reynolds land was flooded and Lake Oconee (a Creek word meaning great waters), the state's second largest lake, was formed. Out of the remaining property, Reynolds heirs established a lake and golf community called **Reynolds Plantation**.

The family's ancestral home, scheduled for demolition, was dismantled and relocated on a knoll overlooking the entrance to Reynolds Plantation. This steamboat Gothic house is one of the few left in the South. Its most distinctive feature is the elaborately carved and decorated trim on the porch that sweeps around two-thirds of the house, like wrap-around decks on the old steamboats. The inside is decorated to look as though people were still living in the house; it does not feel like a museum. Behind the house is a fully equipped summer kitchen and a playhouse.

Though Reynolds Plantation is basically a resort community, accommodations are available to travelers. Outstanding golf courses include the Plantation Course, rated by *Golf* magazine as one of the "top ten new resort courses in the world." Designed by U.S. Open Champions Fuzzy Zoeller and Hubert Green in association with designer Bob Cupp, this course opened in 1988. In 1992 the Jack Nicklaus Great Waters Course opened. Tennis, swimming, boating and water sports are also featured. The shores of **Lake Oconee** are dotted with other golf resort communities such as Harbor Club and Port Armor.

The water level on this 19,000-acre lake remains constant regardless of the climatic conditions because a unique set of pumps built into Wallace Dam allows water below the dam to be pumped back into the lake as needed. The lake has more than 374 miles of shoreline, and there are two public recreation areas totaling 85 acres: Old Salem and Parks Ferry. These parks offer swimming, fishing, boat ramps, plus picnicking and camping facilities. The Georgia Power Company can supply information about public access to the lake; call (706) 485-8704. The waters of Lake Oconee are stocked with striped, largemouth and white bass, bream, crappie and catfish. Wildlife is found in abundance in and around the lake. The area harbors deer, wild turkey, foxes, rabbits and other small game as well as countless waterfowl.

Directions: From I-20 take Exit 53 and head north on Route 44 to Greensboro. For Reynolds Plantation of Lake Oconee take Route 44 south to the well-marked entrance on the left. For Old Salem Park: After you take Exit 53, head south on Route 44 for 7 miles. Turn right onto Linger Longer Road. Drive 1.5 miles, turn right and follow signs to Old Salem Park.

Magnolia Springs State Park and Bo Ginn National Fish Hatchery

Fish and Shells, Birds and Dogs

Andersonville is Georgia's most notorious Civil War prison camp, but Camp Lawton outside Millen also held Union prisoners. The camp was built on this site because of the area's natural springs. The 40,000 prisoners held here had a better source of water than those at Andersonville because Magnolia Springs's crystal clear water flows at an estimated nine million gallons per day.

When Sherman's march through Georgia brought him close to Millen, the prisoners were evacuated to Savannah and the camp abandoned. Sherman burned a great portion of Millen. All that remains of the prison camp are two huge timbers, once part of the walls, that were recovered from the stream.

Today the 948-acre park is a sylvan recreational spot within Georgia's coastal plain. The park has a swimming pool, four playgrounds, five cottages, picnic shelters and 26 tent and trailer sites. There are two nature trails and the wildlife is abundant. You may spot rabbits, deer, turtles, alligators and a large selection of native birds. Bird watchers have sighted red-cockaded woodpeckers, wood storks and Canada geese in the icy-cold spring water pool that is home for many species of birds, reptiles, fish and aquatic plants. You may bring your own boat or rent a canoe or fishing boat. There is a dock and the lake is ideal for fishing and water skiing. The park office is open 8:00 A.M. to 5:00 P.M.; for information on park accommodations call (912)982-1660.

A footbridge leads from the park to the adjacent **Bo Ginn National Fish Hatchery and Aquarium**. The hatchery was established in 1950 and since then has raised three million fish annually for stocking and research purposes. There are 27 ponds within the 127-acre warm-water hatchery. Since the population of striped bass, also known as rockfish, began declining the hatchery has focused on propagating that species.

When you visit the hatchery you can see the holding house, production ponds, raceways and spawning pens. There is also a 26-tank aquarium that displays fish raised at the hatchery as well as bluegill, sturgeon, channel catfish, perch, bowfin and a host of other specimens. The aquarium is open at no charge from 9:00 A.M. to 4:00 P.M. daily.

After exploring these spots, continue up the road to Waynesboro, the "Bird Dog Capital of the World." It's also a major cotton growing region. As you head into town on Route 25, if you turn left on 4th Street (it becomes Herndon Road) and proceed about seven miles, you will be in cotton country. Cotton grows on both sides of the road for as long and deep as you can see.

Exhibits on both cotton and bird dogs can be seen at the **Burke County Museum** at 536 Liberty Street in the heart of Waynesboro. Housed in the 1858 J. D. Robert House, the museum is open Monday through Friday from 9:00 A.M. to 5:00 P.M. and Saturday from 1:00 to 5:00 P.M. An entire room is filled with tools and equipment needed for cotton production. There's a turn-of-the-century cotton scale; the average bale weighed between 480 and 500 pounds. The details of marketing and selling cotton are covered as well as the dangers of the boll weevil.

If you are in the area in January and February you might want to watch the Georgia Field Trials, one of the oldest hunting dog competitions in the nation. They have been held here since 1905. The dogs are judged on how well they run the birds. You can watch these trials from wagons that follow the action, criss-crossing the fields with the dogs.

Each year the National Shoot to Retrieve Field Trial Association and Quail Unlimited, "QU Dog of the Year Trial" is held at the Boll Weevil Plantation, a hunting and fishing preserve just outside Waynesboro. This historic plantation encompasses 5,771 acres and has excellent quail, deer, wild hog and dove hunting as well as six lakes for fishing. For more information call (706)554-6227.

While you are in the Waynesboro area you also might want to head nine miles east of town (take Route 56 for five miles and then Route 80 for four miles) to a shell bluff on the Savannah River. You can find giant oyster shells on the sandy bluff overlooking the river. There are thousands of these shells sticking out of the sandy soil. The bluff is adjacent to the Georgia Power Vogle Nuclear Power Plant, and you can stop at the plant's Visitor Center to see exhibits on nuclear power.

Directions: From I-16 take Route 121 north, it merges with Route 25 just before Millen. Five miles north of Millen on Route 25 is the entrance to Magnolia Springs State Park.

Meadow Garden and Woodrow Wilson Boyhood Home

Houses with History

George Walton conquered a string of adversities in his rise from humble beginnings to his position of prominence in Georgia. The date of his birth is uncertain; it's given as any time from 1740 to 1750. What is known is that his father died within months of George's birth, and his mother died before he was seven. He was reared near Farmville, Virginia, by his uncle.

Apprenticed by age 15 to a carpenter, Walton had little formal schooling but did undertake extensive independent studies. In 1769 Walton moved to Savannah, where his elder brother lived. George studied law and in five years took the oath of allegiance to the British king, a step necessary to join the bar. Within two years he had one of the most successful legal practices in Georgia.

Early in his legal career, Walton plunged into politics, becoming a leading activist in the state. He was a member of the colony's first Council of Safety and the early Committee of Correspondence. In 1776 Walton was appointed to the Continental Congress in Philadelphia, and he arrived just in time to join Button Gwinnett and Lyman Hall in signing the Declaration of Independence for Georgia. George Walton had the distinction of being the youngest of all the signers.

Walton became a colonel in the Georgia militia and was wounded and captured during the siege of Savannah in November–December 1778. It wasn't until the following September 1779 that the British exchanged Walton for a navy captain of theirs.

Later that fall Walton was elected governor. When the newly elected legislature met a few months later in January 1780, they picked someone else for governor. Walton returned to the Continental Congress. He went from there through a succession of offices: chief justice, justice of the State Superior Court, delegate to the state constitutional convention (1788), governor (1789-90), U.S. senator (1795-96).

It was while serving as governor that Walton moved from Savannah to the new capital in Augusta. At this time he built **Meadow Garden** cottage on the northern edge of the city on confiscated Loyalist land that he had acquired. Despite his high offices, his economic situation was not strong. George Walton's wife was more than a decade younger than he. When they married in September 1778 he was 28 and Dorothy Camber, either 14 or 15. By the time they moved to Meadow Garden they had had two sons, Thomas Cambor and George Jr. To protect his family, Walton never listed the Meadow Garden property in his own name because he wanted to ensure that it would be passed to his son at his death.

When Walton lived at Meadow Garden the house had but two rooms and no hallway. In 1835 it was enlarged to the 1½-story Sandhills Cottage style frame house you see today. The house is furnished with late 18th- and early 19th-century pieces. Octavia Walton LaVert, the granddaughter of George Walton, was born after the signer's death, but she remembers the family's claim that George Walton "filled the inside with books and the outside with mulberry trees." In the parlor, which contains the house's finest architectural feature, a lovely late Georgian mantel, visitors can see a portrait of George Walton.

Meadow Garden is open for tours Tuesday through Saturday from 10:00 A.M. to 3:00 P.M. The house is closed Sundays and major holidays.

The **Woodrow Wilson Boyhood Home**, 419 7th Street on the corner of Telfair Street, is diagonally across the street from the First Presbyterian Church of Augusta where Wilson's father was minister.

Tommy Wilson, as the future president was called in his youth, was 12 months old in 1856 when his father was transferred to Augusta from Staunton, Virginia. The Wilsons lived in Augusta until 1870. Years later in a speech Woodrow said, "My earliest recollection is of standing at my father's gateway in Augusta, Georgia, when I was four years old, and hearing someone pass and say that Mr. Lincoln was elected and there was to be war. Catching the intense tones of his excited voice, I remember running in to ask my father what it meant."

Tommy Wilson lived in Augusta through the highly impressionable years of one to 13. Here you discover an individual

much more full of fun than the scholar-politician he would become. He organized a secret club, the Lightfoot Baseball Club,
whose logo was a Red Devil, an idea borrowed from the label of
a commercial deviled ham. Fellow members were Joe and Phil
Lamar (Joe went on to become a justice of the U.S. Supreme
Court), sons of the Reverend James Lamar who lived next door,
and Pleasant Stovall (who went on to become Ambassador to
Switzerland). Boyish mysteries and adventure were concocted
in the dark barn behind the manse, where the only light came
through apertures high in the brick wall. Old-time Augusta residents still recall a town matron telling Tommy Wilson that he
and his friends would never amount to anything. Their favorite
playgrounds were around the city's great cotton warehouses.

As the Civil War progressed, Tommy saw his father's church
turned into a hospital. From his bedroom window he could hear
the cries of the wounded soldiers. The churchyard eventually
was used as a federal prison camp that held hundreds of Union
soldiers under guard.

The Woodrow Wilson Boyhood Home was built in 1859 in the
restrained Greek Revival Style. It looks much as it did when
Tommy Wilson lived there. His father's book-lined study was to
the left of the front door and the formal parlor, to the right.
Tommy's bedroom was at the back on the second floor. Restoration work is still being done, and the house will be furnished
with period pieces. Call Historic Augusta to arrange a tour
(706)724-0436.

Directions: Take I-20 to Augusta. You can pick up city maps
at the Visitor Information in the Historic Cotton Exchange at 32
Eighth Street at Riverwalk.

Robert Toombs House and The
Washington Historical Museum

Near Misses

For a brief time Washington was the temporary capital of Georgia,
and native son Big Bob Toombs was very nearly the president
of the Confederacy. Such are the brushes with history of this
scenic antebellum town, the first city to be chartered in honor
of George Washington.

Robert Toombs was one of Georgia's most impassioned and
charismatic politicians. His stellar gifts were offset by his ebul-
lient lifestyle. He was expelled from the University of Georgia
for his drinking, gambling and carousing (although not for his
earlier offense of trying to kill two fellow students who had

The Washington Historical Museum houses one of the best collections of Civil War memorabilia in the South.

thrashed him). He lost his chance to be the president of the Confederacy by getting drunk in front of delegates to the provisional government. He went on to become secretary of state of the Confederacy, then bored by the routine, he quit to take up arms. As a brigadier general he bravely led his men but still had trouble taking orders and staying sober. Eventually he resigned his commission. Late in the war he once again took up arms as a colonel in the Georgia State Guard.

When Toombs first served in the U.S. Congress, he was considered a moderate, but with Abraham Lincoln's election he argued for secession. On January 24, 1860, he thundered, "Defend yourselves, the enemy is at your door. . ." In trying to persuade his fellow Georgians to fight the North, Toombs said, "We can whip the Yankees with cornstalks." After the war, when questioned about that boast, Toombs replied, "We could have, too. But the damn Yankees wouldn't fight with cornstalks!"

On another occasion when Toombs was giving a speech from the back of a train to a gathered throng, a man came through the crowd waving a telegram about the Chicago Fire. Toombs quipped, "the wind is with us." Local lore has it that a line on the oak tree outside the Toombs house shows where the Union troops were going to hang Toombs if they caught him. It's unlikely that story is true, but they did hope to imprison him. Toombs hid in the north Georgia mountains and then went into exile in Cuba and Europe until 1867. Returning to the United States, he refused to apply for a pardon, thus never regaining U.S. citizenship. This unreconstructed rebel declared, "I am not loyal to the existing government of the United States and do not wish to be suspected of loyalty."

A 25-minute film on Robert Toombs, who died in 1885, only touches the surface of this colorful Georgian. It does give information that will help you appreciate all that you see when you visit Toombs's home.

Joel Abbot, Connecticut physician and Georgia congressman, built the core of the **Toombs House** in 1797. Abbot later moved the house to its present location and added several appendages. When Toombs purchased the house in 1837, he also made changes, turning the kitchen into a law office and adding the Doric-colonnaded facade. Later he rebuilt the east wing and installed brass hardware, plumbing and gaslights.

Your tour starts in the warming kitchen and continues through the basement area where you'll see exhibits on the restoration work. On the main floor most of the books and much of the furnishings you see belonged to Toombs. Upstairs is a bedroom where Toombs's good friend Alexander H. Stephens, vice-president of the Confederacy (see selection), often stayed. A message from the host reads: "Welcome to the home of R. Toombs. Where the tradition of warm hospitality will always live."

The Robert Toombs House State Historic Site is open year-round Tuesday through Saturday 9:00 A.M. to 5:00 P.M. and Sunday 2:00 to 5:30 P.M. Closed on major holidays. A nominal admission is charged.

The town of Washington has four historic districts and within three blocks of the town square there are 13 sites on the National Register of Historic Sites. The last Cabinet meeting of the Confederacy met in May 1865, in Washington at the Heard House. At this meeting Jefferson Davis signed the last official papers dissolving the Confederate government. The courthouse, a fine example of Romanesque Gothic architecture, now stands where the Heard House once stood, and a marker notes the historic last meeting.

The Mary Willis Library, founded in 1888 by Dr. Francis T. Willis in his daughter's memory, is the state's oldest free public library. The library's genealogical and rare book collection attracts the serious researcher, and the priceless Tiffany stained-glass windows attract appreciators of beauty. The library also has the iron-bound chest in which Jefferson Davis carried out what was left of the Confederate treasury when Richmond was abandoned in April 1865. The treasury, estimated at over half a million dollars, was moved from one Southern city to another to keep it from Federal hands. A portion was seized when Davis was captured and also $100,000 held in a Washington bank. Washington was the last town to shelter the fortune, and there are those who believe some of the gold is still buried somewhere in Wilkes County.

For more about the history of Washington and Wilkes County visit **The Washington Historical Museum**. The earliest portion of the antebellum mansion that houses the museum was built around 1835. When Samuel Barnett, Georgia's first Railroad Commissioner, acquired the house in 1857, he greatly enlarged it. The furnishings are typical of an elegant Georgia home of the mid-19th century.

Civil War relics gathered by the Last Cabinet Chapter of the United Daughters of the Confederacy are exhibited at the museum. This collection is one of the finest in the South. In addition to Jefferson Davis's camp chest, it includes a Ku Klux Klan regalia from the Reconstruction days, General Robert Toombs's uniform and fascinating old photographs.

The museum is open Tuesday through Saturday from 10:00 A.M. to 5:00 P.M. and Sundays 2:00 to 5:00 P.M. A nominal admission is charged. While you're at the museum pick up a brochure with a driving tour map that will lead you to some of Washington's charming old homes.

Directions: From I-20 East take Exit 58, Washington/Warrenton. Turn left on Route 278 and go approximately one mile and turn right onto Route 47. In Washington make a right turn on Route 78, which is Robert Toombs Avenue. Go east to the house at 216 Robert Toombs Avenue.

Thomson Upcountry Plantation Tour

Camellia City of the South

During the Colonial period the area along Georgia's fall line, some 30 miles above Augusta, was called upcountry. The plantations in this region were working estates associated with the land; their architecture came to be known as Plantation Plain.

McDuffie County is fortunate to have the oldest house in the state with its design intact. In 1785, when most settlers were hewing logs for their cabins, Thomas Ansley, a settler from New Jersey, built his three-story home from field stones following the styles popular at the time in the Delaware Valley. Ansley, who is a sixth-generation ancestor of Jimmy Carter, and his family were Presbyterian, not Quaker. They nevertheless joined the Quaker settlement of Wrightsborough, which was established in 1768. Quakers from Greensboro and Hillsboro in North Carolina received a land grant from the Governor of the Colony of Georgia that included most of McDuffie County. After the Revolutionary War, the Quakers moved to Ohio and Indiana. The Wrightsboro church and cemetery, seven miles northwest of Thomson, date back to the Quaker period. This area marks the southernmost point of Quaker migration in North America.

The **Rock House** was added to the National Register of Historic Places in 1970 and in 1981 benefited from a complete restoration that reveals the detailing in the stonework and woodworking. The field stones were cut from nearby granite outcroppings. A technique called parging, which is similar to plastering, gives the interior walls a contoured look. They are also whitewashed.

You can view the house on a drive-by tour or arrange to see the inside by stopping by the Thomson-McDuffie Tourism Convention and Visitors Bureau. Their office is in the Thomson Depot at 111 Railroad Street, or you can call (706)595-5584.

The Thomson Depot is worth a visit, since the town was established as a railroad stop and was named for J. Edgar Thomson, who surveyed the area for the Georgia Railroad. He went on to become the third president of the Pennsylvania Railroad. The Thomson Depot, built in 1860, is now a community center. In the center of town there is a marble statue of a woman cradling a Confederate flag, one of the few monuments that honor Confederate women.

Overlooking the town is **Hickory Hills**, the antebellum home of Senator Tom Watson. An outstanding orator and popular political figure of the late 19th century, Watson is considered the father of Rural Free Delivery mail service. He ran for vice-president of the United States on the Populist ticket in 1896 and was the presidential candidate of the People's Party in 1904 and 1908.

The cabin where this agrarian rebel was born sits on the grounds of Hickory Hill. The lovely white-columned mansion, listed on the National Register of Historic Places, is privately owned and is not open for tours.

Two other architecturally interesting old homes are also privately owned and can only be appreciated from the road. The 1805 **Alexandria Plantation**, is a Virginia-style brick house built by Spotsylvania native Colonel Thomas Carr. He moved to Augusta to practice law then built this upcountry plantation. The boxwood gardens around this elegant house are worth noting. The second of the drive-past visual treats is **Snowhill**, an antebellum plantation house. In the fields near Snowhill look for the "cookie" cows, a distinctive breed whose black-and-white markings make them look like Oreo cookies. The owners of Snowhill also own the 1810 West Inn Bed-and-Breakfast in Thomson. This typical Piedmont Plains Plantation house has five attached dependencies. The inn is furnished with 19th-century antiques and equipped with 20th-century conveniences, (706)595-3156.

If you are traveling on your own you can pick up a map at the Thomson-McDuffie Tourism CVB and explore. If you are with a group, you can arrange an escorted Upcountry Plantation Tour that includes the significant attractions in and around Thomson. The tour takes between 2 and 2½ hours. The CVB office is open Monday through Friday from 9:00 A.M. to 5:00 P.M. except for Wednesday morning. On weekends, call ahead to arrange to get a driving tour map (706)595-5584. A substantial portion of Thurmond/Clarks Hill Lake is in McDuffie County (see selection).

Directions: From I-20 Thomson is directly off the interstate at Exit 59, Route US 78/GA 17. To get to the old town site of Wrightsborough, seven miles west of Thomson take Route 78 to where it intersects Wrightsboro Stagecoach Road. Turn left on Wrightsboro Stagecoach Road and proceed to church and old town site. You turn right on this road to get to the plantation houses. From Exit 60 follow Route 150 and turn left on Stagecoach Road. This is the historic Wrightsborough Road established in 1769. It's also part of the William Bartram Trail, a scenic route followed by the noted botanist who visited Wrightsborough in 1773 and 1774.

State Parks

Alexander H. Stephens State Historic Park, Crawfordville (see selection).

Elijah Clark State Park, Lincolnton (see selection).

George L. Smith State Park, Twin City; fishing lake, boat rental, picnicking and camping, (912)763-2759.

Hamburg State Park, Sandersville; scenic 1921 gristmill and museum, boating, fishing, hiking and camping, (912)552-2393.

Magnolia Springs State Park, Millen (see selection).

Mistletoe State Park, Appling; lake with beach, water skiing, boat ramp and dock, fishing, nature trails, picnicking, tent and trailer sites, cottages and camping, (706)541-0321.

Watson Mill State Park, Comer; covered bridge, fishing, boat and canoe rentals, picnicking and camping, (706)783-5349.

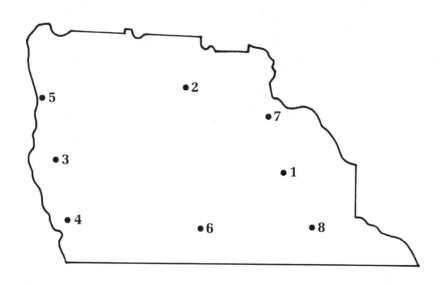

PLANTATION TRACE

1. **Adel**
   Reed Bingham State Park
2. **Albany**
   Chehaw Wild Animal Park
   Museum of Art
   Thronateeska Heritage Center
3. **Blakely**
   Kolomoki Mounds State Park
4. **Donalsonville**
   Seminole State Park
5. **Fort Gaines**
   Dill House
   Lake Walter F. George
   George T. Bagby State Park

6. **Thomasville**
   Lapham-Patterson House and
   Hardy Bryan House
   Pebble Hill Plantation and
   Susina Plantation Inn
   Thomas County Historical
   Society Museum and Cultural
   Center
7. **Tifton**
   Georgia Agrirama
8. **Valdosta**
   Crescent
   Drexel Park
   Lowndes County Historical
   Society Museum

═══Plantation Trace═══

Traces of the past are evident throughout this southwestern region. Stretching back into prehistory are remnants of one of the continent's largest Indian population centers. This thriving center vanished by the 14th century, but seven mounds remain to suggest the enormity of the accomplishment of the Swift and Weeden Island Indians at Kolomoki Mounds State Park near Blakely.

On a high bluff above the Chattahoochee River in Fort Gaines are reminders of another Indian era. Rough logs cabins and a replica of a frontier fort evoke Georgia's early days when newcomers were threatened by Creek and Seminole Indians. An authentic Creek Indian village is being added at Chehaw Wild Animal Park, where you'll see indigenous and exotic animals in a setting designed by naturalist Jim Fowler.

Traces of 19th-century rural life can be seen at the Georgia Agrirama in Tifton. Fields are tilled, household chores done, syrup prepared and shops and businesses once again sell handcrafted products and old-fashioned sodas.

A glimpse of the wide verandas and white columns of antebellum plantations can be seen in Thomasville and Valdosta. Many of these Southern homes were built by wealthy Northerners as shooting plantations. The Thomas County Historical Society provides a look at plantations off limits to the traveling public. Sportsmen still enthusiastically support many of these retreats, but one—Pebble Hill—is now a house museum.

Chehaw Wild Animal Park and Albany

Zoo in the Forest

A mile outside Albany, at Chehaw Park's 100-acre wild animal habitat, elephants, zebras, elk, bison, bears and deer roam as freely as they would in the wild. Visitors standing on the suspension bridge over the one-acre bobcat enclosure must have

This elephant roams free in the Chehaw Wild Animal Park.

keen eyes to spot the elusive cats in the southwest Georgia vegetation.

This wild animal park was designed in 1974 by Albany native Jim Fowler of Wild Kingdom fame. Plans are in progress to expand and redesign some exhibit areas, moving animals from cages and netted enclosures to natural environments. At the present time over 150 exotic and endangered animals are exhibited.

At the entrance to the habitat area is a gift shop, housed in a former South Georgia tenant house. Once expansion is complete this area will be expanded to include an interpretive and information center. A children's village and an orientation village are also on the drawing boards. This "zoo in the forest" presents animals from across the North American continent and from around the world. A major emphasis, however, is placed on native animals and vegetation, exemplified by the Georgia Woods and Swamp exhibit.

Within Chehaw Park's 779 acres there are other recreational options including camping, fishing in both Muckalee Creek and Lake Worth, picnicking, jogging and biking. Younger visitors spend their time at the playgrounds, a Native American museum and the Creek Indian Village.

Chehaw Park opens at 9:00 A.M. and the gates close at 5:00 P.M. A lighted Christmas exhibit in the park is presented 6:00 to 9:00 P.M. from immediately after Thanksgiving through the Christmas season. A nominal admission is charged to the park, and the holiday exhibit charges a small fee per car.

Albany, Georgia's fifth largest city, offers other diversions including the **Albany Museum of Art** that moved into its new quarters in 1983. The museum's east gallery showcases Georgia's established and emerging artists. The outstanding African gallery reflects the cultural mix of the city. The colorful mask collection intrigues young visitors. There is also a collection of decorative art. Museum hours are Tuesday through Saturday from 10:00 A.M. to 5:00 P.M. and Sunday 2:00 to 5:00 P.M. A suggested contribution is solicited. The museum has a gift shop filled with artistic and educational items and sponsors lectures, workshops, classes and special tours.

Another attraction is the **Thronateeska Heritage Center** housed in part in Albany's 1913 Union Station train depot. Here you'll see a museum that focuses on southwest Georgia history and the natural sciences. Also part of Heritage Center is the Model Train Display, the only one in the state located in a railroad car. Wetherbee Planetarium, in the Railway Express building, presents four to five different shows each year. The complex encompasses the 1854 Jarrard House; the 1847 Hilsman kitchen; the 1858 Tift Warehouse and the Fryer-Merritt House built in the 1880s but remodeled in 1912.

The Thronateeska Heritage Museum of History & Science is open Monday through Friday from NOON to 5:00 P.M. and Saturday 2:00 to 5:00 P.M. The Train Display operates Wednesday,

Saturday and Sunday from 2:00 to 4:30 P.M. The Wetherbee Planetarium has a show on Saturday at 3:00 P.M.

Four miles south of Albany is **Radium Springs**, the state's largest natural spring. Recreational opportunities are again available at this once popular swimming spot where the waters, at a year-round temperature of 68 degrees, have been enjoyed from prehistoric time. Archaeological excavations indicate the presence of a nomadic village here before the birth of Christ. The Creek Indians called the spring Skywater, and religious ceremonies were conducted using the curative water. The first settlers called it Blue Springs. In the early 1920s the water was tested and traces of radium were discovered, as were a variety of minerals. The springs were renamed, and the area developed as the Radium Springs Club Casino and Lodge, which operated until the late 1960s. With the lodge now restored and open as a restaurant, swimming is again permitted in the spring waters.

Directions: From I-75 take Route 82 west to Albany. If you're coming from the north from I-75 at Cordele take Route 300 south. Once in Albany take Route 91 north to Chehaw Wild Animal Park. The Albany Museum of Art is at 311 Meadowlark Drive at Gillionville Road next to Darton College. Thronateeska Heritage Center is at 100 Roosevelt Avenue. Radium Springs is south of the city on Radium Springs Road.

Fort Gaines and Lake Walter F. George

Indian Tales

Fort Gaines, on a bluff overlooking the Chattahoochee River, is one of the oldest continuously occupied towns in the South. Its history dates back even before the arrival of European settlers. In New Park Cemetery, a summer house sits on the Indian mound that dates back to 300 A.D. At the mouth of the Cemocheechobee Creek there are remains of an Indian village dating from 700 A.D. In the Indian language Cemocheechobee meant "a blind horse staggering through the woods," and the name reflects the crooked course of the creek. Relics from a mound in the Cemocheechobee village can be seen at the Clay County Library.

There were three forts built here. The first was erected after Andrew Jackson forced the Indians to cede territory to the United States in payment for the cost of the Creek wars. The state of Georgia did not want to accept what they called "sterile and unprofitable land," but in 1818 legislators reluctantly added the former Creek lands to the state.

The first fort was built in 1816 under the direction of General Gaines, who commanded a large district that included this former

Indian village. The 100-square-foot fort had two blockhouses enclosed by a stockade eight feet high. Gaines used the fort as his headquarters. Later the fort was garrisoned by federal troops under the command of John Dill.

One of Fort Gaines's historic houses, the **Dill House**, was built with money obtained unknowingly from the Indians. At the end of the War of 1812, the Indians, encouraged by the British, chose not to recognize the peace treaty and dared the American settlers to enter their territory. Fort Scott was under siege and General Gaines sent reinforcements. An Indian war was expected and on November 28, 1817, a boat filled with wounded and ill soldiers and their families was intercepted as it headed for the safety of Fort Scott.

Two wounded men escaped, but the rest of the party were killed and scalped except for the young bride of Sergeant Stuart. Elizabeth Stuart was held captive as the Indians raided and pillaged in Georgia and Florida, committing atrocities that triggered the first Seminole War. Mrs. Stuart noticed that the Indians kept the coins they obtained during their raids but threw away the paper money. She retrieved the bills and pinned them to her petticoat with briars and palm needles.

Elizabeth Stuart was rescued by General Andrew Jackson's forces in Spanish Florida and sent to Fort Gaines. Widowed but wealthy, she met and married General John Dill. Her petticoat money paid for the Dill House that still stands on the corner of Washington and Commerce streets.

The fort was rebuilt and manned again during the Indian uprising in 1836 when 300 women and children fled to safety from Indian raids. The fort's capacity was stretched even further when settlers fleeing aboard the steamer *Georgian* sought safety within the fort's walls. A third fort was built on the same location during the Civil War in 1863 with cannons facing downstream to prevent the Union navy from reaching the Columbus Confederate Naval Yard (see Confederate Naval Museum selection).

Fort Gaines continued to prosper as a steamboat town until highways and the boll weevil changed the economy of the South. To preserve the past, a frontier village has been built in the shadow of what was once the old fort. In front of the collection of authentic frontier structures is the only Indian statue in the Old Creek Nation. The statue, by local artist Philip Andrews, commemorates Otis Micco who, along with the others in his village, was ordered to leave by General Andrew Jackson. The frontier buildings are not yet furnished.

There is a walking and cycling tour booklet that will provide historical background and anecdotes about private homes and other points of interest in and around Fort Gaines. Driving tour cassettes are also available at the Fort Gaines library and at Lake

Walter F. George Lodge in **George T. Bagby State Park**. The 300-acre park is on the shores of the 48,000-acre lake. There is a swimming beach, marina, bait and tackle shop, pedal boat and canoe rentals, a public boat ramp, tennis courts, nature trails and picnic sites. The park also has a lodge with 30 guest rooms, five two-bedroom cottages, a group shelter and a restaurant overlooking the lake. Camping is available at the Corps of Engineers' Cotton Hill Park, less than a mile away (912-768-3061).

Be sure to take the time to stop at the Corp of Engineers' local headquarters, another spot to obtain information on Fort Gaines and the recreational opportunities on Walter F. George and George W. Andrews lakes. The Walter F. George Lock and Dam is the third deepest lock east of the Mississippi River. It has a lift of 88 feet, and the inside dimensions are 82 feet by 450 feet. It was opened to navigation in 1963.

The Corp of Engineers resource manager's office has displays on the construction of the dam and on the cultural development of the area. There is an audio-visual program, exhibits and a wide range of printed material. The visitor area is open Monday through Friday from 8:00 A.M. to 4:00 P.M. During the summer the visitor area is open on weekends from 9:30 A.M. to 5:30 P.M.

Directions: From I-75 take Route 37 west to Fort Gaines. George T. Bagby State Park is north of town on Route 39.

Georgia Agrirama

Digging Into the Past

Georgia's 95-acre living history museum brings to life the years between the Civil War and the 20th century. More than 35 structures make up the four distinct areas at the Georgia Agrirama. There are two farm communities, a rural town and an industrial complex.

Visitors explore at their own pace, but authentically clad interpreters are on hand throughout the buildings demonstrating the lifestyle, activities and work of a vanishing way of life. The tour begins with a traditional southern pine belt farmstead of the 1870s. The farmhouse is the 1886 Clark cabin, a one-room log cabin from the area. Since George Flournoy Clark didn't have access to a sawmill he cut and peeled the logs he needed to build his cabin. The loom you'll see in the cabin is over 150 years old. Spinning and weaving came back into vogue after the Civil War because the area lacked resources and transportation and had to rely on handmade material. The farmstead area has a barn, storage crib, smokehouse, sugarcane mill and syrup shed. You'll see from the crops planted here that subsistence farmers in this re-

Visitors to Georgia Agrirama and its living history demonstrations explore the lifestyles of rural Georgia prior to 1900.

gion did not grow only one crop; they grew cotton, corn, peanuts, sugarcane, oats and other crops.

The 1870s farmstead is the farthest point on your tour. Heading back to the main area you'll pass a rural settlement that includes a one-room school, church, preacher's house and cemetery. The Agrirama holds workshops in the schoolhouse for school children from Georgia and neighboring states. Students are dressed in costumes of the era, and they do class work and take a lunch break just as their counterparts did over a century ago. One part of the schoolroom wall is painted with a black compound, the original blackboard. Students could write with chalk on this black wall and then wash it clean. There is even an old potbellied stove. The church, where traditionally a preacher would visit on a circuit roughly once a month, once stood outside Albany. The Wesley Methodist Chapel was built in 1882 using only hand tools.

Things were more progressive by the 1890s as you'll see by the sprawling farmstead next on your tour. Adapted from the dogtrot design of the early pioneers, this framed farmhouse has a wide porch and central breezeway with rooms off each side. The **Gibbs farmhouse** was built in 1896. Allen Gibbs had 13 children, seven by his first wife and six by his second. It was customary to have one room as a guest room; the latch was left off deliberately so visitors could easily find hospitality no matter when they arrived. Guests repaid their hosts by relating the news they had collected on their travels. Across the breezeway from the guest room is the front room. It was not called a parlor since it doubled as both a living area and a bedroom. When you visit you can watch the interpreters performing such daily tasks as sweeping the yard with brush brooms, cooking over the open hearth, changing the feather beds and making soap.

Dependencies surround the farmhouse like the storage house, smokehouse, chicken house, sugarcane mill and shed, buggy shed, barns, corncrib, seed cotton house and privy. There is also a kitchen garden where the vegetables, herbs and fruits are typical of those grown here in the 1890s. With the rise of one-crop agriculture in the South, the small freeholders had difficulty maintaining their land. Many lost their farms and became sharecroppers living in tenant houses like the one you'll see across the road from the Gibbs farmhouse.

Farmers were dependent on the local miller to grind their crops. The miller's house on your tour was built in 1880 by Benjamin Cravey. Much of the community's social life centered around the **miller's house** and **gristmill**. The miller was often the postmaster, justice of the peace, or notary public, as well as the only source, limited though it might be, of store-bought goods. His elevated status can be discerned by the three-hole privy, which was considered very "high cotton." The miller's water mill at the Agrirama was built in 1879 near Warwick. The mill still grinds corn into meal and grits that can be purchased at the Country Store.

One of the high points of young children's visits to the Agrirama is the steam-powered logging tram that runs during the summer months from the gazebo behind the gristmill into the piney woods and then back to the sawmill. You also can take the nature trail through the wetland area to the mill. Georgia had a thriving forest industry, with farmers harvesting trees just like other crops. Costumed interpreters man the sawmill that brings to life the years between 1870 and 1910 when much of the yellow pine forest was cut. The sawmill has a maximum daily output of 10,000 board feet, though no longer is that much produced. They do sell specialty lumber.

Pine trees were also a source of turpentine, and the naval stores industry was also of importance to South Georgia. The Agrirama has one of the few wood-fired turpentine stills that is operational. Pine trees were not killed when they were tapped for gum or sap. You can watch the process by which the gum is distilled into turpentine and its by-product rosin. Nearby is a cooper's shed where the barrels necessary to store the sap were assembled. There is also a company store, or commissary, like those that once served the employees of the lumber and turpentine industries.

The Georgia Agrirama showcases all the elements of rural life, including the interdependence between the farmers and those living in rural towns. Communities developed around railroad stations, as it was the trains that brought in the products of the industrial age. The town section is still growing. At present it contains a railroad depot, blacksmith shop, printing office and telephone exchange, doctor's office, cotton ginhouse and warehouse, plus a Masonic Lodge. You can even get a soda at the marble-topped fountain in the drug store. One favorite is the Rebecca Special, which has cherry, vanilla, strawberry syrups and carbonated water.

One last exhibit honors the founder of Tifton: the 1886 **Captain Henry Harding Tift Home**. Representing the entrepreneur class that settled in South Georgia, this gracious Victorian house reveals the artistic touches of Elizabeth Willingham, Tift's wife. Bessie was a graduate of Monroe Female Academy in Forsyth, and she painted several of the landscapes you'll see in the house. The Tifts had three sons and raised their oldest son's two children after his wife died. Like the 1890s farmhouse, this house too was always filled with guests. The tradition of hospitality continued across the years and across economic lines.

The Georgia Agrirama is open year-round on Tuesday through

Saturday 9:00 A.M. to 5:00 P.M. and Sunday 12:30 to 5:00 P.M. Admission is charged and family passes can be purchased; for prices call (912)386-3344.

Throughout the year there are special events scheduled at the Agrirama. In January there is a Winter Homecoming featuring the music and food of rural Georgia. February is the time for a special celebration of the region's Black Heritage. The fun continues in late March with a Spring Frolic featuring 19th-century games, music, food and storytelling. In late April there is a Folk Life Festival with sheepshearing, rail splitting, logrolling and craft demonstrations. Also the Wiregrass Opry begins country music and dancing shows on selected Saturdays April through October. In late May they hold the turpentine still firing. The 4th of July abounds with old-fashioned fun including watermelon-eating contests, footraces and children's games. In early September, quilts, fresh fruits, vegetables and baked goods are displayed at the County Fair of 1896. The weekends in October are devoted to cotton ginning, while cane grinding begins in mid-November. In mid-December a 1890s Christmas Celebration is held.

Directions: From I-75 take Exit 20 in Tifton. The Georgia Agrirama is directly off the interstate.

Kolomoki Mounds State Park

Seven Hills in Georgia

The land we now know as Georgia was crossed by Paleo-Indian hunters in the Archaic period. Artifacts uncovered at Macon and other points give evidence that aboriginals followed large game into this area. The Kolomoki region in the southwestern corner of Georgia was occupied in the Middle Woodland period, around 200 to 400 A.D., by the Swift Creek community. This first group to settle around Kolomoki probably numbered only a few hundred people. From this third-century group the population increased slowly, peaking about 700 to 900 A.D., in the Weeden Island period, with a population close to two thousand people.

The seven mounds that visitors see at Kolomoki Mounds State Park were probably built during the third through ninth century by the Swift Creek and Weeden Island Indians. This is not only one of the largest archaeological sites in the southeast; it also has one of Georgia's oldest great temple mounds.

The best place to become oriented to the Kolomoki site is at the **museum**, which is built in part over Mound E. This burial mound is not recreated; the rocks and dirt are original. Only the skeletal remains are not natural, although these realistic copies are placed exactly where the three Indian skeletons were found in the burial pit. The museum has a ten-minute video program highlighting the excavation work and the history of the people who once lived here. Artifacts and exhibits provide additional details. A diorama gives a visual picture of the funeral ceremony of a Kolomoki chief. The Indian Museum is open Tuesday through Saturday from 9:00 A.M. to 5:00 P.M. and from 2:00 to 5:30 P.M. on Sunday. A nominal admission is charged.

Pick up a self-guided tour map at the museum before heading out to explore the site. Across the street from the museum are two small mounds. The first of these, the oval-shaped Mound F, is 60 feet long, 50 feet wide and 6 feet high. Pottery shards from the Weeden Island period were found in this mound. Archaeologists discovered a white square clay platform inside the mound.

Continuing up the road you will see Mound G. The Mercier family, who had a plantation on this land, were buried within the mound. Back on the same side of the road as the museum, visitors will see Mound D, 20 feet high and 100 feet in diameter. This large, elaborate mound was excavated and rebuilt in the early 1950s. The mound was built in one continuous undertaking to bury one of the tribe's chieftains and his servants, slaves, wives and trophy skulls.

The nearby Mound II is thought to have been for the burial ceremony of the leader interred in Mound D. Within this satellite mound, like in Mound F, there is a clay platform.

Straight ahead is the rectangular truncated pyramid style **Mound A**, with base measurements of 325 by 200 feet and a height of 56 ½ feet. Georgia's largest temple mound was erected over 1,000 years ago as a religious center for the Kolomoki people. Archaeologists have calculated that it took two million basket loads of earth to build this mound. There are steps to the top, and the view encompasses the entire archaeological site area. From this vantage point it is easy to see the gully that lies behind the mound. The exact purpose of this ditch has been debated. One explanation is that it served as a covered way to obtain water during sieges, while others argue that it was simply a source for the dirt used to build the mound. Since the latter theory would only have accounted for one foot of the construction, that seems an unlikely guess. Although this mound may have been started during the Swift Creek period, at least the last two caps were in the Weeden Island period.

To the north and south of this temple mound are smaller mounds. Mound B is a post mound possibly used as a goal for games. Mound C is something of a mystery. Although it is thought to have been built during the Weeden Island period, it is not a burial mound. Apparently it was erected from sweepings of the plaza area that extended in front of the temple mound. The 1,500 to 2,000 residents who lived here built a village of thatched houses that arched around the plaza.

Once you've seen the mounds there are other recreational options at the 1,294-acre Kolomoki Mounds State Park. Within the park are two lakes, Lake Kolomoki and Lake Yahola. Both have boat launching areas and are open for year-round fishing. Lake Kolomoki, the lower lake, also has a fishing pier. The park's pool is open Tuesday through Friday from 11:00 A.M. to 6:00 P.M. and on weekends remain open until 7:00 P.M. There is also a miniature golf course and a playground.

The Kolomoki Mounds State Park Nature Trail winds through a hardwood forest. Indigenous wildlife includes white-tailed deer, fox, gray squirrel, wild turkey, raccoon and hundreds of woodland birds. The natural world you see on this trail is much like the one the ancient Indian cultures experienced. Along the way are numbered posts, indicating various trees and plants.

The park has 20 tent and trailer campsites, seven picnic pavilions and numerous picnic tables. There is also a 100-capacity group camp available with swimming pool and ballfield. Park hours are 7:00 A.M. to 10:00 P.M.

Directions: From I-75 at Cordele take Route 300. From I-75 at Tifton take Route 82 west to Albany and pick up Route 62 west into Blakely to Route 27 north. One mile north on Route 27 from Blakely, turn left at the sign for Kolomoki. In roughly five minutes you will see the park's entrance.

Lapham-Patterson House and Hardy Bryan House

Rose in Bloom

Since Thomasville has an eclectic mix of architectural styles, it is an ideal classroom for the study of building arts. One of the most elaborate examples is the Lapham-Patterson House, a Victorian Queen Anne estate built in 1884-85 by Charles W. Lapham of Chicago at a cost of $4,500.

As a result of the Chicago Fire, which Lapham barely survived, he suffered lung damage and wintered in Georgia to escape the harsh northern winter. His understandable fear of fires prompted him to ensure that every one of the 19 rooms in his winter cottage had at least one exterior door. In all, the house has 45 doors; 26 are exterior. It is also possible to step outside through many of the windows. Each room also had a fire extinguisher. On your tour you'll see one of the originals.

A fear of fire led the original owner of the 1884 Lapham-Patterson House to design his home with 45 doors.

CREDIT: TOURIST DIVISION, GEORGIA DEPARTMENT OF INDUSTRY & TRADE

For its time, the Lapham house was a veritable temple of technology with its own gas lighting system, hot and cold running water, indoor plumbing and modern closets. It is also noted for its decorative exterior touches like the fish-scale shingles and Oriental-style porch decorations. Nowhere inside is there a 90-degree angle; nothing is symmetrical or centered. Another singular feature is the double-flue chimney in the dining room with built-in stairs. Extending over the dining room is a cantilevered balcony where minstrels played for guests. The interior floor boards are of local longleaf pine. The last pure stand of this pine is in Thomas County.

The cow's head ornamental design on the woodwork of the third floor balcony is supposedly the image of Mrs. O'Leary's cow, the one that started the Chicago Fire. Indeed, according to some, the entire third floor looks like a fireman's hat.

Lapham was married and had five children, but in 1906 he and his wife were formally separated. *She* was required to pay *him* $35.00 alimony a month! In 1893 Lapham lost his business and he sold the house a year later. His former wife went west and became a cattle rancher. Ironically, she perished by fire when a kerosene lamp ignited her clothes.

In 1905 the house was purchased by James G. Patterson, and his family owned it until it was sold to the city in 1970. Four years later it opened as a museum furnished with Lapham family furniture and other Victorian pieces. This National Historic Landmark property, at 626 N. Dawson Street, is open Tuesday through Saturday 9:00 A.M. to 5:00 P.M. and Sunday 2:00 to 5:00 P.M. A nominal admission is charged. Interested visitors can watch a 22-minute film on Victorian architecture. A gift shop sells some unusual books and paper dolls. For additional details you can call (912)225-4004.

If you continue down Dawson Street for two blocks to 830, you'll see the exterior of the Hanna-McKinley House. This High Victorian Renaissance Revival House was built in 1883 and for a time served as the "White House of the Nation." Industrialist Mark Hanna invited southern Republican leaders to vacation at his winter cottage in Thomasville. It was in his sun parlor in 1896 that party delegates nominated William McKinley for the presidency. McKinley promised to visit Thomasville if he won, and he did. Locals claim he is "the only President who ever kept his word about anything!"

Another house open for tours, although by appointment only, is the **Hardy Bryan House** at 312 N. Broad Street. This is the city's oldest two-story house. Furnished with Federal period pieces, this Classic Revival house is now the headquarters of Thomasville Landmarks, Inc.

Springtime is especially inviting in Thomasville. Thousands of azaleas bloom throughout the city in late March; then in April the roses begin blooming. Every business in town and most of the private homes have rose beds. The fourth Friday in April and the week preceding is the Annual Rose Festival with a parade, rose show, picnic, beauty pageant, country fair, historic tours and a myriad of other activities. One additional natural feature that should not be overlooked is the **Big Oak** on the corner of Monroe and Crawford streets.

The live oak, circa 1680, is Thomasville's most beloved landmark. To put this great oak in perspective, it is significant to know that its limb span is 162 feet, making it two feet higher than Niagara Falls, at least in some places along the falls (at some spots the falls reach a depth of between 170 and 175 feet). The tree supports a colony of resurrection ferns. This harmless plant appears dry and dead, but when it rains the fern resurrects itself and turns a lush green.

Thomasville is one of 26 cities in Georgia designated a Main Street city. It has a collection of interesting shops and eateries. One of the best places for lunch is Melissa's at 134 South Madison Street directly across from a row of upscale shops in Madison

Square. The evening meal can be enjoyed at Somewhere for Dinner, a captivatingly titled restaurant at 116 N. Broad Street.

If you want more information about Thomasville you can write to Destination Thomasville. Address is the Tourism Authority, P.O. Box 1540, Thomasville, GA 31799.

Directions: From I-95 take Exit 4 to Valdosta and continue west on Route 84 to Thomasville. From I-75 take Exit 32 near Cordele. The Georgia/Florida Parkway 300 will take you to the perimeter of Thomasville.

Pebble Hill Plantation and Susina Plantation Inn

Hunting in Style

Plantations conjure up images of antebellum homes, but although Pebble Hill Plantation existed before the Civil War, the original section, built by county founder Thomas Jefferson Johnson, was torn down. The second house, built in 1850, burned in 1934. What you see today is a splendid Georgian and Greek Revival-style mansion completed in 1936 after the plantation grounds were acquired by Howard Melville (Mel) Hanna. The architect was Abram Garfield, the son of the 20th president.

Mel Hanna, a wealthy Cleveland businessman, was the brother of Mark Hanna. Mark gained fame as the behind-the-scenes manipulator who propelled his good friend William McKinley to the presidency. Mel Hanna gave this Georgia property to his daughter Kate, who directed the construction of the lavish 3,000-acre shooting plantation. She in turn passed it on to her daughter, Elizabeth "Pansy" Ireland Poe whose taste you will see reflected at Pebble Hill. Miss Pansy owned the property until 1978 and established a private foundation to operate the estate as a house museum. Until Pebble Hill opened in 1983 none of the grand shooting plantation could be toured.

You'll discover a world unto itself in the 37 acres, overgrown with longleaf pine. The estate includes stables, dairy, carriage house, dog kennel, cottages, garages, servants' quarters, laundry, a fire engine house, family schoolhouse, cemetery and formal gardens surrounding the mansion. As you enter the grounds a sign warns: "Slow Down, I Mean It!" signed, "E.I. Poe."

Visitors to Pebble Hill join an illustrious list. Guests of Pansy Poe included the Duke and Duchess of Windsor, Cornelia Otis Skinner and Jimmy Carter.

Pansy Poe had two life-long passions—horses and collecting—

and both of these loves are reflected at Pebble Hill. Begin exploring the estate at the **Visitors Center**, part of the stable complex. Included in this complex is the cow barn where Pebble Hill's prize-winning Jerseys were stabled, the dairy, and horse stables with a tack room filled with carved saddle racks. There's also a carriage house with old hunt wagons and carriages. One of the wagons was used when President Eisenhower stayed here.

You'll see several small buildings as you head for the north entrance of the main house where the conducted tours begin. The living areas have remained just as Pansy decorated them, filled with items from her collections. Shelves and display cases have been added in some rooms to showcase more items including porcelain, silver, crystal, glassware and memorabilia. The interconnected themes of wildlife and the sporting life are captured in a variety of ways throughout the house. There are 33 original Audubon prints.

The tour ends in the main drawing room, one of the loveliest rooms in the house. The walls are covered with an enormous painting of wild birds that was cut to fit the panels surrounding the huge windows, thus creating the illusion of bringing the outside inside.

Seeing the way of life captured at Pebble Hill—one of privilege and luxury—is like walking onto the set of the television show "Lifestyles of the Rich and Famous." A portrait of Pansy Poe with her pony and shepherd dog gives you a glimpse of what she was like in her early twenties.

Hour-long tours start every 15-minutes for groups of up to eight. Children younger than first-grade level are not permitted in the house although they can explore the grounds. Pebble Hill is open Tuesday through Saturday 10:00 A.M. to 5:00 P.M. and Sunday 1:00 to 5:00 P.M. with the last tour beginning at 4:00 P.M. There is an admission to the grounds and an additional charge for a house tour. Pebble Hill is closed the day after Labor Day until October 1 plus on Thanksgiving, Christmas Eve and Christmas Day. Don't miss the gift shop, which is filled with an appealing array of handcrafted items. For additional information you can call (912)226-2344.

Seven miles down the road you'll come to **Susina Plantation Inn**, a true antebellum plantation house. It was designed in 1841 by John Wind. On the National Register of Historic Places, the house sits back from the road in tree-shaded splendor. You can stay in one of the eight antique-filled bedrooms or dine at Susina (the dining room does not accept credit cards); for reservations call (919)377-9644. Guests enjoy the lighted tennis court, swimming pool, croquet court, fishing pond and jogging trails.

Directions: From I-75 take Route 84/221 west to Thomasville. Pebble Hill Plantation is five miles south of Thomasville on Route 319. Continue down Route 319 for Susina Plantation Inn.

Quail Hunting Plantations

Timeless Gentlemen's Sport

As you drive through wooded stretches of southwest Georgia, it's easy to miss the hunting plantations tucked away out of sight. Discreet signs mark the turn-offs that lead down rutted dirt roads to the lodges where visitors enjoy a bit of the Old South.

The Thomasville area, which extends over the border into Florida, has more than 70 private estates—hunting preserves of wealthy northern businessmen. Throughout the Plantation Trace region, however, there are private hunting preserves that do open to the public. In fact, Albany is considered the "Quail Capital of the World."

Georgia's quail hunting season runs from October through March, with two distinct phases. From mid-November through February hunters on their own can shoot native wild birds, while from October through March the preserves that run commercial operations can book hunting trips. Hunters staying at one of the region's plantations are customarily met at the airport, and their food, lodging, dogs and guide are included in the price of the hunt. Plantation staff can also arrange for hunting licenses.

The search for bobwhite quail begins in the morning when hunters are transported to prime areas. Most plantations have hunt wagons, modified jeeps, each of which normally has two hunters and a guide. The wagons also transport the bird dogs. Once an ideal location is reached, the dog handler releases a pair of dogs who immediately begin their search for game.

When they sight their prey, the dogs lock on the birds and point. The hunters shoot when the handler flushes the covey. Quail hunting is a buddy sport, rather than one that stresses solo tracking. Shooting the birds is secondary to working with the dogs and hunting. There are those who believe quail is the ultimate hunting experience, combining as it does good guns, good dogs and good company. The hunt generally lasts all morning and after a lunch-time break (you will undoubtedly be served quail sometime during your stay) resumes in the afternoon. The daily limit under state law is 12 birds, but hunters can pay an additional charge per bird and exceed the limit when hunting on a commerical property.

Novice hunters or those whose skills are rusty can take instruction at most plantations. The plantations usually have skeet ranges for practice sessions. During deer season, some plantations also offer an early morning or late afternoon deer hunt.

Contributing to the success of quail hunting in and around Albany is **Quail Unlimited** (P.O. Box 10041, Augusta, GA 30903). Their primary concern is quail management and preserving the quail's habitat. This task is made easier because quail rarely travel more than a mile from the spot where they are hatched. On the first weekend in February, Quail Unlimited hosts an annual Celebrity Hunt giving hunters the chance to shoot with sports figures like Dave Butz, Jack Youngblood and Will Clark and entertainers like Bruce Boxleitner, Gerald McCraney, Richard Crenna and Patrick Duffy.

It hasn't been verified, but hunters say good bird dogs have a disdainful glare that they give those who miss their shot.

Hunting Plantations:

Bevy Burst
Lynn Gray
Route 2, Box 245
Edison, GA 31746
912-835-2156

Cane Mill Plantation
John Thompson
Route 3, Box 531
Albany, GA 31707
912-432-9241

Covey Rise Plantation
Route 1, Box 30
Camilla, GA 31730
912-336-7068

Dogwood Plantation
Sidney Gainey
Route 3, Box 274
Cairo, GA 31728
912-872-3508

Foxfire Plantation
Jimmy Vaughn
P.O. Box 26
Thomasville, GA 31799
912-226-2814

Idle Grass Plantation
Paul Trulock
P.O. Box 70
Climax, GA 31734

Partridge Pea Plantation
Glenn Dowling
P.O. Box 70971
Albany, GA 31707
912-432-0289

Pinefield Plantation
Charles Cannon III
Route 2
Moultrie, GA 31768
912-324-3240

Quail Country of Worth Co.
Davis King
P.O. Box 1110
Albany, GA 31708
912-883-0500

Quail Country
Tom Newberry
Route 1, Box 690
Arlington, GA 31713
912-725-4645

Riverview Plantation
Cader Cox
Route 2, Box 515
Camilla, GA 31730
912-294-4904

Rosin Pine Plantation
Ruby Turner
P.O. Box 36
Barwick, GA 31720
912-735-2095

Samara Plantation
Harold Ivey
P.O. Box 356
Norman Park, GA 31771
912-796-3065

Soggy Bottom Hunting Lodge
Jerry Nolan
Doverel, GA
912-883-4748

Southern Style Shooting Preserve
John Peek
P.O. Box 199
Thomasville, GA 31799
912-228-0987

Sugar Mill Plantation
J. Groover
Route 1, Box 422
Ochlocknee, GA 31773

Tallawahee Plantation
Ken Bangs
Route 5, Box 135B
Dawson, GA 31742
912-995-5937

The Covey Shooting Preserve
P.O. Box 427
Barwick, GA 31720

The Millpond
Oscar Tye
Route 1, Box 22
DeSoto, GA 31743
912-874-6720

Three Creeks
J.M. Simmons
P.O. Box 795
Bainbridge, GA 31717

Wise Olde Pine Plantation
Mickey Wise
Route 2, Box 39
Americus, GA 31709

Wolf Creek Plantation
Jerry Ricks
P.O. Box 37
Rebecca, GA 31873
912-567-9339

Wynfield Plantation
Larry Ruis
2413 Tarva Road
Albany, GA 31707
912-883-7878

Reed Bingham State Park

Buzzard's Roost

Buzzards may not be aesthetically pleasing, but with wing spans of up to six feet they are impressive. You can see thousands of these carrion-eating birds of prey at Reed Bingham State Park where they come to roost each winter. The buzzards bask in the

Catfish, crappie, bream and bass draw fishermen to the numerous lakes and rivers of Southwest Georgia.

sun with wings outspread, soar on the air currents or perch in almost stereotypical fashion on denuded trees.

Reed Bingham has two types of vultures, turkey and black buzzards. The former are slightly larger brownish birds with red heads, while the latter are dull sooty-black birds. In flight the turkey has slow wing beats in contrast to the black buzzards' very rapid ones. The buzzards can be seen in the trees along the marshy banks of the Little River that flows through the park before meeting the 375-acre lake that is Reed Bingham's focal point during the warmer months.

While they are the most dramatic, buzzards are but one species of wildlife visitors will see at the park. If you take the 3.5-mile coastal plains **nature trail**, you're apt to see gopher tortoise, indigo snakes, deer, waterfowl and even perhaps an alligator. The trail encompasses a diverse array of ecological systems including pine flatwoods, upland pine woods, river swamp, flood plain, freshwater pond, southern mixed hardwoods, cypress gum swamp, fields, a sandhill area and the bay.

Hiking is just one of the recreational options at this 1,605-acre park. During the summer there is a beach wading area that is open Memorial Day weekend through Labor Day weekend. The lake is also a popular spot for fishermen who try for bass, crappie and bream. There are four boat ramps and three fishing piers, 11 shelters for picnickers and 120 tent and trailer sites for campers. The park has two playgrounds, one near the wading area and another near the camping area. A trail leading from the playground area winds through a butterfly and hummingbird sanctuary. A miniature golf course is also located near the campgrounds.

The park hosts three special annual events: the Annual Easter Egg Hunt, entertainment and fireworks on July 4th and Buzzard Day. The latter, on the first Saturday in December, is the park's big day with pontoon rides to the buzzards' roosting areas plus educational programs and an arts and crafts show.

Reed Bingham Park is open 7:00 A.M. to 10:00 P.M., and the park office is open 8:00 A.M. to 5:00 P.M. For camping details call (912)896-3551.

If you are in the area in mid-October be sure to stop at the **Sunbelt Agricultural Exposition**. Viewed by many as the premier farm show in the country, this show is in its second decade of operation. The exposition has more than 600 corporate exhibitors covering 80 acres at Spence Field, six miles southeast of Moultrie on Route 33. For specific dates call the Colquitt Country Economic Development Corporation, (912)890-1983.

Directions: From I-75 take Exit 10 at Adel and head west for six miles on Route 37. The park is on your right. For the Sunbelt Agricultural Exposition continue west on Route 37 to the intersection with Route 33; then follow the signs to Spence Field.

Thomas County Historical Society Museum and Cultural Center

The South's Original Winter Resort

Tours in Newport, Rhode Island, Martha's Vineyard, Massachusetts, and Hollywood, California, take visitors past locked gates and carefully screened mansions and give a filtered look at the lifestyles of the rich and famous. Far less known is Thomasville, where sheltered hunting plantations provide seasonal sport for political and entertainment personalities.

You won't be able to glimpse these lavish private estates from the road, but you can see photographs and discover their history at the **Thomas County Historical Society Museum**. These gracious Southern plantations survived because Northerners used and purchased them as hunting retreats (see Quail Hunting Plantations selection). A number of them were even built by Northern industrialists. There are roughly 70 of these plantations in Thomasville and the surrounding area extending as far south as Tallahassee. Only one, Pebble Hill (see selection), is open to the public. A second, Susina, is open as a bed-and-breakfast. Historical Society exhibits tell the story of these fabulous houses.

It was to **Greenwood Plantation** that Jacqueline Kennedy retreated for six weeks after her husband's assassination. The antebellum plantation was Margaret Mitchell's inspiration for Ashley Wilkes's Twelve Oaks. Decades earlier Eisenhower had visited Millstone on five occasions to take part in the quail hunting. Ted Turner owns a hunting estate, Welaunee, just south of the Georgia state line.

The Northerners did not merely invest in these stately old plantations. Many stayed at inns and guest houses in town, leading to the development of a great Hotel Era that lasted for 30 years. The museum chronicles the years when Thomasville was the Miami of its day with 15 hotels, 25 boarding houses and 50 cottages. The Piney Woods opened in 1885 and was a great success, though it did have to deal with the embarrassment of snow in 1895. The Mitchell House was noted for serving ice water, even though the ice had to be brought in from Massachusetts. In a time when the average wage was 50 cents a day, rooms at the swank Thomasville hotels cost $4.00 a day. B.F. Goodrich and Cornelius Vanderbilt often took suites at the Mitchell House costing $11.00 a night, the equivalent of $700 today. John Masury, one of the world's wealthiest men, built two hotels in Thomasville plus a cottage (more lavish than the word implies). He also had a baronial estate on Long Island.

The answer to what the locals thought about this infusion of Northern money is given in this oft-repeated local saying: "Yankees are worth two bales of cotton and are twice as easy to pick."

In addition to the exhibits, the museum offers brief slide presentations on the Hotel Era, Plantation Life and Faces and Lifestyles. There is also a fascinating exhibit on patent medicines with such blatant advertisements as the one for Las-I-Co that asks: "Are You a Man in Name only?" and offers a cure that will induce superb manhood. There is also Peffer Ner-Vigor that claims to cure brain fag (fatigue). The museum is open daily 2:00

to 5:00 P.M. except Friday. It is closed on major holidays. Admission is charged.

Once you have perused the exhibits stroll around the grounds where you'll see a 1893 Queen Anne bowling alley, the only one like it in the state and one of the oldest in the world. The barn-like structure was built in February 1893 specifically to accommodate the bowling alley. There is also a log house from the pioneer years and a typical 1877 middle-class family home.

In the Orientation Room of the Thomasville **Cultural Center** you will find additional exhibits on the town's history from 1825 to the present. This center is in Thomasville's first tax-built school where the actress Joanne Woodward's father was once the principal. The Woodwards lived in the brown bungalow you see across the street at 528 E. Washington Street.

The cultural center has four state-of-the-art galleries on the lower level, an auditorium for cultural performances, a museum shop and a genealogical and fine arts library. The library is a major repository of materials for family research in the southeast and Atlantic coastal region. Library hours are Monday through Friday 9:00 A.M. to 5:00 P.M. with an hour lunch break at NOON. The cultural center is open Monday through Friday from 9:00 A.M. to 5:00 P.M. and weekends from 1:00 to 5:00 P.M. Admission is free, except for guided tour groups.

Directions: From I-75 at Valdosta take Route 84 west to Thomasville. The Museum is at 725 N. Dawson Street and the Cultural Center at 600 E. Washington Street.

Valdosta

Vale of Beauty

Valdosta, whose springtime beauty has earned it the soubriquet of Azalea City, has three National Register Historic Districts. The Downtown, Victorian Fairview and Midtown Patterson Street District offer distinct architectural points of interest. The Valdosta-Lowndes County Main Street Program likes to quote William Hickling Prescott who said, "The surest test of the civilization of a people. . .is to be found in their architecture, which presents so noble a field for the display of the grand and the beautiful and which...is so intimately connected with the essential comforts of life."

The **Downtown District** can be explored as part of the Historic Driving Tour or by using a walking tour brochure. The district exemplifies the diversity of design found in Valdosta and includes the Neo-Classical Lowndes County Courthouse, the Beaux

Arts City Hall and the Late Victorian storefronts along Ashley Street. Three churches within the district offer striking contrasts. The First Baptist Church, one block west of the corner of Central and Toombs, mixes Queen Anne and Romanesque styles. The stained-glass windows and elaborate wood-and-truss ceiling are worth noting. The Victorian First United Methodist Church, on the corner of Patterson and Valley, has towers, spires, pointed gables, buttresses and rich Gothic interior woodwork. On the corner of Patterson and Magnolia, First Presbyterian Church's Corinthian columns indicate its Neo-Classical style.

Valdosta's Tourism Welcome Center, open Monday-Friday 9:00 A.M. to 5:00 P.M., is in the **Barber-Pittman House**, at 416 N. Ashley Street. This Neo-Classical mansion was built by E. R. Barber, one of the original owners of the Coca-Cola Company of Valdosta. Another lovely Neo-Classical mansion, just outside the boundaries of the Historic District, is the Converse-Dalton-Ferrell House. It has been restored by the Valdosta Junior Service League. The delicate interior woodwork is highly prized. This house, circa 1902, is on the National Register of Historic Places.

The **Fairview National Register Historic District** just east of the downtown area boasts some eye-catching Victorian homes. The J. T. Roberts House, 206 Wells Street, started out in 1840 as a Plantation Plain house, but the addition of wings, towers and Victorian gingerbread changed its style. The Monroe-Sutton House, 303 Wells Street, is an elaborate Queen Anne mansion with towers, gazebo, turrets and stained glass. A change of pace is seen at the Winn-Wilson-Hamm House, 208 Wells Street, which combines Mediterranean and Prairie styles.

North of these districts is the **Midtown Patterson Street District**. The **Crescent**, Valdosta's only historic house open regularly for tours, is on the outskirts of this district. This distinctive oval plantation house was built in 1898 for $17,000 for Senator William S. West. The 13 white Doric columns represent the original colonies. Originally the Senator planted live oak trees like spokes of a wheel extending out from each column. Only a few of these oaks still stand. The Valdosta Garden Center which now owns the house began extensive renovations in 1950. The house is now decorated in an eclectic mixture of styles. A diversity was also achieved in the original design by making each of the 14 fireplaces different. One unusual feature of the house is the third floor ballroom, which still has its original piano (now badly in need of tuning).

The garden is Valdosta's most picturesque site, there is a tiny white chapel that is much in demand for weddings and an octagonal schoolhouse set amid a lovely boxwood parterre garden. This is also an official day lily garden of the American Hemerocallis Society. The Crescent, at 200 N. Patterson Street, is open Monday through Friday from 2:00 to 5:00 P.M.

Drexel Park is located in the Patterson District and it is a not-to-be-missed springtime destination as it is abloom with azaleas and dogwoods. A park-like ambience is also present in the Sunset Hill Cemetery that dates back to the 1860s. You'll discover an intriguing collection of mausoleums and memorials.

If you want to learn about the past inhabitants and the history of Valdosta, visit the Lowndes County Historical Society Museum at 305 W. Central Avenue. One of the town's most notorious native sons was John Henry Holliday, the son of a city mayor. Young Holliday attended the Pennsylvania School of Dental Surgery and then returned to Valdosta to practice dentistry. Going west in hopes of improving his tuberculosis, Doc Holliday later became noted as a gunfighter and gambler. He died at age 36 in Glenwood Springs, Colorado, not as Hollywood indicated in the gunfight at the O.K. Corral. The museum has exhibits on Holliday, artifacts from the Civil War, regional history and a genealogical library. Hours are Monday through Friday from 2:00 to 5:00 P.M. and on Sunday from 3:00 to 5:00 P.M.

Directions: Exits 3,4,5 and 6 off I-75 lead into Valdosta. It is 13 miles north of the Florida state line. Stop by the Valdosta Convention & Visitors Bureau at Exit 5 for additional information.

State Parks

George T. Bagby State Park, Fort Gaines (see selection).
Kolomoki Mounds State Park, Blakely (see selection).
Reed Bingham State Park, Adel (see selection).
Seminole State Park, Donaldsonville; on 37,500-acres, offers
    swimming in Lake Seminole, water skiing, fishing, pioneer
    camping, boat ramp and dock, 10 cottages and 50 tent and trailer
    sites, (912)662-2001.

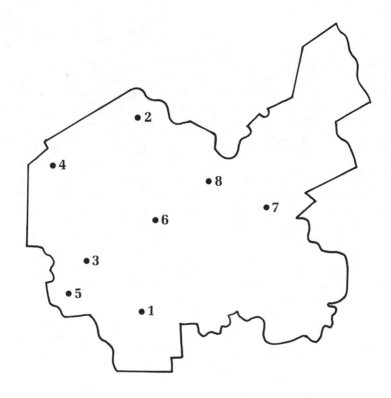

MAGNOLIA MIDLANDS

1. *Douglas*
   General Coffee State Park
   Pioneer Village
   Sunbelt Greenhouses
   The Rocks

2. *Dublin*
   Dublin-Laurens Museum and
   Chappell's Mill

3. *Fitzgerald*
   Blue and Gray Museum

4. *Hawkinsville*
   Black Swan Inn
   Double Q Farm
   Gooseneck Farms
   Harness Horse Training Facility

5. *Irwinville*
   Crystal Lake
   Jefferson Davis Memorial Park
   and Museum

6. *McRae*
   Little Ocmulgee State Park

7. *Reidsville*
   Gordonia-Altamaha State Park

8. *Vidalia*
   Ladson Genealogical Library
   Vidalia Onion Farms

═══Magnolia Midlands═══

The roots of tourism in this south central region are deep in its soil. From this soil farmers in Vidalia harvest the sweet onions the region made famous. On this hard red clay, harness racers train during the mild winter months. This was the ground Confederate President Jefferson Davis covered on his last night of freedom before being captured by Federal troops. And as you'll discover at Fitzgerald's Blue and Gray Museum, this is also the land Northerners came back to settle after the War Between the States.

Blue and Gray Museum

Yankee Land in Dixie Land

Unless you live in or around Fitzgerald, it's unlikely that you've heard the story of Georgia's Colony City. It's a fascinating but true story about a group of Union veterans who established a colony in a pine forest ten miles from the spot where Jefferson Davis, the President of the Confederacy, was captured (see Jefferson Davis Park and Museum selection).

At a time when hatred still burned in most Southerners, these aging Northerners, anxious to escape the bitter winters and unrelenting drought in the North and West, purchased 50,000 acres in the heart of South Georgia. Indianapolis newspaper editor P. H. Fitzgerald, a former Union drummer boy, spearheaded the concept. Using the pages of his paper to publicize the idea and to obtain the support of Georgia Governor Northen, Fitzgerald formed the American Tribune Soldiers' Colony. The veterans began to arrive at their new colony in the summer of 1895.

The Blue and Gray Museum in Fitzgerald has photographs from the first days of this settlement, such as the one of Mrs. Fox and her daughters standing in front of their boarding house in

1895. The museum exhibits household goods, personal memorabilia, tools and equipment from the colony's earliest days. There are war relics from both the Union and the Confederate armies.

More than 2,700 colonists moved to this Georgia community, including men who had marched with Sherman, others who had been prisoners at Andersonville and even one who had taken part in the capture of Jefferson Davis. Before the land was surveyed and distributed the men lived in shacks, tents and covered wagons. As a gesture to assuage the ill feelings the local residents felt towards them, the colonists named many of their streets for Confederate generals, although others were named for Grant and Sherman. Soon roll call was being held at the newly built bandstand, and historians claim the colonists ranged from Maine to California and from Washington to Florida, as some Confederate veterans also joined the colony. When schools opened in the fall of 1896, attending were children from 38 states and two territories.

One of the country's first public works projects, a tourist hotel built by the Colony Company in 1896-1898, was Georgia's largest frame building. Originally called the Grant-Lee, but changed to the Lee-Grant out of deference to local sensitivities, this was a popular spot for Southerners who came to get a look at the transplanted Northerners.

This same sensitivity was shown when the satisfied colonists celebrated their first year in their new home. They planned a harvest festival and built the Corn and Cotton Palace to house their exhibits. Two parades were planned, one for the Union veterans and one for Confederate veterans, but when the band began to play all former soldiers marched together. Fitzgerald was a town where both sides met in harmony, and veterans of both sides of the war established the town's Blue and Gray Park.

Outside of the museum there are few reminders of Colony City. One such landmark, however, is the W.R.C. Hall on South Main Street. The Womens Relief Corps was an auxiliary to the Grand Army of the Republic. Fitzgerald was one of the few cities in the South where that organization had a post, and in the Colony City there were three such posts.

The Blue and Gray Museum is in the restored Atlanta, Birmingham and Coast Railroad depot, built in 1909. This Spanish-style depot now also houses city offices. The museum is open Monday through Friday from 2:00 to 5:00 P.M. April through September. It also is open by appointment; call (912)423-3337.

Directions: From I-75 take Exit 26, Route 32/125 east. You will pass Crystal Lake then Irwinville. When Route 125 splits, head north for ten miles to Fitzgerald.

Dublin-Laurens Museum and Chappell's Mill

Lady of the Camellias

The Laurens County Historical Society sponsors a museum in Dublin's old Carnegie Library, now listed on the National Register of Historic Places. This museum has the largest single collection of the work of Georgia artist Lila Moore Keen, who is noted for her paintings of camellias, magnolias and other Southern flowers.

This historical museum also exhibits local memorabilia, Indian artifacts and a collection of photographs depicting scenes of Georgia in the late 1800s. There are works from rural folk potters, agricultural tools and an assortment of letters, diaries, journals and charts. The museum, at the intersection of Bellevue Avenue, Church Street and Academy Avenue, is open Tuesday through Friday from 1:00 to 4:30 P.M.

If you visit around lunch time stop at **Ma Hawkins Restaurant** on Jackson Street. It serves the best home cooking in the area, including a lemon meringue pie that's hard to beat. You can pick up a walking tour map of the downtown area and explore the historic district. Bellevue Avenue is lined with restored Greek Revival and Victorian homes. Old-timers still talk of the days in the 1920s and 1930s when Henry Ford used to stop at the gas station in the 300 block of Bellevue on his way from Richmond Hill to Macon.

Dublin was a major cotton producer, leading the state in production from 1891 through 1913. In 1912, the area had an all-time record crop, producing more cotton than the entire state of Missouri. It was this cotton boom that resulted in the major buildings of Dublin including the First National Bank Building at Jefferson and Madison, constructed in 1912.

The railroad reached Dublin in 1891, and soon two lines served the city. A new railroad park at the intersection of Martin Luther King and South Jefferson streets is in the formative stages. The park will have a caboose with exhibits from the railroad days. The caboose also will serve as a visitors' welcome center. A new riverfront park is also planned for the west bank of the Oconee River. To be included is a river walk, hotel, restaurants, shops and offices. The site encompasses the location of the first ferry landing at Dublin. Even before Europeans settled the area, Indians forded the Oconee River on a trail that came through the center of town. At this point the Oconee was flat and shallow with a rock base. There was a large sand bar that aided those crossing the river. It was only a few miles north of here that

DeSoto and his expedition crossed the river in the 1540s. Fording the river was only possible when the waters were low. When they ran high a ferry was needed, and even before the Scotch-Irish settled around Dublin, Jencks Ferry was operating. The first ferry may have been run by Creek Indians who had large cotton plantations in the area. Soon there were many ferries on the Oconee River, and one, the Dublin Ferry, operated until 1921.

Another establishment that dates back to the region's early days is **Chappell's Mill**, ten miles north of Dublin. This mill, on the banks of South Sandy Creek, has been producing cornmeal since 1811. The rustic mill annually grinds around 15,000 bushels of corn into meal on mill stones that are five centuries old. According to local lore, the mill barely survived Sherman's troops during the Civil War. Legend says Confederate surgeon Major James Barnes Duggan, on leave at his home just north of the mill, learned that Sherman's men were burning a path of destruction on their March to the Sea. Duggan raced to a bridge-crossing near the mill and persuaded a local woman to set the bridge on fire. When the Union men stopped to douse the fire, Duggan fired shots over their heads, then fooled the Federal detachment into thinking he was leading troops, hidden around the bend, in their direction. The Union soldiers abandoned the bridge and rode back to rejoin the main Union army.

You will notice that the mill does not have a picturesque waterwheel. The original was replaced in 1938 by a water-run turbine that generates power for the mill. The mill, located on Route 441, is open Monday through Wednesday from 8:00 A.M. to NOON. It occasionally is open on Thursday and Friday as well. Call before visiting (912)272-5128.

Since 1966, Dublin's fame has spread due to the popularity of the annual St. Patrick's Festival. The month-long festivities include a parade, arts and crafts exhibits, sporting events, dances (including a street dance that customarily draws thousands), musical entertainment and the world's largest pot of Irish stew. Using an 80-gallon pot, the ladies of Dublin's Christ Episcopal Church prepare enough stew to serve 400 people. For information about the festival call (912)272-5546.

Directions: From I-75 take I-16 east. Dublin is at the intersection of I-16 and Route 441.

General Coffee State Park

Pioneers in the Georgia Sandhills

General Coffee State Park is exemplary of community effort: The land was donated by county citizens and the park's pioneer village built through community effort. The park's name honors General John Coffee, a local planter who achieved fame as an Indian fighter and U.S. Congressman.

Nearly 1,500 acres include four small lakes created by Seventeen-Mile River that flows through the swampy cypress terrain. Indigenous wildlife includes the endangered gopher tortoise and indigo snake as well as a variety of small animals, waterfowl and woodland birds. Some trails that wind through the park are the River Swamp Trail and the Gopher Loop around the camping area. Additionally, there is a five-mile horse trail, although as yet the park does not have stables or mounts for hire. The three-mile nature trail is especially appealing in the spring when the wildflowers are in bloom.

After the nearby community of Douglas celebrated the 1976 Bicentennial, the local Exchange Club donated a log cabin to the park. The cabin is the nucleus of a series of houses and barns called **Pioneer Village**. A permanent exhibit is housed in each, ranging from rough-hewn furnishings to antique farm implements and household items. The agricultural museum includes penned farm animals and cultivated local crops. A blacksmith shop is staffed for special events, and during the cane season the syrup cooker is in use.

The park also has tent and trailer sites, seven picnic shelters, a swimming pool and bathhouse and a playground area. There are plans to add a horse arena, cabins and cottages. The park is open 7:00 A.M. to 10:00 P.M. daily.

As you pass through Douglas, take a drive down Gaskin Avenue—silk stocking row and the town's original residential area. In the spring the street is lined with blooming dogwoods and azaleas. Nature lovers may want to stop at **Sunbelt Greenhouses**, a 37-acre complex with 12 acres of greenhouses. The public is welcome to explore the state's largest greenhouse operation. Sunbelt is a wholesale grower of bedding plants and poinsettias, and if you time your visit right you will see thousands of blooming plants. In an average year Sunbelt may have as many as 225,000 poinsettias. The peak blooming season is mid-November to early December. Sunbelt is on West By-Pass Route 20 and is open Monday through Friday from 9:00 A.M. to 4:00 P.M. There are no retail sales.

Two hunting preserves are located in the Douglas area. Quail Ridge, (912)384-0025, is six miles southeast of town on Route 3 and offers quail, duck and dove hunting. You can arrange for guides, field transportation and trained dogs. Ten miles north of Douglas on Route 221 is the Moore's Southern Hunting Preserve that also arranges hunts for individuals and groups; call (912)384-8363 for information.

Also in the Douglas area, 16 miles north of the town on Route

107, is The Rocks, a Nature Conservancy property with wild orchids and waterfalls; woodland trails lead to caves and scenic bluffs. Nine varieties of orchids have been discovered here, including several endangered species.

Directions: From I-75 take Route 158 east to Douglas. From Douglas take Route 32 for six miles to General Coffee State Park.

Hawkinsville Harness Horse Training Facility

Divas and Kiwis, Pecans and Pulaski

Heroes of the American Revolution are remembered in central Georgia. The county of Pulaski, created in 1808, was named for Polish General Casimir Pulaski who was killed defending Savannah from the British. Hartford, the original county seat, honored Nancy Hart, a Revolutionary War character (see Hart State Park selection). In 1804, the city of Hartford lost a bid to become Georgia's capital by one vote. In 1836, the county seat was moved across the Ocmulgee River from Hartford to Hawkinsville, named for Revolutionary soldier Colonel Benjamin Hawkins.

In 1894, Hawkinsville inaugurated a spirited rivalry to determine who had the fastest trotter or pacer in the county. The Wiregrass Exposition, combining races and a fair, was held for four years on land that is today the Hawkinsville Harness Horse Training Track and Stables, one of the county's biggest businesses and its biggest tourist draw.

Since 1927, harness horse trainers, after a season of racing in the northern and midwestern states, head to the Hawkinsville area. The proximity of stock farms, mild winters and ideal track conditions lured the breeders and trainers to the area. In 1975, the city built an 86-acre training and racing facility that has made Hawkinsville the Harness Horse Capital of Georgia.

The facility has a mile-and-a-half long track of high quality red Georgia clay, an ideal racing surface. There are 480 permanent stalls, bunkhouses and accommodations for grooms and stablehands, plus two blacksmiths shops, tack shops and hay rooms. During the winter months, you can watch training sessions. Come early in the morning to see the most activity.

Twenty years ago the first Hawkinsville Harness Horse Festival was held, and over the years it has grown in popularity. Trophies and blankets are awarded to the winners in the 18 races. Residents of Hawkinsville "adopt" a horse, and if they choose a winner, they too, are awarded a prize. The festival, held on the first weekend in April, includes a barbecue cook-off, arts and

Harness horse racing is big business and the main tourist attraction in Hawkinsville.

crafts, sporting events and historical tours. For more information call the Hawkinsville-Pulaski County Chamber of Commerce at (912)783-1717.

Tours of several historic houses are given during the April festival and as a fund raiser in December. A home often open on these occasions is **Taylor Hall**, listed on the National Register of Historical Places. In 1824, the county's first physician, Robert Newsom Taylor, used Creek Indian labor to construct this house on the Ocmulgee River in Old Hartford. After that community declined, the house was dismantled in 1836 and ferried across the river to Kibbee Street in Hawkinsville. During the Civil War, Union troops camped on the front lawn to preserve order after General Robert E. Lee surrendered the Army of the Confederacy in 1865.

Two other houses of note are on Kibbee Street: The Arnold House, #324, dating back to 1877, or earlier, and the McAllister-Anderson House, #328. The latter, built around 1905, is the only solid-brick house in the county.

One of Hawkinsville's Southern Colonial-style mansions has been renovated and opened as an inn and restaurant. The Black Swan, named for a steamboat that carried passengers and produce up the Ocmulgee River from Savannah, was built for a successful cotton planter and hotelier James P. Brown. Victorian furnishings fill the six guest rooms. The restaurant is open Monday through Saturday from 11:30 A.M. to 1:30 P.M. and from 6:00 to 10:00 P.M. Reservations are suggested; call (912)783-4466.

The best known landmark in Hawkinsville is the **Old Opera House**, built in 1907 and now listed on the National Register of Historic Places. This is one of only three opera houses in the state; the others are in Columbus and Macon. When visiting his aunt in Hawkinsville, Oliver Hardy, of the comedy duo Laurel and Hardy, sang with a quartet on the stage of the Opera House. Performers are still treading the boards of this legitimate theater. Just outside the theater is Katie, the world's oldest horse drawn LaFrance fire engine.

Items that fill the rooms of some of the town's historic old homes may well have come from the Hawkinsville Antique Mall where 27 dealers exhibit in 36 booths. You can check out the fine antiques and collectibles daily from 10:00 A.M. to 5:00 P.M.; on Sunday the Antique Mall opens at 1:00 P.M.

Discriminating shoppers will also want to stop at the **Butler Brown Gallery**, on Route 3 in Hawkinsville. Brown is a native Georgian whose work has hung in the White House. Private and corporate collections in the U.S. and abroad include Brown's work. Signed and regular-edition prints of many of his rural Georgian landscapes are sold in his gallery.

The Hawkinsville area boasts two agricultural products that visitors enjoy. The **Double Q Farms**, 1475 Route 26, is the largest kiwi fruit producer in the state, although they only began growing kiwi in 1986. Most kiwi is grown in California, but this successful farm sells about 70 tons a year. In the last part of October, you can pick your own or purchase fresh kiwi or kiwi products, like kiwifruit jam, kiwipepper jam, and kiwipeach jam, at the farm's gift shop. Products can be mail ordered by calling (800)732-5510.

Another popular local product is pecans and pecan candy from

Gooseneck Farms. Located on Route 129 just two miles south of Hawkinsville, this farm has been in the pecan business only ten years, although their pecan trees are more than 100 years old. Their gift house sells a delicious array of fresh pecan produce. They also do a mail order business; call (800)537-6965 for details.

Directions: From I-75 southbound, take the I-475 By-pass after Foysyth; this will rejoin I-76 south of Macon. Continue south on I-75 to Exit 41, Perry/Fort Valley. Turn left and take Route 341 south through Perry. Hawkinsville is 22 miles southeast of Perry on Route 341.

Jefferson Davis Memorial Park and Museum

Last Stop for the Leader of the Confederacy

On May 10, 1865, the President of the Confederacy was captured on ground now part of the Jefferson Davis Memorial Park. The Confederate cabinet had met for the last time a week earlier in Washington, Georgia (see Washington Historical Museum selection). General Lee had surrendered his Confederate Army, and there was a threat of a "price on the head of Mr. Davis." Davis and a small staff and escort were en route to the trans-Mississippi region, where records indicate that he planned to unite the forces of several Confederate officers who had not yet surrendered their troops.

Davis had made his way from Sandersville to Dublin where he was reunited with his wife and daughter. Then with his family, aides and a small group of supporters he arrived at Abbeville. The group was camped in a pine forest near Irwinville when they were surrounded by the Fourth Regiment of the Michigan Cavalry. Davis was taken prisoner and held two years in a prison in Virginia before being released. He was never brought to trial.

This site is now on the National Register of Historic Places. A monument stands on the spot where Davis was captured. Nearby is a bronze marker indicating where two Michigan cavalrymen and their horses were accidently killed by Union crossfire.

A small **museum** has memorabilia from the Civil War including flags, weapons, newspaper clippings and old photographs. Museum staff fill in the details on the events that occurred here. Many false stories have been told including the one that said Jefferson Davis escaped in women's clothes. Reports indicate that he was suffering from a malaria attack and was wearing a rain cape in the cool, gray, early morning hours.

The museum is open Tuesday through Saturday from 9:00 A.M. to 5:00 P.M. A nominal admission is charged. There are nature trails and a picnic table.

When the weather is hot, you can cool off at nearby Crystal Lake, a water park with natural sand beaches, water rides, slides, flumes and tubes. The park is open weekends only in April, May and September. From Memorial Day through Labor Day, it is open daily starting at 8:00 A.M. The admission covers all rides and attractions; call (912)831-4655 for current schedule and prices.

Directions: From I-75 take Exit 26 Route 32/125 east. You will pass Crystal Lake before reaching Irwinville. Turn left at the bronze signs indicating the Jefferson Davis Memorial Park and Museum.

Ladson Genealogical Library and Vidalia Onions

American Roots

Vidalia is home to one of the southeast's major research libraries, the John E. Ladson Jr. Historical and Genealogical Foundation Library, a branch of the Ohoopee Regional Library System. Individuals researching family and state histories are welcome to consult the collection's 25,000 books and pamphlets, plus the 4,000 items on microfilm.

The non-circulating collection is organized using the Dewey Decimal Classification and includes state and county histories; county, census and church records; Confederate rosters; biographies; and genealogical collections of individual families and groups of families. On file are various genealogical quarterlies from all over the United States.

A rare book room has a 1656 volume, The Antiquities of Warwickshire Illustrated. The main shelves include Genealogies of Mayflower Families, a 40-volume set of The Domesday Books and Burke's Peerage, Baronetage and Knightage.

All that is required to use the collection is a valid form of identification. All research must be done in person; the library does not have the staff to do personal research for the public. Visitors should be aware that access to the library is by a flight of steep stairs.

The Ladson Genealogical Library is open Monday through Friday 9:00 A.M. to 1:00 P.M. and 2:00 to 6:00 P.M. It is closed on major holidays. For information you can call (912)537-9395 or 537-8186.

Vidalia is more widely known as the home of Georgia's famous mild, sweet-tasting **onions**. The mild climate and unique soil around Vidalia produce the special taste of this delicious member of the lily family. Onions were sacred to the ancient Egyptians, but even during the Middle Ages when they were as valuable as gold they did not represent as lucrative an industry as they do today in Georgia, where they are a 30-million-dollar industry. Vidalia onions, grown in 20 southeast counties, are harvested from May through mid-June. During the spring harvest season more than 20 million pounds are stored in several controlled-atmosphere facilities and later sold throughout the year.

You can stop at the Stanley Farms Vidalia Onion Factory to see their climate controlled storage facilities, the sorting and grading areas and the country store where you can purchase a wide variety of Vidalia onion products. Fresh Vidalia onions are available from May through August. For mail order information call (800)227-ONION.

South of Vidalia is the **Edwin I. Hatch Visitors Center** and its exhibits on how nuclear energy supplies electrical power in Georgia. Nuclear fission is explained, and visitors can light a lamp from electricity produced here. There is no charge to visit this facility open Monday through Friday 9:00 A.M. to 5:00 P.M. Adjacent to the center is a roadside park with picnic tables over-looking the Altamaha River.

Directions: From I-75 take I-16 east from Macon; then take the Soperton exit, Route 15/29 south, until the intersection with Route 280. Turn left on Route 280 to Vidalia. If you are traveling west on I-16 take the Lyons exit, Route 1 south. Just past Lyons turn right on Route 280 for Vidalia. If you want to reach the Hatch Plant from Vidalia take Route 15/29 south (that is Jackson Street and Center Drive), which connects with Route 1, then continue south on Route 1.

Little Ocmulgee State Park

Sandhills and Sandtraps

Hundreds of years ago the 1,374 acres on which Little Ocmulgee State Park stands were under an ocean. As the water receded, dunes were left that, with the passage of time, became inland sand ridges. Within the park, the 2.3-mile Oak Ridge Trail winds through these Georgia sandhills. It takes about an hour to hike the trail. There is a shorter 1.7-mile Magnolia Loop Trail, which begins in the low-lying bay swamp, or pocosin. Growing in the pocosin are loblolly bays, swamp red bays, sweet bays and evergreen shrubs. The water is a yellowish-brown color because of the tannic acid from the decaying vegetation and plant roots. When you climb the first sandhill you'll see Spanish moss hanging from the trees. This draping plant, part of the bromeliad family that includes the pineapple, is not a parasitic growth. The moss gets its sustenance from air. It's unwise to gather Spanish moss because during most of the year it is inhabited by a plethora of small bugs and mites.

The large shrubs growing beside the trail are yaupon holly. The leaves of this plant were gathered by the southeastern Indians to make a "black drink." This highly caffeinated tea was used to purge the body during ceremonial occasions. In fact, the botanical name for the yaupon holly is Ilex vomitoria. The trail winds through a dwarf oak forest. You'll see the longleaf pine that produces the largest cone of any pine in the East, as well as turkey oats, post oaks and wiregrass.

Many visitors to Little Ocmulgee strive to stay out of the sand, at least on the 18-hole Wallace Adams Memorial course, one of the state's best public courses. The park has one of the state's best golfer's getaway packages; for details call (912)868-7474. Young duffers can try their luck on the miniature golf course that is a replica of the park's regulation course. A restaurant overlooks the sixth tee of the golf course.

Hiking and golf are only two of the recreational opportunities at Little Ocmulgee State Park. Fishermen can try their luck in the 265-acre lake. The world record largemouth bass was hooked in the Ocmulgee River in 1932; it weighed 22 pounds and four ounces. Private boats can use the boat ramp, and boats and canoes can be rented. Overnight accommodations include the 30-room Pete Phillips Lodge, ten cottages along the lake and tent and trailer sites. There are four lighted tennis courts, a swimming pool, guided nature walks and canoe trips on the Ocmulgee River. Little Ocmulgee State Park is open 7:00 A.M. to 10:00 P.M., although the park office hours are only 8:00 A.M. to 5:00 P.M.

Directions: Traveling south, take I-75 to Macon and pick up I-16 east towards Savannah. Continue on I-16 to Exit 14, Dublin, and head south on Route 319/441 for 31 miles to Little Ocmulgee State Park. Heading north on I-75 take the Cordele exit, and take Route 280 east to McRae. Just east of McRae, take a left on Route 319/441 north and travel two miles to the park.

State Parks

General Coffee State Park, Douglas (see selection)
Gordonia-Altamaha State Park, Reidsville; a 280-acre park with a 12-acre lake offering fishing, paddle boats and a boat dock, plus swimming pool, camping, picnicking and a 9-hole golf course, (912)557-6444
Little Ocmulgee State Park, McRae (see selection)

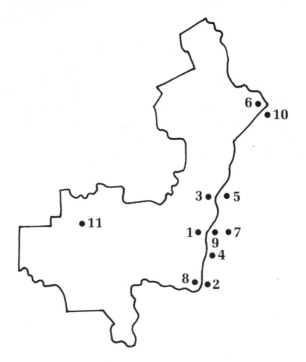

COLONIAL COAST

1. **Brunswick**
   Hofwyl-Broadfield Plantation
   Marshes of Glynn
   Sunbury State Historic Site

2. **Cumberland Island**
   Dungeness Historic District

3. **Darien**
   Fort King George State Historic
   Site

4. **Jekyll Island**

5. **Sapelo Island**

6. **Savannah**
   Forts Jackson, McAllister,
   Pulaski, Screven
   Historic District and Homes
   Juliette Gordon Low Birthplace
   and Andrew Low House
   King-Tisdell Cottage and Beach
   Institute
   Ships of the Sea Museum
   Wormsloe State Historic Site

7. **Sea Island**
   The Cloister

8. **St. Marys**
   Crooked River State Park
   Kings Bay Naval Submarine
   Base
   Orange Hall

9. **St. Simons Island**
   Christ Church, Frederica
   Fort Frederica National
   Monument and Bloody Marsh
   Battle Site
   Little St. Simons Island
   Museum of Coastal History

10. **Tybee Island**
    Museum and Lighthouse

11. **Waycross**
    Heritage Center and Southern
    Forest World
    Obediah's Okefenok and
    Okefenokee Swamp Park
    Okefenokee National Wildlife
    Refuge
    Stephen C. Foster State Park

──────Colonial Coast──────

Brilliant days, molten-hued sunsets, sun-dappled sand and endless expanses of golden marsh grass beckon travelers to the coastal islands the Spanish called the Golden Isles—Sea Island, Jekyll, St. Simons and Little St. Simons. Georgia has protected her golden treasures: On Cumberland Islands and Sapelo, there are places where you can walk along an unpopulated beach, and yours will be the only footprints in the sand.

You can chart your course by the trees. The island trails are palmetto-lined, the drives of old colonial plantations like Wormsloe are oak lined and the canoe paths in the Okefenokee Swamp are flanked by moss-bedecked cypress.

The queen of the coast is Savannah, where the past is glimpsed through delicate iron garden gates and fretwork-trimmed porches that enhance the oak-shaded homes from the 18th and 19th century. Four protective forts remind visitors of the bloody struggles for the coast. The Ships of the Seas Museum evokes the rich maritime legacy of this bustling port, and the homes of prominent residents reveal their lifestyle.

Discriminating travelers have been vacationing in this coastal region for centuries. In the 1800s some of America's wealthiest industrialists formed a private club and spent their summers at Jekyll Island. Now that private playground is open to all, and knowledgeable travelers have beaten a path to this shore.

Brunswick

Poetic Inspiration

In 1877, Sidney Lanier sat under what is now called the Lanier Oak and wrote his famous poem, *The Marshes of Glynn*. From this historic tree in Overlook Park you can see the vast marshlands that inspired one of his most beloved works. He wrote:

> *Ye marshes, how candid and simple and*
> *nothing-withholding and free*

Ye publish yourselves to the sky and
offer yourselves to the sea!
Tolerant plains, that suffer the sea and
the rains and the sun,
Ye spread and span like the catholic
man who hath mightily won
God out of knowledge and good out of
infinite pain
And sight out of blindness and purity
out of a stain.

The expanses of golden marshes, the days of bright golden sun and brilliant golden sunsets prompted the Spanish adventurers who came to Georgia's coastal islands in the 1500s to call them the "Golden Isles." The four islands are Sea Island, Jekyll, St. Simons and Little St. Simons (see each selection).

At the gateway to the Golden Isles is the seaport of Brunswick, noted as the western-most harbor on the eastern seaboard. Brunswick calls itself the "shrimp capital of the world." The shrimp docks, at the foot of Gloucester Street, come alive in late afternoon when the boats come in with their catches. Visitors gather at **Mary Ross Waterfront Park** to watch the shrimpers and the setting sun. Shrimpers unload all along Bay Street, and travelers sample the catch-of-the-day at numerous Brunswick restaurants. Brunswick stew, a dish made along the coast predominantly from seafood, was created in this part of Georgia more than a century ago. This stew is now enjoyed far beyond the boundaries of the Golden Isles. (Elsewhere the dish is prepared with meat.)

Brunswick, established in 1771, did not follow the lead of other American towns and cities that changed their British street names after the War of Independence. The name for the city honors Braunsweig, Germany, King George II's ancestral home. The streets still have Old English names like Gloucester, Norwich and London. Brunswick is on the National Register of Historic Districts, and its downtown area has undergone a revitalization as part of the Main Street Program.

The streets of Southend Brunswick are lined with old homes noted for their turn-of-the-century architecture. The finest example of "carpenter gothic" in Georgia is the **Mahoney-Mc-Garvey House** at 1709 Reynolds Street opposite the Courthouse. The 1907 courthouse itself is impressive and made even more so by the moss-covered live oaks and exotic trees including a Chinese pistachio and a tung tree that surround it. Another striking public building is the "Old" City Hall, a Richardsonian Romanesque structure built in 1890.

At the intersection of Route 17 and the St. Simons Causeway is a Visitors Center for Brunswick and the Golden Isles. You can

Moss-covered live oaks and exotic trees surround Brunswick's impressive courthouse.

watch a color film on the area and pick up brochures and maps. On display is the pot in which Brunswick's stew was first prepared. Outside on the grounds is a replica of a Liberty Ship, one of more than 100 that were built in the Brunswick shipyards during World War II. The Visitor Center is open daily 9:00 A.M. to 5:00 P.M.; closed on holidays.

On the east side of town opposite the Marshes of Glynn Overlook Park, is the **Mary Miller Doll Museum** at 1523 Glynn Avenue. Here are celebrity dolls, foreign dolls and antique dolls including pre-Civil War china-head and bisque-head dolls—more than 3,000 dolls, one of the region's largest collections—also uncounted doll dresses, accessories and toys. The museum is open Monday through Saturday from 11:00 A.M. to 5:00 P.M. and charges a nominal fee.

Directions: From I-95 southbound take Exit 8, North Golden Isles Parkway. Take a left and travel approximately three miles into Brunswick. From I-95 northbound take Exit 6, South Golden Isles Parkway. Take a right and travel six miles into Brunswick. Visitors can also take Exit 7, Route 341, Newcastle Street, into Brunswick.

The Cloister and Sea Island

Vacation Mecca for the Cognoscenti

Long a retreat for heads of state, royalty and the cognoscenti, The Cloister, a world-renowned Five-Star resort on Sea Island, welcomes both overnight guests and daytrippers. All visitors are free to stroll the grounds, enjoy a meal in the main dining room and browse through the shops.

Five-mile-long **Sea Island** was uninhabited and virtually unknown until the causeway from Brunswick to St. Simons was completed in 1924. By that time the resort potential of this sleepy Georgia coastal island was recognized by area businessmen, who sought a developer. Local enthusiasts interested Ohio auto magnate Howard E. Coffin in Sea Island. Coffin already owned Sapelo Island and a large holding on St. Simons, including Retreat Plantation, an antebellum cotton plantation (see Sapelo and St. Simons selections).

Coffin formed Sea Island Investments, Inc. (subsequently renamed the Sea Island Company) and embarked on the creation of a luxury resort. He originally intended to develop the resort on his St. Simons plantation, but his young cousin, and Sapelo Island supervisor, Alfred William (Bill) Jones, persuaded him to develop Sea Island instead. Jones was put in charge of the company.

The problems inherent in the remote location were all resolved. Public utilities were brought in, an electrical plant constructed, a telephone system installed and a road system established. Shuttle service from Savannah and Jacksonville was in place even before The Cloister opened. Resort architect Addison Mizner designed the main hotel and River House in the Spanish-Mediterranean tradition. Over the years sprawling villas with sunny patios and cloistered terraces were added.

President Calvin Coolidge attended the ceremonial opening on October 12, 1928. He was but the first of many presidents to visit this Georgia resort; others include Dwight D. Eisenhower, Gerald Ford, Jimmy Carter and George Bush. The Bushes are among many well-known honeymooners who have stayed at The Cloister, including Vice President and Mrs. Alben Barkley, General and Mrs. William Westmoreland and Treasury Secretary William Simon and his wife. Sir Winston Churchill's daughter Sarah got engaged while staying at The Cloister and was married at the home of Alfred W. Jones. More than 33,000 honeymooners have enjoyed the hospitality of The Cloister.

Guests at the resort use the 36-hole **Sea Island Golf Club** on the grounds of Coffin's Retreat Plantation (ruins of the old plantation can still be seen on the course that Bobby Jones said was "one of the world's finest"). There is also an 18-hole course at the St. Simons Island Club plus a golf learning center, two pools and a spa at the Beach Club, 18 tennis courts, horseback riding, sailing, biking, fishing, boating and miles of private beach. Meals are included and a full schedule of activities each day, culminating in live music each evening, except Sunday.

It's fun to stroll around the grounds of this island playground and visit the trial gardens and greenhouses, open weekdays from 8:00 A.M. to 4:00 P.M. A walking tour map pinpoints 36 trees, shrubs, vines and flowering plants. Daytrippers may help themselves to the brochure "Walking The Cloister Grounds" at the Bell Stand in the lobby. Garden enthusiasts who would like to take home plants such as they see on their walk can find them for sale at the Island Landscape Center adjacent to the Sea Island Stables on St. Simons Island.

Directions: From I-95 heading south take Exit 8 (traveling north use Exit 6). Both connect with Route 17 east that leads to the Sea Island Causeway, the last link to The Cloister entrance.

Cumberland Island

Wilderness Magnet

In 1972, Georgia's largest and southernmost barrier island became a National Seashore, and 8,840 acres were designated as **The Cumberland Island Wilderness Area**. According to the Wilderness Act of 1964, "A Wilderness, in contrast with those areas where man and his own works dominate the landscape, is. . .recognized as an area where man himself is a visitor who does not remain."

Cumberland Island is 18 miles long and three miles wide. The fact that only 300 travelers are permitted to visit the island daily ensures that the unspoiled nature of the island is maintained. Visitors explore on foot; there are no vehicles for hire, nor are visitors permitted to bring in bikes. There are no stores on the island. Visitors are advised to bring with them everything they need during their time ashore.

Hearty adventurers will enjoy camping in this pristine wilderness. Reservations must be obtained in advanced by calling (912) 882-4335. There is a developed campground at Sea Camp Beach with restrooms, cold showers, drinking water and the option of a campfire. There are also four primitive back-country sites where minimum impact camping is permitted. Diametrically opposite this no-frills overnight experience is **Greyfield Inn**, the only travelers' accommodations available on the island, excepting an occasional private home for rent.

In 1881, Lucy and Thomas Carnegie built a second lavish Dungeness mansion on the site of the earlier mansion built on the island by Revolutionary War General Nathanael Greene in 1783. Greyfield Inn was built in 1901 as a vacation home for Lucy and Thomas Carnegie's daughter, Margaret Ricketson. In the 1960s Margaret's daughter opened the lovely 1,300-acre island property as an inn. The inn accommodates only 18 guests, and reservations are a must. Call (904) 261-6408 for details.

Most visitors to the island spend only a few hours, but that is time enough to fall in love with the natural beauty of Cumberland. Visitors approach the island aboard the ferry that departs from St. Marys (see selection). From their first glimpse, visitors are struck by the undulating beauty of the marsh grasses. When the tide is in it is hard to distinguish between the grass and water. Not merely eye-catching, the marsh is also the most productive land acre per acre of any on the planet. One must wait for the tide to go out before seeing the long-legged wading birds: great blue, little blue and Louisiana herons; snowy and American egrets; white ibis and wood stork (an endangered species).

Accessible only by hiking trails is the island's **maritime forest**. The weirdly contorted live oak have a visual appeal that is appropriately enhanced by the spidery web of Spanish moss draped from their boughs. A wide range of wildlife lives under this dense canopy. Hikers and campers may encounter feral (domesticated animals that have gone wild) pigs and horses, deer, raccoons, armadillos, snakes and alligators.

On the Atlantic side of the island is a seemingly endless expanse of **beach**—the longest stretch of undeveloped beach in the East. It is an unalloyed joy to walk along a beach where there are no footprints except your own, where there are scarcely any signs of man's intrusion, where only a few people may invade your solitude. Far more numerous are the shore birds that dash back and forth across the tightly packed sand or drop gracefully head-first into the surf in search of food. The undeveloped dunes, anchored by sea oats and viny plants, are nesting spots for female loggerhead turtles that come ashore each year to lay their eggs.

The first ferry stop is at **Dungeness Dock**. Visitors start their exploration in the Ice House Museum, then walk the trail that covers the Dungeness Historic District. Several outbuildings such as the ice house have survived from the original estate. Within the museum are photographs from the Carnegie era, as well as exhibits that enrich a visit to the island.

Cumberland Island was inhabited by marine-oriented Indians 4,000 years ago. Piles of shells, called middens, are all that remain of the Timucuan Indians, who lived undisturbed on the land they called Missoe (Sassafras) until 1566 when the Spanish governor of Florida ordered a fort built on the island. Once San

Pedro, as the fort was called, was complete, a Franciscan mission on the island attempted to convert the Indians. A few pot shards have been unearthed that date back to the Spanish occupation. Control of Cumberland Island slipped from Spanish to English hands in the 1730s, and in 1736 General James Oglethorpe named the island Cumberland. Toonahowie, one of the Indians who advised Oglethorpe, suggested the name in remembrance of the Duke of Cumberland, whom he had met when he traveled to England. The English built two forts on Cumberland Island and a hunting lodge called Dungeness.

After the Revolutionary War, General Nathanael Greene bought land on Cumberland Island intending to harvest live oaks for the shipbuilding industry. At his death in 1783 his widow Catherine inherited the property. She married Phineas Miller and together they built Dungeness, a four-story tabby mansion. In 1818, General Lighthorse Harry Lee, who had been a comrade-in-arms of Nathanael Greene, became ill while sailing from Barbados. Lee was put ashore at Cumberland Island where he died. Buried for a time on the island, his body was disinterred in 1913 and re-buried at Lexington, Virginia, beside his son, Robert E. Lee.

For a time there were cotton plantations on Cumberland Island, but that era ended when the Union army transported the island slaves to Amelia Island. After the Civil War, some of the freed blacks returned, and a settlement was established in the 1890s for black workers. One of the few remaining buildings from this old community near Halfmoon Bluff is the First African Baptist Church built in 1893, then rebuilt in the 1930s.

In 1881, Thomas Carnegie, the brother of financier Andrew, bought a large holding on Cumberland Island. He and his wife, Lucy, began building a palatial estate on the fire-damaged ruins of the Greene home. Like Nathanael Greene, Thomas died shortly after his mansion was finished, and his wife inherited most of the island.

The blue-blazed Dungeness Trail takes visitors past the ruins of the Carnegie mansion. Because ruins and most of the out-buildings are unstable, visitors are advised to keep their distance, a warning that is automatically heeded once they learn that the diamondback rattler, one of the island's three poisonous snakes, makes its home among the ruins. Speaking of possible dangers on this or any of the other 50 miles of trails that criss-cross the island, visitors should check themselves for ticks (carriers of Lyme disease). Care should be taken in the surf because sharks are not uncommon in these waters.

The second ferry stop at **Sea Camp**, has a beach and developed campsites, plus a Visitor Center adjacent to the dock. During the summer season there are ranger-led walks and interpretative programs. Fishing on Cumberland Island is popular, and red bass, spotted trout and bluefish abound. The Cumberland Sound is another good fishing area but requires a license. Likely catches include croaker, drum, trout and red bass.

The ferry runs between St. Marys and Cumberland Island daily, departing the mainland at 9:00 and 11:45 A.M. Island departures are at 10:15 A.M. and 4:45 P.M. From October to March there is no ferry service on Tuesday and Wednesday. For reservations and current fares call (912)882-4335 on weekdays between 10:00 A.M. and 2:00 P.M. The ferry does not accommodate cars, bikes or pets.

Since there are no stores on the island, visitors often bring a picnic lunch. Picnic baskets can be ordered from Seagle's Restaurant (see St. Mary's selection) opposite the ferry dock in St. Mary's. If you want to order a picnic in advance, call 912-882-4187. It's advisable to wear comfortable hiking shoes and carry insect repellant and sun screen.

Directions: To reach St. Marys from I-95 take Route 40 east.

Fort Frederica National Monument and Bloody Marsh Battle Site

European Enemies Met on Southern Soil

Spanish and English quests for empire collided at Fort Frederica on St. Simons Island. Oglethorpe, the founder and leader of the Georgia colony, established Fort Frederica in 1736, three years after landing at Savannah. Fort Frederica, which had the distinction of being "the largest, most regular, and perhaps most costly" British fortification in North America, was established as a bulwark against Spanish aggression.

Under Oglethorpe's direction, the settlers—44 men and 72 women and children—built a fortified town. Oglethorpe laid out the military town in 84 lots; giving each family a lot for their home and 50 acres for crops. Settlers built palmetto huts, soon replacing them with substantial homes of wood, brick and tabby, a crude concrete made of oyster shells. By the 1740s the village looked like a town in the English Midlands, with numerous tradesmen and craftsmen, a public baker and a tavern keeper. Since there was no slavery, the settlers did their own field work, augmenting their diet by fishing and hunting. A visitor described Frederica as "a pretty strong Fort of Tappy (sic), which has several 18 Pounders mounted on a Ravelin in its Front, and commands the River both upwards and downwards; and is surrounded by a quadrangular Rampart, with 4 bastions, of Earth well stockaded and turfed, and a palisadoed Ditch." The town was named for King George II's only son, Frederick.

Built in 1736, Fort Frederica was established to protect British interest from Spanish encroachment.

Nearly 1,000 people lived in Frederica then, and Spain felt threatened by this growing settlement so near her Florida domain. Oglethorpe, anticipating armed conflict, returned to England to raise an army. He returned to Georgia with his own 630-man regiment of British regulars, the 42nd Regiment of Foot.

Oglethorpe garrisoned these troops at Frederica and at Fort St. Simons, a new fort built on the south end of the island. War broke out between England and Spain over the slave trade in 1739, and less than a year later Oglethorpe, with 900 troops and Indian allies, attempted to capture the Spanish colonial capital at St. Augustine. Unable to breach the defenses of the Castillo de San Marcos, Oglethorpe returned to Frederica. The Spanish couldn't overlook Oglethorpe's aggression, so they gathered an armada of 2,016 men and 33 warships and attacked Fort Frederica in early July 1742.

The highwater mark of the Spanish invasion of British territory was reached on July 7th, when they pushed to within one mile of Fort Frederica. A determined effort by the British repulsed their attack at Gully Hole Creek. Later that day, Oglethorpe's men ambushed a column of Spanish Grenadiers at **Bloody Marsh**, so named because the marshes ran red with blood. Following the British victory, the Spanish withdrew from the island, never to return to Georgia.

With the Spanish threat eliminated, the reason for Frederica's existence was also eliminated. Oglethorpe returned to England in 1743, and the regiment garrisoned at the fort was disbanded in 1749. Lacking their former military customers, the town's businesses closed, leaving it by 1755 virtually a ghost town. Some of the town buildings survived a major fire in 1758, but Frederica fell into total ruin soon after that.

You can still see the tabby ruins of Frederica. Using the site's walking tour map, you find eight points of interest, including the foundations of several old houses, the barracks, fort and protective wall and moat. Before exploring the old military town, see the 25-minute film, narrated by John Ireland, on daily life in colonial Frederica. The film is shown every 30 minutes from 9:00 A.M. to 4:00 P.M. (4:30 P.M. in the summer). During the summer months, rangers lead daily walking tours, and on weekends there are black powder weapons demonstrations.

Fort Frederica is open 8:00 A.M. to 5:00 P.M., during the summer it remains open one hour later. There is an admission fee for each vehicle. At the Bloody Marsh Battle Site, some distance from the fort, there is a historic marker.

Directions: From I-95, Exit 8, take the Golden Isles Parkway to the St. Simons Causeway (if you are traveling on I-95 from the south take Exit 6). Once you cross the bridge, for Fort Frederica turn left on Sea Island Drive and then left again onto Frederica Road, and follow this road to the National Monument. For the Bloody Marsh Battle Site, once you cross the bridge go straight on Demere Road past the airport and bear left at the historic marker sign.

Fort King George State Historic Site

Scene from the Colonial Past

When you enter the gates of Fort King George in Darien, let your imagination populate the earthen fort with British soldiers, like those who built and garrisoned the fort between 1721 and 1728. Actually, most of the fort was built by South Carolina Provincial scouts, civilians and slaves substituting for the British who were suffering from scurvy.

Interpreters wear hand-sewn uniforms from original 18th-century patterns to look like Colonel John **"Tuscarora Jack" Barnwell's soldiers**. These men, from His Majesty's 41st Independent Company, had to endure the unfamiliar, steamy colonial climate—made even more unbearable by their cumbersome, wool uniforms. Many soldiers were felled by insect-transmitted diseases, as well as by Indians. During the first year of the fort's existence more than two-thirds of the garrison died. On the site of this old fort is one of the oldest British military cemeteries in North America.

The area around the rebuilt fort has not changed over the past 300 years. You'll see the marshes that bedeviled the British, the river (although man's intervention has somewhat altered that), the distant barrier islands and abundant wildlife.

Old documents from the British Public Records Office were used to reconstruct the cypress blockhouse to the exact dimensions of the original building. Tools and construction methods used were identical to those of the past. The blockhouse has three stories: a magazine room, a room with gun ports in the walls for cannon and muskets and a large protruding top floor. Also rebuilt during the reconstruction in 1988 was a log palisade in the moat that protects two sides of the fort.

Artifacts unearthed at the fort provide a glimpse of 18th-century life in this coastal Georgia wilderness for the British, as well as for the Indians and the Spanish priests who came to the New World to convert them. Scholars think that decades before the fort was built the site was a Guale (pronounced "Wally") Indian village and possibly a Spanish mission site.

The fort was abandoned a year after fire destroyed the barracks and damaged the blockhouse and palisades. In 1736, subsequent to the fort's closure, General James Oglethorpe encouraged a group of Scottish Highlanders to settle in this area. These Scots developed the town of **Darien**. By the 1800s a thriving timber industry had developed which lasted until 1925. There are tabby and brick ruins of three sawmills on the Fort King George site.

Fort King George Historic Site is open Tuesday through Saturday from 9:00 A.M. to 5:00 P.M. and Sunday 2:00 to 5:30 P.M. Closed on Thanksgiving and Christmas Day. There is a nominal admission fee. A video on the fort's historical background as well as exhibits can be seen at the Visitor Center.

Darien is Georgia's second oldest town and while in the area you should explore its historic squares and ride past the timber barons' homes. Route 99 through "The Ridge" takes you past quaint Victorian sea captains' residences.

Directions: From I-95 take Exit 10, and travel east for one mile on Route 251. Turn right on U.S. 17 to Darien. Approximately one mile through Darien turn left on Route 99 and follow the signs to the fort. You can stop at the Darien Welcome Center at Route 17 by the Altamaha River bridge to obtain additional information and to purchase tickets for the Sapelo ferry (see selection).

Four Forts of Savannah

Bastions of Defense

The Indians, the Spanish and the British threatened the security and sovereignty of Savannah. From her earliest days, Fort Jackson, Fort Pulaski, Fort Screven and Fort McAllister guarded her flanks.

Although **Fort Jackson** is the oldest standing fort in Georgia, it was not the first on this site. The structure standing today was begun in 1808 on the site of an earlier colonial fort on Salter's Island. The Revolutionary War battery was purchased by the Federal government in 1808 and garrisoned to protect Savannah from the British during the War of 1812. The fort was rebuilt in 1842 and served as a Confederate headquarters during the Civil War. An audiovisual program in the fort gives more of the military history of Fort Jackson.

A moat surrounds Fort Jackson, and artifacts that reflect the fort's history are displayed in the fort's casemates. The fort's original 32-pound cannon is the largest black-powder cannon still fired in the country.

Fort Jackson is open daily 9:00 A.M. until 5:00 P.M. From July through mid-August the fort stays open until 7:00 P.M. and the fort presents "Trooping of the Colors" and cannon firing demonstrations on selected days. A nominal admission is charged.

The first seacoast fort built to protect Savannah was **Fort Pulaski**, constructed between 1829 and 1847, on marshy Cockspur Island in the Savannah River, at a cost of one million dollars. West Point graduate Robert E. Lee was one of the engineers who built Fort Pulaski. It was named to honor Revolutionary War hero Casimir Pulaski, a Polish count who was killed during the unsuccessful siege of Savannah in 1779. A seven-foot-deep moat surrounds the brick fort. On the other side of the drawbridge is an area known as the demilune, where cannons were placed to protect the fort's wooden gate.

The hallway that forms an entranceway to the fort is called the sallyport. There is a small door, called a wicket, set into the larger door. In times of trouble soldiers could enter individually through this small door and follow a covered brick walkway to their rooms. Only the officers had a bed to themselves. In the guardroom and barracks two men shared each bed, and there were sometimes as many as 16 men in a room.

Other rooms you'll see include Father Whalen's Quarters which also served as a chapel, the officers' and enlisted men's mess, the dispensary, the quartermaster's office and supply room and the commanding officer's quarters.

The massive seven-and-a-half-foot solid-brick walls, backed with massive masonry piers, were considered impregnable until April 11, 1862. Before that time U.S. Chief of Engineers Joseph G. Totten had claimed, "You might as well bombard the Rocky Mountains as Fort Pulaski." On that April day, however, Northern soldiers fired on the fort from Tybee Island, located a mile away. Colonel Charles H. Olmstead surrendered the fort 30 hours after bombardment began because the southeast angle was shot away exposing the fort to infantry attack.

During this bombardment the new **rifled cannons**, which had been in use since the beginning of the war, demonstrated their true worth. The use of these new cannons marked the end of masonry fortifications. A rifled cannon is on exhibit at the top of the granite steps inside the fort. Rifled cannons had spiral grooves cut in them. Instead of being perfectly round, the projectiles these new cannons fired were bullet-shaped. They traveled faster and farther, and the spin made them better balanced so they could hit their intended target from farther away.

Fort Pulaski, just 15 miles east of Savannah, is open daily 8:30 A.M. to 5:15 P.M. Extended hours may be available during the summer; call ahead for information (912)786-5787. The fort is closed on Christmas Day. A small fee is charged, children under 17 and seniors are admitted free. There is a visitor center, museum, book store, picnic area and nature trails and in the summer, demonstrations and daily talks at the fort. Fort Pulaski is one of ten National Parks in Georgia.

A third fort loomed south of Savannah on the bank of the Great Ogeechee River. Built in 1861-62, **Fort McAllister** is the best preserved example of Confederate earthwork fortifications. Designed to protect Savannah's back door, the fort also protected an important railroad trestle and the rice plantations along the Great Ogeechee River. It was named for one of these plantations. Between 1862 and 1863, the fort repulsed seven attacks by armored Union vessels. It was a major target of Sherman's army and the fort finally fell on December 13, 1864. The earthworks and bombproofs withstood heavy firing and after restoration look just as they did during the Civil War.

Fort McAllister State Historic Site is open 9:00 A.M. to 5:00 P.M. Tuesday through Saturday and Sunday 2:00 to 5:30 P.M. A small fee is charged. The site has a museum with Civil War artifacts, a 1.3-mile hiking trail, boat ramps and a dock, camping and picnicking facilities.

The fourth fort protecting Savannah was just past Fort Pulaski on Tybee Island. **Fort Screven** was built in 1875 along the Atlantic Ocean beach. The fort was garrisoned during the Spanish-American War and both World Wars. During World War II it was commanded by General George C. Marshall. Fort Screven has not been restored, and private homes sit atop its walls. The Tybee Museum is located adjacent to the fort (see Tybee Island).

Directions: From I-16 in Savannah take M.L. King Boulevard to Bay Street and turn right. Go east on Bay Street to the convergence with Presidents Street extension. Continue on Presidents Street for one mile and turn left at the Fort Jackson sign. The fort is three miles east of Savannah on the Savannah River. For Fort Pulaski you also take Presidents Street to U.S. Route 80. The entrance is on the left off Route 80. For Fort McAllister State Historic Site take Exit 15 off I-95. Turn right on Route 17 to Richmond Hill, then make a right on Route 144. Take Route 144 for six miles, then turn left on Spur 144 that ends at the park entrance.

Hofwyl-Broadfield Plantation

Coastal Rice Empire

Only a few of the South's great rice plantations survived the Civil War. Hofwyl-Broadfield was one of the lucky ones. It was begun in 1806-07 when William Brailsford of Charleston, South Carolina, cleared cypress swamp land along the Altamaha River for rice cultivation. At his death in 1810, his son-in-law, James M. Troup, assumed management of Broadfield. Troup bought the property in 1834, enlarging it several years later by buying the adjoining New Hope Plantation. When Troup died in 1849 he was in debt, though he did own 7,300 acres of land, 357 slaves and several homes. His son, a Dr. Troup, managed the estate until 1856 when it was divided so that each of his three sons could inherit a plantation of his own.

One of these plantations, West New Hope, was renamed **Hofwyl** by Ophelia Troup Dent, in honor of the Swiss Agricultural school her husband attended. Exhibits and photographs at the Visitor Center trace the life and culture of this Altamaha River empire.

Visitors come to a deeper appreciation of the mystery and the history of this rice plantation as they stroll along the path at the edge of the marsh. The **trail** skirts the tabby rice mill ruins where the rice was processed. Only the largest and wealthiest plantations had their own mill, and most planters sent their grain to mills in Savannah or Charleston.

The path continues along the top of the rice field dike. As you look out over the freshwater marsh, it is hard to believe that it was probably once a virgin cypress swamp. It took hundreds of slaves to clear and level such jungle-like terrain. Once that was done, miles of ditches and dikes had to be hand dug. Some of these dikes date back to William Brailsford's day.

As you stand on the dike you'll see a narrow channel used to transport the heavily ladened rice flats on which rice was floated to the mill or seed was carried to the fields to be planted. The flats also hauled earth away from the ditches. As Edward D. King wrote in his 1775 book, *The Great South*, "A rice plantation is, in fact, a huge hydraulic machine, maintained by constant warring against the rivers."

The trail's farthest point is the antebellum **plantation house**. The grounds around the simple white frame house are planted with magnolias, camellias, palms and centuries old, moss-ladened live oaks. A small flower garden and a brick-lined spring house add more charm.

Guides conduct tours of the house, furnished as it was when it was willed to the state in 1973 by Miss Ophelia Troup Dent. The family furnishings span decades. On Ophelia's mother's bed is a bedspread knitted in the 1850s. There's a Charleston secretary in the parlor with six secret compartments.

Outside, notice the duplex design of the servants' quarters, a common plantation practice. After 1915, when rice ceased to be planted at Hofwyl-Broadfield, the plantation became a dairy farm. The ice house, garage, milling barn and bottling house date from that period.

If you take the mile-long path in summer, be sure to use insect repellant as mosquitoes are a problem. You also may encounter fire ants and snakes, but they normally stay off the path. During most of the year, wildlife abounds in and around the plantation, which borders the Butler Island Wildlife Management Area. You may glimpse a raccoon, wild hog, fiddler crab, hawk or waterfowl.

Hofwyl-Broadfield Plantation State Historic Site is open year-round. Hours are 9:00 A.M. to 5:00 P.M. Tuesday through Saturday and 2:00 to 5:30 P.M. on Sunday. Closed on Thanksgiving, Christmas and New Year's. A nominal admission is charged.

Not far from Hofwyl-Broadfield is **Sunbury State Historic Site**. In 1776 when the delegates from the 13 colonies met in Philadelphia to declare their independence, they also took steps to protect the newly proclaimed country from the British. One step authorized by the Continental Congress was the construction of a fort near the seaport of Sunbury to protect Georgia's coast.

Fort Morris was built on a low bluff on the Medway River and garrisoned by 200 patriots. The fort withstood two British attacks. On November 25, 1778, when the British demanded the fort's surrender, Col. John McIntosh's defiant answer was, "Come and take it." The British declined the invitation and withdrew to the south. The fort fell on January 9, 1779, the last remaining colonial outpost in Coastal Georgia. British troops left the thriving town of Sunbury in ruins when they evacuated Georgia in 1782. The harbor never regained its former prominence.

During the War of 1812, the remains of Fort Morris were rebuilt into a smaller fort, called **Fort Defiance**. It is the earthworks from this fort that visitors see today. There is a small museum in the Visitors Center with exhibits on the forts and the colonial port of Sunbury. The center is open Tuesday through Saturday from 9:00 A.M. to 5:00 P.M. and Sunday 2:00 to 5:30 P.M. A small admission fee is charged.

Directions: From I-95 take Exit 9, then east on Route 99 one mile to U.S. 17 south. Hofwyl will be about 200 yards on U.S. 17 south on the left. At Midway, turn right off Route 17 on Sunbury Road, Route 38, for Sunbury State Historic Site.

Jekyll Island

Industrial Barons' Private Kingdom

Before 1886 Jekyll Island's history duplicated the other major barrier islands of Georgia—Sapelo, Cumberland, St. Simons and Sea Island. Originally Jekyll was inhabited by the Guale Indians, then the Spanish missionaries and ultimately the English settlers. Oglethorpe named the island for Sir Joseph Jekyll, a contributor to the Georgia colony. Oglethorpe's trusted adviser and military officer, William Horton, had a thriving plantation on the island and provided food for the English troops. Today only the shell of his home survives.

The shell of Horton's plantation home contrasts sharply with the 240-acre **Jekyll Island Club Historic District** that covers the southern half of the island. The 30 restored buildings in this district represent what in 1904 was called the "richest, the most exclusive, the most inaccessible Club in the world." They are part of one of the largest restorations undertaken in the southeastern United States.

Originally Jekyll Island was purchased by members of New York's Union Club as a private hunting club. It proved so popular that membership soon expanded. Members included the leaders of the Industrial Revolution such as J.P. Morgan, Joseph Pulitzer, Vincent Astor, William K. Vanderbilt, William Rockefeller and Marshall Field. It was estimated at one time that one-sixth of the world's wealth was owned by members of this club.

Landscape architect Horace W.S. Cleveland aimed to create a "paradise" that would enhance the natural beauty of the island; the design of the members' cottages and clubhouse was simple and unpretentious as a result.

The Club House in Jekyll Island's Historic District, once "the richest, most exclusive and most inaccessible club in the world."

Visitors can take an historical or, during certain seasons, an architectural tour of the Jekyll Island Club Historic District. The daily **tram tours** wind through the district stopping at several cottage and spots of interest. The mansion-sized cottages open for tours look as if their owners may, at any moment, appear to welcome their guests. The cottages are furnished with many original pieces.

Tours begin at the **Jekyll Island Museum's Orientation Center**, housed in the 1897 stables. The center is open daily 9:30 A.M. to 4:00 P.M. The room used for the Museum Shop still has its original horse stalls. Exhibits include a model of the original village, old photographs and a replica of a "red bug," the name given to the dune buggies younger members of the elite once raced along the island beaches. A 12-minute orientation film is shown at the center. For a walking tour there is a comprehensive self-guided brochure.

The tram tour includes stops at the **DuBignon Cottage**, a singularly appropriate stop since this cottage was built in 1884 for John Eugene du Bignon, the great-grandson of Christophe Poulain du Bignon, the man who acquired full ownership of Jekyll Island around 1800 after it passed from the hands of William Horton's descendants. In 1885 John Eugene du Bignon acquired the island, and with his brother-in-law, Newton S. Finney, sold it to the wealthy New York club members.

Du Bignon was one of the original members of the Jekyll Island Club, and his cottage originally stood on the present site of the Sans Souci Apartment. It was moved in 1896 and over the years became known as the "Superintendent's Cottage." This Queen Anne Style house with its wrap-around porch is furnished in high Victorian style. The parlor is brilliant red, and the upstairs bedrooms are lavender and hot pink. Clawfooted tubs, potted palms, lace curtains, swags and other decorative staples of the period abound.

Indian Mound Cottage, circa 1892, is furnished to represent its appearance in 1917 when Standard Oil director William Rockefeller and his family wintered here. (William was John D.'s brother.) Rockefeller substantially altered the shingle-style cottage he purchased at the death of inventor Gordon McKay (the creator of a machine to sew the upper part of shoes to the sole, a popular invention during the Civil War when the government needed shoes for soldiers). The cottage is named for the mound located in the front yard. It was once much bigger but since it obstructed the view, Rockefeller had it reduced. During his tenure Rockefeller added the covered driveway, the north and south dormer windows, and extended the living room and the bedroom above it to form a large rounded bay. Visitors may notice the absence of a kitchen. Meals were prepared by outstanding chefs and served in the clubhouse in a convivial atmosphere. If members without kitchens wanted to eat in, the meals would be brought to their cottages in charcoal-warmed carts. Some cottages, such as Mistletoe and Hollybourne, had complete kitchens.

The third house visited on the tour is **Mistletoe Cottage** designed in 1900 for Henry Kirke Porter, a U.S. Representative from Pennsylvania. Porter, who manufactured light locomotives, leased his cottage to John Claflin, founder of Lord and Taylor. Claflin eventually bought the cottage, and for the last part of his life, before his death in 1938, he was the oldest living Charter Member of the Club.

Mistletoe Cottage is a Dutch Colonial Revival house with a gambrel roof. Of special note here is the collection of sculpture by Russell Fiore. Fiore, who has lived on Jekyll Island for a quarter of a century, is a noted sculptor whose work can be seen in Washington, D.C., at the Supreme Court building, the National Archives and the Samuel Gompers Memorial.

Visitors opting for the seasonal architectural tour will tour the **Villa Ospo**, Crane Cottage and Faith Chapel. The Spanish Colonial Revival style Villa Ospo, built in 1927, was one of the last cottages built during the Club era. The 1915 San Diego Exposition influenced John Russell Pope's design for Walter Jennings's island home. Club president Jennings' cottage was the only one in the district to have an attached garage. A begrudging acceptance of cars on the island was forthcoming in 1901. In the beginning, however, the use of cars was restricted to only a few hours a day. Their speed could not exceed 6 mph and they had to stop for horses. Within the Villa Ospo, visitors will see a photographic exhibit of other Jekyll Island historical buildings.

The Italianate **Crane Cottage**, built in 1917 by architect David Adler for Richard T. Crane, was the largest private residence constructed by a Club member. The Crane Company of Chicago manufactured plumbing fixtures, so it is not surprising that the cottage had 17 bathrooms. Many of the architectural features of this house were copied directly from 16th-century Italian villas.

The architectural tour also stops at the cypress-shingled **Faith Chapel**. Architectural touches include six animal heads carved on the interior roof trusses and terra-cotta gargoyles surrounding the steeple. The stained-glass window on the west facade was done by Louis C. Tiffany. A father-and-daughter team, David Maitland Armstrong and daughter, Helen, created the stained glass above the altar.

The Great Depression severely curtailed the activity of the Jekyll Island Club, but members continued to vacation here through the 1942 season. This last season was shortened due to wartime rationing and the shortage of employees. It signaled the end of an era. In 1947 the state of Georgia purchased the island, and it is now leased to the Jekyll Island Authority.

For information and reservations on the tours that run from 10:00 A.M. to 3:00 P.M. daily call (912)635-4036 or 635-2119. The center is closed Christmas Day and New Year's Day. If you want to feel like a member of the Jekyll Island Club, plan to enjoy a meal or an overnight stay at the Jekyll Island Club Hotel, a Radisson Resort. For details call (800)333-3333 or (912)635-2600. After extensive renovation the hotel reopened in 1986 on the 100th anniversary of its initial launching, once again offering outstanding cuisine amid pristine settings.

The Jekyll Island Club is but one of ten hotels on the island; there are also rental cottages and campgrounds. Island amenities include ten miles of beach, four golf courses (the island is Georgia's largest public golf resort), a tennis center, charter boat sightseeing and fishing trips from the two marinas, and Summer Waves, a 11-acre family water park. There are more than 20 miles of paved trails for bicycling. For island information call the Jekyll Island Convention and Visitors Bureau at (800)841-6586 or (912)635-3636.

Directions: From I-95 take Exit 6 onto the Jekyll Island Causeway. Continue ten miles to Jekyll Island.

Juliette Gordon Low Birthplace and the Andrew Low House

Homes of Girl Scouts Founder

Anyone who has ever been associated with the Girl Scouts would appreciate a visit to the Juliette Gordon Low Birthplace in Savannah. Interpreters wear Girl Scout uniforms and speak of Ms. Low so knowingly it's hard not to feel they are personal friends. Visitors are quick to discover the advantage that Juliette Low made of what many would consider a major handicap—her near total loss of hearing. She claimed her disability never permitted her to hear the word "no". Guides at the house tell you that Ms. Low said, "It was so hard to listen, I just talked all the time."

She certainly succeeded in talking the ladies of Savannah into supporting her idea of an organization for young girls modeled after the Boy Scouts. In 1911 Juliette Low met Robert Baden-Powell who founded the Boy Scouts. When he began registration, 6,000 girls signed up, and his sister Agnes Baden-Powell formed the Girl Guides. Juliette became interested in the Girl Guides and on March 12, 1912, in Savannah, 18 girls attended the organizational meeting for the American Girl Guides, the original name of the Girl Scouts. In the Victorian Age, Mrs. Low's belief that young women were entitled to an education, career and a family was quite a radical concept. Also ahead of its time was her burgeoning organization that encouraged girls to wear bloomers, go on camping trips and earn badges in subjects like electrical work, farming, ecology and astronomy.

Juliette Gordon Low, called Daisy by her friends, grew up in Savannah with a strong interest in the arts. The second of six children, she wrote poems and plays, sketched and acted. She eventually became a gifted painter and sculptor. On her parents' 29th wedding anniversary, Juliette married a wealthy Englishman, William Mackay Low.

The Regency townhouse where Juliette Gordon was born, on Halloween in 1860, is now the **Girl Scout National Center**, also the first Registered National Historic Landmark in Savannah. The house, built between 1818 and 1821, is restored and furnished to look as it did in 1886 when Juliette was married. Roughly 40 percent of the furnishings are family pieces and the rest are of the period. Examples of Juliette's art work can be seen, including the bust she did of her father and her own self-portrait. She also did a bust of her favorite niece, Daisy Gordon, who was the first registered member of the American Girl Guides. In the library there is a copy of the lovely portrait painted of Juliette Low in 1887 by Edward Hughes. The original hangs in the National

Portrait Gallery in Washington, D.C. Hanging over the fireplace in the south parlor is Juliette's portrait of her mother which she copied from an original painted in 1856 by G.P.A. Healey.

Juliette may have inherited her tendency to attract drama. Her great-grandmother was kidnapped by the Iroquois Indians at the age of six and held for four years before being returned to her grieving family. Juliette's mother Nellie, while at Yale University, literally knocked her future husband off his feet when she slid down the banister and collided with him. Later at age 81, when she was bedridden, Nellie overheard her children downstairs discussing her funeral arrangements. Knowing that the doctor had forbidden her to use the stairs, they were surprised suddenly to see her standing at the door. One of the children asked, "How did you get down?" "I slid down the banister, of course," came the retort.

Juliette Gordon Low had a penchant for eccentric stunts like driving on the wrong side of the road—she drove on the right side in England and on the left in America. She wore real vegetables in her hats, and once went trout fishing with Rudyard Kipling in a formal evening dress.

Visiting the Juliette Gordon Low House is as rewarding as making a new friend. Her birthplace at 142 Bull Street is open Monday through Saturday (except Wednesdays) from 10:00 A.M. to 4:00 P.M. and Sunday 12:30 to 4:30 P.M. The house is also closed on Sundays in December and January and on major holidays. Admission is charged.

After Juliette married William Mackay Low she became the third mistress of the **Andrew Low House**. William had inherited the home from his father Andrew. Andrew Low was married twice, his first wife, Sarah Cecil Hunter Low, having died a few short months after the death of her infant son. Five years later Andrew married Mary Couper Stiles Low, and William was one of their four surviving children.

William Mackay Low died on June 8, 1905; at the time the couple were separated and divorce proceedings were underway. Juliette spent several years traveling between the British Isles and Savannah. She lived in this Savannah house on and off from 1905 until she moved here permanently just a few months before her own death on January 17, 1927. One of her longest periods of residency was during World War I, when U.S. citizens were barred from travel across the Atlantic.

The Andrew Low House has been restored to its early appearance. Seventeen coats of paint were removed from the oversize double front doors and the pilaster capitals. The interior doors were returned to the mahogany-grained appearance and the silver plating on the hardware restored. The Carriage House, on the grounds of the Andrew Low House, was the first Girl

Scout Headquarters in the U.S. Juliette Low left the Carriage House to the Girl Scouts of Savannah.

The house has served as the headquarters of The National Society of The Colonial Dames of America in the State of Georgia since 1928. It is furnished with period antiques. Open weekdays from 10:30 A.M. to 4:00 P.M. and Sundays NOON to 4:00 P.M., it is closed on Thursdays, major holidays and December 13 through the 27th. Admission is charged.

Directions: From I-16 in Savannah take M. L. King Boulevard and turn right on Oglethorpe Avenue. The Juliette Gordon Low Birthplace is on the northeast corner of Oglethorpe Avenue and Bull Street. For the Andrew Low House continue on Oglethorpe to Abercorn Street and turn right. The Andrew Low House is at 329 Abercorn Street facing Lafayette Square.

King-Tisdell Cottage and Beach Institute

Negro Heritage Trail

The first African slaves entered the port of Savannah in 1749, so whether you explore the city's African-American heritage on your own or take a group tour of the **Negro Heritage Trail**, the place to start is at the docks along the Savannah River. The group tours present the black perspective of Savannah's history and are sponsored by the King-Tisdell Cottage Foundation.

The King-Tisdell Cottage, built in 1896, was rented by mill owner and builder W.W. Aimar until 1910, when it was purchased by Eugene Dempsey King. He died in 1941, and his widow remarried Robert Tisdell, a Savannah longshoreman. On her death, Tisdell married Alma Porter, but after spending a few years in the cottage, they moved. The cottage remained vacant until 1980 when it was saved by the city and given to the Association for the Study of Afro-American Life and History. Although moved to a new location, the cottage represents a coastal black residence of the 1890s. The cottage has intricate gingerbread ornamentation on the porch and dormers. The decorative fretwork is done in a wheels-and-spindles pattern that is unique to this cottage.

The cottage, at 514 East Huntington Street, is open for tours weekdays 12:30 to 4:30 P.M. and weekends 1:00 to 4:00 P.M. One room is furnished with period items, and the rest of the rooms on the two main floors are used to display art objects and documents relating to black history.

Additional exhibits of black artists are hung at the **Beach Institute**, at 502 East Harris Street. This building was constructed in 1867, during postwar Union occupation of the city, as a school for freed slaves. Besides the changing exhibits of art and sculpture there is a gift shop that features books and handcrafted items created by Afro-American artists.

The King-Tisdell Cottage and Beach Institute are on the Negro Heritage Trail. The route also includes a drive past homes built by "free persons of color," long before Emancipation. You'll also see the site where Sherman promised newly freed slaves "forty acres and a mule."

No tour of Savannah's black heritage would be complete without a stop at the **First African Baptist Church of Savannah**, at 23 Montgomery Street. The First African Baptist Church is one of the oldest black churches in the country. The first pastor George Leile was ordained May 20, 1775. The church survived occupation by both the British during the Revolutionary War and the Yankees after the Civil War. The second pastor of this church was the slave Andrew Bryan, ordained with the permission of his owner Jonathan Bryan. In 1826, the first Black Sunday School in the country was organized here. The Heritage Tour passes the old cemetery where the church's first pastor is buried; also buried here are black soldiers from both the Union and Confederate army.

The Negro Heritage Trail Tour is offered Monday through Saturday at 10:00 A.M. and 1:00 P.M. It starts at the Savannah Visitor's Center parking lot at 301 Martin Luther King, Jr. Boulevard. There is a charge. For details and reservations either for individuals or for groups, call (912)234-8000.

Directions: From I-95 take Route 16 into Savannah, turn left on Martin Luther King Boulevard for the Savannah Visitor's Center. The Center is on the corner of Liberty Street. For the Beach Institute take Liberty Street to East Broad Street and turn right. Make another right on East Harris Street for the Beach Institute. For King Tisdell Cottage return to East Broad and continue on it to Huntington Street and make a right for the Cottage.

Obediah's Okefenok and Okefenokee Swamp Park

The Southeast's Paul Bunyan

Obediah Barber and his father Isaac moved from Bryan County to the northern border of the Okefenokee Swamp in the early 1800s. When Obediah was only six years old he accompanied Isaac on a journey to help Georgia State surveyors establish a boundary between the state of Georgia and the territory of Florida.

When he was grown, Obediah stood over six-and-a-half feet. His great height, sense of honor and integrity earned him the nickname, the Southeast's Paul Bunyan. One of the best-known frontiersmen, he was a noted hunter and trapper. During his 84 years he had three wives and 20 children.

In 1871, Obediah built a one-story cabin with wooden-pegged walls and puncheon floor that is still standing. The cabin and outbuildings have been restored. Additional outbuildings have been added to give a well-rounded look at life in and around the Okefenokee Swamp in the 1800s. There is a blacksmith shop, smokehouse, out-kitchen, gristmill, livestock barns, tobacco barn, print shop, moonshine still, cane mill, pavilion and two museums. Various native plants and trees are noted on the self-guiding map of the homestead. Crops that grew in Obediah's time are planted here once again, and there are pens and cages with wild and domestic farm animals. Various native plants and trees are noted on the self-guiding map of the homestead.

Obediah's Okefenok offers bluegrass music and entertainment on its homestead stage. There is a diner and gift shop. For those with more time there is a half-mile nature trail. Obediah's Okefenok is open Monday through Saturday from 10:00 A.M. to 5:00 P.M. and Sunday from 2:00 to 4:00 P.M. Admission is charged.

At the annual event, "Autumn in the Okefenok," in mid-November, visitors can watch cane grinding and syrup making. There's also a hog butchering demonstration in mid-March and an annual Indian Pow Wow in late April.

Moving away from the edge of the swamp towards its interior, you come to **Okefenokee Swamp Park** where the denizens of this eerily beautiful sanctuary live. Since 1946, visitors have been able to go where only trappers and adventurers once traveled. This grant area of nearly a half million acres is part of the National Wilderness System. The park's boat tours take visitors on the original Indian waterways that reflect the serene beauty of the overhanging trees.

The park attracts Hollywood producers as well as nature lovers. Numerous feature films have been shot in these dramatic environs. You understand why when you spot your first alligator. Waterfowl are abundant and you may see more elusive inhabitants such as bobcats and bears.

In addition to the unique swamp tours, Okefenokee Swamp Park presents wildlife shows, interpretative exhibits, wilderness walkways, native animal habitats, a serpentarium, a Pioneer Island and a 90-foot-tall observation tower.

The Okefenokee Swamp Park is open June through August

Abundant waterfowl, wild animals and lush vegetation thrive in waterways of Okefenokee Swamp Park.

from 9:00 A.M. to 6:30 P.M. The park closes an hour earlier from September through May. It is closed on Christmas Day. A nominal admission is charged. Boat tours run on the hour and the half-hour starting at 9:30 A.M. There is a reptile show and video presentation in the Serpentarium throughout the day; check the schedule when you arrive.

A limited number of visitors can be accommodated on the **Deep-Swamp Excursion,** a two-hour, ten-mile, guided boat tour into the swamp. Depending on water level these trips depart three times a day: 10:00 A.M., 1:00 and 3:00 P.M. There is an additional fee for this trip, but the short 1½-mile trips that run throughout the day are included in the general admission. Visitors also can rent canoes.

Directions: From I-75 take Route 84 east to Waycross. Obediah's Okefenok is eight miles south of Waycross. Take Route 520, the South Georgia Parkway, then turn right on either Brunel or Gilmore Street to reach Swamp Road, the access road for Obediah's Okefenok. For the Okefenokee Swamp Park stay on Corridor Z and exit on Route 1/23 southeast. Turn right on Route 177.

Okefenokee Heritage Center and Southern Forest World

Magic Wilderness

The 600 square miles of Okefenokee Swamp constitute the largest national wildlife refuge in the Eastern United States. Once part of the ocean floor, the dense swamp and freshwater prairies have a long history that is explored at the Okefenokee Heritage Center in Waycross.

Exhibits start with the first men to live in the Okefenokee, roughly 4,500 years ago. Indians arrived in the swamp shortly after its formation and remained until about 1850 A.D. Flint artifacts, potsherds and broken clay pottery dating from about 2000 B.C. are exhibited at the center.

During this early Archaic Period the Indian population was slight, but it increased in the Woodland Period. Exhibited pottery and wooden paddles from the Woodland era are decorated with stamped linear designs.

The next inhabitants were of the Weeden Island Culture, mound builders who settled in small villages instead of the temporary camps of the earlier Indians. Weeden pottery, as you will see in the display, was decorated with incised and punctuated designs. Some cord-marked pottery uncovered in the area suggests contact with coastal Indians. Once the Weeden Island period ended, Indian population in the swamp was minimal, though there are records of a Timucuan village in the 1600s.

Most of the exhibits in the Heritage Center are from the Weeden Island People, the Choctaws and the Creeks who inhabited the Satilla River Region. With the influx of European settlers into the Okefenokee area, between 1800 and 1860, violence erupted into the Creek Wars of 1814 and 1819. Sporadic raids against settlers continued between 1835 and 1842 when the Seminole War in Florida spilled over into Georgia.

The last Indian massacre in Georgia was in July 1838, when Maximillan Wildes, his wife and six children (plus a neighbor's child), who lived on the northwestern edge of the Okefenokee Swamp, were slain by Seminoles. Troops under General Charles R. Floyd drove most of the Indians from the Swamp, and by 1850 they had been eliminated from the area.

The settlers who came to this area between 1818 and 1870 are also represented in exhibits. The front portion of the oldest standing house in Waycross (circa 1871) has been moved to the center for display. You can see a replica of the second county courthouse from Waycross too. Local residents had a disagreement about whether the courthouse should be in the country or in the city.

One night the city lawmakers headed out into the country, dismantled the courthouse and moved it into the city of Waycross. There is a schoolroom and household furnishings from settlers who were part of the communal group known as the Ruskin Commonwealth. This group espoused collective ownership of land, machinery, tools and farm animals. All members worked the same amount of time and received payment redeemable at the group's commissary.

The center has gallery space for rotating art shows, workshops and classes. Adjoining the gallery is an exhibit honoring cartoonist Walt Kelly, creator of the Okefenokee's most well-known inhabitant, Pogo. Kelly's New York studio is recreated with his personal belongings. The piano is there on which he composed and accompanied songs on his album, "Songs of Pogo."

The 20-acre complex includes a 1905 logging train, 1912 Baldwin steam locomotive and tender, the Old Nine Depot, a 1900s print shop and a 1840s farm house.

Next to the Heritage Center is **Southern Forest World** that tells the history and importance of forestry, the state's number one industry. Favorite exhibits for younger visitors include the talking tree that presents an overview on forestry, the 15-minute video on Smokey the Bear and the second floor giant loblolly pine. An interactive forestry quiz focuses on the South's managed forests. Two former denizens of the forest are displayed: one is a 493-pound bear, a one-time state record holder; the other is a mummified dog that "barked up the wrong tree." Supposition is that the dog chased a raccoon up the hollow tree and got stuck inside. The chemicals in the tree bark mummified the dog and when the tree was felled the dog was still stuck inside.

The Okefenokee Heritage Center is open Monday through Saturday from 9:00 A.M. to 5:00 P.M. and Sunday from 1:00 to 5:00 P.M. The Southern Forest World is open Tuesday through Saturday from 9:00 A.M. to 5:00 P.M. and it is closed on Sunday. A nominal admission is charged at both museums.

Directions: From I-95 take Route 520/82 to Waycross. Both attractions are two miles west of Waycross between U.S. 1 and U.S. 82 on North Augusta Avenue.

Okefenokee National Wildlife Refuge

Land of the Trembling Earth

There is something scary and magical about ground that quivers beneath one's feet. The name Okefenokee is derived from a Choctaw Indian word that means "trembling earth." It is the peat beds overlaying the sandy floor of the swamp that cause the ground to tremble. In some places peat deposits reach 15 feet, but in other areas they merely form a thin unstable layer. This decaying vegetation releases tannic acid that stains the water a tea-colored brown, producing a highly reflective surface that is perfect for mirror-image photography.

The swamp is a vast peat bog that fills a huge saucer-shaped depression covering about 438,000 acres. This depression was once under the Atlantic Ocean but is now 103 to 128 feet above sea level, higher than the surrounding area. Most of the water that replenishes the swamp is rainwater, although there are some creeks that feed into the swamp. The swamp drainage is the source of origin for the St. Marys and the Suwannee Rivers.

The Okefenokee is one of the largest and most primitive swamps in the country. It is the second largest National Wilderness Area east of the Mississippi; only the Everglades is bigger. One of the principal differences between the two is that the Everglades is a riverine system, encompassing the tail waters from nearby rivers as well as coastal marsh and mangrove swamps, and the Okefenokee is totally fresh water and the headwaters for two rivers.

The Okefenokee National Wildlife Refuge, protecting 396,000 acres of the swamp, has three entrances: north, west and east. The north entrance is the **Okefenokee Swamp Park** just south of Waycross (see selection). The 82-acre **Stephen C. Foster State Park** on Jones Island (18 miles northeast of Fargo off Route 177) is the west entrance. There is a museum, a half-mile nature trail and more than 25 miles of waterway for public day use. Visitors can rent motorboats, canoes or johnboats. Another option is a guided boat tour of the Okefenokee. The park is open from 7:00 A.M. to 7:00 P.M. from mid-September through February; the rest of the year the park closes at 8:30 P.M. The office hours are 8:00 A.M. to 5:00 P.M. year-round. S.C. Foster State Park also has nine cottages and 66 tent and trailer sites, plus picnic facilities and educational programs.

The refuge's east entrance via the **Suwannee Canal Recreation Area** lies 11 miles southwest of Folkston off Route 121/23. An Information Center orients visitors and has exhibits highlighting the refuge's complex ecosystem. Over 225 birds have been identified within the Okefenokee Swamp, as have 42 species of mammals, 58 species of reptiles (including more than 10,000 alligators), 32 species of amphibians and 34 species of fishes. Before exploring, take the time to see the 20-minute National Geographic film on the Okefenokee.

From the Information Center parking lot you can take a 4.5-mile wildlife observation drive or explore the more than 4.5 miles of hiking trails that lead to observation towers, photography blinds and a restored homestead. (For another restored home-stead in the Okefenokee see Obediah's Okefenok selection.)

To appreciate this aquatic world, you need to get out on the water. You arrange boat rentals or guided boat tours at the **Su-wannee Canal Recreation Concession**. Canoes can be rented for day use and for overnight trips. You also can rent camping equip-ment including Coleman stoves and lanterns, sleeping bags and foam pads, cookware and other items. With advance reservations you can arrange guided nighttime boat tours.

Many of the more than 120 miles of boat trails that wind through the swamp branch off the **Suwannee Canal**. It offers access to the swamp's most extensive open areas like the Chesser, Grand and Mizell prairies. These prairies are shallow expanses of dark, reflective water dotted with aquatic plants that blossom throughout the year. The prairies are punctuated with small is-lands on which shrubs and trees have taken root. Cypress trees everywhere are draped with Spanish moss. Locals tell the story of the burly, hairy sea captain who wanted to wed an Indian girl. He arranged the marriage with her father, the tribal chief, but she ran away before the ceremony. The sea captain found the reluctant bride up in an oak tree where she was hiding. It is said that Spanish moss is the beard of that old sea captain caught forever in the branches of the tree.

The Suwannee Canal serves visitors well by providing access to the swamp's core, but it never served its original purpose. The 11.5-mile Suwannee Canal, begun in 1891 with work continuing for the next three years, was an attempt to conquer the swamp by draining it into the Atlantic Ocean by way of the St. Marys River. The problem was that digging the ditch exposed small springs that continued to feed water into the swamp. Recognizing the enormity of the project, the authorities abandoned it. A 30-minute walk along Canal Diggers Trail reveals man's intrusion into the Okefenokee. There are dunes left by the canal diggers, and you see pines planted to replace the virgin forest that had to be cut to pay the expenses of the canal company.

The Suwannee Canal Recreational Concession is open from 8:00 A.M. to 6:00 P.M. from mid-September through February and from 7:00 A.M. to 7:30 P.M. the rest of the year. For information on rental prices call (912)496-7156. Advance arrangements must be made for wilderness camping. Call no more than two months in advance, (912)496-3331.

Directions: From I-95 take Route 40, the Okefenokee Parkway, west for 20 miles to Folkston. There you take Route 121 eight miles southwest to the east entrance of the Okefenokee National Wildlife Refuge. The entrance will be on your right. The parking lot for the Information Center is three miles from the entrance.

St. Marys

Get a Feel for the Past

If St. Marys had kept its Indian name, tourism might have slowed to a trickle, because no visitors could have said where they'd been. A Timucua Indian Queen, reputedly the most beautiful Indian woman in the southeast, named the large village located here Thlathlothlagupka.

The first European visitor was Jean Ribault, a French Huguenot, who sailed into the St. Marys River and named it the River May, for the time of his arrival. The name was changed to Mary some time during the Spanish occupation of Georgia, 1566 to 1686. Local legend claims that one of the two cannons you'll see on the walking tour of St. Marys is from the *Amelia*, a wrecked Spanish vessel that foundered in a storm just offshore. (This walking trail is the first in the state to have 38 historical markers with raised letters and Braille interpretations to help the sight-impaired.)

The land on Buttermilk Bluff on the north bank of the St. Marys River was purchased in 1787 by twenty proprietors for the sum of $38 each. The city was laid out in August 1788 and formally recorded on January 5, 1789.

A decade after St. Marys was established, George Washington died on December 14, 1799. The day he was buried at Mount Vernon, a boat docked at St. Marys bearing a flag-draped casket in homage to Washington. The empty casket was ceremonially buried in the median of Osborne Street and live oak trees were planted, the last of which died in 1987. West of Osborne on Bartlett Street, as old as the city itself, is **Oak Grove Cemetery**, where soldiers from every war America has fought are buried. There is an unusual walled section set aside for the French-inscribed graves of Acadian settlers in St. Marys who were driven out of Nova Scotia.

One of St. Marys' most elegant homes was built in the 1820s for Reverend Horace Pratt by the father of his first wife, Jane Wood. This is disputed by some historians who claim Pratt built the lovely Greek Revival mansion himself during his second marriage to Isabel Drysdale. The house was called **Orange Hall** because it was surrounded by orange trees. By the 1840s the house was described as ". . .one of the showplaces of the town."

Today Orange Hall, on Osborne Street between Weed and Conyers, serves as the city's Welcome Center. Besides picking up information on the area, visitors can tour the house. A nominal fee is charged. The rooms on the main floor are filled with period pieces as are the bedrooms upstairs.

Two of the town's attractive homes have been converted to bed-and-breakfasts. The **Historic Spencer House Inn**, (912)882-1872, built in 1872 by a St. Marys' collector of customs, was renovated and restored and is now an inn. The 1885 **Goodbread House**, in the heart of the National Register Historic District of St. Marys, abounds with Victorian touches. It has seven fireplaces, high ceilings and period antiques, (912)882-7490. Another popular spot is the recently renovated and aptly named Riverview Hotel, (912)882-3242, which has 18 guest rooms and Seagle's Restaurant where you can enjoy fresh seafood specialties. Seagle's prepares picnic lunches for visitors heading for Cumberland Island (see selection) or the Okefenokee swamp (see selection).

Kings Bay Naval Submarine Base in St. Marys is the Atlantic home for Trident submarines. The Trident squadron of submarines make up about one third of the nation's underwater deterrent force.

Certainly a most unusual landmark is what the natives call the **Toonerville Trolley**, a 1920s railcar with a body of a wooden truck built to run on tracks. This conveyance carried passengers to and from the main North-South rail line in the nearby town of Kingsland. Cartoonist Roy Crane rode into St. Marys on the trolley and stayed at the Riverview Hotel. He wandered around town drawing, then featured the trolley and local sites in his 1935 comic strip "Wash Tubbs."

St. Marys is the point of departure for the Cumberland Queen, a ferry boat that makes daily trips to and from Cumberland Island National Seashore, Georgia's most southern and largest barrier island (see selection).

Located near the tabby ruins of McIntosh Sugar Mills just outside St. Marys is **Crooked River State Park**, a 500-acre facility on the river's south bank. The park has a 1.5-mile nature trail, an Olympic pool and bathhouse, saltwater fishing, a boat ramp, 11 cottages and tent and trailer sites.

Another recreational spot is the 6,800-yard, par 72 **Osprey Cove Golf Course** laid out by PGA Tour Champion Mark McCumber. The course, overlooking the salt marshes, is open to the public. To reserve tee times call (800)352-5575.

Directions: From I-95 take Exit 2, Route 40, east to St. Marys. For Crooked River State Park take Georgia Spur 40 north.

St. Simons Island

God's Little Acres

Follow in the footsteps of Spanish explorers 400 years later and explore St. Simons, the largest of Glynn County's Golden Isles.

One of the oldest navigational beacons still in use on the East Coast, St. Simons lighthouse offers a breathtaking view of the Golden Isles.

Five miles from the Georgia mainland, this Manhattan-size island offers an interesting mix of historical reminders, unspoiled natural beauty, abundant wildlife, elegant resort properties and diverse recreational options.

There is a self-guiding driving tour to follow, but it's far more fun to take the hour-and-a-half trolley tour of the island. Daily tours leave from the village pier from March through Labor Day weekends at 11:00 A.M., 1:00 and 3:00 P.M. The rest of the year there is an 1:00 P.M. tour Tuesday through Sunday. To reserve a spot, call (912)638-8954.

The pier was built in the 1880s by Captain Dart. During that era when ferry-transported visitors from the mainland arrived at the pier, they were met by a mule-pulled trolley. Four mules pulled St. Simons first trolley along tracks laid out on the beach. Following this early lead, the latest of the trolleys to transport visitors around St. Simons began operating in 1992. These trolleys, however, are on wheels not tracks.

Trolley tour guides tell stories about the early history of St. Simons as visitors bump along the island streets, past the up-to-date boutiques and eateries that line the village's main drag. Directly facing the fishing pier where passengers board the trolley is **Neptune Park**, named for Neptune Small, a slave on Retreat Plantation. Small, serving his owner Henry Lord King during the Civil War, recovered King's body from the battlefield at Fredericksburg, VA, and brought it back to Georgia so he could be laid to rest at his family home. The King family gave Small the land that is now Neptune Park. The rich cultural heritage of St. Simons' African-Americans is celebrated each year on the third weekend in August during the Georgia Sea Island Festival.

Directly behind the park is the **Old Casino Building**. It now houses the St. Simons Chamber of Commerce where visitors can pick up maps and brochures on the island. The office is open Monday through Friday 9:00 A.M. to 5:00 P.M. and Saturday from 10:00 A.M. to 2:00 P.M.

Down from this building is the **St. Simons Lighthouse**, now part of the Museum of Coastal History. The lighthouse stands on the site of Fort St. Simons, a colonial fort built under General James Oglethorpe's direction (see Fort Frederica selection). The fort was destroyed by the Spanish on their retreat from the Battle of Bloody Marsh in 1742. In the 1800s, John Couper owner of the land sold the point for a token dollar to the federal government so that a lighthouse could be built.

During the Civil War, the Confederate army made the beacon part of Fort Brown, but when the Confederates abandoned the island they destroyed the lighthouse so that Northern troops could not use it as a navigation point. The 106-foot lighthouse that stands today was built in 1872. Now fully automated, it is one of only five tower lights in Georgia. Its third-order Fresnel lens can be seen 18 miles from shore. Anyone with the fortitude to climb the 129 steps to the top will be rewarded will a breathtaking glimpse of the Golden Isles spread beneath their feet. The vast salt marshes that one sees are only part of the half million acres of salt marshes in the state.

Maritime exhibits fill the lighthouse keeper's cottage and in the adjacent 1890 brick oil house there is a well-stocked gift shop with books, illustrations and hand-crafted items. The museum is open Tuesday through Saturday from 10:00 A.M. to 5:00 P.M. and Sunday from 1:30 to 5:00 P.M. Admission is charged.

Around the point on which the lighthouse stands, along the Atlantic Ocean, is **Massengale Park**, St. Simons public beach. There are several miles of beach, bathhouse facilities and picnicking areas.

Whether you take the self-guided driving tour or the narrated trolley tour you must plan to spend some time at Fort Frederica and the site of the Battle of Bloody Marsh (see selection). On the trolley tour you will be driven into the fort, but you get such a quick overview, that you want to be sure to return and explore on foot.

Another must stop on St. Simons is **Christ Church**, Frederica, a picturesque chapel built on the site where John and Charles Wesley held services under the oak trees in 1736. The Reverend Charles Wesley was both chaplain and secretary for Indian Affairs during Oglethorpe's tenure. The first Episcopal Church was built on this site in 1820 but was destroyed during the Civil War. Anson Dodge, Jr., son of a local lumber baron, was greatly impressed by the ruins of the first Christ Church. After he became a minister he rebuilt the church in memory of his wife who died of cholera during their honeymoon abroad. Anson's wife, Ellen, was buried under the altar. Anson was eventually married again, to Anna Deborah Gould, the granddaughter of the lighthouse keeper. The second wife is buried in the Christ Church cemetery. After Anson's death, his first wife was reburied in the cemetery by his side.

Visitors who take the trolley tour will spend some time in the **cemetery** hearing stories about the colorful personalities who lie buried there. The oldest marked grave dates back to 1803. Buried here is Henry Lord Page King, the young soldier brought back by the family slave from the Fredericksburg battlefield. John Couper, a friend of Thomas Jefferson and fellow horticulturalist, is also buried here. Couper grew olive trees on St. Simons from cuttings sent to him by Jefferson.

Within the cross-shaped church, with its trussed Gothic roof, is a Tiffany stained-glass window. A few of the pews are original, and a plaque indicates where Presidents Coolidge, Carter and Bush sat while attending services here.

St. Simons, lying between the mainland and Sea Island, provides access to **The Cloisters**, an upscale resort (see selection). The resort's golf course is on St. Simons on the grounds of industrialist Howard E. Coffin's Retreat Plantation, renowned for its superior quality Sea Island cotton. The majestic Avenue of Oaks that once led from the plantation to the interior of the island has been protected and preserved. Tabby ruins mark the site of the plantation's slave hospital, and a lone chimney marks the place where the antebellum mansion once stood. An arboretum created by Ann Matilda Page King in the 1800s has also been preserved. St. Simons' live oaks have their own place in history books. Timber from these trees was used to build the U.S.S. *Constitution*, "Old Ironsides," and the Brooklyn Bridge. A historical marker at Gascoigne Bluff denotes the area from which the live oak timbers were cut.

Additional plantation sites are indicated along Lawrence Road leading to St. Simons' northern end. The road leads to Hampton River Club Marina where boats take visitors to Little St. Simons Island. Guided day tours to this private island run from June through September; call (912)638-7472 to arrange passage.

The same family has owned 10,000-acre **Little St. Simons** barrier island since the turn of the century. For years it was the family retreat of Philip Berolzheimer, who built a hunting lodge for his family, friends and business associates. The lodge is now an inn with 12 rooms, serving no more than 24 guests. Nature is the draw at this elegant retreat: seven miles of beaches, nature trails through the thick wooded maritime forest and along the marshes and ponds that support a wide array of wildlife. The trails are used for birding, nature walks and riding. The inn is open to individual guests in March, April, May, October and November. During the summer months the inn rents exclusively to groups that rent the entire island. For information call (912)638-7472.

Directions: From I-95 traveling from the south take Exit 6, Route 17, and from the north, Exit 8, the Golden Isles Parkway. Both lead to the St. Simons Causeway that crosses to the island. At the end of the Causeway take Kings Way, then turn right on Mallory Street straight to the pier and the trolley.

Sapelo Island

No Barrier to Beauty

Georgia's fourth largest barrier island lies 30 minutes by ferry from the Hudson Creek dock. The boat trip offers expansive views of Doboy Sound and the marshy banks of Sapelo Island. Seagulls follow in the wake of the *Sapelo Queen* and passengers can see great egrets, clapper rails, pelicans and other marsh birds foraging along Sapelo's coast. As the ferry approaches the south side of the ten-mile-long island, the abandoned 1820 lighthouse can be seen rising out of the marsh grass. Sapelo's history is a colorful mix of ethnic groups and a trio of wealthy private owners who controlled the island for more than two centuries before it became a public trust managed by the state.

The best way to see the island is to take an **island tour**. These are arranged in advance at the McIntosh County Chamber of Commerce Welcome Center at 105 Fort King George Drive in Darien. Reservations may be made by calling (912)437-6684 or 437-4192. Tours are given on Wednesday and Friday at 8:30 A.M. and 12:30 P.M. and on Saturday at 9:00 A.M. and 1:00 P.M. On the last Tuesday of each month from March through October a day-long tour is given.

The advantage of these tours is that they provide a jitney that transports you around the island. Like Cumberland Island, although not to the same degree, there are large portions of Sapelo that are unspoiled. Cumberland does not allow vehicles, so all exploring is done on walking trails. The Sapelo tours provide a more accessible look at one of the state's primitive barrier islands.

Island tours take visitors to an information center to view a video on Sapelo's history. Along the east bank of the Duplin River at Kenan Field on Sapelo there is an Indian site where a 158-acre Indian village stood sometime between 1,000 and 1,600 A.D. Burial mounds and the remains of buildings and earthen embankments have been studied by archaeologists. The clay pottery they found is the oldest unearthed in North America.

In 1566 Spanish Jesuit priests established a mission named for Jose A. Zapala (the anglicization of this Spanish name is Sapelo). The mission was withdrawn in 1570 after the local Indians killed several of the priests. Three years later the Franciscans established the Convent of San Jose de Zapala that thrived for more than a century until 1686.

Sometime during the early colonial period, Mary Musgrove, the half-breed daughter of an Indian chief who was Oglethorpe's interpreter, obtained Sapelo and several other barrier islands from the local Indians. The Indians used the islands as hunting grounds until 1757 when the Creeks ceded the islands to England.

In 1760, Sapelo was sold to Englishman Gray Elliot, but it wasn't extensively cultivated until 1762 when Patrick MacKay, a Scotsman and Indian trader, purchased the island. The northwest portion of Sapelo is still called Mackay's Old Fields. Subsequent owners continued Mackay's farming efforts until in 1789

Sapelo and other nearby islands were sold to a group of French noblemen fleeing their country's revolution who purchased Sapelo for 10,000 pounds sterling. The French settlers owned and inhabited Sapelo from 1789 to 1802.

In 1802 Thomas Spalding inherited a portion of the island from his father-in-law and purchased a 4,000-acre tract on Sapelo's south end. Spalding established a Sea Island cotton and sugar operation, and for the only time in its history, Sapelo sustained an income-producing plantation. Before his death Spalding owned all but a small 650-acre portion of Sapelo. The tabby ruins of Spalding's sugar mill built in 1809 and its adjacent boiling house can be seen adjacent to the information center. The center has photographs of Spalding's south end mansion built in 1807-1810.

Spalding died in 1851 and his Sapelo Island holdings were badly damaged during the Civil War. Following the war, roughly 400 of his freed slaves returned to Sapelo to farm. Spalding family members also returned to continue farming the island, although the fields were fallow and the main house in ruins.

The only part of Sapelo still in private hands is **Hog Hammock**, a community of descendants of Spalding's black slaves. Most of the community's residents are elderly and most speak the Gullah dialect. Tour participants will stop at a small gift shop, the Pig Pen, while passing through Hog Hammock.

The island limped along for decades after the Spalding years, before it was purchased in 1912 by Howard Coffin, a Hudson Motor executive from Detroit who had discovered it on a hunting trip and decided to establish a residence and business on the island. Coffin owned most of Sapelo and he developed a commercial fishing operation and a dairy farm.

You can see the mansion Coffin built in 1925 on the foundation of the old Spalding house. He added a swimming pool that visitors see as a reflecting pool today. He also added statuary such as *The Awakening* that stands in front of the mansion. Listening to the tour guide's description of the "Circus Room," with its canopied-tent ceiling, and the indoor glass solarium with a tiled swimming pool, makes visitors wish they could glimpse the interior. Guests who did enjoy these luxurious surroundings include President and Mrs. Calvin Coolidge in 1928 and President Herbert Hoover and his wife in 1932.

When the Depression endangered some of Coffin's projects and he decided to concentrate on Sea Island, he sold Sapelo Island to Richard J. Reynolds, the tobacco heir from Winston-Salem, North Carolina. Reynolds continued the dairy established by Coffin. He also modernized the main house and turned the guest house into a summer camp for underprivileged boys.

One of Reynolds's most enduring contributions was the establishment of a marine research foundation on the island, now the **University of Georgia Marine Institute**. During the island tour, visitors will stop at the headquarters of this facility to see marine exhibits that include examples of indigenous fish, sponges, corals as well as birds, reptiles and amphibians. Portions of the island are protected as part of the Sapelo Island National Estuarine Research Reserve and as the R.J. Reynolds State Wildlife Refuge.

For a more detailed account of the history of Sapelo read Buddy Sullivan's *Early Days on the Georgia Tidewater* and his *Sapelo: A History*.

Directions: From I-95 take Exit 10 and travel east for three miles on Route 17 to Darien. The well-marked Welcome Center is right on Route 17.

Savannah's Historic District

America's Mona Lisa

Anita Raskin in her introduction to *Sojourn in Savannah* writes, "Savannah is a Lady. . .who keeps her treasures polished for the pleasure of her guests. Enjoy her jewel-like parks and squares, her prize collection of heirloom oaks, her matchless muster of 18th and 19th century houses. . .Savannah is America's Mona Lisa. . .You may never fathom the secret of her smile, but like those who love and live with her, you will know the endless rich rewards of trying."

Savannah, situated on the 40-foot Yamacraw Bluff, 15 miles above the mouth of the Savannah River, is a city for pedestrians, laid out in an easily accessible pattern of 21 historic squares. The **National Historic Landmark District** covers 2½ square miles and includes more than 1,100 architecturally significant buildings, most of which have been restored and continue to be in use.

Adjacent to the historic area is the **Victorian District/Landmark District**, one of the largest collections of Victorian architecture in the country. Strolling the streets of this district provides ample opportunity to notice details. You'll see delicate fretwork on the porches of the old houses and glimpse gracious gardens through intricate wrought-iron gates. Before visitors begin their leisurely inspection, it helps for them to have had a bus or tram tour of the historic district. On these tours they hear fascinating stories about the history and the people of this former colonial capital.

The **Savannah Visitors Center** at 301 Martin Luther King, Jr. Blvd. (in what was once the Central of Georgia Railroad Station)

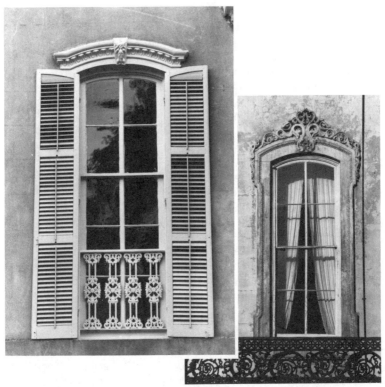

Savannah's intricate wrought-iron gates, fretwork-decorated porches and embellished windows capture the gentility and grace of the Old South.

has information on all the city's attractions and tours. A slide presentation provides historical background and a glimpse of the landmarks. The Visitors Center is open weekdays 8:30 A.M. to 5:00 P.M. and weekends 9:00 A.M. to 5:00 P.M. Most of the trolley, bus, carriage and tram tours depart from the Visitors Center and pick up participants at selected hotels.

The **Savannah History Museum**, in an adjunct to the Railroad Station beside the Visitors Center, has exhibits on Savannah's past as far back as the Indian era. Most popular are the authentic cotton gin much like the original built by Eli Whitney, a Baldwin steam locomotive and railroad memorabilia, uniforms and weapons from the Revolution and the Civil War. Savannah's pivotal role as a port is covered in the featured video, *Savannah the Survivor*, along with an overview of Savannah's history seen from General Oglethorpe's perspective. The museum is open daily from 9:00 A.M. to 5:00 P.M. except on major holidays. An admission is charged.

The **Historic Railroad Shops**, the oldest and most complete railroad repair and manufacturing facility still standing in the country, is located in the block next to the History Museum. On this site where restoration is in progress, you can view a video that offers oral history gathered by two former employees of the Central of Georgia Railroad. The Shops house the country's oldest, wheeled portable steam engine as well as machinery of the type used in this facility at the turn of the century. Open Monday through Saturday from 10:00 A.M. to 4:00 P.M. and Sunday NOON to 4:00 P.M. except on major holidays. Guided tours are given each day at 1:00 P.M., at other times visitors may explore on their own. Admission is charged.

After the Visitors Center, before you start touring or exploring, stop at the **Massie Heritage Interpretation Center**, at 207 East Gordon Street. Here you'll see three exhibits that will enhance your appreciation of Savannah's historic district: a city model showing the layout of Savannah's buildings; an architectural exhibit that shows the influence of Greek, Gothic, and Roman architecture; and a display on Savannah's Victorian era.

The interpretative center is located on the southeast corner of Abercorn and Gordon streets in Massie School, Georgia's oldest public school. The Greek Revival school, now on the National Register of Historic Places, was built in 1855 by John Norris. Its architectural features include a gable roof, wood cupola and cornice, and a connecting passageway between two sections of the building. A 19th-century classroom has been recreated on the second floor. It is used for elementary school field trips to give youngsters a sample of old-fashion education techniques. The center is open Monday through Friday from 8:30 A.M. to 4:30 P.M.

Several hours can be spent investigating the city's **historic churches**. The French Gothic Cathedral of St. John the Baptist on Lafayette Square is noted for its stained-glass windows, marble altars, Persian rugs and wall murals. Christ Episcopal Church is noted for historic, not architectural details. It was in this Bull Street Church that John Wesley founded the world's first Protestant Sunday School. The First African Baptist Church, at 403 West Bryan Street, was established by the oldest Negro congregation in the country (see King Tisdell Cottage selection). In 1826, the church opened the first Negro Sunday School. Visitors can listen to taped recordings about events associated with the church. In 1885, Woodrow Wilson was married at the Independent Presbyterian Church at 25 West Oglethorpe Avenue. The only Gothic synagogue in the country is the Mickve Israel Temple at 20 East Gordon Street. The oldest Torah in America is among the 1,790 historical books in the synagogue's collection. The Temple is open weekdays 10:00 A.M. to NOON.

Savannah tour guides regale visitors with anecdotes about famous residents and historic events, but once an overview is gained it's fun to walk through the various districts. Be sure to check out the antique shops, boutiques and galleries in the historic district, also on the restored Riverfront and in the newly remodeled City Market.

Art lovers should visit **Telfair Mansion and Art Museum**. Opulent period rooms in the 1819 mansion designed by William Jay reveal the lifestyle of the Telfairs, a wealthy 19th-century Savannah family. The Telfair collection is the South's oldest public art museum. Hours are Tuesday through Saturday 10:00 A.M. to 5:00 P.M. and Sunday 2:00 to 5:00 P.M. Admission is charged.

Music, notably jazz and blues, is an integral part of Savannah's charm. There is a Jazz Society Center in the Old City Market where jazz enthusiasts listen to music, do research and buy memorabilia. During the summer the Coastal Jazz Association features a jazz music festival. One of the city's most popular clubs is **Hard Hearted Hannah's**, owned by legendary jazz bass violinist Ben Tucker. On Tuesday through Friday night from 6:00 to 9:00 P.M. Emma Kelly plays and sings. She is one of Savannah-native Johnny Mercer's favorites, and among the 6,000 songs in her repertoire are most of Mercer's compositions. When Emma finishes her set, Ben Tucker and Friends play. It's not unusual for big name musicians to drop by and sit in with the group. Hard Hearted Hannah's is in the Desoto Hilton, at Liberty and Bull Streets.

Savannah has more than its share of good places to eat and drink. You may see a card that lists what questions travelers to Georgia can expect to be asked first. In Atlanta they will be asked their business; in Macon, their religion; in Augusta their mother's maiden name; in Savannah, they're just asked what they want to drink.

Dining spots are numerous, diverse and good. It's hard to beat the bountiful, family-style breakfast and lunch served at Mrs. Wilkes Boarding House, 107 W. Jones Street, a Savannah tradition where no reservations are taken and lines start forming well before opening time. If you want to dine in historic surroundings stop at either the Pirate's House, 20 E. Broad Street, or the Olde Pink House, 23 Abercorn Street. For seafood along the river try the River House, 125 W. River Street.

If you plan to overnight in Savannah, stay in one of the outstanding historic inns, such as newly redecorated East Bay Inn, a restored cotton warehouse across from Riverfront at 225 East

Bay Street. River Street Inn has private balconies overlooking the Savannah River. The Ballastone, 14 E. Oglethorpe Avenue, considered by many including *Brides* and *Glamour Magazine* to be one of the nation's most romantic inns, has 18 rooms decorated with period furnishings. The Eliza Thompson House, Five West Jones Street, is a 1847 Federal Style Inn located in the heart of the historic district. The popular Four-Diamond Gastonian, 220 East Gaston Street, is furnished with English antiques, has such modern amenities as jacuzzi baths and cable television and serves full Southern-style breakfast—the best of all worlds. Other inns of note include the Foley House Inn, The Haslam-Fort House, Presidents' Quarters, Old Harbour Inn and Liberty Inn. Although not technically an inn, the Mulberry, the city's only Four Diamond hotel, is luxuriously furnished in the style of a small historic establishment.

Directions: From I-95 take Route 16 to Martin Luther King, Jr. Boulevard and turn left. The Savannah Visitors Center is at 301 Martin Luther King, Jr. Blvd.

Ships of the Sea Museum

Ships that Sailed the Seven Seas

It would be hard to imagine a more appropriate spot for a maritime museum than the four-story waterfront building that houses the Ships of the Sea Museum. It's just steps away from the bustling Savannah River traffic. Museum visitors often glance up after contemplating the intricate details of a Viking warship and see, passing by the window, one of the floating container ships. The carriers and tankers that ply the waters average 800 to 900 feet in length.

Ships of the present vie for attention with fascinating ships of the past. The museum has an outstanding collection of more than 50 ship models and over 75 ships in a bottle. The ship replicas, ranging from palm-size to eight feet in length, are works of art and you don't have to be a nautical buff to appreciate them.

Of special interest to Georgians is a model of the *Anne*, the 200-ton British galley on which General James Oglethorpe sailed to his new colony with his first 112 colonists. Another vessel that arouses local pride is the S.S. *Savannah*, the first steamship to cross the Atlantic. She sailed from Savannah to Liverpool in 29 days and 11 hours. The world's first atomic-powered cargo ship, was also named for the city, the N.S. *Savannah*.

Only one model, the *See Madchen*, includes its 12-man crew and interior cabin furnishings. There are models of historic vessels and representative examples of ship designs from around the world. Ships of the Seas Museum allows visitors to take photographs of their ships and other collections; the friendly staff will even snap a shot of you and your family.

Peter Barlow, a retired British Royal Navy Commander, constructed many of the museum's ships in a bottle. All of the miniature ships were modeled after actual vessels, and one in fact, the *Titanic*, is shown as it sinks in the Atlantic on April 14–15, 1912.

The museum has additional collections of interest including shells, figurines, figureheads, hatchcovers and scrimshaw. Within the museum there is a ship's carpentry shop filled with tools of the trade. The Ships of the Sea Museum is open daily 10:00 A.M. to 5:00 P.M. It is closed on major holidays. Admission is charged.

One prize possession of the museum is the lantern that belonged to Florence Martus, **Savannah's Waving Girl**. After you finish touring the museum, stroll over to the waterfront park east of the museum and see the statue erected to her. Florence was born in 1868 and spent almost all of her life with her brother, the lighthouse keeper on Elba Island. It was Florence's custom to greet every ship that entered or left the Savannah River. Legend claims that for 44 years, from 1887 to 1931, she "waved a white cloth during the day and a lantern at night." The romantics like to claim she was looking for her lover who went to sea. Whatever her reason she became an international personality, known by seamen from the 137 countries that navigate the waters of Savannah.

The red brick buildings along the bluff above the Savannah River were located on Factors' Row. The name came from the cotton brokers who brought prosperity to 19th-century Savannah. The brokers were called cotton factors, and they worked in these old brick buildings, now converted into offices and business space. The building's third floor opened onto the area where cotton and other products were bought and sold. The lower floors served as warehouses for cotton and naval stores. One of the red brick buildings houses the Ships of the Sea Museum today.

The ramps that lead down the bluff from Bay Street to River Street are paved with cobblestones brought as ballast on early sailing ships. Factors' Walk, halfway down the ramp, is highlighted by connecting bridges that lead to offices, apartments, inns and restaurants on the upper level.

An interesting dining spot, two blocks away from the Ships of the Sea Museum, is the Pirates' House Restaurant in the Historic Trustees' Garden, the first economic garden in the colonies. Plants and herbs from around the world were brought here to test whether they would acclimate to Georgia.

The Pirates' House at East Broad and Bay Street was originally an inn for seamen including—legend has it—blood-thirsty pirates. Robert Louis Stevenson's *Treasure Island* has many references to Savannah, and some of the action is supposed to have been set in the Pirates' House. Captain Flint, who reputedly buried the treasure on which the story is based, is said to have died in an upstairs room at the old inn.

The restaurant is both an authentic house museum and an award-winning dining establishment. Lunch is served from 11:30 A.M. to 2:30 P.M. and dinner from 5:30 until 9:45 P.M. Late afternoon desserts, coffee, cocktails and Sunday brunch buffet are also served. For reservations call (912)233-5757.

Directions: From I-16 in Savannah take M.L. King Boulevard to Bay Street and turn right. The Ships of the Sea Museum is at 504 East Bay Street. The riverfront entrance is at 503 East River Street.

Trio of Savannah Historic Homes

Master Builders

A trio of houses in Savannah's historic district convey the height of architectural achievement in three distinct styles. The **Davenport House** is an outstanding example of Georgian design. Although the house was not constructed until 1815, its design is a holdover from the colonial period. The Owens-Thomas House represents the Regency Period and the Green-Meldrim House is one of the South's finest Gothic Revival mansions.

Architect Isaiah Davenport spent five years designing and building his home. From the beginning in 1815, he planned to use it as a showcase for his architectural talents. He used a pattern book to provide the basic design for the elegant English brick exterior but added a number of his own inspirations such as the English cast-iron downspouts shaped like open-mouthed fish.

While Isaiah was having his dream house built, he lived with his family in a small house next door. When the big house was completed the little one was torn down and the space used for an ornamental garden. Years later the Davenport House very nearly was lost to the wrecker's ball but fortunately became the first of many historic homes to be rescued by the preservation society. Seven Savannah women worked to save the Davenport House, raising $22,000 to buy the house before it was leveled for a funeral parlor parking lot. After their success the preservation society surveyed two square miles of the historic district and embarked on a mission to restore several more outstanding properties within the district.

The Davenport House's exquisite interior woodwork and plasterwork have been restored, and it is once again filled with priceless Chippendale, Hepplewhite and Sheraton furniture. Also exhibited is a superior collection of Davenport china (not related to the family), a popular china made in England in the 19th century. The mantle piece in the front parlor is original; it was purchased by a social worker who returned it to the house during the restoration.

The stairs, with their supporting iron rods, are original. Across from Isaiah and Sarah's master bedroom was the bedroom used by their six sons. Their daughter Cornelia had the room behind her parents'. The beds are on casters so they could be moved to catch the summer breeze; the need for cross ventilation also accounted for the fact that each room opened into another room. On the third floor there is a toy room filled with antique play equipment such as a stove and tea set, a wagon pulled by a horse and doll furniture.

The house and 18th-century style garden, on the northwest corner of State and Habersham Streets, are open Monday through Saturday from 10:00 A.M. to 4:00 P.M. and Sunday from 1:30 to 4:00 P.M. Admission is charged. Fans of Eugenia Price's novel *Savannah* will be interested to learn that the house appears in her book, and also that a portrait in the house inspired the heroic character of Mark Browning.

The **Owens-Thomas House and Museum** nearby is one of the finest examples of Regency architecture in the country. This urban villa was designed one year later than the Davenport House, by noted English architect William Jay, and built between 1816 and 1819 at a cost of almost $90,000. The house was always maintained, so no extensive restoration has been necessary. The floors and window panes are original, as are the European marble mantles. Visitors are surprised by the vivid hues: the walls in the dining room are bright red, those in the hall deep green, and in the parlor, orange. The built-in cabinet in the dining room displays a 126-piece set of blue and white Canton china.

When the Marquis De LaFayette visited Savannah in 1825, he stayed in the Owens-Thomas House, addressing the crowds from his bedroom balcony. Local legend claimed he spoke for more than two hours in French, but it is now believed that he spoke only thirty minutes. The house has bedrooms on the first floor and boasted inside plumbing as early as 1819. The lighted mirror in the dressing room was lit by candles in holders on the sides of the frame.

An unusual architectural detail is the bridge over the staircase leading from the back to the front of the house. The upstairs has bedrooms, a dressing room and library. The library desk is finely crafted from a variety of woods. The lower floor is devoted to a kitchen, laundry room, wine cellar and larder.

The Owens-Thomas House, 124 Abercorn Street on Oglethorpe Square, is open Tuesday through Saturday from 10:00 A.M. to 5:00 P.M. (the last guided tour is at 4:30 P.M.) and Sunday and Monday from 2:00 to 5:00 P.M. There is also a gift shop and formal walking garden. The house is closed in January and on major holidays. Admission is charged.

Of the three homes, the latest to be built was the **Green-Meldrim House** constructed in the early 1850s for Charles Green, an Englishman who had moved to Savannah in 1833. New York architect John S. Norris was hired to design and build the house, which became the city's most elaborate house at a cost of $93,000. Many of the flagstones, bricks, laths and planks were brought from England as ballast on Mr. Green's ships. Norris designed Savannah's Custom House and several other private homes. A hallmark of his houses are graceful curved stairways such as the one visitors see at the Green-Meldrim House.

Noteworthy architectural features include the three sets of doors at the front entrance and elaborately carved American black walnut in the downstairs rooms. The doorknob, hinges, keyhole escutcheons and covers are silver-plated. The matching chandeliers and large mirrors in gold-leaf frames were brought from Austria when the house was constructed.

Mr. Green made his house available to William Tecumseh Sherman when the general's March to the Sea brought him to Savannah in December 1864. It was from this house that Sherman sent his famous telegram to President Lincoln offering him the city of Savannah as a Christmas present. Sherman's chaplain conducted Christmas services in St. John's Church, adjacent to the Green home.

At the death of Charles Green in 1881, the house was inherited by his son Edward Moon Green who sold it on July 14, 1892, to Judge Peter W. Meldrim. In 1943, the Meldrim family sold the house to St. John's Church, and it is now the Parish House for this Episcopal Church. It has been restored and furnished with period pieces. The house can be toured Tuesday, Thursday, Friday and Saturday from 10:00 A.M. to 4:00 P.M. Admission is charged. The house is closed from mid-December through mid-January and for the two weeks prior to Easter.

Directions: From I-16 in Savannah take M.L. King Boulevard to Bay Street and turn right. Continue up Bay Street to Habersham Street and make a left. The Davenport House will be on Columbia Square. For the Owens-Thomas House take State Street west for two blocks to Oglethorpe Square. From here turn left on Abercorn Street to Harris Street and turn right. Take Harris Street to Bull

Street, where you will find the Green-Meldrim House, opposite the DeSoto Hilton Hotel on Madison Square.

Tybee Island

Savannah's Summertime Playground

The beachfront community of Tybee, 18 miles from Historic Savannah, takes its name from the Indian word for salt. Seven flags have flown over the salt marshes surrounding the island since it was occupied by Indians. During colonial days the flags of Spain, France and England flew here, and there were times when pirate flags flew. The town was part of the Confederate States of America; then Union soldiers captured Tybee Island and used its northern shore to bombard the supposedly impregnable walls of Fort Pulaski across the Savannah River (see Four Forts of Savannah selection). And, of course, the flag of Georgia flies over Tybee.

Thirty-six years after Fort Pulaski fell, the federal government constructed Fort Screven on the northern side of Tybee Island (see fort selection). Adjacent to the fort is **Tybee Museum**, housed in a 1897 Coastal Artillery Battery. In the battery's winding tunnels you'll see Indian artifacts, displays on Georgia's colonial settlement and exhibits covering the military history of the area. There is memorabilia from the resort era (1880–1930s) and also a doll collection and a gun collection that includes one of the world's longest guns, a 10-foot-long punt gun. From the museum's observation deck you can watch sea traffic entering and leaving the port of Savannah.

Tybee Museum is open From October through March, Monday through Friday (closed Tuesdays) NOON to 4:00 P.M. and weekends 10:00 A.M. to 4:00 P.M. From April through September it is open daily (except Tuesday) from 10:00 A.M. to 6:00 P.M. Closed on major holidays. A nominal admission is charged. Children accompanied by adults are free. Also on the lighthouse and museum grounds is the Tybee Island Art Center offering island art for sale.

Across the parking lot from Fort Screven and the museum is the **Tybee Lighthouse**, which is open concurrently with the museum. The Tybee Island Lighthouse is one of approximately 46 lighthouses in the United States that are accessible to the public. Of these, three are located in Georgia; the other two are on St. Simons Island and on Cockspur Island at Fort Pulaski.

The present 154-foot-tall lighthouse was built in 1867, replacing the one erected in 1736. When you visit you can climb the

178 spiral steps of the tower for a panoramic vista of the salt marshes, Atlantic Ocean and Savannah suburbs. You also can see the keeper's cottage. There is a small gift shop. A nominal admission is charged.

Most of the side streets of Tybee provide access to the beach. The wide sandy expanse is a great getaway year-round. The town has a small commercial district for browsing, shopping and eating.

On the way back to Savannah you can detour off the Island Expressway to the **Oatland Island Education Center** and have a look at the animals. The local Board of Education operates this 150-acre complex. Visitors are welcome to take the self-guiding trails past the 12 animal areas. There are habitats for alligators, panthers, bobcats, small mammals, deer, bears, wolves and bison as well as several aviaries.

The access road to the Oatland Island Education Center leads past the offices of **Wilderness Southeast**, a non-profit educational organization that sponsor's wilderness camping trips. These wilderness courses provide an up-close look at different ecosystems, such as the canoeing trip in Georgia's Okefenokee Swamp. Another Georgia trip they sponsor explores Cumberland Island (see selection). Other courses take participants around the world to diverse destinations such as the Amazon, Costa Rica and the Bahamas. For additional information call (912)897-5108.

Directions: From I-16 take U.S. 80 from Savannah east from the city to Tybee Island. Make a left turn on Polk Street for Tybee Museum.

Wormsloe State Historic Site

Tabby Ruins, End of Hope

Even readers of Gothic novels might think a character named Noble Jones was a bit much, but just such a person sailed from England with Oglethorpe in 1733. Noble Jones was a physician and carpenter from Surrey. When he settled in the wilds of colonial Georgia, he also became a soldier, constable, rum agent, surveyor and, for 18 years, a member of the Royal Council.

Between 1739 and 1745, Jones constructed a fortified home, **Wormsloe**, on the Isle of Hope, on 500 acres he leased not far from the Savannah settlement. Jones and his family spent part of the year at Wormsloe and the other part at their home in Savannah. During the 1740s England and Spain were fighting for control of this part of Georgia. After Oglethorpe conducted an unsuccessful siege of the Spanish settlement at St. Augustine, he expected a retaliatory Spanish invasion of Georgia. He made

Wormsloe a command post for a company of boatmen to protect the colony's coast.

In 1756 Jones was given a royal grant for Wormsloe. Noble Jones was one of the few original settlers to survive. Most fell victim to hunger, the plague, the environment or the Indians and Spanish. Wormsloe remained for many years the only Savannah plantation to be held by the same family that settled the land. In 1973, descendants of Noble Jones gave the property to the Georgia Heritage Trust, retaining a three-story mansion and gardens on the property for their own use.

Today all the public can see of Wormsloe are some tabby ruins and a long avenue of 400 live oaks, Georgia's state tree, that were planted along the drive in the 1890s by Jones's great-great-grandson, Wymberley Jones DeRenne. There is a gravesite monument to Noble Jones, who was once buried here. He is now interred at Bonaventure Cemetery.

Tabby was the building material for much of Georgia's colonial coast. It was made by mixing equal parts of sand, water, lime and oyster shells and poured into wooden molds. As the tabby hardened, the wooden molds were moved up, and the next layer poured. Due to this time-consuming process, it took roughly six years to build the Wormsloe house. More than 8,000 bushels of lime alone were used in the construction of this house. The oyster shells were taken from shell mounds left by Indians who inhabited the region thousands of years earlier.

What you see are the remains of the fortified house built in 1745, the last original architectural reminders of Oglethorpe's years in Savannah. The Visitor Center has a model of Wormsloe. The center also displays artifacts uncovered at Wormsloe. An audiovisual program provides background on the establishment of Georgia, the thirteenth British colony founded in the New World.

Throughout the year special programs are presented in the colonial living-history demonstration area. Authentically garbed staff provide a glimpse of the daily life and chores of Georgia's earliest settlers. In this area are copies of typical outbuildings that would have stood around the Wormsloe house. Small wattle-and-daub huts, like those reconstructed here, were used as quarters for indentured servants, the marine boatmen stationed here and, eventually, for the slaves who worked the plantation. There is also a fenced garden and small crops of indigo and cotton.

An interpretive trail displays copies of prints done in 1723 by Mark Catesby, who drew the wildlife he encountered in this part of Georgia. Two of the birds pictured are now extinct: the Carolina parakeet and the ivory-billed woodpecker.

Wormsloe State Historic Site is open Tuesday through Saturday 9:00 A.M. to 5:00 P.M. and Sunday 2:00 to 5:30 P.M. There is a nominal admission fee. Picnic tables are available.

While in the area take a drive along **Bluff Road**. This part of the Isle of Hope is designated as a historic district on the National Register of Historic Places. On the high shell bluff you'll see a row of picturesque homes, some dating back to the early 1800s.

Another nearby point of interest you many want to visit is the **Marine Extension Service** on Skidaway Island. This free aquarium is part of the University of Georgia, and it offers educational programs to students from the southeastern part of the state. The aquarium focuses on the marine and estuarine animals of Georgia. It has over 200 live animals representing about 50 species. Visitors also learn about Gray's Reef National Marine Sanctuary that is 17.2 miles east of Sapelo Island (see selection). The aquarium is open 9:00 A.M. to 4:00 P.M. on weekdays and Saturday from NOON until 5:00 P.M. Films are shown on Saturdays at 1:00 and 3:00 P.M.

Another worthwhile stop is **Skidaway Island State Park**, a 506-acre barrier island. It combines a mile-long Sandpiper Nature Trail, the three-mile-long Big Ferry Nature Trail, a Junior Olympic swimming pool, a playground, picnic facilities and camping sites. The park hosts educational programs on birding and seafood.

Directions: From I-95 take Exit 16, Route 204, Abercom Expressway. At Montgomery Crossroads turn left and then bear right on Skidaway Road. Wormsloe's imposing masonry archway entrance is on your right at 7601 Skidaway Road. The site is ten miles southeast of Savannah's historic district. For the Marine Extension Center take a left on Ferguson Avenue after you leave Wormsloe and then take the Diamond Causeway and make a left on McWhorter Drive. The Marine Extension Service will be at the end of McWhorter Drive. Skidaway Island State Park is directly off the Diamond Causeway; signs indicate the entrance.

State Parks

Crooked River State Park, St. Marys (see St. Marys selection)

Laura S. Walker State Park, Waycross; gateway to the Okefenokee Swamp Park, home of the red-cockaded woodpecker, fishing, boat dock and ramp, swimming pool, picnicking, nature trails, tent and trailer sites and pioneer camping, (912)287-4900

Skidaway Island State Park, Savannah (see selection)

Stephen C. Foster State Park, Fargo (see Okefenokee National Wildlife Refuge selection)

Interior of the Cathedral of St. John the Baptist in Savannah, the oldest Roman Catholic Church in Georgia.

CREDIT: TOURIST DIVISION, GEORGIA DEPT. OF INDUSTRY & TRADE

Calendar of Events

Remember that each year telephone numbers and dates of events change. To get an up-to-date twice yearly "Georgia Days" listing of the state's special events contact the Tourist Division of the Georgia Department of Industry, Trade and Tourism, (404)656-3590.

JANUARY

Early:

"Tales from the Briar Patch," Atlanta, Wren's Nest, (404)753-7735

Mid:

National King Week & Martin Luther King, Jr. National Holiday Observance, Atlanta, King Center, (404)526-1956

Primitive Flintlock Musket and Rifle Competition, Midway, Sunbury State Historic Site, (912)884-5999

Late:

Rattlesnake Roundup, Whigham, (912)762-4215

Winter Homecoming, Tifton, Georgia Agrirama, (912)386-3344

FEBRUARY

Early:

Groundhog Day, Lilburn, Yellow River Game Ranch, (404)972-6643

Georgia Heritage Festival, Savannah, (912)233-7787

Quail Unlimited Celebrity Hunt, Albany, (803)637-5731

Camellia Festival, Ft. Valley, Massee Lane Gardens, (912)967-2358

Fasching Karnival, Helen, (706)878-2271 (month long)

Mid:

Savannah Onstage, Savannah, Historic Downtown Churches, (912)236-5745

Late:

Black Heritage, Tifton, Georgia Agrirama, (912)386-3344

Founder's Day, Pine Mountain, Callaway Gardens, (800)282-8181

Fat Saturday Mardi Gras Celebration, Augusta, (706)724-0436

Camellia Show, Atlanta, Atlanta Botanical Garden, (404)876-5859

MARCH

Early:

St. Patrick's Festival, Dublin, (912)272-5546 (month long)

Celebration of Spring, Pine Mountain, Callaway Gardens, (800)282-8181

First Saturday Festival, Savannah, Waterfront, (912)234-0295

Athens International Festival, Athens, (706)546-1805

Mid:

Spring Wildflower Day, Lumpkin, Providence Canyon State Park, (912)838-6202

Claxton Rattlesnake Roundup, Claxton, (912)739-3820

Old-Fashioned Hog Butcherin', Waycross, Obediah's Okefenok, (912)287-0090

Forsythia Festival, Forsyth, (912)994-9239

Irishfest, Savannah, (912)234-0295

Late:

Georgia Folk Festival, Perry, Georgia National Fairgrounds Agricenter, (912)452-9327

Georgia Cherry Blossom Festival, Macon, (912)751-7429

Spring Frolic, Tifton, Georgia Agrirama, (912)386-3344

Azalea Festival, Pine Mountain, Callaway Gardens, (800)282-8181

Discovery Week, Jefferson, Crawford W. Long Museum, (706)367-5307

Tour of Homes & Gardens, Savannah, (912)234-8054

APRIL

Early:

Dogwood Festival, Perry, (912)987-5138

Spring Festival, Lumpkin, Westville, (912)838-6310

River Days at Chehaw, Albany, Chehaw Park, (912)888-5000

Dogwood Days Festival, Pine Mountain, (706)663-4338

River Days Festival, Albany, (912)888-5000

Spring Fling Pig Jig, Tifton, (912)386-1333

Harness Horse Festival, Hawkinsville, (912)783-1717

Seafood Festival, Savannah, (912)234-0295

Antebellum Jubilee, Stone Mountain, Stone Mountain Park, (404)498-5637

Scottish Days, Indian Spring, Indian Spring Hotel, (706)775-6734

Okefenokee Spring Fling, Waycross, Okefenokee Swamp Park, (912)283-0583

Mid:

Peanut Plantin Pickin Phestival, Dawson, (912)995-2011

National Mayhaw Festival, Colquitt, (912)758-2400

Sheep to Shawl Day, Atlanta, Atlanta History Center, (404)814-4000

Salisbury Fair, Columbus, Chattahoochee Promenade, (706)322-0756

Sweet Auburn Festival, Atlanta, Auburn Avenue, (404)344-2567

Gold Panning Championship & Craft Show, Dahlonega, Blackburn Park, (706)864-3711

Easter Sunrise Service, Tybee Island, (912)786-5444

Late:

Rose Show and Festival, Thomasville, (912)225-5222

Festival on the Square, Moultrie, (912)985-1922

Night in Old Savannah, Savannah, (912)355-2422
Great Hahira Pick-in, Hahira, (912)247-ARTS
Crawfish Festival & Rodeo, Woodbine, (912)576-3211
Earth Day Celebration, Gainesville, Elachee Nature Science Center, (404)535-1976
Folk Life Festival, Tifton, Georgia Agrirama, (912)386-3344
Indian Heritage Day, Jonesboro, Stately Oaks Plantation, (404)473-0197
Jonquil Spring Festival, Smyra, (404)434-3661
Old Jonesboro Day, Jonesboro, (404)473-4358
Sidewalk Arts Festival, Savannah, (912)238-2487
Calico Days At Cotton Row, Augusta, Riverwalk, (706)722-3175
Big Shanty Festival, Kennesaw, (404)423-1330
Magnolia Fine Arts & Crafts Festival, Newnan, (404)254-3703
Mossy Creek Barnyard Festival, Perry, (912)922-8265
Enchanted Valleys Rhododendron Festival, Hiawassee, (706)896-4966
Taste of Toccoa, Toccoa, (706)886-2132
Confederate Memorial Day, Kingston, (706)336-5385
Confederate Memorial Day, Savannah, (912)238-1779

MAY

Early:

Revolutionary Rendevous, Hartwell, Hart State Park, (706)376-8756
Mayfest in the Mountains, Helen, Festhalle, (706)878-3677
May Day, Westville, Westville Village, (912)838-6310
Antebellum Spring Festival, Roswell, Town Square, (404)640-3253
The Love Affair, Tifton, (912)386-3558
Blessing of the Fleet, Darien, (912)437-4192
Mayfest on the Rivers, Rome, (706)295-5576
Cabbage Patch Kids Baby Show & Adoption Event, Cleveland, (706)865-2171
Madison in May, Madison, (706)557-2740
Spring Garden Tour, Marietta, (404)429-1115
Howard Finster Art Festival, Summerville, Dowdy Park, (706)857-1048
First Saturday Festival, Savannah, (912)234-0295
International City Festival, Warner Robins, Perkins Field, (912)922-8585
Lake Blackshear Catfish Festival, Cordele, (912)273-1668
Rose Society's Rose Show, Millen, (912)982-4981
Red Carpet Festival, Dalton, (706)278-8667
Art & Handicraft Show, Calhoun, (706)629-4749
Storytelling Festival, Atlanta, Atlanta History Center, (404)814-4000
Georgia Frontier Days, Calhoun, New Echota Historic Site, (706)629-4749
Great Griffin Mayfling, Griffin, City Park, (404)228-8200

Historic Marietta Arts & Crafts, Marietta, Historic Marietta Square, (404)528-0616
Old Clinton's War Days, Gray, Old Clinton, (912)986-3384
Springfest, Stone Mountain, Stone Mountain Park, (404)498-5635
Antique Car Rally, Cairo, (912)377-3663
Arts-On-the-River Weekend, Savannah, (912)651-6417
Prater's Mill Country Fair, Dalton, Prater's Mill, (706)259-5765

Mid:

Old Capital Celebration, Milledgeville, (912)452-4687
Berry/Ford Festival, Mt. Berry, Berry College Campus, (706)236-2256
Spring Music Festival, Hiawassee, (404)896-4191
Armed Forces Day, St. Marys, Kingsbay Submarine Base, (912)673-4714
Chehaw National Indian Festival, Albany, Chehaw Park, (912)436-1625
Plains Country Days, Plains, (912)824-5445
Arts in the Park, Toccoa, (706)886-2132
Country by the Sea, Jekyll Island, (912)635-2232
Morven Peach Festival, Moren, (912)775-2167
Civil War Battle of Resaca Reenactment, Resaca, (706)629-9128
Wildflower Festival of the Arts, Dahlonega, (706)864-3711

Late:

Decatur Arts Festival, Decatur, 401/371-9583
Atlanta Peach Caribbean Carnival, Atlanta, (404)344-2567
Arts in the Park, Blue Ridge, (706)632-2144
Turpentine Still Firing, Tifton, Georgia Agrirama, (912)386-3344
Andersonville Antiques, Crafts and Civil War Artifacts Fair, Andersonville, (912)924-2558
Coosa Valley Arts & Crafts Show, Rome, Lock and Dam Park, (706)291-0766
Memorial Day Celebration, Richmond Hill, Ft. McAllister Historic Park, (912)727-2339
Memorial Day Ceremony, Andersonville, National Historic Site, (912)924-0343
Memorial Day Weekend Beach Music Blast, Lake Lanier Islands, (404)932-7275
Memorial Day Weekend Military Encampment and Reenactment, Midway, Sunbury State Historic Site, (912)884-5999
Taste of the South, Stone Mountain, Stone Mountain Park, (404)498-5635

JUNE

Early:

Hot Air Balloon Race & Festival, Helen, (706)878-2271
Cave Spring Arts Festival, Cave Spring, Rolator Park, (706)777-8855

Lock n'Ham Jam Barbecue Cookoff and Country Festival, Augusta, Lock & Dam Park, (706)826-4702

Reach of Song, Hiawassee, Georgia Mountain Fairgrounds, (800)262-7664

Mid:

Sugar Creek Bluegrass Festival, Blue Ridge, (706)632-2560

Weinman Rock Festival, Cartersville, William Weinman Mineral Museum, (404)386-0576

Beach Music Festival, Tybee Island Beach, (912)234-5884

Georgia Peach Festival, Fort Valley-Byron, (912)825-3733

Late:

Quilt and Antique Car Show, Indian Spring, Indian Spring Hotel, (706)775-6734

Dahlonega Bluegrass Festival, Dahlonega, Blackburn Park, (706)864-3711

Indian Cooking Day, Cartersville, Etowah Indian Mounds Historic Site, (706)387-3747

Toombs' Birthday Reunion, Washington, Robert Toombs House, (706)678-2226

JULY

Early:

Fantastic Fourth Celebration, Stone Mountain, Stone Mountain Park, (704)498-1754

Robins AFB Open House and Air Show, Warner Robins, Robins Air Force Base, (912)926-2177

4th of July Fest, Hampton, Atlanta Motor Speedway, (494)946-4721

4th of July Music & Fireworks, Moultrie, Reed Bingham State Park, (912)985-2131

Celebration on the Levee, Rome, Banks of the Oostanaula River, (706)295-2787

Chattahoochee River Tube Parade, Helen, (706)878-2181

Family Day July 4th Celebration, Dahlonega, (706)864-3711

Fort Gaines Firecracker Festival, Fort Gaines, (912)768-2247

Fourth of July Sand & Surf Spectacular, Pine Mountain, Callaway Gardens, (800)282-8181

Independence Day Celebration, Dublin, (912)272-5546

Independence Day Celebration, Richmond Hill, Ft. McAllister Historic Park, (912)727-2339

Independence Day Folklife Celebration, Juliette, Jarrell Plantation Historic Site, (912)986-5172

Jekyll's July 4th Festivities, Jekyll Island, (912)635-3636

July 4th Beach Concert & Fireworks Extravaganza, Lake Lanier Islands, Beach and Water Park, (404)932-7200

July 4th Observance, Andersonville, (912)924-2558

Old Fashioned Independence Day Celebration, Tifton, Georgia
Agrirama, (912)386-3344
Lower Muscogee Creek Tribe Pow-Wow, Whigham, Tama Tribal Town,
(912)762-3165
Steam Engine Festival, Cumming, (404)889-0309
Watermelon Days Festival, Cordele, (912)273-1668

Mid:

Anniversary of the Bloody Marsh Battle, St. Simons Island, Ft.
Frederica National Monument, (912)638-3639
Forsyth Performing Arts Festival, Savannah, Forsyth Park, (912)651-6417
Dillard Blue Grass Festival, Rome, (706)291-0216
Prunifolia Azalea Day, Pine Mountain, Callaway Gardens,
(706)663-5086
Civil War Encampment, Atlanta, Atlanta History Center,
(404)261-1837

Late:

Moccasin Creek Arts & Crafts Festival, Clarkesville, Mocassin Creek
State Park, (706)947-3194
Vann House Days of Indian Heritage, Spring Place, Chief Vann
House, (706)695-2598

AUGUST

Early:

National Black Arts Festival, Atlanta, (404)7307315
Fairy Tale Festival, Lookout Mountain, Rock City Gardens,
(706)820-2531
Georgia Mountain Fair, Hiawassee, (706)896-4191
Family Farm Day, Juliette, Jarrell Plantation State Historic Site,
(912)986-5172

Mid:

Beach Music Festival, Jekyll Island, (912)635-3400
Wild Foods Walk, Cartersville, Etowah Indian Mounds, (404)387-3737
Harvest Celebration at Chateau Elan, Braselton, Chateau Elan,
(706)441-9463

Late:

Homemade Ice Cream Festival, Newnan, (706)254-3703
National Park Day at Ft. Frederica National Monument, St. Simons
Island, (912)638-3639
Fannin County Fair, Blue Ridge, (706)632-3919
Nacoochee Valley Native American Indian Festival and Pow Wow,
Helen, (706)878-2938

SEPTEMBER

Early:

Civil War Encampment, Ft. Oglethorpe, Chickamauga Battlefield, (706)866-9241

Labor Day Folklife Celebration, Juliette, Jarrell Plantation State Historic Site, (912)986-5172

Labor Day County Fair of 1896, Tifton, Georgia Agrirama, (912)386-3344

Perry Craft Show, Perry, Georgia National Fairgrounds, (404)860-4902

Art in the Park, Marietta, Historic Marietta Square, (404)429-1115

Powers' Crossroads County Fair & Art Festival, Newnan, (706)253-2011

Old Fort Days, Ft. Oglethorpe, (706)965-5201

Mid:

Savannah Maritime Festival, Savannah/Wilmington & Tybee Island, (912)238-4434

Oktoberfest, Helen, Fest Halle, (706)878-3677

Kingston Historical Festival, Kingston, (706)336-5841

Yellow Daisy Festival, Stone Mountain, Stone Mountain Park, (404)498-5702

Ellijay Quilt Exhibit & Fair, Ellijay, (706)635-5605

Southern Jubilee, Macon, (912)742-8155

Chattachoochee Mountain Fair, Clarkesville, (706)754-2363

Covington Square Arts and Crafts Festival, Covington, (706)760-8846

Autumn Fall Festival, Dublin, (912)277-3733

Cherokee Festival-Homecoming, Calhoun, New Echota Historical Site, (706)629-8151

Clogging Hoedown, Tifton, Georgia Agrirama, (912)386-3344

Fala Day, Warm Springs, FDR's Little White House, (706)655-3511

Late:

Barnesville Buggy Days, Barnesville, (706)358-2732

Coosa Valley Fair, Rome, (706)291-9951

North Georgia State Fair, Kennesaw, (404)423-1330

Possom Hollow Arts & Crafts Fair & Country Music Show, Dexter, (912)875-3104

Creek Homecoming at Etowah Indian Mounds State Historic Site, Cartersville, (404)387-3747

Heritage Day at Bulloch Hall, Roswell, (404)992-1731

OCTOBER

Early:

Cold Sassy Days, Commerce, (706)335-2954

SciTrek October Odyssey, Atlanta, SciTrek, (404)522-5500

Great Locomotive Chase Festival, Adairsville, (706)773-3451

Indian Games Day, Cartersville, Etowah Indian Mounds, (404)387-3747
Miller Lite Chili Cookoff, Stone Mountain, Stone Mountain Park, (404)872-4731
Mule Day, Washington, Callaway Plantation, (706)678-2013
Cherry Jubilee Street Party, Macon, (912)741-8005
Old Grist Mill Days, Juliette, (912)994-3670
Rock Shrimp Festival, St. Marys, (912)882-6200
Town and Country Arts and Crafts Festival, Lincolnton, (706)359-4300
Andersonville Historic Fair, Andersonville, (912)924-2558
Cotton Pickin' Country Fair, Gay, (706)538-6814
Georgia Marble Festival, Jasper, (706)692-5600
Indian Summer Festival, Suches, (706)747-3169
Octoberfest, Roswell, (706)642-2055
Big Pig Jig, Vienna, (912)268-8275
Georgia Peanut Festival, Sylvester, (912)776-6657
Cherokee Rose Storytelling Festival, Carrollton, (404)832-1161
Blue Grass Festival, Blue Ridge, (706)632-2560
Garden Center of Greater Atlanta Fall Flower Show, Atlanta, Atlanta Botanical Garden, (404)876-5859
Montpelier Station Arts & Crafts Festival, Macon, (912)781-2370
Corn Tassel Festival, Gainesville, (404)532-6206

Mid:

Pioneer Rendevous, Lincolnton, Elijah Clark State Park, (706)359-3458
Sorghum Festival, Blairsville, (706)745-4745
Georgia National Fair, Perry, Georgia National Fairgrounds, (912)988-8000
Chic-O-Pen Festival, White, (706)386-8089
Cotton Patch Craft Fair, Madison, (706)342-1536
Okefenokee Festival, Folkston, (912)496-2536
Appalachian Fall Color Festival, Dahlonega, (706)864-5162
Fall Festival and Battle Re-enactment, Jonesboro, Stately Oaks Plantation, (404)473-0197
Golden Isles Arts Festival, St. Simons Island, (912)638-8770
New Salem Mountain Festival, Rising Fawn, Lookout Mountain, (706)398-1988
Prater's Mill Country Fair, Dalton, (706)275-6455
Georgia Apple Festival Arts and Crafts Fair, Ellijay, (706)635-7400
Tybee Indian Summer Festival, Tybee Island, (800)444-CHARM
Chrysanthemum Festival, Pine Mountain, Callaway Gardens, (800)282-8181
Atlanta International Wine Festival, Atlanta, Georgia World Congress Center, (404)873-4482
Moonshine Festival, Dawsonville, (706)216-1297

Sunbelt Agricultural Exposition, Moultrie, (912)386-3459
Heritage Holidays Festival, Rome, (706)291-3819
Scottish Festival and Highland Games, Stone Mountain, Stone
    Mountain Park, (404)396-5728
Fall Music Festival, Hiawassee, (706)896-4191
African Violet Show, Atlanta, Atlanta Botanical Garden,
    (404)876-5859
Chiaha Arts & Crafts Fair, Rome, Coosa River, (706)235-4542
Dahlonega Gold Rush Days, Dahlonega, (706)864-3711
Mossy Creek Barnyard Festival, Perry, (912)922-8265
Mountain Harvest Sale, Blue Ridge, (706)374-5988
Oktoberfest, Augusta, Riverwalk, (706)823-6600
Pogo Fest, Waycross, Memorial Stadium, (912)283-3742
Red Top Mountain Arts & Crafts Festival, Cartersville, Red Top
    Mountain State Park, (404)975-0055
Brown's Crossing Craftsmen Fair, Milledgeville, (912)968-5382
Olde Madison Days, Madison, (706)342-4454

Late:
Tour of Southern Ghosts, Stone Mountain, Stone Mountain Park,
    (404)469-1105
Georgia Trust Haunted Castle, Atlanta, Underground Atlanta,
    (404)881-9980
Dillard Blue Grass Festival, Rome, (706)291-0216
Big Red Apple Festival, Cornelia, (706)776-4565
Pinetree Festival, Sparta, (706)444-5715
Fair of 1850, Lumpkin, Westville, (912)838-6310
The Early Creeks, Cartersville, Etowah Indian Mounds, (404)387-3747
Chrysanthemum Show, Atlanta, Atlanta Botanical Garden,
    (404)876-5859
Civil War Days, Indian Spring, Indian Spring Hotel, (706)775-6734
Pine Mountain Fall Harvest Festival, Pine Mountain, (706)663-4000
Haunted House, Helen, Fest Halle, (706)878-3677
Historic Halloween Carnival, Tifton, Georgia Agrirama, (912)386-3344
Great Halloween Caper, Atlanta, Zoo Atlanta, (404)624-5630

NOVEMBER

Early:
Crawford W. Long Days, Jefferson, Crawford W. Long Museum,
    (706)367-5307
Founder's Day, Pine Mountain, Callaway Gardens, (800)282-8181
Heritage Day, Lumpkin, Westville Historic Village, (912)838-6310
Stewart County Wild Game Cook-Off & Crafts Fair, Lumpkin,
    (912)838-6310
Grecian Festival, Augusta, Riverwalk, (706)724-1087
Toccoa Fall Harvest Festival, Toccoa, (706)886-2132

Mid:

Cane Grinding & Craft Festival, Oatland Island, Oatland Island
 Education Center, (912)897-3773
Mule Day, Douglas, (912)384-3302
Calico Holiday Arts & Crafts Show, Moultrie, (912)386-3459
Fall Encampment, Darien, Ft. King George Historic Site,
 (912)437-4770
Cane Grinding and Syrup Making Day, Juliette, Jarrell Plantation
 State Historic Site, (912)986-5172

Late:

Foothills Dulcimer Festival, Dawsonville, Amicalola Falls Lodge,
 (404)475-4283
Jekyll Island Craft Show, Jekyll Island, (407)860-4902
Swine Time Festival, Climax, (912)246-0910
Holiday Bazaar, Jonesboro, Stately Oaks Plantation, (404)473-0197
Christmas at the Fort, Ft. Gaines, (912)768-2695
Warm Springs Thanksgiving, Warm Springs, FDR's Little White
 House, (706)655-3511
Christmas Open House in Historic Madison, Madison, (706)342-2153
Festival of Lights, Augusta, Riverwalk, (706)821-1754
Children's Lights for the Future, Columbus, Riverwalk Promenade,
 (706)322-1613
Lighting of the Chateau, Braselton, Chateau Elan, (706)441-9463
Holiday Celebration, Stone Mountain, Stone Mountain Park,
 (404)498-5702
BabyLand's Appalachian Christmas, Cleveland, BabyLand General
 Hospital, (706)865-2171

DECEMBER

Early:

Mountain Country Christmas, Young Harris/Hiawassee,
 (706)896-4966
Buzzard Day, Adel, Reed Bingham State Park, (912)896-3551
Festival of Trees, Ft. Valley, Massee Lane Gardens, (912)967-2358
Christmas at Deer Lick, Douglasville, Deer Lick Park, (404)920-7132
Christmas at Callanwolde, Atlanta, Callanwolde Fine Arts Center,
 (404)872-5338
Warm Springs Christmas, Warm Springs, FDR's Little White House,
 (706)655-3511
Jekyll's Christmas, Jekyll Island, (912)635-3636
White Columns & Holly, Macon, (912)743-3401
Legends of Christmas, Lookout Mountain, Rock City Gardens,
 (706)820-2531
Cottage Christmas, Macon, Sidney Lanier Cottage, (912)743-3851
Lighting of the Gardens, Pine Mountain, Callaway Gardens,
 (800)282-8181

Candles and Carols of Christmases Past, Rome, Martha Berry
  Museum and Oak Hill, (706)291-1833
Crescent Christmas Open House, Valdosta, Crescent Complex,
  (912)247-6747
Dahlonega's Old Fashioned Christmas Celebration, Dahlonega,
  (706)864-3711
Christmas at Chehaw, Albany, Chehaw Park, (912)430-5275
Christmas at Hay House, Macon, (912)742-8155
Coosa River Christmas, Rome, (706)295-5576
Holiday Reflection Lake Allatoona, Cartersville, (706)974-8716
Log Cabin Christmas, Ellijay, Elijah Clark State Park, (404)359-3458
Christmas at Bulloch Hall, Roswell, (404)992-1731
Poinsetta's Display, Atlanta, Atlanta Botanical Garden, (404)876-5859
Christmas and Kwanzaa, Atlanta, Herndon Home, (404)581-9813

Mid:

Tybee Island Family Christmas Celebration, Tybee Island,
  (800)444/CHARM
Yuletide Season, Lumpkin, (912)838-6310
Christmas Candlelight Tours, Juliette, Jarrell Plantation State Historic
  Site, (912)986-5172
Pebble Hill Plantation Candlelight Tour, Thomasville, (912)226-2344
Natural Christmas Decorations Day, Cartersville, Etowah Indian
  Mounds, (404)387-3747
Moravian Christmas, Dalton, Chief Vann House, (706)695-2598
Christmas Candlelight Tour of Homes, St. Marys, (912)882-6200
1890's Victorian Christmas Celebration, Tifton, Georgia Agrirama,
  (912)386-3344
Season of Reflections, Athens, State Botanial Garden of Georgia,
  (706)542-6154
Winter Muster, Richmond Hill, Ft. McAllister Historic Park,
  (912)727-2339
Fort King George Christmas, Darien, (912)437-4770

Late:

Fort Frederica's Holiday Celebration, St. Simons Island, Ft. Frederica
  National Monument, (912)638-3639
First Night Athens, Athens, (706)353-1421
First Night Macon, Macon, (912)741-8005
New Year's Eve Gala, Braselton, Chateau Elan, (706)441-9463
Dropping of the "Great Peach", Atlanta, Underground Atlanta,
  (404)523-2311

Georgia Regional Representatives

For more information contact the following offices:

PRESIDENTIAL PATHWAYS
Becky Basset
801 Front Avenue (31901)
Columbus, GA 31902
(706)649-7228

CLASSIC SOUTH
Jeannie Buttrum
Post Office Box 657
600 Broad Street Plaza
Augusta, GA 30913
(706)721-3276

ATLANTA METRO
Barbara Daniell
Post Office Box 1776
285 Peachtree Center Avenue
Suite 1000 (30303)
Atlanta, GA 30301-1776
(404)656-3596

PLANTATION TRACE
Mary Jo Dudley
Post Office Box 767
235 East Lee Street (31742)
Dawson, GA 31742-0706
(912)995-3035

HISTORIC HEARTLAND
Becky Morris
Post Office Box 1851
131 South Clark Street
Milledgeville, GA 31061
(912)453-4756

COLONIAL COAST
Kitty Sikes
Post Office Box 786
1803 Gloucester Street
Suite 209
Brunswick, GA 31520
(912)264-3256

NORTHEAST MOUNTAINS
Cheryl Smith
Post Office Box 3116
1010 Ridge Road
Gainesville, GA 30503
(706)535-5757

MAGNOLIA MIDLANDS
Carol Spires
Post Office Box 1139
215 West Jackson Street (31021)
Dublin, GA 31040
(912)275-6888

NORTHWEST MOUNTAINS
Dawn Townsend
Post Office Box 2497
700 West Line Street (30701)
Calhoun, GA 30703
(706)629-3406

Index

Acknowledgments

I would like to thank two longtime friends, and fellow members of the Society of American Travel Writers, for encouraging me to write about Georgia: Karin Koser of the Georgia Department of Industry, Trade and Tourism and Jenny Stacy of the Savannah Convention & Visitors Bureau.

My two years of research work in Georgia were made easier by the friendly and knowledgeable assistance of the Regional Representatives I worked with as I traveled through the state. My special thanks to: Becky Basset, Presidential Pathways; Kitty Sikes, Colonial Coast; Dawn Townsend, Northwest Georgia Mountains; Cheryl Smith, Northeast Georgia Mountains; Carol Spires, Magnolia Midlands; Jeannie Buttrum, Classic South; Mary Jo Dudley, Plantation Trace; Barbara Daniell, Atlanta Metro; and Becky Morris, Historic Heartland. I want to add a special word of appreciation to Mary Anne Thomas, Georgia's Hospitality Training Representative, with whom I was fortunate enough to travel on several memorable occasions.

My visits to the state's many attractions were aided by the friendly assistance of the staff at each site. I wish that space permitted to list each and every new friend I met traveling through Georgia. Some whose special kindness I would like to recognize are: Theresa Jenkins, Marietta; Diana Shadday, Rome; Shelda Rees, Rock City; and finally to Deborah Greaney, formerly of Dahlonega and now with the Dillard House, who arranged a delightful first anniversary dinner for my husband and me.

About the Author

Jane Ockershausen became a best-selling author by concentrating on the growing weekend-travel market. Her seven travel guides include books on Virginia, Maryland, North Carolina, Philadelphia and Washington, D.C. She has also written a popular guide to historic sites in and around the nation's capital entitled *One-Day Trips Through History*. Jane has spent the last two years traveling the nine regions of Georgia researching *The Georgia One-Day Trip Book*.

Jane was a correspondent for *The National Geographic Traveler* for several years. For three years she wrote a weekly regional column for *The Washington Times*, and for six years she wrote a regular feature in *AAA World, Potomac Magazine*. Her byline has appeared in *The Washington Post, The Baltimore Sun, The Chicago Tribune, The Buffalo News, The Dallas Times Herald, The Oregonian* and *The Pittsburgh Post Gazette*. She has also written for *The Washingtonian Magazine, Mid-Atlantic Country Magazine* and *Historic Preservation Magazine*.

A member of the Society of American Travel Writers and the American Society of Journalists and Authors, Jane has lectured at the Smithsonian Institution and addressed conferences on travel and tourism in Missouri, Virginia, North Carolina and Georgia.

TO HELP PLAN YOUR TRAVEL IN THE MID-ATLANTIC AREA

THE WALKER WASHINGTON GUIDE   **$8.95**
The seventh edition of the "Guide's guide to Washington,"
completely revised by Katherine Walker, builds on a 25-year
reputation as the top general guide to the capital. Its 320
pages are packed with museums, galleries, hotels, restaurants, theaters, shops, churches, as well as sites. Beautiful
maps and photos. Indispensable.

INNS OF THE BLUE RIDGE   **$11.95**
More than 125 country escapes in six mountain states,
Virginia to Georgia, all personally visited. Selections include country manors, farmhouses, hunting lodges,
B&Bs—a complete range from the luxurious to the laid-
back. Nuts and bolts info tells the what, where, how much
and other details to help make the right choice. Maps and
photos.

MARYLAND ONE-DAY TRIP BOOK   **$10.95**
From boiling rapids and rugged trails high in the western
mountains to frontier forts, horse country, Baltimore's urban
treasures, the Chesapeake Bay and the plantations and preserves of the Eastern Shore, Maryland is more than you can
imagine!

THE WEST VIRGINIA ONE-DAY TRIP BOOK   **$11.95**
Over 150 diverse, affordable day adventures in the magic
mountain state, including excursions to historic mansions,
craft centers, caverns, art museums, Civil War battlefields,
state parks, even a palace of gold and a miniature Swiss
village. Very accessible info on fishing, skiing, white water
rafting. Maps/photos/charts.

ONE-DAY TRIPS THROUGH HISTORY   **$9.95**
Describes 200 historic sites within 150 miles of the nation's
capital where our forebears lived, dramatic events occurred
and America's roots took hold. Sites and arranged chronologi-
cally starting with pre-history.

THE VIRGINIA ONE-DAY TRIP BOOK   **$8.95**
Jane Ockershausen Smith, one of the most experienced travel
writers in the Mid-Atlantic area, admits to being surprised by
the wealth of things to see and do in the Old Dominion. With
101 sites divided into seven geographic regions, this is the
perfect guide for anyone who is anywhere in Virginia.

NORTH CAROLINA ONE-DAY TRIP BOOK   **$11.95**

150 excursions throughout the Tarheel State that beckon day-trippers of all ages and interest. The state slogan says "The beauty only begins with the scenery"—we've organized all of it into seven geographic regions for easy planning, supplemented with maps and seasonal information.

Also:

Florida One-Day Trips (from Orlando). What to do after you've done Disney. **$7.95**

Call it Delmarvalous. How to talk, cook and "feel to hum" on the Delaware, Maryland, and Virginia Peninsula. **$7.95**

A Shunpiker's Guide to the Northeast. Wide open routes that shun turnpikes and interstates between Washington and Boston. Maps and directions included. **$9.95**

Footnote Washington. Tracking the engaging, humorous and surprising bypaths of capital history by one of the city's most popular broadcasters. **$8.95**

Walking Tours of Old Washington and Alexandria. Paul Hogarth's exquisite watercolors of grand old buildings, lovingly reproduced and arranged in seven guided walking tours. **$24.95**

Order Blank for all EPM books described here. Mail with check to:

EPM Publications, Inc.
Box 490, McLean, VA 22101

Title	Quantity	Price	Amount	Shipping
_____	_____	_____	_____	_____
_____	_____	_____	_____	_____
_____	_____	_____	_____	_____
_____	_____	_____	_____	_____

Subtotal   _____

Virginia residents add 4 1/2% tax   _____

Orders totaling up to $15 add $3.00 shipping/handling   _____

Orders totaling more than $15 add $4.00 first item, $.50 add'l   _____

Name _____

Street _____

City _____ State _____ Zip _____

                                    Total _____

Remember to enclose names, addresses and enclosure cards for gift purchases.
Please note that prices are subject to change. Thank you.